Born in Nigeria in 1960, Onyekachi Wambu arrived in Britain after the Biafran War. Educated in London and at the universities of Essex and Cambridge, he has worked as a journalist since 1983, and edited the *Voice*, the leading black newspaper, in the late 1980s. He currently presents a show on Spectrum Radio. He is also a TV producer and director, and has made numerous documentaries for the BBC and Channel 4. He lives in south London.

Hurricane Hits England

*An Anthology of Writing
about Black Britain*

Onyekachi Wambu, Editor

Preface by E. R. Braithwaite

CONTINUUM   NEW YORK

2000

The Continuum International Publishing Group Inc
370 Lexington Avenue, New York, NY 10017

Printed in the United States of America

Library of Congress Cataloging-in-Publication Data

Empire Windrush
Hurricane hits England : an anthology of writing about Black Britain / edited by
Onyekachi Wambu ; preface by E.R. Braithwaite.
p. cm.
First published in Great Britain under the title: Empire Windrush.
ISBN 0-8264-1261-0 (alk. paper)—ISBN 0-8264-1262-9
1. English literature—Black authors.   2. Immigrants—Great Britain—Literary
collections.   3. Blacks—Great Britain—Literary collections.   4. English literature—
20th century.   5. Immigrants—Great Britain.   6. Blacks—Great Britain.
I. Wambu, Onyekachi, 1960– II. Title.

PR1110.B5 E47 2000
820.8'0896041—dc21
00-024085

For Monica, Emeka, and Chika – We usually
love the children of the woman whom we love

ACKNOWLEDGEMENTS

The seers Colin Prescod, Mike Phillips, Henry Letts. Anne Ogidi, Harold Wilson, Georgia de Chamberet, Helen Denniston and Carl Daniels for all their help elsewhere.

Clean water does not know any boundary; the
one that is boundary-conscious contains ashes
YORUBA PROVERB

Thou shalt neither vex a stranger, nor oppress
him: for ye were strangers in the land of Egypt
EXODUS 22: 21

CONTENTS

EMPIRE REVISITED

THE NEW BRITAIN

PREFACE

I arrived in Britain even as Hitler was planning to annex parts of Europe and unashamedly threatening the rest. I was on my way to Cambridge University, because, in those days, educational institutions in British Guyana were limited to what was little more than high-school level, and any Guyanese with hopes and aspirations beyond those offerings had no choice but to seek their fulfilment in Britain or the United States. I chose Britain.

In my first year at Cambridge, war was declared and I, like most able-bodied young men, including some, like myself, from Britain's Colonial Empire, responded to the general mobilization, easily persuaded that I was included in the call to arms, and readily seduced into believing myself included in the 'We' of 'We shall fight them on the beaches and in the fields . . . ' I volunteered for Aircrew service in the Royal Air Force and served as a fighter pilot.

In 1945, I returned to Cambridge and resumed my education, older and considerably wiser for the wartime experience. I applied myself single-mindedly to my studies, secure in the belief that those of the 'We' who had survived the conflict would be welcome participants in the massive task of reconstruction which lay ahead.

In 1949, armed with degrees in Physics and the residual disciplines of military life, I sought employment in many of the well-advertised areas for which I believed myself to be eminently qualified. Great was my amazement and chagrin when, time after time, I was denied employment, with elaborate casualness and courtesy, for reasons which seemed to have nothing to do with my abilities or qualifications. In due course, I was forced to confront the simple fact that, relieved of the threat of German invasion, the British had abandoned all pretence of hand-in-hand brotherliness and had reverted to type, demonstrating the same racism they had so roundly condemned in the Germans.

Acting on someone's suggestion, I applied for one of the teaching posts advertised by the London County Council, to relieve the increasingly acute shortage of teachers, especially in some of the less-favoured schools in London's East End. I was accepted. My intention was to use the job as a security blanket while extra-murally pursuing my Doctoral Degree.

My work as a teacher among those whom a certain member of Parliament labelled 'The Great Unwashed', forced me to deal quietly with my own implosive anger and resentments. Even within the school I encountered instances of bigotry and intolerance from some students and members of the faculty, but I was determined to keep the job, come what may. To that end I tried to develop strategies for stimulating and holding the interest of my students and began a daily diary of events, chronicling everything that occurred in the classroom, and weekly reviewing those events that I might discover anything which helped or hindered the learning environment. I carefully examined what was done and how it was done, what was said and how it was said, and gradually came to understand the interplay of forces between the students and me. In short, I learned from them how to teach them.

To Sir, With Love is an amalgam of those personal reviews and, it would seem, the beginning of my interest in writing. It is perhaps inevitable that, learning from that first attempt, nearly all my books are records of personal experiences in predominantly white situations. It is perhaps equally inevitable that some residual anger and bitterness sometimes circumvent my best intentions and spread themselves across the page.

From all this it is clear that I came to writing somewhat accidentally. Before *To Sir*, I had never given any thought to writing, believing that writers were specially gifted people, who had something important to say and the wit, imagination and eloquence necessary for saying it. This view was confirmed and reinforced when I read works by black writers like Sam Selvon, George Lamming, Andrew Salkey, C. L. R. James and others. I was consumed with admiration and delight, but had no ambition to join their ranks, preferring to read and occasionally listen to their informed observations on what it meant to be an intelligent, ambitious black person in post-war Britain.

In 1958, I was seconded to the London County Council's Child Welfare Department, and had a close, unblinkered view of the quickly deteriorating relationship between the indigenous British, at all levels, and their black counterparts. As the number of blacks increased, so did the stresses and rifts, giving rise to many ugly incidents of disharmony and intolerance, the most dramatic of which were the Notting Hill riots.

Successive British governments either blithely ignored the continuing racial strife or treated it with benign neglect. Other issues affecting both the blacks and the British clamoured for attention, especially the aggressive demands for independence from the former colonies. Unhappily, the British press in general and the conservative press in particular, did very little in their reporting to ease racial tensions. The blacks in Britain had no significant leadership which could rally and represent black interests, and no forum from which to present their case. Some black writers attempted, with little success, to engage the British public in a dialogue about those much-vaunted Christian virtues and values which had long been preached in the Colonial territories, but which now failed the simplest examination when subjected to rigorous testing in the 'Mother Country'.

The British public was disinclined to listen, and the British Government was unwilling to act, so the situation festered. Neither gentle persuasion nor the more climactic riots produced any noticeable change in attitudes and the situation was further polarized by politicians who sought to exploit the racial tensions for political gain.

Through all this, black men and women continued to write of the agony and ecstasy of living in a society which had long been conditioned to view them as less than equal; yet each in his or her particular style and through his or her particular experience added a significant and vibrant thread to the tapestry which is post-war Britain. They wrote of the British society as they found it, distressingly alien, yet painfully familiar, and, in writing, held an unwelcome mirror to Britain's reluctant gaze. For them, 'back home' was a persistant reminder of promises to keep.

Today, in celebrating the fiftieth anniversary of the SS *Empire Windrush*'s arrival on Britain's shores, we celebrate those black men and women and take pride in their achievements, however minimal the effect might have been on the racial status quo. We also celebrate the new band of brothers and sisters, many of them British by birth though black by ancestry, who are undeniably a part of the new Britain. They can and will write from the unique perspective of being part of the British fabric of seeing and feeling and knowing every nuance of the complexities of life in Britain. In them and with them lies the hope of recreating and maintaining that dialogue which is the first, infant step to racial harmony.

E. R. Braithwaite
Washington, DC, 1998

INTRODUCTION

According to an African proverb, 'The world acknowledges that you live only when you speak.' Just as in the growth of people from embryo to adulthood, the speakers of the proverb understood that the move from silence to life involves various stages of the spirit within manifesting itself. First, the noise of the initial incoherent babbling of the baby, then development of fluency and language, and finally the lucid communication of the consciousness of this self and identity through the highest forms of expressions available to humans – the mysterious symbolic languages we convey through the artistic endeavors of music, painting, sport, and dramatic story telling. At the highest stages one is left with a fully formed sensibility.

Over the last fifty years, a new consciousness has come into being. The people who carried it were settlers. They made one of the most spectacular migrations of the last century, over four million of them returning from the farthest outposts of the British imperial world back to the center of the Empire itself. During the last century of massive upheavals and migrations, their story has been buried, dominated by the big movement of various European communities to the United States. Like those who journeyed to the United States, the trigger for their passage was labor shortages and political convulsions within Europe. But unlike their fellow American voyagers, they came only for a short period, to make enough money to return to their own countries. But most stayed, transforming themselves and the British island which they began to call home. Though they have yet to achieve a similar transformative impact on the world, Americans are slowly beginning to catch a glimpse of their sensibility as it begins to assert itself.

On a popular level, supermodel Naomi Campbell has been a lonely and obscure shape on the radar screen for the last ten years. But 1999 was a good year for sightings. Providing a little in-your-face focus was dreadlocked boxer Lennox Lewis, who, by beating Evander Holyfield, became the first British undisputed World Heavyweight Champion in nearly a hundred years. At another, but more sublime level, artist Chris Ofili's controversial picture, *Madonna,* dominated the 'Sensation' showcase of contemporary British art at New York's Brooklyn Museum. However, like Naomi Campbell before them, these two recent dramatic outings came with very little back-story attached. Americans notice them but appreciate little of their internal realities or their deepest desires. They know even less about the self-belief or unique set of struggles that bring into being such greatness.

This lack of a broader point of view merely repeated an earlier pattern when the first truly global manifestation of this sensibility became apparent in the 1960s. It was projected through a serious best-selling book that achieved an international reputation after it was made into a Hollywood film, starring Sidney Poitier. E. R. Braithwaite's fictional autobiography, *To Sir, with Love,* and his portrayal by Poitier in the film version, thrust the new black population in Britain into global consciousness. But with much confusion. It is probable that many people watching the film were unable to go beyond Sidney Poitier's celebrity, and understood it only as a story about an 'American teacher in London,' as well as a way of recasting America's racial drama in a far away, and therefore, less threatening theatre. For those who were able to go beyond the mask of Poitier's celebrity, the confusions might have persisted. Here, ultimately, was an American of West Indian origin, playing another man from the West Indies, living in Britain. But beneath all the layers of the actor's masks, who was this real man being portrayed? And why was the new milieu in London important to the human drama of *To Sir, with Love?*

E. R. Braithwaite, though not born in Britain, is a man of Empire. Like other ex-Empire writers who have established formidable international reputations, such as C. L. R. James, V. S. Naipaul, George Lamming, Salman Rushdie, and Ben Okri, Braithwaite continues to be perceived as an individual. He is not understood as part of a historical movement centered on Britain in the last half of the 20th century: a movement which produced particular ways of seeing and which has left a distinctive legacy, a legacy that is being built upon by a new generation.

To clear up the confusions, it is best to comprehend the rather complicated relationship between the new migrants or 'post–Empire' people and their British hosts, as well as the historical baggage they carried to their new country. And one of the best gateways to this understanding of the 'Hurricane that hit England' is the literature that was produced as the migration unfolded.

The landing of the SS *Empire Windrush* at Tilbury Docks on June 21, 1948, began a process that has steadily and radically transformed Britain. *Empire Windrush* was the first ship bringing home the people of Empire as settlers. They had, of course, come in the past from Africa, the Caribbean, Hong Kong, and the Indian subcontinent as students, sailors, artists, political activists, and slaves. But this time they were coming as free men and women, seeking work. They were coming at a time of immense change. Britain was recovering from an exhausting and ruinous war, which had sapped her will to hang onto her former possessions. Already in 1947, India and Pakistan had slipped out of her orbit, embarking on a new path in their own universe. After Empire, the pillars on which her identity had traditionally been constructed – Crown, Church, and political union between the nations of England, Scotland, Wales, and Ireland – would also begin to fracture. So although these men were coming 'home,' they were coming to a home that was rapidly changing, one that did not have the energy to sustain what it once was, but was nevertheless trapped in the old idea of itself.

The emotions that spilled out as Britain negotiated the path from greatness to relative decline were just too raw. The newcomers caught the foul icy blast caused by the disorientation of their former empire builders. They watched their hosts lurch from preening imperial arrogance one minute to excruciating self-pity the next. Irvin, a Birmingham-based West Indian, talking to writer Dervla Murphy in her book *Tales from Two Cities,* laments the opportunities that were lost in those early days:

> What a chance Britain's missed! If this country wasn't so racist it could have paid off some of its old debts in the twentieth century . . . you understand what I'm saying? It could've let us escape from our past. You're a reading lady, you know our history. We were dirt, for centuries, no more or less important than work-animals. Then we were needed here, and that was a good feeling. To be needed, as people. To make our own decisions, to cross the sea independently, paying our own fares, travelling to earn a fair wage for honest work. That felt real good. A lot of us dreamed about saving to go home to start

something of our own. In the early days most of us didn't come to settle – people forget that. We didn't come to invade cities and take them over. We had stupid ideas about how much we could earn and save in a few years – we were just ignorant about Britain. We thought here we'd be equal. Nothing special, just equal . . . But it was never like that and we had to adjust to the way it was and make the best of it. If it was the other way, if ourselves and our kids got equal treatment, we could have been so happy!

Despite the anger and disappointment experienced by this first generation, British identity has changed and become more forward-looking and gently inclusive over the last fifty years. A large part of the reason has to be attributable to the presence of the 'post–Empire generation' and the discourse of freedom and equality they brought with them. In confronting the racism and exclusion they faced, they also discovered things about their capacity to survive and reconstruct a new identity, which would ironically help, unshackle them from their past. Guyanese novelist and poet David Dabydeen likened the experience of the newcomers from the colonies to that of Dorothy arriving at the castle of the Wizard of Oz.

Descending in the millions, they came in awe and in search of a missing part of themselves, which they believed had been stolen. Starting from the margins, they walked with a terrified boldness toward the center of the power that had held their imaginations enthralled, humiliated their bodies, taken over their economies, and captured their souls. The walk was over a stony landscape of contesting ideas and values about the equality, universality, and possibilities of the human family. When they finally arrived at the huge hall where the center oi power lay, the first thing they discovered was that they had themselves changed beyond recognition.

Next, expecting to see a coherent and supreme intelligence, they found, instead, that there was no center, only aspects and fragments of luminous power confusedly darting back and forth in a spectacular hall with a thousand angled mirrors. When they peered closer into the mirrors they saw only their own image reflected. And they were shocked to have come all this way, only to find themselves.

Rumanian Mircea Eliade tells a similar story, which convinces us that it is the journey itself and the contact with the 'Other' (despite the pain and humiliation that accompanies it) through which liberation is possible. In a piece arguing that the influence of primitivism in Rumanian art did not originate in Africa but from old Rumanian folk art itself, Eliade nevertheless admits that it is the way in which Rumanians rediscover their folk art that is fascinating—and particularly appropriate for us here.

For Eliade, the answer lies in a parable: a desperately poor man dreams, three nights in a row, of finding a pot of gold buried under a bridge in the capital city. Wanting the riches, he travels to the capital, where a soldier demands to know what he is up to. Reluctantly the poor man tells him, but the soldier simply laughs and recalls a similar dream he himself has had. The soldier dreamed he had gone to the house of a poor man in the provinces, where a pot of gold lay buried in the poor man's garden. Only, the soldier sneered at his victim, he did not go foolishly searching for the poor man's gold when he woke up because he realized it was only a dream, and he was not ignorant and superstitious! But the poor man would not be swayed. Ignoring the soldier's insults, he returned home and dug in his garden where the soldier had mentioned. Sure enough he found a pot of gold buried there.

The moral is obvious – the greatest wealth is within you. But Eliade adds an important rejoinder: it is only the contact with the stranger, someone very different from you, who might even despise you, that releases you to find your own treasure. By sharing in the 'dream' of another for awhile, you ironically gain a way into those dreams of yours that you never knew you owned. For when you try on another mentality, you make accessible aspects of yourself not available to you when you think and feel as you ordinarily do.

The Empire was an extraordinary collection of peoples, cultures, and civilizations that was knitted together by English administration, values, and language. It defined everybody, both periphery and center, bonded them together in sometimes exploitative and strained relationships. Center and periphery shared 'dreams' (not all pleasant), transformed and eventually humanized each other. After South Africa's liberation, and the hand back of Hong Kong, both now face each other, in law at least, as equals. Everybody appears on the brink of a new relationship. But for the children of Empire the long walk to this moment of equality has been a journey fraught with the struggle to break out of a major paradigm.

Writers have been at the forefront of unraveling the economic and psychological relationship on the Plantation – this being the para-

digm at the heart of Empire. With the Master occupying the Big
House in the middle, the colonized subjects in surrounding 'slave
quarters' have been wondering, over 400 years, how to break out:
to stop being black, yellow, and brown constructs; to recover their
own equilibrium.

From the dawn of the Empire, the literature in English of the various people in the 'slave quarters' has been preoccupied with these
concerns. The earliest examples, from ex-slaves Olaudah Equiano and
Ignatius Sancho in the eighteenth century, have been about the recovery of self, through autobiographical narratives. Their books, as
well as being campaign tracts against slavery, also sought to declare
through a first-person insistence, the individual's humanity.

Over the years, the preoccupation of much of the literature has
been with this troubled quest for identity and liberty, as men were
wrenched away into a 'New World' and older notions of self col-
lapsed. This is largely the world of the wretched, having to re-
make themselves constantly in a hostile world, with wretched
tools. It is necessarily bleak, tragic, and sad. But there was also
great diversity in the Empire. Its people came from ancient civilizations in Africa, the Indian subcontinent, and the Far East. In
these spaces, although recovery of self was important, the project
could also be founded on older existing literatures, notions of self,
culture, and worldview.

Out of this mixture in the post–Empire world of Britain, an extraordinary group of writers has emerged, a group that has changed
and transformed the style, substance, and themes of English litera-
ture. It has been a rich vein: from the first wave of C. L. R. James,
George Lamming, V. S. Naipaul, Wilson Harris, Samuel Selvon,
Andrew Salkey, and E. R. Braithwaite; to the second wave of Salman
Rushdie, Ben Okri, Mike Phillips, Timothy Mo, Buchi Emecehta,
Grace Nichols, Caryl Phillips, Linton Kwesi Johnson; to those who
have emerged in the 1990s such as Hanif Kureshi, S. I. Martin, Diran
Adebayo, Bernadine Evaristo, and Andrea Levy.

Their subject matter and interests (and those of the other excellent
writers who for reasons of space could not be included in this collection) have ranged widely, but as they express their many preoccupations, they have returned again and again to the big overriding
issue of the post–Empire imagination, which is what to do with the
plantation and how to break the paradigm. Do you burn down the
plantation and begin again? Or do you eschew the inevitable chaos

caused by burning down the house, realize that it is the only economy in town, and hope that over the years through good behavior
and assimilation of the values of the Big House, you will eventually
be admitted? First as faithful servant and trusted Uncle Tom, then
as mimic, before eventually as equal.

The post–Empire imagination has produced two giants who represent these two dialectical poles of thinking. Interestingly, both
were born on the Caribbean island of Trinidad. One is V. S. Naipaul,
who is of Asian descent; the other is C. L. R. James, of African
descent.

Naipaul, who declined to be included in this anthology, is a conservative patrician. He has mapped out over a series of controversial,
classic texts such as *A House for Mr. Biswas, The Mimic Men, A
Bend in the River, In a Free State,* and *An Area of Darkness,* a vision
of cautious evolution, which some have said borders on outright self-
abnegation. In the absence of a viable alternative, he has argued for
an acceptance of the culture and values of the 'Big House.' In *The
Enigma of the Arrival,* he even seems to be suggesting the possibility
of a strange sort of mystical rebirth through this process. Fearful of
chaos, he believes that the older civilizations in Asia or Africa, or
the new constructs like the plantation economies of the West Indies,
had not adapted well to the modern world. Many of their revolts
were simply gestures against humiliation. And beyond that they constructed fantasies that confused excitement with liberation. If the
slave has not built the structure, how does he take over?

For Naipaul, the 'Big House' was the result of the inexorable
march of history, the combined energies and genius of the best aspects of the world's different cultures. It was not really owned by
any one Western culture, but was the inheritance of all, if all were
bold and realistic enough to want to inhabit it. To do that you needed
to study the intricate details of the house and the relationships inside,
in order to move beyond mimicry to understanding its real pulse
and heartbeat. Sudden flamboyant flourishes which pretended to
speed up the process of understanding, should be viewed with suspicion. No sudden vision would reveal another dispensation. As Naipaul wrote in his essay 'Power,' in *The Overcrowded Barracoon,* the
'vision of the black millennium, as much a vision of revenge as of
a black world made whole again', is fantasy.

Naipaul's vision has been most robustly challenged by C. L. R.
James, the Marxist revolutionary, who although a generation older

than Naipaul, always seemed to dazzle with youthful enthusiasm, whether for cricket, West Indian independence, or African liberation. His scope and ambition were extraordinary, mixing disciplines, genres, and subjects with brilliance and insight. Literature, politics, criticism, and philosophy are all deployed as organic parts of the same argument. In *Beyond the Boundary,* cricket is used as a tool to dissect the psychological, as well as social and economic, conditions of the Caribbean. James's flights of the imagination, anchored in Marxist dialectical materialism, led him to the possibility of constructing and reconstructing himself – in order to create the New Man.

James has been one of the leading thinkers of the postcolonial society and the father of Caribbean literature. *Minty Alley* was the first major English novel out of the region. *The Black Jacobins,* his seminal historical account of the successful slave revolt in Haiti at the end of the eighteenth century, rejects Naipaul's caution, and positively embraces the future, despite the violence and chaos. He has walked a thin but careful line between nationalism and internationalism, race and class, believing that the paradigm of the Plantation will shift since the economics of the world is shifting, and new classes of people have a better understanding of themselves and their role in history. The world will not be remade quietly, and we must not be frightened to dream and impose our dreams on a chaotic reality. We particularly need to keep faith with the poor and marginalized – to quote Martinican writer Aimé Cesaire: 'There will be room for all at the rendezvous of victory.'

It is significant that both these writers who dominate the landscape and imagination of black British writing are from the Caribbean, and not Africa, India, or China. From the Islands they take on the imperial center, as well as all the other civilizations – African, Indian, Chinese, Amerindian, and European – which are to be found in the Caribbean. Their subject is Empire: its collapse and the way it continues both to shape and haunt the modern world. In his travels in Africa, India, and Latin America, Naipaul traverses its known limits with his dour pessimism. On the other hand, James's writings on the English Caribbean, Haiti, and revolutionary France, as well as his involvement in Kwame Nkrumah's African revolution, reveal his grasp of the epicenters of change in the project of bringing an end to Empire.

These two men have been hugely influential on the output of the rest of the post–Empire writers, even where this influence has merely been expressed as an opposition to their ideas. It was certainly stronger among the older generation of writers as can be seen from the 'Jamesian' preoccupations of people such as Jan Carew, Andrew Salkey, and George Lamming. Although we hear less of it in the works of the '90s generation, there are still echoes of their ideas in the inevitable clash of cultural values that engulfed Salman Rushdie after *The Satanic Verses,* and in the arguments that raged in the 1970s over the use of dialect in black British writing and over the Black Power movement. Salman Rushdie has even suggested a literary solution to the dilemma of the plantation: 'To conquer English may be to complete the process of making ourselves free.'

Within this broader understanding, the output of writers since the 1950s has also closely mirrored the day-to-day experiences people were going through in Britain. This anthology has been structured to reflect the emotional roller coaster that people went through over the last half of the century. So the first wave of writers naturally concentrated on the themes of home, the journey, and, while settling in Britain, the enormous obstacles that confronted people, such as race prejudice, marginalization, and rejection. The anger of the 1958 race riots in the Notting Hill district of London, when cryptofascist Teddy Boys attacked the new settlers, marked the beginning of a deeper despondency and the beginning of a revolutionary worldwide fight-back in the 1960s. The anger and militancy of Third Worldism and Black Power were its obvious manifestations. By the 1970s such radical activism overlapped with economic recession, and the emergence of the first generation of British-born children of the migrants.

With writers like Linton Kwesi Johnson, the new generation began to express its frustrations through poetry and the theatre, about being born and brought up, but not accepted in Britain. A fresh riot in Notting Hill, this time at the 1976 carnival, prompted another watershed in the development of this generation's British identity, and the search backward, through Rastafarianism and other separatist ideas, for a comfort zone.

However, this younger generation and their elders before them had to contend with the disappointments of independence back home. The new countries, released from the imperial yoke, had in many cases sunk into recession, crisis, and corruption. By the 1980s there was no going back. At least, not in the old romantic sense. This would become a critical moment in the evolution of the post–Empire sensibility. Many of the older generation of writers such as E. R. Braithwaite, Andrew Salkey, Sam Selvon, and George Lamming had already left Britain to seek pastures new and plan the remaking of their original Caribbean homeland. Except this time it would be from Canadian and American settings. While for the new generation, Britain remained the journey's end. In order to make sense of the paradigmatic shift involved in their unequivocal choice, this British–born generation found a voice in novels. Looking back to their own childhood, these writers began, like Caryl Phillips in *The Final Passage,* to rewrite the story of the arrival of their parents. They also began, uniquely, to map out the contours of their own identity as British people—not as rejected outsiders, but critical insiders. This generation of writers, such as Hanif Kureshi, Diran Adebayo, S. I. Martin, and Andrea Levy, crossed the bridge from the post–Empire experiences of the first generation carrying two worlds in their hearts, to the different landscape of multicultural New Britain, which they now inhabit.

At the end of the 20th century, the contours of that identity have become blurred and less black and white. Now the grasp of Britain is surer, writers are increasingly moving away from the limitations of the biographical narrative (or what African American writer Al Murrey calls the 'social-science fiction monster') into the multiplicity of genre fiction in order to capture the complexity of the New British landscape. Having moved into the Wizard's Castle in Oz, they can more readily separate reality from myth because they profoundly understand the institutions and levers that manipulate illusion. So with the ground more solid, people will begin to fly. For years, Mike Phillips ploughed a lonely path in crime fiction. One suspects he will not be alone for long. This, and the other huge gaps that continue to be scandalously apparent in other genres (travel, particularly within Britain, science fiction, satire, horror, spy thriller, adventure- and historical-drama) will soon begin, one hopes, to be filled in dramatic new ways.

Outside of the missing-genre gaps, the other bizarre development in literature about the post–Empire generation is the lack of curiosity shown by white writers, beyond official reports for the race-relations industry or newspaper journalists responding to social crises. When writing for television or the stage, white writers have attempted portraits of post–Empire Britain with varying degrees of success. But few novelists or poets have attempted complex portraits that reveal internal worlds. Given that the presence of brown, black, and yellow people over the last half of the 20th century caused so much angst and soul-searching, this development is rather astonishing. Five white writers have been included in *Hurricane Hits England.* We have the enthusiasm of Colin MacInnes who eagerly embraced the world of the new migrants and understood that they were the harbingers of a social revolution; Roy Kerridge, who grew up with an African stepfather and has embedded himself in the culture of the black church; Elizabeth Taylor, whose story 'The Devastating Boys' cleverly reveals the confusing caution many white Britons expressed toward the post–Empire generation; Irish writer Dervla Murphy, who spent time inside the Asian and African-Caribbean communities of Bradford and Handsworth, Birmingham; and finally anti-migrant right-wing reactionary politician Enoch Powell, who projected the fear and irrational hatred toward the newcomers, typical of so many others. Though controversial, Powell is in this collection because, beyond his obsession with immigration, he was the standard-bearer for a vision of Britain (white, nondevolved, anti–European, and traditional monarchist), which has largely been swept away – with the help of the post–Empire generation and their descendents such as Naomi Campbell, Lennox Lewis, and Chris Ofili.

ONYEKACHI WAMBU
Spring 2000

THE RESTLESS URGE

No Nation now but the imagination
DEREK WALCOTT, 'The Schooner Flight'

JOHN AGARD

John Agard was born in Guyana and has lived in Britain since 1977. He has published several books of poetry for children and adults including *Mangoes & Bullets* and *Lovelines for a Goat-Born Lady* (Serpent's Tail). He was awarded the 1982 Casa de las Americas poetry prize for his collection *Man to Pan*. His latest collection is *From the Devil's Pulpit* (Bloodaxe Books).

'Boomerang' (taken from his collection *A Stone's Throw from Embankment*) was written in 1993, the year John spent as the first writer in residence at the South Bank Centre. The collection meditates on the activities and exhibitions taking place at the centre. Here, he is inspired by 'Boomerang', which was part of Aratjara, the largest aboriginal exhibition ever seen in Europe.

Boomerang

Featherless bird
I will nest in the eye of wind

Crescent moon
fashioned by hand
I will slice the sky of your gaze

Crooked stick
I will aspire to the gift of wings

Rainbow wood
I will bridge what is and is not imagined
forever curving towards the path of origin

Hurl me from your hand. But remember
I am the dream the wind has given you.

STUART HALL

Stuart Hall was born in Jamaica and arrived in England in 1951 to study at Oxford. As one of the editors of *Universities*, *Left Review* and *New Left Review* in the 1960s, he has been a key figure in the New Left. Through his extensive writings and leadership of the Centre for Contemporary Studies at the University of Birmingham, his work has been central to the formation and development of cultural studies as an international discipline. His concerns have ranged over a wide field: cultural studies and the relationship with Marxism; Postmodernism and 'New Times', race, ethnicity and identity. He has been one of the seminal thinkers in the construction of the black British identity, and in the anti-Stalinist and post-communist discourses on the left.

In this interview by Kuan-Hsing Chen, Stuart Hall discusses his background and the way it informed his work.

from *Stuart Hall, Critical Dialogues in Cultural Studies*
The Formation of a Diasporic Intellectual I

The Colonial Situation

KHC: In your later work on race and ethnicity, diaspora seems to have become a central figure – one of the critical sites on which the question of cultural identity is articulated; bits and pieces of your own diasporic experiences have, at certain points, been narrated quite powerfully, to address both theoretical and political problematics. What I am interested in is how the specificities of the various historical trajectories came to shape your diasporic experiences, your own intellectual and political position.

SH: I was born in Jamaica and grew up in a middle-class family. My father spent most of his working life in the United Fruit Company. He was the first Jamaican to be promoted in every job he had; before him, those jobs were occupied by people sent down from the head office in America. What's important to understand is both the class fractions and the colour fractions from which my parents came. My father's and my mother's families were both middle-class but from very different class formations. My father belonged to the coloured lower-middle-class. His father kept a drugstore in a poor village in the country outside Kingston. The family was ethnically very mixed – African, East Indian, Portuguese, Jewish. My mother's family was much fairer in colour; indeed if you had seen her uncle, you would have thought he was an English expatriate, nearly white, or what we would call 'local white'. She was adopted by an aunt, whose sons – one a lawyer, one a doctor – trained in England. She was brought up in a beautiful house on the hill, above a small estate where the family lived. Culturally present in my own family was therefore this lower-middle-class Jamaican, country manifestly dark skinned, and then this lighter-skinned, English-oriented, plantation-oriented fraction, etc.

So what was played out in my family, culturally, from the very beginning, was the conflict between the local and the imperial in the colonized context. Both of these class formations were opposed to the majority culture of poor Jamaican black people: highly race-and-colour conscious and identifying with the colonizers.

I was the blackest member of my family. The story in my family, which was always told as a joke, was that when I was born, my sister, who was much fairer than I, looked into the crib and said, 'Where did you get this coolie baby from?' Now 'coolie' is the abusive word in Jamaica for a poor East Indian, who was considered the lowest of the low. So she wouldn't say, 'Where did you get this black baby from?', since it was unthinkable that she could have a black brother. But she *did* notice that I was a different colour from her. This is very common in coloured middle-class Jamaican families, because they are the product of mixed liaisons between African slaves and European slave-masters, and the children then come out in varying shades.

So I always had the identity in my family of being the one from the outside, the one who didn't fit, the one who was blacker than the others, 'the little coolie', etc. And I performed that role throughout. My friends at school, many of whom were from good middle-class homes, but blacker in colour than me, were not accepted at my home. My parents didn't think I was making the right kind of friends. They always encouraged me to mix with more middle-class, more higher-colour friends and I didn't. Instead, I withdrew emotionally from my family and met my friends elsewhere. My adolescence was spent continuously negotiating these cultural spaces.

My father wanted me to play sport. He wanted me to join the clubs that he joined. But I always thought that he himself did not quite fit in this world. He was negotiating his way into the world. He was accepted on sufferance by the English. I could see the way they patronized him. I hated that more than anything else. It wasn't just that he belonged to a world which I rejected. I couldn't understand how *he* didn't see how much they depised him. I said to myself, 'Don't you understand when you go into that club they think you are an interloper?' And, 'But you want to put me into that space, to be humiliated in the same way?'

Because my mother was brought up in this Jamaican plantation context, she thought she was practically 'English'. She thought England was the mother country, she identified with the colonial power. She had aspirations for us, her family, which materially we couldn't keep up with, but which she aspired to, culturally.

I'm trying to say that those classic colonial tensions were lived as part of my personal history. My own formation and identity was very much constructed out of a kind of refusal of the dominant personal and cultural models which were held up for me. I didn't want to beg my way like my father into acceptance by the American or English expatriate business community and I couldn't identify with that old plantation world, with its roots in slavery, but which my mother spoke of as a 'golden age'. I felt much more like an independent Jamaican boy. But there was no room for that as a subjective position, in the culture of my family.

Now this is the period of growth of the Jamaican independence movement. As a young student, I was very much in favour of that. I became anti-imperialist and identified with Jamaican independence. But my family was not. They were not even identified with the ambitions for independence of the national bourgeoisie. In that sense, they were different from even their own friends, who thought, once the transition to national independence began, 'Well, at least we'll be in power.' My parents, my mother especially, regretted the passing of that old colonial world, more than anything else. This was a huge gap between their aspirations for me and how I identified myself.

KHC: So you are saying that your impulse to 'revolt' partly came from the Jamaican situation. Can you elaborate?

SH: Going to school as a bright, promising scholar and becoming politically involved, I was therefore interested in what was going on politically, namely, the formation of Jamaican political parties, the emergence of the trades unions and the labour movement after 1938, the beginnings of a nationalist independence movement at the end of the war; all of these were part of the postcolonial or decolonizing revolution. Jamaica began to move towards independence once the war was over. So bright kids like me and my friends, of varying colours and social positions, were nevertheless caught up in that movement, and that's what we identified with. We were looking forward to the end of imperialism, Jamaica governing itself, self-autonomy for Jamaica.

. . .

KHC: How important was Marx, or the tradition of marxist literature [on your intellectual development]?

SH: Well, I read Marx's essays – the *Communist Manifesto*, *Wage Labour* and *Capital*; I read Lenin on imperialism. It was important for me more in the context of colonialism, than about Western capitalism. The questions of class were clearly present in the political conversation about colonialism going on in Jamaica, the question of poverty, the problem of economic development, etc. A lot of my young friends, who went to university at the same time I did, studied economics. Economics was supposed to be the answer to the poverty which countries like Jamaica experienced, as a consequence of imperialism and colonialism. So I was interested in the economic question from a colonial standpoint. If I had an ambition at that point, the ambition was not to go into business like my father, but to become a lawyer; becoming a lawyer was already, in Jamaica, a major route into politics. Or, I could become an economist. But actually, I was more interested in literature and history than economics. When I was seventeen, my sister had a major nervous breakdown. She began a relationship with a young student doctor who had come to Jamaica from Barbados. He was middle-class, but black, and my parents wouldn't allow it. There was a tremendous family row and she, in effect, retreated from the situation into a breakdown. I was suddenly aware of the contradiction of a colonial culture, of how one lives out the colour–class–colonial dependency experience and how it could destroy you, subjectively.

I am telling this story because it was very important for my personal development. It broke down forever, for me, the distinction between the public and the private self. I learned about culture, first, as something which is deeply subjective and personal, and at the same moment, as a structure you live. I could see that all these strange aspirations and identifications which my parents had projected on to us, their children, destroyed my sister. She was the victim, the bearer of the contradictory ambitions of my parents in this colonial situation. From then on, I could never understand why people thought these structural questions were not connected with the psychic – with emotions and identifications and feelings because, for me, those structures are things you live. I don't just mean they are personal; they are, but they are also institutional, they have real structural properties, they break you, destroy you.

It was a very traumatic experience, because there was little or no psychiatric help available in Jamaica, at that time. My sister went through a series of ECT treatments given by a GP, from which she's never properly recovered. She never left home after that. She looked after my father until he died. Then she looked after my mother until she died. She took care of my brother who became blind, until he died. That's a complete tragedy, which I lived through with her, and I decided I couldn't take it; I couldn't help her, I couldn't reach her, although I understood what was wrong. I was seventeen, eighteen.

But it crystallized my feelings about the space I was called into by my family. I was not going to stay there. I was not going to be destroyed by it. I had to get out. I felt that I must never put myself back into it, because I would be destroyed. When I look at the snapshots of myself in childhood and early adolescence, I see a picture of a depressed person. I don't want to be who they want me to be, but I don't know how to be somebody else. And I am depressed by that. All of that is the background to explain why I eventually migrated.

ROY HEATH

Roy Heath is from Guyana. He came to England at the age of twenty-four, to read Modern Languages at London University. He has been been teaching since 1959, all the while pursuing a career as a novelist. His first novel, *A Man Come Home*, was published in 1974. His second, *The Murderer*, won the Guardian Fiction Prize in 1978 and was followed by a trilogy about the Armstrong family: *From the Heat of the Day, One Generation* and *Genetha*.

Kwaku – Or the Man Who Could Not Keep His Mouth Shut charts the career and outrageous adventures of Kwaku Cholmondeley, part conman, part everyman, part holy fool. It follows its hero from his childhood dreams of a glorious destiny, to his search for the perfect wife, the ideal job and the easy life. He pursues his dreams of wealth, happiness and position with a fanaticism that is defeated only by his own magnificent failings.

from *Kwaku – Or the Man Who Could Not Keep His Mouth Shut*
The Centre of Attention

Although Kwaku had left his idiocy behind, there were moments when he said and did things that surprised him and confounded those around him. One evening when the storytelling comrade among the group he used to frequent ran out of stories and the youths took to arguing about the superiority of the members of their respective families, one boy declared that his brother, who worked on a timber grant, had fourteen gold teeth in his mouth, a disclosure which earned him a minute of reverential silence. Then Kwaku, for no reason whatsoever, declared for everyone to hear that his mother had bigger bosoms than the mother of anyone else present. And immediately a commotion broke out, for Kwaku's mother had died when he was an infant.

'But she dead!' one youth shouted scornfully.

'I know,' replied Kwaku. 'I say she *had*, not that she *got*.'

'You mean you remember she bosom, though you was a baby,'

pitched in another youth who seized the opportunity to put down Kwaku.

'My father tell me,' protested Kwaku.

'But he run away years ago,' the first youth reminded him. 'And you was a lil' boy.'

'He tell me *before* he go away.'

'You mean,' said another youth, 'just before he run away he call you and say, "Son, I runnin' away an' leaving you. But before I go I got something to tell you. You mother had the biggest bubby in the village."'

Kwaku was now indeed the centre of attention, but not in the way he had expected. The more words he wasted in defending himself, the more impatient his companions became, until one youth said, 'Don' worry with him, he stupidy.'

So the argument came to an end and the youth whose brother had capped his teeth with gold became the centre of attention once more.

Another time Kwaku was on his way home on Blossom's rickety bicycle, which was making so much noise that pedestrians and vehicles had ample time to avoid him, despite the fact that the cycle was not provided with a lamp as the law required. Rounding the bend on the Public Road he saw a number of lights moving about in the distance and, on approaching, saw that there had been an accident. Two cars were locked together by their front bumpers and glass was shattered on the grass verge between the road and the lotus-covered trench.

'Any witnesses?' Kwaku heard one of the three policemen ask.

He had dismounted and placed Blossom's cycle carefully against a wayside tree lest it fell apart. Then he boldly stepped up and said, 'I'm a witness,' though the accident must have occurred some time before he arrived. And he and the others who were on the scene at the moment of the mishap were asked to give their names and addresses.

On the morning of the case, four months later, Kwaku was obliged to walk the eleven miles to court, for Blossom, the previous day, had refused to lend him her bicycle.

'It old,' she observed, 'and the way you does ride it would die on the way.'

Blossom's husband-to-be backed her up, mistakenly seeing in Kwaku a rival for Blossom's affection.

Kwaku set out for court at five o'clock and arrived at ten minutes past nine just after the hearing began, looking like a cat that was fed at the same time as the dog of the house and out of the same receptacle.

He was made to sit on the bench where the other witnesses were ranged, awaiting their turn to be called into the courtroom.

'How long this thing going last?' a young woman next to him enquired.

But before Kwaku could answer, an old man on her right said, 'Can be all day. You bring food?'

'Just as I did think,' muttered the woman.

Kwaku had no money. He was to start work as a shoemaker the following week and his uncle would neither oblige by cooking early in the morning nor allow Kwaku to cook a meal for himself, for all his pepper and salt would disappear mysteriously and the food would be inedible.

Kwaku was called at five minutes to four in the afternoon, after the prosecution witnesses had testified and the magistrate had warned that his clerk-of-court had to go home at six o'clock.

By this time Kwaku was hungry and irritable and regretted bitterly his hastiness in putting himself forward as a witness to the accident. And the sight of the well-fed magistrate, who must have been eating fried chicken during the recess, so incensed Kwaku that he decide to teach him a lesson and misbehave in the witness box.

'Will you swear on the Bible, please?' the uniformed gentleman asked.

'I don't swear,' declared Kwaku. 'My uncle tell me never to swear.'

'Your what?' asked the magistrate, his eyes blazing.

'My uncle,' said Kwaku defiantly. 'And the church say you musn' swear, too.'

'You'd better do as you're told,' ordered the magistrate, 'or you'll take the consequences.'

So Kwaku swore. Then he was asked to tell what he saw on the road on the evening of the accident and he spoke his prepared account.

'I was coming down the road on my new bicycle . . . '

The magistrate looked at his watch.

' . . . and slam, the yellow car turn out of the village road and knock into the blue car.'

'So one car was yellow and the other blue, eh?' asked the middle-aged counsel for the prosecution sarcastically. 'And what was the colour of your glasses?'

'My what?' Kwaku said.

'Your glasses.'

'I don't wear glasses,' Kwaku protested.

'Precisely! Without glasses the cars were both black!'

'Not when I see the accident,' Kwaku corrected him.

The very thing the magistrate feared came to pass. A long-winded witness was going to spoil everything.

And Kwaku did. When six o'clock came the magistrate refused to carry on without his clerk-of-court, and the case was put off until another date. The driver of the car, who had been charged with dangerous driving and who thought that things had been going well for him until Kwaku came into court, gave him such a withering look he was forced to avert his eyes.

Four weeks later Kwaku had to ask for a day off from his new job in order to attend court once more. It was granted him, without pay. He borrowed Blossom's bicycle, promising to buy her a new one from his wages if it did not last the journey. He arrived at the courthouse before the sun came up, when nothing was astir, save a flock of jumbee birds pecking in the damp grass, and the only sound was the high, plaintive wail of a birdcall.

Sitting down on the lowest step of the whitewashed court-house staircase he looked about him, at the tiny house opposite with its unpainted shutters, at the boats and the wooden bridge over the drainage canal. The villagers were asleep while he, from another village, was kicking his heels, anxiously awaiting the arrival of a hostile magistrate, who was bent on intimidating him just because he could not hold his tongue. He began to call to mind his follies, which passed before him like a troop of galloping horses. And he resolved that after the court case he would curb his tongue, even if he had to chain it. He would also take care to show Blossom the gratitude she deserved. Which other woman in the world would consecrate a school friendship as she had done, at the risk of her relations with a husband-to-be? And what sort of life lay before his future wife and children if he fell prey to every impulse?

Day broke and with it came the noise and bustle of animals, men and their machines. Asses brayed, dogs barked, goats bleated, buses hummed like giant bees and magistrates slammed their car doors ostentatiously, in the manner of those men who dare not lay a finger on their wives and bang the window instead.

No sooner did the proceedings begin than the magistrate interrupted his clerk-of-court.

'There are those,' he began threateningly, 'who forget who they are. I am here and they are there; and they forget that. Oh, yes! I warned when the case was last heard of the problems that would arise if it went beyond six o'clock. But certain long-winded people . . . '

And at this point the magistrate glared at Kwaku.

' . . . certain people who don't like taking advice, even when it comes from others in power – *in power* – go on and on and on as if it was morning time. But I'm giving this advice once again. Do not let us hear unnecessary chatter about the colour of cars; because *I* have to go early today. Not the clerk-of-court, but *I*. I hope that's clear.'

The magistrate was now sweating profusely and frothing at the mouth as if he had been stung by a scorpion. When he recovered his composure he took up a thick, elegantly bound law-book, raised it and was just about to bring it down on the clerk-of-court's head, as it seemed, but changed his mind and smashed it on to the desk in front of him instead, in order to stress how serious his warning was.

Kwaku was made to take his place in the witness-box, aware that all eyes were on him and that the magistrate was crouching at his desk, ready to spring on him and bring him to order. And in a quarter of an hour the proceedings were at an end. The accused driver was found guilty of dangerous driving and Kwaku was allowed to leave the courthouse under the scrutiny of the powerful magistrate.

'Lucky he din' make us charge you with perjury,' remarked the constable who had brought the prosecution case. '"Blue car and yellow car!" You ever see a yellow car in this country?'

Kwaku was about to say that his father owned a yellow car once, but luckily he bit his tongue and put on such a pained expression that the policeman believed he was about to burst into tears for the lies he had told.

On his way home under the heat of the morning sun Kwaku decided that, as he had little control of what he said and did, he would get married and so acquire a sense of responsibility. He was once told by his uncle that the tormented look he noticed on all married men's faces was simply the outward sign of a sense of responsibility. And already, on the way home, he was planning how best he would go about the business of choosing a wife from among the village girls.

SAM SELVON

Sam Selvon was born in Trinidad of Indian parentage. A wireless operator with the Royal Navy and a journalist on the Trinidad *Guardian*, he arrived in Britain in 1950. *The Lonely Londoners*, a classic text, was his first novel to be set in London. He wrote two further novels centred around Moses (the protagonist from *The Lonely Londoners*), *A Brighter Sun*, and various collections of short stories. He later moved to Canada, where he died in 1994.

A Brighter Sun catches Trinidad in the turbulent throes of the Second World War. For Tiger, young and inexperienced, these are years in which to prove his manhood and independence. With his child bride Urmilla – shy, bewildered and anxious – two hundred dollars in cash and a milking cow, he sets off into the wilderness of adulthood. The following passage is the opening of the novel.

from *A Brighter Sun*

On New Year's Day, 1939, while Trinidadians who had money or hopes of winning money were attending the races in the Queen's Park Savannah, Port of Spain, a number of Jewish refugees fleeing Nazi persecution in Europe landed on the island. There was an almost instant increase in the rental of residences and business places, and later more refugees were refused entrance. A development plan costing fourteen million US dollars was approved by the Secretary of State for the Colonies but nipped in the bud when war was declared. In April, when pouis blossomed and keskidees sang for rain, local forces were mobilized. In May a German training ship with a crew of 270 paid a visit. Emergency regulations were introduced, mail and telegrams censored, the churches prayed for peace, and the adjacent territorial waters were proclaimed a prohibited area. A man went about the streets of the city riding a bicycle and balancing a bottle of rum on his head. An East Indian, reputedly mad, walked to the wharf and dipped a key in the sea and went away muttering to himself. A big burly Negro called Mussolini, one-legged and arrogant, chased a small boy who was teasing him and fell down, cursing loudly, much to the amusement of passers-by. In September much rain fell; it was the middle of the rainy season. Usually it is Indian summer weather – the natives call it *petite carème* – lasting for a month. It is the best time for planting crops. War was declared and measures necessary for the preservation of internal order were intensified, and wartime regulations brought into force.

All activities concentrated on the 'war effort' in 1940. Money collected in various ways was sent to England. Six young men from the Air Training Scheme left to join the RAF. Negotiations between England and America for bases in the island came to a head when a United States Major discussed the actual locations of the proposed bases with the Governor. Air-raid precautions were introduced. French residents pledged their support to General de Gaulle, and a man named Lafeet died in a hut far in the hills of the Northern Range, and nobody knew anything until three weeks later. A model township was opened on the outskirts of the city to relieve the housing shortage. Land was rented to the peasantry in a 'grow more food' campaign. Teachers' salaries were increased and two buses placed at the disposal of schoolchildren to convey them from remote places to the handicraft and housecraft centres. The biggest budget in the history of the colony was passed. There were thirty-six strikes. Sugar and banana industries declined; the drop in sugar was the worst in four years.

In Chaguanas, a sugar-cane district halfway down the western coast of the island, the biggest thing to happen, bigger even than the war, was Tiger's wedding. The whole village turned out for it, Negro and Indian alike, for when Indian people got married it was a big thing, plenty food and drink, plenty ceremony.

Tiger didn't know anything about the wedding until his father told him. He didn't even know the girl. But he bowed to his parents' wishes. He was only sixteen years old and was not in the habit of attending Indian ceremonies in the village. But he knew a little about weddings, that Indians were married at an early age, and that after the ceremony friends and relatives would bring him gifts until he began to eat; only then would they stop the offerings.

Every night and every morning for a week close relatives came and rubbed him down to prepare his body for married life. On the morning of the wedding he bathed. They dressed him in a wedding gown and put a crown on his head. His father said, 'Boy, dese people not so rich, so don't stayam too long to eat.'

At the back of the bride's house, a great tent of bamboo and coconut branches had been erected. Five goats and six sheep had been slaughtered, an extravagance which could be afforded only at a time like this.

Tiger looked at everybody and everything with a tight feeling in his throat. He wished he knew more about what was going to happen to him.

As part of the ceremony he had to rub a red powder through the path in the middle of her head when a white sheet was thrown over them. As he did this he lifted the veil and looked at her face. She must have been about his age. She had black, sad eyes, long hair, un-developed breasts.

'What you name?' he asked breathlessly.

'Urmilla,' she whispered timidly.

Tiger didn't think that he would have to look at that face for the rest of his life. The whole affair had been arranged for him; he didn't have anything to do with it. He wondered if she could cook, but he didn't ask himself if she knew anything about what boys and girls did when they got married, because he didn't know either. He was aware of a painful exhilaration; painful because neither of them understood, exhilarating because it was something different in his monotonous life.

They offered him a cow and a hut in Barataria and two hundred US dollars in cash, besides smaller things. He didn't know where Barataria was. He didn't know what to expect, or whether he should wait for more gifts before beginning the feast. And then on a sudden impulse – perhaps it was fear, uncertainty – he took up a piece of *meetai* and bit it. That ended the offerings.

Afterwards his father caught him alone for a minute and hissed, 'Yuh fool! Could have gettam plenty more thing! Yuh eatam too quick, stupid boy!'

But it didn't matter to Tiger. Vaguely, like morning mist, he found himself wondering what life was going to be like.

As was the custom, the bride had to spend three days at his home, then they would spend three days at her family's. After that, they could go and live in their own house.

When Tiger had handed Urmilla over to his mother, all the boys and girls from the neighbourhood came up and started to call out to him.

'Tiger! So yuh married now!'

'Yuh is a big man now, boy!'

Some of the older folk drove them away, but Tiger would have liked for them to come. He was familiar with them, he could make jokes and talk. But now he was a man. He would have to learn to be a man, he would have to forget his friends. After all, he thought, they still little children!

In the next three days his mind was in a turmoil. He went out into the canefields where he had toiled with his father and brothers. Wind blew strongly here: he liked to lift his head and smell burned cane. What had life been for him? Days in the fields, evenings playing with other children, *roti* and *aloo* in the night. Sometimes they sang songs. His father had a drum, and when it was Saturday night the neighbours came and they drank and sang. And now all that was gone. He felt a tremendous responsibility falling on his shoulders. He tried not to think about it.

The third day his mind was in a riotous fever. He sat in the yard under a mango tree with Ramlal, an old Indian who often consoled him when he was beaten by his father or mother.

'What I must do?' he asked Ramlal, and Ramlal laughed.

'Is how yuh mean, boy?'

'I mean – I don't know what to do when I go with the girl.'

'What, boy! Never seeam your *bap* and *mai* when dey sleeping in de night?'

'Yes, but—'

'Well, is dat self. You doam same thing. You gettam house which side Barataria, gettam land, cow – well, you go live dat side. Haveam plenty boy chile – girl chile no good, only bring trouble on yuh head. You live dat side, plantam garden, live good.'

In those few words Ramlal summed up things for Tiger. But he didn't feel any sexual excitement at the thought of being alone with Urmilla. Even when he had looked at her face under the *purdah* – the white sheet thrown over them – for to him everything was a whirling, swift event, in which he was told to do this, and do that, and he obeyed.

The last three days at Urmilla's parents he was glad for this putting off of the unknown, this stretching of the few days before the overwhelming river burst over its banks and swept him off his immature feet.

The village of Barataria is situated about four miles east of the capital Port of Spain. Most of it lay on the southern side of the Eastern Main

Road, until the war started and people began to look for places to live, the city being overcrowded with servicemen and jobseekers. House owners in the city put a few sticks of furniture in their rooms and charged exorbitant rents for 'furnished' apartments. Crafty men advertised themselves as house agents who could get you a house for a small fee. Once involved, it was a matter of paying small amounts from time to time, and when at last you saw the house you either didn't like it or had to pay a year's rent in advance. One Negro British Guianese did so well that he opened an office and advertised widely. In three months' time he had a staff of three and was extending business to cover second-hand miscellany. In six months he had a car; by the time the government decided to put up a rent tribunal he had built two houses and had a thousand dollars put away in the bank.

The private estate that owned Barataria leased lots to enterprising housebuilders. In a short time bungalows were going up, to be bought or rented before completion. Roads were laid out, starting a little north of the main road, to run through the village for about half a mile. The railroad connecting other districts to the capital ran parallel to the main road, about one hundred yards south of it. Some of the roads crossed the railway lines. There were ten, running north to south. Then there were thirteen, running across these east to west. The down roads were called avenues, and numbered from one to ten. The cross ones were called streets, and numbered from one to thirteen. The roads were built roughly, with rocks and stones. If a taxi driver was asked to leave the main road and enter the village he said, 'Who, me? My car on dem macadam and big stone? Not me, papa!' In the rainy season puddles of water and mud made the village just like the Laventille Swamp which bordered the western side of the area. The drains were never completely dry, as the land was level and drainage difficult. Mosquitoes bred by the thousands and frogs croaked the night away. Gardeners who had been living in Barataria before the house-hunt started remained in the back streets, near twelfth and thirteenth streets, still living in their thatched huts. Most of them were East Indians. The concrete bungalows near the railway and main road went to middle-class families of various nationalities.

First man to put up a shop was a Chinese. It was at the corner of sixth street and sixth avenue, about the busiest spot in the village. Another opened a laundry. At the corner of sixth avenue and the main road, a good business spot because local trains halted there, shops – groceries, parlours, sweetshops, barber saloons – and general trade

opened up. An Indian woman put a table with a coal-pot on the side-
walk and made *roti* to sell with curried potatoes at twelve cents
apiece. With beef or mutton it was a shilling. An ice company put an
icebox and a scale, selling ice at a penny a pound and snowball –
shaved ice with syrup and condensed milk – from four to six cents. If
you only had a penny you could get a 'press' – the shaved ice was
rammed into a small aluminum cup and taken out and dipped in
syrup.

The main road streamed with traffic all day and night. Those who
worked in the city could wait at the halt for a train or catch a bus or a
taxi on the main road, arriving at their place of work in ten or fifteen
minutes' time. The main road itself was wide and asphalted, with
sidewalks. Between seventh and eighth avenues a concrete bridge
with iron rails spanned a small river. In the wet season the river ran
under another bridge fifty yards from the main road, in tenth avenue,
and emptied itself in the swamp. Villagers called the bridge on the
main road Jumbie Bridge because they were superstitious about it.
They said that every year an accident was bound to happen there.

The village was almost as cosmopolitan as the city. Indians and
Negroes were in the majority. In the back streets the Indians lived
simply, observing their customs and tending their fields, bringing
their produce to sell in sixth avenue or going to the market in San
Juan, a town bordering the eastern side. The earth was black and rich;
they grew vegetables in their yards, kept a few chickens and perhaps
a few cattle or a donkey. The Negroes were never farmers, and most
of them did odd jobs in the village or the city. But it didn't need any
knowledge of farming to dig a hole and put down tomato seeds; the
land was so rich that nearly every villager grew peppers or bananas or
string beans.

The government erected a school on sixth avenue; many children
used to run away and hunt crabs or cascadura fish in the swamp
instead of attending. Opposite the school was a large savannah on
which cattle and donkeys grazed and children played. Anything
would do for a bat and ball to play cricket. A coconut-palm branch,
properly cut and shaped, made an excellent bat; fruit seeds, empty tin
cans, even stones, served as an inexhaustible stock of balls.

So the people poured in from the overfilled city, and though they
grumbled at the mosquitoes and the stones in the streets on which
they 'stumped' their toes, others followed them, filling up the area,
which was not even a mile long or half a mile wide.

It was evening time when Tiger and Urmilla arrived in Barataria. A cow moaned in a field. A radio played jazz music, jarring on the quietude. Across the level stretch of land on the border of the swamp the sun sank splendidly in a pool of red, saffron, deep purple, and the coconut trees behind the land which Tiger was to rent later cast long, last shadows.

Tiger lit a fire of green bush so that the smoke would drive away the mosquitoes. Then he milked the cow under the rose mango tree. Urmilla watched him from the kitchen window. They had hardly exchanged any words since leaving Chaguanas. They had come to the hut and went about putting things away like two people who did not know each other.

There were two chairs, a small table, and some cooking utensils. The hut was one room. The floor and walls were smooth mud. The roof was thatched with palm leaves. The kitchen was behind and separated from the hut. It was, in fact, a miniature of the hut, except that there was an earthen fireplace, dug in the ground. And it was in a dilapidated condition, leaning to one side.

When Urmilla tried to lift the massala stone with which she would grind curry, she found it was too heavy. She turned shyly to her husband and asked him to lift it for her. It was the first time she had spoken to him directly. She swept the floor with a broom made from the stems of palm leaves, put wood in the fireplace, and went to catch water at the standpipe near the corner of the street.

Later they ate *roti* and *bigan* in silence. Tiger chewed slowly, tasting the food. At least she could cook, he told himself.

After the meal he sat on the floor with his legs drawn up under him. 'Get the cigarettes for me,' he commanded.

Urmilla hastened to obey.

Tiger had never smoked. He had only seen his father and the others. But he had decided that he was not going to appear a small boy before his wife. Men smoked: he would smoke. He would drink rum, curse, swear, bully the life out of her if she did not obey him. Hadn't he seen when his father did that? And didn't he know what to do when they went to bed? But he refused to think much about later, in the bed. Unknowingness folded about him so he couldn't breathe. He was afraid.

Urmilla handed him the cigarettes and matches. He pulled one out of the pack, beat the end on the box of matches, put it between his lips, lit it clumsily and inhaled.

All this time Urmilla was fascinatedly looking at him. And when Tiger began to cough so that his eyes ran water she knew. Ordinarily she would not have dared to laugh. But her emotions were too tightly drawn, like ropes across her breasts. And she felt that if she laughed the tautness would snap and set her free.

It flashed in Tiger's mind that this was rudeness and that he should slap her into respect for him when she laughed. And then the humour of the situation broadened like a ring in a pond and pushed other thoughts out of its path. Tightness in Tiger went as he burst into a fit of laughter. They laughed until they felt less afraid of each other. The joke of the cigarette was just a starter; the rest of their laughter was to drown out uncertainty, the knowledge that they would do something soon which they had never done before. And after they laughed, for the first time the thought gave them a thrill.

Urmilla moved away uneasily; Tiger ground the cigarette in the ground.

That night they slept separately on sugar-bags spread on the floor. Tiger crept across the room and huddled up in the corner, afraid of his thoughts and wishing with all his heart that he could fall asleep. Urmilla cried silently in the bags she had folded as a pillow.

When Tiger got up in the morning Urmilla had already milked the cow and was kneading flour. 'Good morning,' she said shyly, not lifting her head. Tiger smiled but he didn't answer. He went out into the yard and cut a toothbrush from the hibiscus fence. He chewed at the end of the stem and scrubbed his teeth with it when it frazzled out. He dipped a calabash full of water from the barrel at the side of the kitchen and dashed it on his face. The sun was halfway up in the sky.

He decided that he had better begin to talk freely with his wife. That way she wouldn't know he was doubtful and fearful of the future.

'Now so, Urmilla, what you doing home by you?' he asked when they sat on the floor to breakfast.

Words came tumbling from the girl like water from a burst dam. 'Oh, Tiger, I have plenty work to do. Clean the house, cook, go out and graze the cattle—'

'Yes, girl, me too. Plenty things to do by my father house. Every day I go in the fields and work, work. In the evening we play. All the boys and girls come, and we play under the mango tree. I wish I was back home now.'

'But, Tiger, we married now! We can't go back to we father and mother house. We have to live here by weself.'

Tiger drank tea from a large enamel cup. 'Yes, I know that. Don't think I don't know. You must remember, first thing is that I is the man in the house and you have to obey me.'

Urmilla said quickly, 'Yes, Tiger.'

'Now second thing,' he said, 'is to get land. We go grow crop and sell. Is San Juan where the estate office is, I going up there now and make arrangement. I don't know the exact spot, but I could always ask somebody.'

He caught a bus on the main road, and by then the sun was high in the sky, and the wind warm and constant. It was easy to find the office, everybody in San Juan knew where it was. He signed a contract, marking a big 'X' for his name, to rent two lots of land. He was worried about the negotiation; he wished his father or one of his uncles was there with him. But the thought made him ashamed. He was married, and he was a big man now. He might as well learn to do things without the assistance of other people.

When he got back to Barataria it was evening. He dropped off by the corner, and seeing the rumshop open, went in. The same spur which had made him smoke now tickled him to get drunk. Only men got drunk, not boys. He remembered once in Chaguanas his father was drinking in a rumshop and he had to go and bring him home. When his father saw him he said, 'Ohe, boy, come an' take ah little one, it go killam all de germs in yuh belly.' And he took a little one, urged by his father's companions, and the rum coursed down his throat as if pitchoil had been soaked in his mouth and a match set to it. Then men had laughed loudly when tears sprang to his eyes.

He ordered a drink.

The men in the rumshop, talking and laughing, looked at him briefly. He stood with the glass in his hand and looked around. Acutely conscious that they were not looking at him, he gulped the rum with an effort and chased it with a soda water. He wanted to buck up his courage and say something to show them he was a man, that he could swallow rum just as they did.

But no one cared if Tiger was a man or not.

Warmth travelled over his body. He went to a dirty table around which two young men were sitting. There was a slop pail near and one of them was leaning from his chair and spitting in it.

'You living in Barataria?' Tiger asked.

'Who is you?' one of them demanded. 'Why yuh want to find dat out?'

'Is just that I newly come here to live. I don't know the place good yet, man.'

'Well, sit down nar,' they invited. 'Have ah liquor wid we. But you must buy.'

It was a chance to prove he was a man. 'Call for another bottle on me, man,' he said, pulling a bill from his pocket. 'All of we is Indian together; let we drink and make merry.'

Already he owned land, he boasted to his companions. He had a house, a cow, a wife. And he thought to himself that he ought to have done it last night, only he couldn't summon up enough courage. Tonight he would show her. Nobody had told him he was still a boy, but they didn't have to speak for him to know.

He got up suddenly from the table. He was feeling giddy. He staggered through the door and he knew they were laughing behind his back, but he didn't care.

Urmilla had lit the kerosene lamp and was waiting anxiously. Through the fog in his brain he could see fear in her eyes.

'Why you stay so long, Tiger?' she asked gladly.

He sulked. He was the man in the house, he could come and go as he pleased. He didn't answer.

They ate in silence. Tiger watched Urmilla out of the corners of his eyes. Now that he had decided to do it, she appeared altogether different. Her hair was glossy in the lamplight, her eyes shining. Almost as if she knew. He wished that he knew more about everything – about planting crops at the right time, about living with a wife, and exactly how to go about the thing. In some way he sensed that unless he did it he would never cease to be a boy, to be treated like a boy.

Later they sat silent. Urmilla shelled pigeon peas she had bought from a passing vendor for the next day's lunch.

He watched her. Did he have to tell her first?

They went to bed. For a long time he lay looking at the thatched roof, making up his mind. Then quietly, like he was stalking a deer, he drew his bags near to his bride.

Urmilla moved and opened her eyes. She knew what was going to happen and she tried not to be afraid. Her mother had said, '*Beti*, whatever happen, don't frighten. You is a woman now.'

It was the same thing with Urmilla: she felt she had to prove herself a woman in front of Tiger.

Young passion burst and swept them so they didn't know really what they were doing. If Tiger had known that this powerful force was going to grip him so that he wouldn't be afraid, it would have been so easy for him to let himself die and switch on the force. Because afterwards he was aware that he of his own accord had taken no part in the thing. A great desire for his wife had come over him, possessing his brain.

Before they fell asleep in each other's arms he told himself that the next time he would just die and let the power do its work.

And the next morning they lay lazily on the bags on the floor, looking at each other with the wonder of the new knowledge.

And they did it again.

GEORGE LAMMING

George Lamming was born in Barbados. He was one of the leading lights of a generation of Caribbean writers who arrived in Britain in the early 1950s. *In the Castle of my Skin*, published in 1953, was his first novel. He followed this with *The Emigrants, Seasons of Adventure, Of Age and Innocence, The Pleasures of Exile, Water with Berries* and *Natives of My Person*. He has received numerous honours and now lives in the Caribbean.

In the Castle of my Skin is a classic novel about Caribbean adolescence, which marked an extraordinary debut. It captures beautifully colonial Caribbean society through the eyes of a bright boy. The following extracts look at the wider context of the lives of those living in a small village, and at the philosophical forces that shaped the world of the boy and his friend.

from *In the Castle of my Skin*

An estate where fields of sugar cane had once crept like an open secret across the land had been converted into a village that absorbed some three thousand people. An English landowner, Mr Creighton, had died, and the estate fell to his son through whom it passed to another son who in his turn died, surrendering it to yet another. Generations had lived and died in this remote corner of a small British colony, the oldest and least adulterated of British colonies: Barbados or Little England as it was called in the local school texts. To the east where the land rose gently to a hill, there was a large brick building surrounded by a wood and a high stone wall that bore bits of bottle along the top. The landlords lived there amidst the trees within the wall. Below and around it the land spread out into a flat unbroken monotony of small houses and white marl roads. From any point of the land one could see on a clear day the large brick house hoisted on the hill. When the weather wasn't too warm, tea was served on the wide, flat roof, and villagers catching sight through the trees of the shifting figures crept behind their fences, or stole through the wood away from the wall to see how it was done. Pacing the roof, the landlord, accompanied by his friends, indicated in all directions the limits of the land. The friends were mainly planters whose estates in the country had remained agricultural; or otherwise there were English visitors who were absentee owners of estates which they had come to see. The landlord, one gathered, explained the layout of land, the customs of the villagers and the duties which he performed as caretaker of this estate. The villagers, enthralled by the thought of tea in the open air, looked on, unseen, open-mouthed.

The wood was thick and wild with tangled weed racing over and along the swollen black roots of the mahogany trees. Patrolling the land at all hours of the day were the village overseers. They were themselves villagers who were granted special favours like attending on the landlady, or owning after twenty years' tenure the spot of land on which their house was built. They were fierce, aggressive and strict. Theft was not unusual, and the landlords depended entirely on the overseers to scare away the more dangerous villagers. The overseers carried bunches of keys strung on wire which they chimed continually, partly to warn the villagers of their approach, and partly to satisfy themselves with the feel of authority. This seemed necessary since the average villager showed little respect for the overseer unless threatened or actually bullied. Many a day poverty, adventure or the threat of boredom would drive them into the woods where the landlady's hens lay and the rabbits nibbled the green weed. They would collect the eggs and set snares for the birds and animals. The landlord made a perennial complaint, and the overseers were given a full-time job. Occasionally the landlord would accuse the overseers of conniving, of slackening on the job, and the overseers who never risked defending themselves gave vent to their feelings on the villagers who they thought were envious and jealous and mean. Low-down nigger people was a special phrase the overseers had coined. The villagers were low-down nigger people since they couldn't bear to see one of their kind get along without feeling envy and hate. This had created a tense relationship between the overseer and the ordinary villager. Each represented for the other an image of the enemy. And the enemy was to be destroyed or placated. The overseer was either authoritarian or shrewd. The villager hostile or obsequious. The landlord's complaint heightened the image, gave it an edge that cut sharp and deep through every layer of the land. And this image, by continual assertion, had become a myth which

like a rumour drifted far beyond the village. Even the better
educated who had one way or another gone to the island's best
schools and later held responsible posts in the Government service,
even these were affected by this image of the enemy which had had
its origin in a layer from which many had sprung and through accidents of time and experience forgotten. The image of the enemy, and
the enemy was My People. My people are low-down nigger people.
My people don't like to see their people get on. The language of the
overseer. The language of the civil servant. The myth had eaten
through their consciousness like moths through the pages of ageing
documents. Not taking chances with you people, my people. They
always let you down. Make others say we're not responsible, we've
no sense of duty. That's what the low-down nigger people do to us,
their people. Then the others say we've no sense of duty. Like
children under the threat of hellfire they accepted instinctively that
the others, meaning the white, were superior, yet there was always
the fear of realizing that it might be true. This world of the others'
imagined perfection hung like a dead weight over their energy. If the
low-down nigger people weren't what they are, the others couldn't
say anything about us. Suspicion, distrust, hostility. These operated
in every decision. You never can tell with my people. It was the
language of the overseer, the language of the Government servant,
and later the language of the lawyers and doctors who had returned
stamped like an envelope with what they called the culture of the
Mother Country.

The landlord was safe. The village was safe. That tension soaring
at times to mutual bitterness had produced this image of the enemy,
and later there emerged an attitude which the overseer wore like a
uniform and which became his substitute for duty. Take no chances.
Be on the look-out always, everywhere. Be fierce. Be strict. Be
aggressive. That was duty. And the overseer was a shadow of the
police constable who patrolled the village at night. He always arrived
alert, ready, prepared. He did not come to explain, inform, interpret
or share experience like other men in the ordinary run of social inter-
course. He came to arrest. Something had to be wrong. The village
might have been asleep, but floating somewhere about, around, perhaps within himself was the large, invisible threatening phantom, the
image of the enemy. My people. Whenever the constable appeared
there was apprehension. People who all the while were relaxed and
composed became fidgety, began to suspect themselves. Sometimes

they slipped along the alley and over to the neighbouring road to warn the villagers there. The constable was around. Nothing seemed wrong, but something must have been. Something had to be wrong. Children hid behind fences or peeped through the jalousies, frightened, waiting.

Once a quarter, or after some calamity like the flood, the landlord with his family drove from road to road through the village. He inspected the damage, looking from one side of the road to the other. Those who were untidy scampered into hiding, much to his amusement, while the small boys who were caught unawares came to attention and saluted briskly. The landlord smiled and his wife beside him smiled too. The daughter seated in the back of the carriage looked down, haughty and contemptuous.

Two horses in an outfit of brilliant polished leather dragged the carriage from road to road through the village, stopping here and there as the fancy took the landlord. The survey lasted all morning, during which he had seen most of the extreme damage and made a rough estimate of the necessary repairs. In the case of floods the repairs were simple. The canals would be re-marked and the wreckage shovelled from the roads. This finished, cartloads of stone and pebbles would be strewn on as a new surface. These would be left for several weeks in their upturned state until vehicles and pedestrians treading upon them from day to day would flatten them out into an even white stretch. The road was new again.

When the carriage disappeared with the landlord and his family, small boys came out to rehearse the scene. Two took the part of the horses and trotted along to the fore, while another three arranged themselves behind as the landlord and his family had done. The boys would trot slowly from road to road pretending to make a similar survey, and discussing among themselves the plans they had for repairs. Earlier, when they had watched the landlord and his friends on the roof of the brick house, they reproduced the scene behind the fence in the open air. They made saucers and cups with a mixture of dirt and water and saliva, leaving them in the sun to bake dry. Then they served tea from the tap of a standing pipe nearby. The make-believe was impressive. The landlord. The overseer. The villager. The image of the enemy. The limb of the law, strict, fierce, aggressive. These had combined to produce an idea of the Great.

The world of authority existed somewhere along the fringe of the villagers' consciousness. Direct contact with the landlord might

have helped towards some understanding of what the others, meaning the white, were like, but the overseer who nominally was a
mediator had functioned like a bridge which might be used, but not
for crossing from one end to the other. The world ended somewhere
along the bridge, and beyond was another plane of reality; beyond
was the Great, which the landlord and the large brick house on the
hill represented. At night the light poured down through the wood
and the house looking down from the hill seemed to hold a quality
of benevolent protection. It was a castle around which the land like a
shabby back garden stretched. When the lights went out, and the
wood was dark, the villagers took note. The landlord's light had
been put out. The landlord had gone to bed. It was time they did
the same. A custom had been established and later a value which,
through continual application and a hardened habit of feeling,
became an absolute standard of feeling. I don't feel the landlord
would like this. If the overseer see, the landlord is bound to know.
It operated in every activity. The obedient lived in the hope that
the Great might not be offended, the uncertain in the fear it might
have been.

      . . .

I know what it is, one boy was saying, I know what it is. He spoke
very well. The old woman isn't an old fool. She knew what she was
saying. She was a slave. We're all slaves. The Queen freed some of
us, but some of us are still slaves.

The boys listened intently as the buzzing soared in another corner.
The head teacher sat quiet, his hands stuck against his forehead.

She wasn't a fool, that old woman. She has a good memory.
When Lucifer, that is the devil, when the devil was sent from his
garden, he carried with him a lot of angels. The angels who were on
his side said they would go with him and they left heaven for the
earth. That is where we are living now. It was a terrible sight the
way they walked out of that garden. But they said they didn't care.
They would get along all right without God. The boys listened. It
was like a Sunday School lesson. They came down to earth, the boy
went on, and they made a home here on the earth. But it didn't last
long. They had got so used to the garden that they couldn't tear
themselves away. They thought they could, but they were wrong.
The garden was like something in the blood. When something is in
the blood you can't get it out unless you take out the blood. They

couldn't manage very well on the earth because they couldn't get rid
of the garden. The garden was in the back of their minds all the time.
They tried to turn their backs against it, but they couldn't turn their
memory. It was deep, deep in them. And then they got very sad.
They couldn't stand one another. The sight of one another on the
earth made them sick. And it wasn't long before they started to fight.
That was the beginning of war. The angels of the devil who were the
first men couldn't stand the sight of one another on the earth. They
couldn't help themselves. It wasn't that they wanted to kill one
another. It wasn't that at all. It was simply that they couldn't help
themselves. And from that day war never stopped. They passed it on
to us from generation to generation. And the older the earth became
the more we got to hate the sight of one another. And the worse the
fighting became. Some of the angels said they would go back to the
garden. Others were ashamed. The devil said he would die first. He
would die before he submitted to returning. But God wouldn't have
them back. He said he wouldn't have them back until they had all
repented. They had to say they were sorry. They had to become
slaves in a sort of way. It was all right for those who didn't want to
stay on the earth. They could do it so easily, but the others found it
very difficult. They couldn't do it so easily. They were slaves. Soon
they all became slaves. You see, they had it deep in them to get out
of the garden. They did want to see something new, something different. But when they saw the something they couldn't stand that. It
gave them a kind of delight to know that there was something else.
If ever God drove them out again they would have somewhere to go.
But they were afraid. They couldn't stand being alone on the earth.
They wanted something to hold on to. And they all agreed to go
back. They say they would repent and go back. And they were
terribly ashamed. They were ashamed because in a way they didn't
want to repent. They feel they could manage. But it was the garden.
They couldn't get the garden out of their minds. And the more they
thought of the garden, the more ashamed they became. And the
more they repented. They were all slaves. And they made us slaves
too. The Queen freed some of us because she made us feel that the
Empire was bigger than the garden. That's what the old woman
meant. The Queen did free some of us in a kind of way. We started
to think about the Empire more than we thought of the garden, and
then nothing mattered but the Empire. But they have put the two of
them together now. The Empire and the garden. We are to speak of

them the same way. They belong to the same person. They both belong to God. The garden is God's own garden and the Empire is God's only Empire. They work together for us. God save the King who will help us to see the garden again. That's all we have to think of now, the Empire and the garden. But the old woman wasn't wrong. We are slaves. We are still slaves of these two. The Empire and the garden. And we are happy to be slaves. It isn't the same as being a prisoner. Nobody wants to be a prisoner. You aren't free when you're a prisoner. But it is different when you are a slave. When you are a slave of the Empire and the garden at the same time, you can be free to belong to both. And you can be free to be ashamed of not thinking enough about them. The more you think of them, the more you are ashamed and also the less you think of them the more you are ashamed. My mother who is a Sunday School teacher has explained it well. There is nothing for us to do, she tells me, but rejoice in our bondage. That is what she calls it. She doesn't say slave. She says bondage. When the time comes we shall be taken out of the bondage by what she calls grace. That's not a girl she's talking about. It's something else. It's a sort of salvation. That's what she says sometimes. Salvation through grace. We're all going to the garden again, free again, and especially those who here on earth belonged to the Empire. We'll be free again. The others will perish. Those who refuse to go back to the garden because they are stubborn, they will perish. And not only through fire. My mother says it's loneliness. They will be lonely in a way they can't stand. The loneliness will make them giddy. Giddy and sick. Because they were stubborn. You can't live without God, my mother says, you can't unless you're prepared to be lonely and sick. And that's more than an ordinary man can stand. Those who choose the garden will find things different. They'll be slaves all right, as the old woman says. They will be slaves, but everything will be better and easier. Very much easier.

The boys had listened patiently. They knew the other's mother was a Sunday School teacher and they felt she spoke with some authority. They were a little afraid. They agreed that if things were as the boy said, it would be better to belong to the Empire and in the end get back to the garden. After all there was nothing to lose by belonging to the Empire. They were all very poor. And moreover the Empire made them put on things like parades. They enjoyed the parades and the flags and the speeches. It made them feel a little more important than they were. Listening to a speech from the inspector! It gave you a feeling of being grown-up and when you marched and saluted you felt like a soldier. A real soldier. They would choose the Empire and the garden. There was nothing wrong with them. And they had everything in their favour. Flowers. Flags. Pennies.

WILSON HARRIS

Wilson Harris was born and educated in Guyana. He worked for the government as a surveyor, which enabled him to travel deep into the Guyanese
interior where the majority of the country's Amerindian population live. He
developed a fascination for their myths and stories, which have shaped his
work. He arrived in Britain in 1958, and soon after published his first novel,
The Palace of the Peacock, part of his four-book *Guyanese Quartet* series.
He is also the author of *The Eye of the Scarecrow*, *Da Silva's Cultivated
Wilderness*, *The Tree of the Sun*, *Angel at The Gate*, and the *Carnival
Trilogy*. He has lived in Britain since 1958.

The Palace of the Peacock is an allegorical quest for the heart of Guyana.
A group of men paddle upstream, into the interior of the country. Dream
sequences merge with allusive fragments from Guyanese history and landscape, as illustrated by the following extract taken from the opening chapter
of the book.

from *The Palace of the Peacock*
Horseman, Pass By

A horseman appeared on the road coming at a breakneck stride. A
shot rang out suddenly, near and yet far as if the wind had been
stretched and torn and had started coiling and running in an instant.
The horseman stiffened with a devil's smile, and the horse reared,
grinning fiendishly and snapping at the reins. The horseman gave a
bow to heaven like a hanging man to his executioner, and rolled from
his saddle on to the ground.

The shot had pulled me up and stifled my own heart in heaven.
I started walking suddenly and approached the man on the ground.
His hair lay on his forehead. Someone was watching us from the
trees and bushes that clustered the side of the road. Watching me
as I bent down and looked at the man whose open eyes stared at
the sky through his long hanging hair. The sun blinded and ruled

my living sight but the dead man's eye remained open and obstinate and clear.

I dreamt I awoke with one dead seeing eye and one living closed eye. I put my dreaming feet on the ground in a room that oppressed me as though I stood in an operating theatre, or a maternity ward, or I felt suddenly, the glaring cell of a prisoner who had been sentenced to die. I arose with a violent giddiness and leaned on a huge rocking-chair. I remembered the first time I had entered this bare curious room; the house stood high and alone in the flat brooding countryside. I had felt the wind rocking me with the oldest uncertainty and desire in the world, the desire to govern or be governed, rule or be ruled for ever.

Someone rapped on the door of my cell and room. I started on seeing the dream-horseman, tall and spare and hard-looking as ever. 'Good morning,' he growled slapping a dead leg and limb. I greeted him as one greeting one's gaoler and ruler. And we looked through the window together as though through his dead seeing material eye, rather than through my living closed spiritual eye, upon the primitive road and the savannahs dotted with sentinel trees and slowly moving animals.

His name was Donne, and it had always possessed a cruel glory for me. His wild exploits had governed my imagination from childhood. In the end he had been expelled from school.

He left me a year later to join a team of ranchers near the Brazil frontier and border country. I learnt then to fend for myself and he soon turned into a ghost, a million dreaming miles away from the sea-coast where we had lived.

'The woman still sleeping,' Donne growled, rapping on the ground hard with his leg again to rouse me from my inner contemplation and slumber.

'What woman?' I dreamed, roused to a half-waking sense of pleasure mingled with foreboding.

'Damnation,' Donne said in a fury, surveying a dozen cages in the yard, all open. The chickens spied us and they came half-running, half-flying, pecking still at each other piteously and murderously.

'Mariella,' Donne shouted. Then in a still more insistent angry voice – 'Mariella.'

I followed his eyes and realized he was addressing a little shack partly hidden in a clump of trees.

Someone was emerging from the shack and out of the trees. She was barefoot and she bent forward to feed the chickens. I saw the back of her knees and the fine beautiful grain of her flesh. Donne looked at her as at a larger and equally senseless creature whom he governed and ruled like a fowl.

I half-woke for the second or third time to the sound of insistent thumping and sobbing in the hall outside my door. I awoke and dressed quickly. Mariella stood in the hall, dishevelled as ever, beating her hand on my door.

'Quiet, quiet,' I said roughly shrinking from her appearance. She shuddered and sobbed. 'He beat me,' she burst out at last. She lifted her dress to show me her legs. I stroked the firm beauty of her flesh and touched the ugly marks where she had been whipped. 'Look,' she said, and lifted her dress still higher. Her convulsive sobbing stopped when I touched her again.

A brilliant day. The sun smote me as I descended the steps. We walked to the curious high swinging gate like a waving symbol and warning taller than a hanging man whose toes almost touched the ground; the gate was as curious and arresting as the prison house we had left above and behind, standing on the tallest stilts in the world.

'Donne cruel and mad,' Mariella cried. She was staring hard at me. I turned away from her black hypnotic eyes as if I had been blinded by the sun, and saw inwardly in the haze of my blind eye a watching muse and phantom whose breath was on my lips.

She remained close to me and the fury of her voice was in the wind. I turned away and leaned heavily against the frail brilliant gallows-gate of the sky, looking down upon the very road where I had seen the wild horse, and the equally wild demon and horseman fall. Mariella had killed him.

I awoke in full and in earnest with the sun's blinding light and muse in my eye. My brother had just entered the room. I felt the enormous relief one experiences after a haze and a dream. 'You're still alive,' I cried involuntarily. 'I dreamt Mariella ambushed and shot you.' I started rubbing the vision from my eye. 'I've been here just a few days,' I spoke guardedly, 'and I don't know all the circumstances' – I raised myself on my elbow – 'but you are a devil with that woman. You're driving her mad.'

Donne's face clouded and cleared instantly. 'Dreamer,' he warned, giving me a light wooden tap on the shoulder, 'life here is tough. One has to be a devil to survive. I'm the last landlord. I tell you I fight everything in nature, flood, drought, chicken hawk, rat, beast and woman. I'm everything. Midwife, yes, doctor, yes, gaoler, judge, hangman, every blasted thing to the labouring people. Look man, look outside again. Primitive. Every boundary line is a myth. No-man's land, understand?'

'There are still labouring people about, you admit that.' I was at a loss for words and I stared blindly through the window at an invisible population.

'It's an old dream,' I plucked up the courage to express my inner thoughts.

'What is?'

'It started when we were at school, I imagine. Then you went away suddenly. It stopped then. I had a curious sense of hard-won freedom when you had gone. Then to my astonishment, long after, it came again. But this time with a new striking menace that flung you from your horse. You fell and died instantly, and yet you were the one who saw, and I was the one who was blind. Did I ever write and tell you' – I shrank from Donne's supercilious smile, and hastened to justify myself – 'that I am actually going blind in one eye?' I was gratified by his sudden startled expression.

'Blind?' he cried.

'My left eye has an incurable infection,' I declared. 'My right eye – which is actually sound – goes blind in my dream.' I felt foolishly distressed. 'Nothing kills *your* sight,' I added with musing envy. 'And your vision becomes,' I hastened to complete my story, 'your vision becomes the only remaining window on the world for me.'

I felt a mounting sense of distress.

'Mariella?' There was a curious edge of mockery and interest in Donne's voice.

'I never saw her before in my dream,' I said. I continued with a forced warmth – 'I am glad we are together again after so many years. I may be able to free myself of this – this – ' I searched for a word – 'this obsession. After all it's childish.'

Donne flicked ash and tobacco upon the floor. I could see a certain calculation in his dead seeing eye. 'I had almost forgotten I had a brother like you,' he smiled matter-of-factly. 'It had passed from my mind – this dreaming twin responsibility you remember.' His voice expanded and a sinister undercurrent ran through his remarks – 'We belong to a short-lived family and people. It's so easy to succumb and die. It's the usual thing in this country as you well know.' He was smiling and indifferent. 'Our parents died early. They had a hard life. Tried to fight their way up out of an economic nightmare: farmers and hand-to-mouth business folk they were. They gave up the ghost before they had well started to live.' He stared at me significantly. 'I looked after you, son.' He gave me one of his ruthless taps. 'Father and Mother rolled into one for a while. I was a boy then. I had almost forgotten. Now I'm a man. I've learnt,' he waved his hands at the savannahs, 'to rule *this*. This is the ultimate. This is everlasting. One doesn't have to see deeper than that, does one?' He stared at me hard as death. 'Rule the land,' he said, 'while you still have a ghost of a chance. And you rule the world. Look at the sun.' His dead eye blinded mine. 'Look at the sun,' he cried in a stamping terrible voice.

THE ARRIVANTS

There are homecomings without home
DEREK WALCOTT, 'Homecoming: Anse La Raye'

GEORGE LAMMING

The Emigrants traces the fate of a group of West Indians who go to Britain in search of a 'better break' and the freedom to redefine themselves. Their vulnerability and their hopes on the voyage are brought out, before their bewilderment at the life of hostels and tenements in Britain. In the extract below they give their first impressions of Britain after their long voyage.

from *The Emigrants*
The Train

Look Lilian look de ol' geyser quiet in de
corner like de whole worl' come to a
standstill . . . he eyes don't wink when he
pull that pipe an' he lookin' only Gawd
knows where he looking like he ain't got eyes
in his head . . . is the way they is in dis
country . . . no talk till you talk. No
speak till you speak, no notice till you notice,
no nothin' till you somethin' . . . 'tis what
ah mean when ah says England . . . when
you lan' up in Englan', ol' man, when you
lan' up here.
    Tornado, . . . but Tornado these
people tell lies too bad. And we say back home
you got to look hard to find the truth, but
Tornado de truth doan' even hide round
here . . . I go back where ah went to tell
de woman she ain't put sugar in de tea, an' you
know, ol' man, you know she swear she put
. . . in broad daylight Tornado she swear
to my face she put as if she think ah doan' know
what sugar taste like, me, Tornado, who

been eating sugar before ah drink tea, the
woman tell me to the front o' my face she
put sugar in dis tea, taste it Tornado, taste
it for yuhself an' tell me if ah mad or she
stupid.

Sugar ration, ol' man, that's why. If she
say she put she put but what she put yuh
won't taste, partner, p'raps if you been lookin'
when she servin' you might ah see somethin'
in the spoon, but what it is you won't taste,
not in yuh tea 'cause sugar ration in this
country.

What ain't ration in dis country Tornado
is there anything ain't ration in dis country.

> Things haven't been the same since the war.
> Where do you chaps come from? The West
> Indies? Been there several times myself. Had
> a nephew was a Governor there some years
> ago.

Would you have a cup of tea? With or
without?

(What she mean with or without.)

Milk and sugar?

(What she mean milk an' sugar.)

Good. Won't be a minute.

Say Tornado what wrong wid dese people
at all? You doan' mean to say people drink
tea when it ain't got milk. They ain't that
poor un, un, Tornado, no tell me de
truth, dey ain't so poor they can't spare a
drop o' milk in they tea, an' what kin' o
talk is dis 'bout with or without. Is it ol'
man that they doan' like sugar. What wrong
wid dem at all. With or without. O Christ
Tornado, will take a long time 'fore I forget
dat . . . with or without.

They have funny taste, partner. You
goin' get some surprises. You wait.

> 'Ave 'alf pint o' bitter John?
> My name ain't John.

Oh no 'arm meant. Jes' gettin' to know
you. 'Alf a pint for me an' my pal . . .
'Ere's yours, John, an' yours, darkie . . .

'E isn't no darkie. 'E's 'avin' a drink with
me, an' that makes 'im my pal.
Understand?

Well w'at you'd 'ave me say. Ah don't
know fercetn't the guy's name. Alllll the
best.

Say Tornado. The thing they call bitter.
You know what ah mean. Well ain't it just
like mauby. Same kind o' taste an' same
kind o' look in the glass. Is that they sell
instead of rum? Where you go to get
something strong.

You know lager beer in down town
Port-o'-Spain. Well that's what they call
bitter. An' you goin' to swell yuh guts up
wid it here, an' it got a good advantage, 'tis
the only advantage, ol' man, it won't ask you
to trot. It goin' leave you as sober as a
gallon o' mauby, an' instead o' vomit as you
vomit back home, it'll be pissing as you
never piss before.

See the chap over yonder standin' like
a black Goliath. He win a football pool las'
year. Sixty thousand pounds. 'Tis w'at every
spade hope to happen to him when he sen'
in the pools.

What spade got to do with it. What
you mean by spade.

The spades? That's me, an' you. Spades.
Same colour as the card. Ever see the Ace
o' spades, ol' man. If ever ah win o' football
pool I'll do just the opposite to what he do.
Instead o' settling down here I'll go home.
I'll live like a lord. I'll show Belmont an'
Woodbrook an' the whole lot of bullshitters
livin' round St Clair, I'll show them the
difference between the rich an' the rest. Ah

got a feelin' someone o' we who make this
trip goin' win a football pool.

How many people go in for dis thing,
the pool.

De whole country. Is a sort of legal
racket, an' dese people'll do anything you
only got to tell dem it legal. So long as the
law give the signal to go ahead, they doan'
ask where, when, or why, they go ahead.
They like to know what they can do an'
what they can't do, an' since they know the
pools is alright they all take to it like fish
to water. De whole country, an' a next
reason, 'course, 'tis 'cause it give them
another reason for buying the evening news.
You have no idea what newspaper mean
to dese people.

We got train back home but ah never see train that big. It big
for so. There was train in Barbados too but not for the same sort
o' purpose at all. The train we had at home was more a excursion
thing. They use to use it to take the Sunday School children to
Batsheba, and the Rocks. But when the war come along they
scrap everything. Train days come to an' end there an' then.

This big alright but they say in the States these things bigger.
They had to make a law dat no man should build a train more
than a mile long. 'Cause they use to be a lot o' fightin' when the
train arrive. People in the back carriage was more than a mile
where they goin' long after the front carriage folks get out.

I never thought ah would have set eyes on England.

If you'd tell me that ten years ago, ol' man, I would have say
you tryin' to poke fun at my head.

But the worl' get small, small, ol' man.

An' also too somethin' happen between people an' people. As
soon as people get to handlin' money, they get a new sort o'
insight 'bout things. If you an' me ever go back folks goin' start
lookin' at we in a different way. Till every Tom, Dick an' Harry
start to come, an' it get so common that it won't mean nothin' no
more to go to England. Would be like goin' from Trinidad to
Tobago.

Feel vaguely that have been here before just as after four years in the other island felt had always lived there. For a moment seemed had forgotten where I was. Stretch of land over yonder reminds so much of home. Every inch cultivated. Earth has colour of clay, and every row even and distinct as though they had measured them. Only light is different. Wish it wouldn't rain for haven't got any rain clothes and heavy coat. They say rain in England is fatal. Put your head in brief case if it comes. Once your head is covered, remember, you're alright.

> Tornado de ground feel harder than back home. W'at dat mean.

> You on strange ground, partner. Yuh foot got to get acclimatized.

> Take off thy shoes from off thy feet for the place thou standest is holy ground.

> People doan' go barefoot here, partner, so you better tell yuh toes to make peace wid yer boots.

Do you know if there were any stowaways on the ship?

Why do you ask me?

Come on. If you know anything speak up. There's nothing to be afraid of.

I don't know. But the chaps standing around here didn't stowaway.

Why do you people come here. Can't you get work at home?

Have a cigarette?

How many o' these did you bring?

> Look I want a drink. Sorry but you'll have to find out all this later.

Do you chaps know if there were any stowaways on the ship?

What you take me for the Almighty Gawd.

Just a question. You know of the Metropolitan Police.

There ain't nothing in dis country Ah don't know 'bout. Ah also know dere's one thing 'bout the English people. They doan' interfere in nobody business.

No stowaways I take it.

If you want to know I'll tell you. Dere's
one but they catch him an' they goin' take him
back to France for trial. Two months in a
French jail an' after back where he come
from.

You don't know what a French jail is
like?

Listen partner, police or no police if you
ask me the wrong question I'll tell you where
to get off. There's more in the mortar than the
pestle. All you in dis country got more for
me than I got for you.

Is work scarce at home?

For some people. If you go down there
they'll make you inspector o' police. Before
the sun hit you twice you won't know who
you is. 'Cause the power you'll command
after that will simply take possession o' you.
Ol' man you'll get in de spirit. Know what
that mean. You'll become one wid Gawd.

In the land of the blind . . .

'Tis the other way round. In the land o'
de one eye the blind is king.

You see, partner, if you can't see, we'll all
start thinkin' that's w'at we got eyes for,
not to see.

You know Bustamante?

Ask him. He come from Jamaica.

Me take to Mr Manley more.

Who's Manley?

Him know 'bout Busta, but him ain't know
'bout Mr Manley. Me always say English
people got everything upside down. The
wrong things catch they eye.

Are there any communists in Jamaica?

Not since Stalin lef'.

When was he there?

He born there.

Come to study?

Where do you chaps come from? You don't

mind me asking, do you. My sister's a
missionary in Africa, says it's a nice place,
and your people very good people. She adores
the Africans. Says we haven't been very nice
always but things are changing. Your people
are gradually getting to understand us, and the
future promises to be brighter. That's what
I've always said, you know. Understanding.
As soon as people get to understand one
another life is easy.

Is it true what the papers say about unemployment?

Of course it is. Don't you expect it. Wherever there's an economic contradiction in the whole process of production and
distribution you'll find that. Wages dropping. Prices soaring.
Finally slump. We haven't got to that yet but I give us three
years. This country is heading for an economic suicide and all
because they won't face facts. There's going to be hard times
ahead, but all you've got to do is keep on the right side of the
fence. Don't listen to the lies you hear. People are so blinded by
lies in this country that they see an enemy whenever a friend
stands up to speak the truth. But history is an open book, and
those who read and understand realise that their duty is to
change. The key word is change. Before anything like peace and
prosperity can come about in this country the whole economic
structure of the society must be changed. They are people who lie
and fight and would even die to keep the old order. They want to
build a new house on old, tottering foundations. You must be
careful. Keep on the right side of the fence and play your part in
the struggle.

You speak excellent English for a foreigner.
Much better than the French.

How nice of you to say that. 'F course
the better classes get much the same
standard of education as you do. I'm really
from the middle class. Among us, that is my
circles an' my circles' circles there isn't an
upper class. In a sense you might say we
were the upper class.

Where is this may I ask?

Grenada. One of the islands. My father is

a magistrate. Was educated here in England.
Where is Grenada? I don't seem to recall the name.
Don't you know? You're kidding. Were you at university?
No, but here is a map of the world. We might look for it.

Excuse, old man, but how much you think
I should give the baggage man.
W'at you talkin' bout?
As a tip.
Tell him you hope de weather change.

WILL PASSENGERS TAKE THEIR SEATS PLEASE

You see dat chap over dere. Well he vex as hell to see we here on dis train. Long ago only he could come, an' when he see dis he start to feel he is not as rich as should be. You know that fellow from Trinidad. Whole family solicitors. They spend six months here and six months at home. Every year. He got a young woman wid him.

'Tis he wife. You doan' know she . . . Chinese girl from Woodbrook. Come into prominence when the Yank was at Point Cumana. When the Yanks went back home everybody say she days did come to a end. But only Gawd know how it happen, ol' man, my friend pick it up, an' who goin' help him wid it now is anybody guess.

I wasn't in Trindad when the Yanks was there.

Well you miss something, ol' man. The Yanks turn Trinidad upside down, an' when they finish they let we see who was who. They is a great people, those Yankee people. It take a man like Lord Kitchener to put they fame in poetry.

WILL PASSENGERS KEEP THEIR HEADS WITHIN THE TRAIN
What him get drunk on so?
The limeys know how to get drunk on
bitter. They make up they min' before they
take a sip. Doan' pay him no mind.
Him turn real stupid but me no say for

certain him ain't better man than the one
me see back down yonder who let coal pot
in he mouth make dumb man outta him.

WILL PASSENGERS KEEP THEIR HEADS WITHIN THE TRAIN
England's a pleasant place
For those that are rich and free
But England ain't no place
For guys that look like ye.
Good night Irene, Good night,
Pam, pan paddan pam pam.

WILL PASSENGERS KEEP THEIR HEADS WITHIN THE TRAIN
On the hill beyond where the grass is, green,
greener than the hedges here, in the sun, look,
like a print of plaster made against plain, look
a white horse. Did you see the white horse.
If you look now you can see it, where the
grass is, green, greener than the hedges
here. And the sun makes it real like an animal
in stride. It looks as if it had been set on
the side so that one flank of ribs rests on
the grass, and the sun seems brighter there,
the grass green, greener, than the hedges here.
Now. The horse. The buildings have come
between us. You won't see it for some time,
that white horse like a plaster print on the
grass. Look how the buildings slip past.
And these, obviously these were destroyed.
Destroyed by fire. Two, three, four of
them, all in a row. These, oh, these were hit
from above. Bombed. The War. Everything
seemed so preserved nearer the sea that it
didn't register. The War. But there was a
War. These buildings were bombed. That is,
bombs fell on them, and they went up in
flames, leaving as a memorial of their
destruction what you see now. The War. It
was fought here, and you read about it.
Heard about it. Saw people who had seen it.

And now the buildings. Of course they were
bombed. And this is the first time you have
been to a country that was bombed. Now
you are in the war zone. England. Am I really
in England. Remember the battles. England
was always the place that fought battles, the
country with some enemy, but England, it
was Britain the books said, for Britain.
It was Britons, Britons never never shall be
slaves. This is England. Look you just missed
it. Ah, there again, there it is, the white
horse. Gone. There ah, there it is. White
against the grass. Who put it there. Look.
There again. Ah, it's gone. Gone. All the
buildings are solid here. These were not
bombed. Or perhaps these were rebuilt. They
have blocked out the white horse. Forever.
The white horse is gone. Only the buildings
now.

How long you been sleepin'?

WILL PASSENGERS KEEP THEIR HEADS WITHIN THE TRAIN

> Look partner dat's where they make the
> blades, partner, all yuh shaving you say you
> shave you do cause o' that place. Look it,
> ol' man, they make yuh blades there.
>
> Ponds, ol' man, look Ponds. They make
> cream there. All those women back home
> depend on what happen in there. Look,
> Ponds Cream. Look Tornado you see that.
> Paint. They make paint there. Look. Paint.
> You dint see that, partner. You see that.
> They make life there. Life. What life partner.
> Where you say they make what.
>
> Life partner. Read it. Hermivita gives life.
> You ain't see it.
>
> In the same direction, look, they make
> death there, ol' man. Look. Dissecticide kills
> once and for all. Read partner. Look what
> they make.

They make everything here on this side.
All England like this.

Everything we get back home they make
here, ol' man

PASSENGERS MUST NOT OPEN DOOR BEFORE ORDERS
Pull yuhself together, ol' man. This is it.
This, ol' man. Look.
Changes very quickly. From the land
down yonder where everything was clean,
cultivated, to this. Now only buildings. And
there aren't any people now. Not here. Down
yonder the man was walking like a man
back home. Slow as if he had all tomorrow
to get where he was going. Now only the
buildings. And it's so dark with the smoke
over the chimneys. The buildings. Perhaps
there might be work in the buildings. Too
many buildings. Must be work. Always say,
what can another wage mean to the whole
business. Must be work. Too many buildings.

WILL PASSENGERS KEEP THEIR HEADS WITHIN THE TRAIN
Gawd bless my eyesight. Never
thought I would have see where
those suspenders come from. Look,
bellybreakers, ol' man, look the
good ol' keep-me-ups we call
bellybreakers.
Tell Edna you see wid your own
eyes where they mix up the lipstick
she use an' she'll say you tellin' lies.
Look Tornado, you see that.
Yeast. They make yeast there.
Get a job inside dat place you'll
fatten yuh guts to busting point.
My Gawd, yeast.
Why they doan' make these
things themselves back home?
We ain't got the buildings man, we

ain't got them big buildings. Look,
partner, look toothpaste. You not
looking good. You doan' want
to say you see dese things. Look
good man.

She slowing down boys. The engine slowin'
down.
Time she did. My bottom sore wid sitting.
Pull yuhself together, chums, this is it.
We comin' in.

It cold Tornado. It get cold sudden as hell.
Button up good ol' man. Keep yuhself warm.
Remember we keep together.

But if a man see one single good break goin'
Doan' miss it.

How much change you got now.
What the Governor lend me.
Dat wont take you more'n two stations
from where we get off.

How far we got to go.
Ah doan' know where you goin.
Wherever ah get a place to sleep.
You know Victoria. Ask for Victoria.
What happen there?
The Colonial Office.
You can sleep there.
Not there. But may be they find something.
We take long to get there. It turn dark.
It only five past five. My clock stop.
I say ten past five. Mine tickin'.
It turn dark Tornado.
Why it so dark Tornado.
Look Tornado. Fire. Smoke.
Where all that smoke comin' from?
I see the smoke. But no fire. What happen now?
We stop ol' man. We stop dead.
Look a train next door.
Maybe they collide. The smoke thick.
We stop sudden as hell.
That smoke Tornado. It ain't look real.

It got a colour like the cold off yuh chest.
We got to wait 'til that smoke clear up.
That ain't smoke ol' man.
It cold Tornado. It get cold sudden as hell.
Button up good, ol' man, keep yourself warm.
It dark Tornado. It take long as hell to get
here. It late.
Five o'clock partner. Only a few minutes past.
But it dark Tornado. Why it so dark, ol' man.
Look. There is a fire in London. Look. Where
all that smoke comin' from.
That ain't smoke, ol' man. There ain't no fire.
Look a train next door. What we waitin' for.
We stop Tornado. We stop sudden as hell.
What happen next.
We got to wait till that smoke clear up.
Open that door, partner.
Where is that Tornado.
Paddington.

Here pavement. Over there luggage.
Beyond crowds. Vague and ragged waiting
to greet friends. You can't see them clearly
because things get thicker like a blacksmith's
shop after something has gone wrong. No
blaze. No fire. Just a thick choking mass of
cloud. The men bend to read the names.
Beyond the people crowd like refugees. As
though something had happened outside
to frighten them into hiding! Only these
voices speak clearly. The strange ones.
The men working on the platform. The
others talk as though they were choked.
Weak. Frightened. They said it wouldn't
be so cold. So cold . . . so frightened . . .
so frightened . . . home . . . go . . . to
go back . . . home . . . only because . . .
this like . . . no . . . home . . . other
reason . . . because . . . like this . . .
frightened . . . alone . . . the whole place
. . . goes up up up and over up and over

curling falling . . . up . . . over to heaven
. . . down to . . . hell up an' over . . .
thick . . . sick . . . thick . . . sick . . .
up . . . cold. . . so . . . frightened . . .
no . . . don't . . . don't tremble . . . no
. . . not frightened . . . no . . . alone
. . . no . . .

What's yer name son?
Collis.
Know where you stayin'?
No.
There's a gentleman up front takin' you
chaps to a London 'ostel.
Thank you.
It's the coldes' spring we've 'ad in fifty
years.
Thank you.

Tornado.
Yes Lilian.
Touch my nose.
It feel alright.
But it feel hard like wood.
'Tis the cold.
How long it stay so.
Ah doan' know.
Tornado, ol' man.
What happen.
When you get outside all this smoke.
What happen?
Would be able to see where you goin'?
Ah doan' know.
How long you stay in the dark like this?
Till you get out.
A day, two days? three days? forever?
Maybe.
Tornado.
What.

Tornado.
What you cryin' for, you's a man, no chil',
why you cry?

Tell me, Tornado, tell me.

What, man, what?

When we get outta this smoke,

When we get outta this smoke, w'at happen
next?

More smoke.

STUART HALL

from *Stuart Hall, Critical Dialogues in Cultural Studies*
The Formation of a Diasporic Intellectual II

KHC: From then on, you maintained a very close relationship with your sister – psychoanalytically speaking, you identified with her?

SH: No, not really. Though the whole system had messed up her life, she never revolted. So I revolted, in her place, as it were. I'm also guilty, because I left her behind, to cope with it. My decision to emigrate was to save myself. She stayed.

I left in 1951 and I didn't know until 1957 that I wasn't going back; I never really intended to go back, though I didn't know it at the same time. In a way, I am able to write about it now because I'm at the end of a long journey. Gradually, I came to recognize I was a black West Indian, just like everybody else. I could relate to that, I could write from and out of that position. It has taken a very long time, really, to be able to write in that way, personally. Previously, I was only able to write about it analytically. In that sense, it has taken me fifty years to come home. It wasn't so much that I had anything to conceal. It was the space I couldn't occupy, a space I had to learn to occupy.

You can see that this formation – learning the whole destructive, colonized experience – prepared me for England. I will never forget landing there. My mother brought me, in my felt hat, in my overcoat, with my steamer trunk. She brought me, as she thought, 'home', on the banana boat, and delivered me to Oxford. She gave me to the astonished college scout and said, 'There is my son, his trunks, his belongings. Look after him.' She delivered me, signed and sealed, to where she thought a son of hers had always belonged – Oxford.

My mother was an overwhelmingly dominant person. My relationship with her was close and antagonistic. I hated what she stood for, what she tried to represent to me. But we all had a close bond with her, because she dominated our lives. She dominated my sister's life. It was compounded by the fact that my brother, who was the eldest, had very bad sight, and eventually went blind. From an early age, he was very dependent on my parents. When I came along, this pattern of mother–son dependency was clearly established. They tried to repeat it with me. And when I began to have my own interests and my own positions, the antagonism started. At the same time, the relationship was intense, because my mother always said I was the only person who fought her. She wanted to dominate me, but she also despised those she whom she dominated. So she despised my father because he would give in to her. She despised my sister, because she was a girl, and as my mother said, women were not interesting. In adolescence, my sister fought her all along, but once my mother broke her, she despised her. So we had that relationship of antagonism. I was the youngest. She thought I was destined to oppose her, but respected me for that. Eventually when she knew what I had become in England – fufilling all her most paranoid fantasies of the rebellious son – she didn't want me to come back to Jamaica, because by then I would have represented my own thing, rather than her image of me. She found out about my politics and said, 'Stay over there, don't come back here and make trouble for us with those funny ideas.'

I felt easier in relation to Jamaica, once they were dead, because before that, when I went back, I had to negotiate Jamaica through them. Once my parents were dead, it was easier to make a new relationship to the new Jamaica that emerged in the 1970s. This Jamaica was not where I had grown up. For one thing, it had become, culturally, a black society, a post-slave, postcolonial society, whereas I had lived there at the end of the colonial era. So I could negotiate it as a 'familiar stranger'.

Paradoxically, I had exactly the same relationship to England. Having been prepared by colonial education, I knew England from the inside. But I'm not and never will be 'English'. I know both places intimately, but I am not wholly of either place. And that's exactly the diasporic experience, far away enough to experience the sense of exile and loss, close enough to understand the engima of an always-postponed 'arrival'.

It's interesting, in relation to Jamaica, because my close friends whom I left behind then went through experiences which I didn't. They lived 1968 there, the birth of black consciousness and the rise of Rastafarianism, with its memories of Africa. They lived those years in a different way from me, and so I'm not of their generation either. I was at school with them, and I've kept in touch with them, but they have an entirely different experience from mine. Now that gap cannot be filled. You can't 'go home' again.

So you have what Simmel talked about: the experience of being inside and outside, the 'familiar stranger'. We used to call that 'alienation', or deracination. But nowadays it's come to be the archetypal late-modern condition. Increasingly, it's what everybody's life is like. So that's how I think about the articulation of the postmodern and the postcolonial. Postcoloniality, in a curious way, prepared one to live in a 'postmodern' or diasporic relationship to identity. Paradigmatically, it's a diasporic experience. Since migration has turned out to be *the* world-historical event of late modernity, the classic postmodern experience turns out to be the diasporic experience.

. . .

KHC: Then you went to England in 1951. What happened then?

SH: Arriving on a steamer in Bristol with my mother, getting on the train to come to Paddington, I'm driving through this West Country landscape; I've never seen it, but I know it. I read Shakespeare, Hardy, the Romantic poets. Though I didn't occupy the space, it was like finding again, in one's dream, an already familiar and idealized landscape. In spite of my anti-colonial politics, it had always been my aspiration to study in England. I always wanted to study there. It took quite a while to come to terms with Britain, especially with Oxford, because Oxford is the pinnacle of Englishness, it's the hub, the motor, that creates Englishness.

There were two phases. Up until 1954, I was saturated in West Indian expatriate politics. Most of my friends were expatriates, and went back to play a role in Jamaica, Trinidad, Barbados, Guyana. We were passionate about the colonial question. We followed the expulsion of the French from Indochina with a massive celebration dinner. We discovered, for the first time, that we were 'West Indians'. We met African students for the first time. With the emerging postcolonial independence, we dreamt of a Caribbean federation, merging these countries into a larger entity. If that had happened, I would have gone back to the Caribbean.

Several West Indian students actually lived together, for a while, in this house in Oxford, which also spawned the New Left. They were the first generation, black, anti-colonial or postcolonial intelligentsia, who studied in England, did graduate work, trained to be economists. A lot of them were sent by their governments and went back, to become the leading cadre of the post-independence period. I was very much formed, politically and personally, in conversation with that, in the early Oxford days.

At the time, I was still thinking of going back to Jamaica, having a political career, being involved in West Indian federation politics, or teaching at the University of the West Indies. Then I got a second scholarship, and decided to stay on in Oxford and do graduate work. At that point, most of my immediate Caribbean circle went home. During that time, I also got to know people on the left, mainly from the Communist Party and the Labour Club. I had a very close friend, Alan Hall, to whom I dedicated an essay on the New Left in *Out of Apathy*.* He was a Scotsman, a classical archaeologist, who was interested in cultural and political questions. We met Raymond Williams together. We were very close to some people in the Communist Party then, but never members of it – people like Raphael Samuel, Peter Sedgwick. Another close friend was the philosopher Charles Taylor. Charles was another person, like Alan Hall and me, who was of the 'Independent Left'. We were interested in marxism, but not dogmatic marxists, anti-Stalinist, not defenders of the Soviet Union; and therefore we never became members of the Communist Party, though we were in dialogue with them, refusing to be cut off by the Cold War, as the rulers of the Labour Club of that time required. We formed this thing called the Socialist Society, which was a place for meetings of the independent minds of the Left. It brought together postcolonial intellectuals and British marxists, people in the Labour Party and other left-wing intellectuals. Perry Anderson, for example, was a member of that group. This was before 1956. Many of us were foreigners or internal immigrants: a lot of the British people were provincial, working-class, or Scottish, or Irish, or Jewish.

When I decided to stay on to do graduate work, I opened a discussion with some of the people in this broad-left formation. I remember going to a meeting and opening a discussion with members of the Communist Party, arguing against the reductionist version of the

* Stuart Hall, 'The "first" New Left: life and times', in Oxford University Socialist Discussions Group, *Out of Apathy: Voices of the New Left 30 Years On*, Verso, 1989

marxist theory of class. That must have been in 1954, and I seem to have been arguing the same thing ever since. In 1956, Alan Hall, myself and two other friends, both of them painters, went away for a long summer vacation. Alan and I were going to write this book on British culture. We took away three chapters of *Culture and Society*,* *The Uses of Literacy*,† Crossland's book on the *Future of Socialism*, Strachey's book, *After Imperialism*; we took away Leavis, with whose work we'd had a long engagement. The same issues were also breaking culturally. We took away the novelist Kingley Amis's *Lucky Jim*, new things that were happening in cinema in the British documentary movement – like Lindsay Anderson's essay in *Sight and Sound*. In August, while we were in Cornwall, the Soviet Union marched on Hungary and by the end of August, the British invaded Suez. That was the end of that. The world turned. That was the formation, the moment of the New Left. We went into something else.

* Raymond Williams, *Culture and Society: 1780–1950*, Penguin, 1958
† Richard Hoggart, *The Uses of Literacy*, Penguin, 1958

SAM SELVON

The Lonely Londoners is an account of major importance, about the first
wave of West Indians to arrive in Britain. A series of episodic sketches centred around Moses, it chronicles the unending search for jobs, homes, money
and women. In among the humour there is great nostalgia for the islands, and
a well of loneliness and pathos surrounding characters such as Big City, Cap,
Daniel and Sir Galahad. In the extract below, Moses introduces the larger-
than-life Cap.

from *The Lonely Londoners*

When Moses did arrive fresh in London, he look around for a place
where he wouldn't have to spend much money, where he could get
plenty food, and where he could meet the boys and coast a old talk
to pass the time away – for this city powerfully lonely when you on
your own.

It had such a place, a hostel, and you could say that in a way most
of the boys graduate from there before they branch off on their own
and begin to live in London. This place had some genuine fellars who
really studying profession, but it also had fellars who was only marking time and waiting to see what tomorrow would bring.

It had a big dining room, and you had was to buy a meal ticket
before you could get any food. Well some of the boys soon get in
with the servant girls and get meal tickets free. Sometimes in the
evening some fellars coming in, watching in the queue to see if they
see a friend who would buy them a meal. Then afterwards in the
lounge they would sit around – the genuine fellars with text-books in
they hand, and some fellars with the *Worker*, and big discussion on
politics and thing would start up. Especially with them who come
from British Guyana and don't want federation in the West Indies,
saying that they belong to the continent of South America and don't
want to belittle themself with the small islands. Meanwhile a
African fellar would be playing the piano – he would give you a

classic by Chopin, then a calypso, then one of them funny African
tune. It had a game them Africans used to play with a calabash shell
and some seeds, and nobody but a African could understand it, and
all the time two–three of them sitting by a table playing this game.
In another room had a pingpong table, and they used to play knock-
out, and some sharp games used to play there. In another room had a
billiards table.

Them was the old days, long before test like Galahad hit London.
But that don't mean to say it didn't have characters. There was a
fellar name Captain. Captain was Nigerian. His father send him to
London to study law, but Captain went stupid when he arrive in the
big city. He start to spend money wild on woman and cigarette (he
not fussy about drink) and before long the old man stop sending
allowance.

Cap had a greenstripe suit and a pair of suede shoes, and he live in
them for some years. He used to wash the clothes every night before
he go to sleep, and when he get up press them, so that though he
wearing the same things they always fairly clean. If he have money,
he would get up in the morning. If not, he would sleep all day, for to
get up would mean hustling a meal. So all day long he stay there in
bed, not really sleeping but closing his eyes in a kind of squint. Come
evening, Cap get up, go in the bathroom and look to see if anybody
leave a end of soap for him to bath with. Come back, press the clothes
and put them on, comb hair, blow the nose in the sink and gargle
loud, watch himself in the mirror, and then come down the stairs to
the dining room, wiping his face with a clean white handkerchief.

The old Cap have the sort of voice that would melt butter in the
winter, and he does speak like a gentleman. So the thing is, after he
sponge on all the fellars he know for meals, he used to look around
for newcomers, and put on a soft tone and the hardluck story.

It have some men in this world, they don't do nothing at all, and
you feel that they would dead from starvation, but day after day you
meeting them and they looking hale, they laughing and they talking
as if they have a million dollars, and in truth it look as if they would
not only live longer than you but they would dead happier.

Cap was a man like that. Cap had plenty work, but he only stay a
few days at any of them. And though he never have money in his
pocket, yet he would be there, there with the boys, having a finger in
everything. Cap only smoking Benson and Hedges – if you offer him
a Woods he would scorn you. If he manage to hustle a pound, he

eating a big meal, belching, buying a pack of B and H, and he ready
to face the world.

Come a time when the warden of the hostel tired hearing Cap talk
about the allowance that coming and never come, and tell him he have
to leave. As luck would have it, Cap was staying in the same room
with Moses, and he tell Moses not to say anything, but he would go
out during the day and sneak back in the room to sleep in the night.

One morning the warden get suspicious and he begin to make a
rounds looking for Cap, and when he come to Moses room the old
Cap get so frighten that he start to rattle. He fly out the bed and went
down on his knees before Moses, clasping his hands as if he saying
prayers.

'Don't say that I am here,' he beg Moses, 'I would get in trouble.'
And he went and hide in the clothes closet.

The warden open the door and look around and ask Moses if anybody else in the room, but he say no.

Captain come out after and start to shake Moses hand and thank
him.

'You will have to go,' Moses say. But though he threaten the
Captain often, Cap still hanging out in Moses room in the hostel.

To make things worse, he start getting up in the night and saying
that he see a white pigeon flying over his bed.

'It ain't have no pigeon in here,' Moses say.

'But I tell you I saw it!' Cap drawing back under the blankets. 'It
must be the spirit of my father from Nigeria.'

Another night Cap wake Moses up. 'Believe me, I saw an angel
with a harp playing over your bed,' he tell Moses.

'Listen,' Moses say. 'The next time you see that angel playing a
—ing harp over my bed, you don't say or do anything. I like harp
music, and he come to inspire me.'

One time Cap make a hundred pound. He hear that some English
fellars who want car used to get Africans to buy them, saying they
leaving the country. In that way they get away from a big set of purchase tax. Then the African would use the car a bit and sell it to the
fellar who finance the venture as second-hand car. The Cap get in this
racket, and make a hundred pound, but it went through his hands so
quick that the morning he wake up broke he was surprise.

Things reach a head at the hostel and he had to pull out. Cap walk
out as if he going for a stroll, with a toothbrush in his pocket. Brazen
as ever, he went to a hotel and put on the soft tone, explaining he was

a student and expected his allowance any day. Cap face so innocent
that the clerk start calling him 'mister' and hustle to get him a room.
No cheap room, one of the best, and Cap insisting on the ground floor
too.

One thing with Cap, he love woman too bad. He is one of them
fellars who would do anything to get a woman, and it ain't have a
night that he not coasting down the Bayswater Road, or drifting
round by the Circus. In fact, all the odd money that he need he get
from women that he pick up here and there about the place. So what
he doing is sleep in the day, and go out in the night to look for cat and
sponge a meal whenever he could.

Well of course the hotel people begin to get uneasy when two
weeks go by and Captain allowance ain't come, and they tell him he
would have to leave. So Cap went out for a walk and didn't come
back. In the winter, it hardly have a place where he ain't do the same
thing, from boarding house to hotel, from room to room. He had to
widen the area after a time. One day you would hear he living
Caledonia, another time he move to Clapham Common, next time
you see him he living Shepherd's Bush. Week after week, as landlord
and landlady catch up with him, the Captain moving, the wandering
Nigerian, man of mystery. Nobody could contact Cap, is only by
chance you bouncing him up here and there about London.

'Where you living now Cap?'

A kind of baby smile, and 'Victoria.'

'Ah,' Moses tell Galahad when he was giving him ballad about
Cap, 'is fellars like that who muddy the water for a lot of us. You see
how it is? One worthless fellar go around making bad, and give the
wrong impression for all the rest.'

Cap had an Austrian girl who was a sharp dresser, all kind of fur
coat in the winter, and in the summer some kind of dress that making
fellars whistle and turn round. As long as Cap had a place to take she,
where have a bed to relax, this Austrian was all right. And for Cap, he
used to take she round by all the fellars he know when he ain't have
no place to stay himself.

This kind of life going on, and the Austrian trying she best to make
Cap look for work.

'Why don't you get a job,' she tell Cap, 'there are many jobs
around, and all your friends are working.'

'Jobs are hard to get,' Cap say cagey, 'it is not as easy as you think.
I have tried many times.'

On one of those many times, the employment exchange send Cap to a railway to get a storekeeping work for seven pounds. When Cap go, the fellar in charge look at him and say yes, it have a work, but is not storekeeping work, and the pay is six ten.

'What kind of work it is?' Cap say. At this stage in his acquaintance with the boys he does forget proper English and many times you would mistake him for a West Indian, he get so hep.

The fellar take Cap to the back of the station, and behind there real grim. The people who living in London don't really know how behind them railway station does be so desolate and discouraging. It like another world. All Cap seeing is railway line and big junk of iron all about the yard, and some thick, heavy cable lying around. It have some snow on the ground, and the old fog at home as usual. It look like hell, and Cap back away when he see it.

'They tell me the pay was seven pounds,' Cap say, backing back.

'They made a mistake,' the fellar say. 'Do you think you can shift that piece of cable?'

'Take it easy,' Cap say.

'Go on, have a try,' the fellar urge.

'Take it easy,' Cap say. 'I will think about it and let you know.'

When he meet Moses he tell him how they was threatening him with this work in the railway.

'Is so it is,' Moses say. 'They send you for a storekeeper work and they want to put you in the yard to lift heavy iron. They think that is all we good for, and this time they keeping all the soft clerical jobs for them white fellars.'

Cap evade work so much that the Austrian start to get vex with him.

'How is it,' she tell Cap, 'that Moses has a job and manages on his salary? Why can't you get a job at the factory where he works?'

She nag Cap so much that at last Cap went to see Moses. He come back and tell the girl yes, he get a night-work same as Moses, and he would be starting right away.

In the night the Austrian come to the tube station with Moses and the Cap, and she buy a platform ticket and went down the platform with them, and she kiss Cap and wish him luck, and Cap and Moses get on the train and went.

When the train reach Notting Hill Gate Cap get off and went to hustle woman as usual.

He do that for a week and the Austrian please that he working so hard. When Friday come she ask Cap how much pay he get.

'This is a place,' Cap say, 'where they don't pay you the first week that you work.'

The second week Cap carry on as usual, catching the tube in the Water and hopping off at the Gate.

When the week over Cap tell the girl that he left the work because it too hard.

How it is, that it have women, no matter how bad a man is, they would still hold on to him and love him? Though the Austrian find out what Cap was doing, she still stay with him. In fact, when things hard she start pawning wristwatch, ring, coat, shoes and anything to get a penny, and she giving Cap all the money. Cap used to send she round by a fellar name Daniel to borrow, and she would go there and cry big water and say how things hard, and the old Daniel, who can't bear to see a woman cry, would lend she five–six pounds.

When Daniel see she later and ask for the money, she say she give Cap to give him. When he ask Cap, Cap say he give the Austrian to give him.

One time Cap was in a thing with two woman. One was a German and the other was English. He borrow eight pounds from the frauline, and as time went by and she can't see him at all, she send the Chelsea police after him. Now Cap have a genuine fear of the law – though he might be the most shiftless and laziest fellar in London, one thing is that he never in any trouble with the law. So when the Chelsea police take after him he was frighten like hell.

Same time, he was in another thing with the English one. She spend some time in Africa and she know a lot of the boys from there. When she was in London she had a big work with a respectable firm, and she always travelling light – toothbrush and toothpaste and soap and towel and night things in a small travelling bag, and after work she going round by one of the fellars she know.

Well Cap get in with this thing, and when the German close in on him, he take a wristwatch off the English girl and pawn it and pay the frauline the eight pounds.

One night Cap take the English round by Daniel, and soon after that Daniel was carrying the girl to ballet and theatre and cinema. The English was smart – Cap not taking her anywhere or spending any money, while this Daniel taking she to all the latest shows. Teahouse of the August Moon and Sadlers Wells and to restaurants in the Circus and in Soho. So the outcome was that she left Cap and begin to go with Daniel.

One night she tell Daniel how Cap take she wristwatch and didn't give it back.

'What!' Daniel say, feeling like a knight rescuing a damsel in distress, 'we have to do something about that!'

He and the girl went to Earl's Court, which part Cap had a room at the time. When Daniel ask the landlady for Cap, she say she don't know where he is, that he went away owing ten pounds rent.

Somewhere in London Cap hear the rumour that Daniel looking for him, so he went to Daniel house one night, where he meet the English girl.

'Cap,' Daniel say, 'how you could do a thing like this, man? You take the girl wristwatch and pawn it! You have to get it back for she right away!'

Cap see he can't get out of the situation no how, so he start to 'buse the English girl, calling she all kind of whore and prostitute, saying how she could go with Daniel. And with that he went away not to see Daniel again until the matter was forgotten.

One powerful winter Cap was shivering with cold, and the sight touch Moses heart. He lend Cap a camelhair coat. When spring come, Moses looking all about for Cap to get back the coat. But he can't see Cap nowhere. Truth is it always happen that Cap see him first and hop off the bus or tube and run to hide. At last Moses run him to earth in Marble Arch one evening.

'Aye, you bitch,' Moses say, 'I looking for you all about. Where my coat?'

'I ain't have it, Moses,' Cap say in the baby voice.

'You best hads get it for me,' Moses say, 'or I set the police after you. I ain't fooling, man.'

At mention of police Cap turn white, which is a hell of a thing to see. And the next day he pass round by Moses house and drop the coat.

And yet when things real desperate with Cap, is Moses self who helping him out. The Austrian used to complain to him about Cap. 'All day he is sleeping, sleeping, I do not know what to do.'

Moses say: 'Listen, I telling you, that man no good for you, he is a worthless fellar who won't do no work, he would sleep with you and then look for somebody else to sleep with two minutes after, why you don't leave him?'

The Austrian ups and went back and tell Captain all what Moses say, and he and Cap had a big quarrel about it.

But still Moses have compassion on him. Round about that time the Captain trousers start to give way under the stress and strain of the seasons, and it was Moses who give him a old pair of pants. Moses couldn't help: everytime he going out with the Cap, Cap walking a little bit in front and asking him: 'See if my backside is showing, boy, this pair of trousers wearing thin.' And he look and see that Cap really in a bad way, and the soft heart was touched once more.

So Cap get a pair of corduroys, and the Austrian girl give him a black blazer jacket.

One night something happen with Cap and Moses nearly go mad laughing when he find out afterwards, because at the time he didn't know nothing. He and Cap uses to coast Bayswater Road, from the Arch to the Gate, nearly every night. Well it had one woman used to be hustling there, dress up nice, wearing fur coat, and every time when the boys pass she saying 'Bon soir,' in a hoarse voice, and the boys answering politely 'Bon soir' and walking on. But on this particular night things was scarce on the patrol and the old Cap thirst bad, so Moses tell him why he don't broach this big woman who always telling them 'Bon soir.'

Cap broach and he take the woman down by Gloucester Road and he was so hurry he couldn't wait but had was to begin as soon as she turn off the lights in the room.

Couple nights after they was talking to some women near a pub, when one of them turn to Captain and say: 'It was you who slept with that man the other night!'

And when the mark burst, Moses get to understand that this 'Bon soir' woman was really a test who used to dress up like a woman and patrol the area.

Moses start one set of laughing, and the old Cap laugh too. He tell Moses he didn't know anything until he begin, when he find the going difficult and realize that something wrong.

Since that time all the boys greeting Captain: 'Bon soir.'

Who can tell what was the yap that hit Cap and make him get married? A man like he, who ain't have nothing, no clothes, no work, no house to live in, no place to go? Yet is so things does happen in life. You work things out in your own mind to a kind of pattern, in a sort of sequence, and one day bam! something happen to throw everything out of gear, what you expect to happen never happen, what you don't expect to happen always happen, and you have to start thinking all over again.

Cap was a fellar like that – a fellar that you never know what he will be doing, which part he will be, what he will say. If you hear that Cap is Prime Minister of England, don't be surprised. If you hear that Cap kill four–five people in the Circus, don't be surprised. If you hear that Cap join a order of the monks and go to Tibet to meditate, be unconcerned.

Cap had a friend in Brighton who had a garage business, who was friending with a French girl. The French girl went back to France and tell she sister how things rosy in Brit'n, and the sister come, and Cap get in with she. This number was a sharp thing and Cap like it more than the regular Austrian. He tell Frenchy how the garage business not doing so well – this time so he give her the impression that he have part ownership in his friend business – and that he would be leaving it and taking up a post with the Nigerian Government. He tell the girl is a better job, and she believe every word he say, partly because his face so innocent, and partly because she can't understand English so well.

So thinking they would soon be off to Nigeria, the girl decide to marry Cap. She went to a vicar and give three weeks notice, and when the time come Cap went, wearing the corduroy trousers and the black blazer jacket and the suede shoes, which was still carrying him around. Them suede shoes, the makers would pay Cap a lot of money if they could get him to advertise how long they last him.

Without a cent in the world, no prospects, nothing at all Cap went to say 'I do.' When the vicar say they have to have a witness Cap run out on the road and was lucky to see a African fellar passing. He explain the position and the fellar say all right, but after the ceremony, when the vicar tell the fellar that he have to sign a book, the test shake his head.

'I not signing anything,' he say. 'I come to witness, and I witness. But I not signing anything.'

All the vicar explain to the test that it was necessary for the witness to sign the registry, the fellar decide that he not putting his name to any paper, and he went away.

Good thing, the vicar wife was in, and she said she would witness.

Cap, not having any address at the time, give Frenchy Daniel address and left the girl, saying he have some business to attend to.

That evening when Daniel come home from work the landlord meet him by the door and say: 'Your wife has come.'

'My wife?' Daniel say, standing up stupid.

'Yes. She is waiting for you in your room.'

When Daniel hear that he fly up the steps to see who it was. He see Frenchy sitting there with all her luggage, waiting on the Captain. She manage to explain to Daniel what she was doing there, and now Daniel in a quandary. He don't know which part to find the Captain. At last he had to leave the girl and go to look, and he decide to try a all-night cafe in the Gate where Cap does always hang out, coasting lime over a cuppa or a cup of coffee, sitting there eyeing every woman, trying to make contact.

As luck would have it he spot the old Cap having a cuppa, sitting down on a stool like if he have all the time in the world and not a worry on his mind.

'Cap,' Daniel say, 'what the hell is this? Your wife home by me, man with all she luggage.'

'Good lord,' Cap murmur, sipping tea and wiping his face with a clean white handkerchief. 'Good lord.'

'Don't just sit there and say good lord, man. Do something.'

'Look, Daniel, this is the way it is.' And Cap say how he have no place to take the wife.

'But Christ man why you get married if you have no place to live?'

'Good lord,' Cap murmur.

Now Cap gambling on Daniel thirst, so when they go back to the room Cap encouraging conversation and getting Frenchy to talk familiar with Daniel, and sure enough the old Daniel had the kettle on to make a cup of tea.

So the night wearing on, and Cap ain't making no move to move, he only sitting down there wondering how to get out of the mooch he find himself in. As for Frenchy, she puzzle that Cap only sitting there and wouldn't get up.

Cap put on the soft tone and ask Daniel to lend him eight pounds.

'Eight pounds!' Daniel say. 'What you think, money growing on tree?'

'I will give it back to you tomorrow,' Cap say, making the sign of the cross with his forefingers and kissing it, as he see the West Indian boys do.

Daniel hesitate a little, but he want to impress the French girl. Now he is a fellar that does take them woman to Covent Garden and Festival Hall, and them girl does have big times in them places, for all they accustom to is a pint of mild, the old fish and chips, and the one and six local. Many times Daniel go round by Moses saying how he take so and so to see ballet, and Moses tell him that them girls won't appreciate those things.

'I want them to feel good that we coloured fellars could take them to these places,' Daniel say, 'and we could appreciate even if they can't.'

'You spending your money bad,' Moses say. 'Them girls ain't worth it.'

But Daniel does feel good when he do things like that, it give him a big kick to know that one of the boys could take white girls to them places to listen to classics and see artistic ballet.

'You don't treat your women right,' he tell Moses, 'as long as you could get them in the yard you satisfy. You don't spend no money on them.'

'Why I must spend my money on them frowsy women?' Moses say.

So with Frenchy sitting there – and Cap giving the impression that anytime Daniel want a little thing with she it would be all right – he fork over the money.

Upon that Cap went out and hail a taxi and take the girl away to a seven-guinea room in a hotel.

And so Cap start the married life. He had to shift out of the hotel when the week was up, but the French girl was getting money from France every week, and they live on that for a long time. Every time she ask him when they going to Nigeria, Cap say he waiting on some papers from the Nigerian Embassy.

Meanwhile the Austrian hear that Cap have another girl, but she didn't know it was so serious. When she find out she went by Moses to moan, but he tell she to go to hell, because he did warn her about Cap.

Cap carrying on the same sort of life like when he was single. He there with the French girl in the night, and when she fall asleep he putting on clothes and going out to hustle just as he used to do before he get married. It don't make no difference to him at all. Eventually Frenchy had to get a work in a store, and nothing please him better. He sleeping all day while she out working, and going out in the night. He make she buy a radiogram and he get some of the latest bop records to keep him company, and now and again he having a little party in the room.

He had a way, every time Moses have a girl visitor, he dropping in and won't leave at all, sitting down there on the bed as if he waiting for Moses to give him a share. This thing happen so often that Moses get damn vex.

One evening when a girl was there the bell ring and Moses went and open the door. From the moment he see Cap he start to get on ignorant.

'Get out, get to hell out, man!' he say, and he push Cap in the road and shut the door.

Still, the Captain living. Day after day you will see him, doing nothing, having nothing, owing everybody, and yet he there with this innocent face, living on and on, smoking Benson and Hedges when things good, doing without a smoke when things bad. Who in this world think that work necessary? Who say that a man must have two pairs of shoes or two trousers or two jackets? Cap with woman left and right – he have a way, he does pick up something and take it home and when he finish and she ask for money, throw she out on the streets. He have a way, he would broach any girl who he see going around with one of the boys.

Yet day after day Cap still alive, defying all logic and reason and convention, living without working, smoking the best cigarettes, never without women.

Sometimes you does have to start thinking all over again when you feel you have things down the right way.

DAVID DABYDEEN

David Dabydeen was born in Guyana. His first collection of poetry, *Slave Song*, was awarded the Commonwealth Poetry Prize and the Cambridge University Quiller-Couch Prize. Alongside poetry, he has written a number of novels. His critical book on the painter Hogarth offered original insights into the presence and position of black people in eighteenth-century Britain. He lectures at the University of Warwick.

'London Taxi Driver' is taken from *Coolie Odyssey*, a collection of poems tracking the experience of the peasant labourers from India to the Caribbean and then to Britain.

London Taxi Driver

From Tooting, where I picked him up, to Waterloo,
He honked, swerved, swore,
Paused at the twin-tubbed buttocks of High Street Wives,
Jerked forward again,
Unwound the window as we sped along,
Hawked and spat.

The talk was mostly solitary,
Of the new single, of missing the pools by bleeding two,
Of some sweet bitch in some soap serial,
How he'd like to mount and stuff her lipsticked mouth,
His eyes suddenly dreamy with designs –
Nearly missing a light he slammed the car stop,
Snatched the hand-brake up.
Wheel throbbed in hand, engine giddy with anticipation.
As we toured the slums of Lambeth the meter ticked greedily.

He has come far and paid much for the journey
From some village in Berbice where mule carts laze
And stumble over broken paths,

Past the women with buckets on their heads puffed
with *ghee* and pregnancy
Past the men slowly bent over earth, shovelling,
Past the clutch of mud-huts jostling for the shade,
Their Hindu flags of folk-defiant rituals
That provoked the Imperial swords of Christendom
Discoloured, hang their heads and rot
On bamboo pikes:
Now he knows more the drama of amber red and green,
Mutinies against double-yellow lines,
His aggression is horned like ancient clarions,
He grunts rebellion
In back seat discount sex
With the night's last whore.

WOLE SOYINKA

Wole Soyinka was born in Nigeria and educated at the University of Ibadan. He arrived in Britain in 1954 to complete an English degree at Leeds University, and later was attached to the Royal Court Theatre (1957–59) as a Play Reader. He is Nigeria's leading poet and dramatist. His plays include: *A Dance of Forests*, *The Lion and the Jewel*, *The Trials of Brother Jero* and *Kongi's Harvest*. He has also written novels, screenplays, criticism and two volumes of autobiography. He won the Nobel Prize for Literature in 1986.

'Telephone Conversation' was first read at the Royal Court Theatre in 1959.

Telephone Conversation

The price seemed reasonable, location
Indifferent. The landlady swore she lived
Off premises. Nothing remained
But self-confession. 'Madam,' I warned,
'I hate a wasted journey – I am African.'

Silence. Silenced transmission of
Pressurized good-breeding. Voice, when it came,
Lipstick coated, long gold-rolled
Cigarette-holder pipped. Caught I was, foully.

'HOW DARK?' . . . I had not misheard . . . 'ARE YOU LIGHT
OR VERY DARK?' Button B. Button A. Stench
Of rancid breath of public hide-and-speak.
Red booth. Red pillar-box. Red double-tiered
Omnibus squelching tar. It *was* real! Shamed
By ill-mannered silence, surrender
Pushed dumbfoundment to beg simplification.
Considerate she was, varying the emphasis –
'ARE YOU DARK? OR VERY LIGHT?' Revelation came.
'You mean – like plain or milk chocolate?'

Her assent was clinical, crushing in its light
Impersonality. Rapidly, wave-length adjusted,
I chose. 'West African sepia' – and as afterthought,
'Down in my passport.' Silence for spectroscopic
Flight of fancy, till truthfulness clanged her accent
Hard on the mouthpiece. 'WHAT'S THAT?' conceding
'DON'T KNOW WHAT THAT IS.' 'Like brunette.'

'THAT'S DARK, ISN'T IT?' 'Not altogether.
Facially, I am brunette, but, madam, you should see
The rest of me. Palm of my hand, soles of my feet
Are a peroxide blond. Friction, caused –
Foolishly, madam – by sitting down, has turned
My bottom raven black – One moment, madam!' – sensing
Her receiver rearing on the thunderclap
About my ears – 'Madam,' I pleaded, 'wouldn't you rather
See for yourself?'

E. R. BRAITHWAITE

E. R. Braithwaite made his reputation with the autobiographical book *To Sir, With Love*, which was later turned into a record-breaking film starring Sidney Poitier, Judy Geeson and Lulu.

Braithwaite had arrived in Britain just before the start of World War II to enter Cambridge University. In his freshman year war was declared and he volunteered for Aircrew in the Royal Air Force, serving as a fighter pilot. After the war he returned to Cambridge and earned a Master's degree in Physics.

He later worked as a teacher and Welfare Officer for the London County Council. In 1960, he left Britain for an appointment with UNESCO in Paris and in 1965 became the newly independent Guyana's first Ambassador to the United Nations in New York.

Braithwaite has taught at New York University and Florida State University. Now an American citizen, he resides in Washington, DC.

Paid Servant is a non-fiction account of the time Braithwaite spent as a social worker dealing with the growing problem of orphaned black children. It paints an absorbing picture of black family life and the struggles faced by the first generation to establish themselves. In the extract below, he describes taking on the job and his interest in Rodwell, a mixed-race orphan who needed placing with a family.

from *Paid Servant*

As the Underground train rocked gently on its way I wondered what would happen if I suddenly shouted to my fellow passengers, 'Would any of you like to foster a little boy?' They'd probably think me mad. Even as a joke I wouldn't have the courage to disturb the heavy quiet, broken only by the occasional quick rustle of a newspaper held in such a way that the effect of semi-detachment was continued along the rows of seats. The fact that elbows touched gave no one the right to glance at his neighbour's paper.

The only reading matter I had was the thick file of case-histories in my briefcase – not appropriate reading for the Underground. I was on

my way to discuss one of the cases with a London County Council
Welfare Officer at her office in the North London Area. A tough case,
but, after all, that was why I was appointed to the job, to deal with the
tough ones.

After nearly nine years as a schoolmaster in England, I had been
seconded from the London County Council's Department of
Education to their Department of Child Welfare, to help and advise
on the many problems created by the heavy post-war influx of immigrants into Britain from the West Indies, India, Pakistan and other
Commonwealth regions. Although I had had no formal training in
Welfare work, I had been rather active, for some years, among many
immigrant groups in different parts of London, encouraging their
efforts to promote self-help schemes of one sort or another.
Apparently, some of these extra-curricular activities attracted some
notice to themselves and it was considered that I had the kind of
experience and continuing contact with West Indian and other immigrant groups which fitted me for the job.

Operating from a centrally situated Welfare Office, I was available
to all the Area offices for consultation with the Council's Child
Welfare Officers who might need help and advice in their dealings
with members of the immigrant groups and their children, and to
assist in the search for foster or adoptive parents for the increasing
number of non-white children who for a variety of reasons, and either
temporarily or permanently, came into the care of the Council – especially the hardcore cases, children who, year after year, remained in
the Council's Nurseries or Children's Homes, without any real hope
of ever experiencing the warmth of family life. It was hoped that I
might have some success with these cases and though I did not quite
agree with the premise on which this hope was based, I was determined to do my best.

Miss Coney was neat; that was the word that came into my mind as
we exchanged pleasantries in her office. Everything about her person
was neat and orderly – the short, grey-streaked brown hair, trimmed
close to her well-shaped head, and the slim, well-proportioned figure
in soft tailored tweeds. She was of medium height, her face small-
boned, with well-balanced features, and a surprisingly full mouth
which would surely have looked sensual with the least touch of lipstick. Her hands were long-fingered, and relaxed, reflecting the
confidence she felt in herself, her assured control of whatever the situation would be.

I asked her for some details of the background of Roddy Williams, the young boy whose case I had come to take over from her.

'Ah, yes,' she replied. 'Rodwell Williams.' Her voice was clear and precise. I noticed that she said 'Rodwell'. She took a slim folder from a pile on her desk and went on . . .

'Not very much on him, I'm afraid. You know about his parents?'

I opened my briefcase and took out the case file on Roddy Williams. Not much there.

Name:	Rodwell Clive Williams
Age:	4½ years
Sex:	Male
Race:	Coloured. Half-Mexican
Father:	Unknown. Thought to have been a United States Serviceman, probably of Mexican origin.
Mother:	Angela Williams, present whereabouts unknown. Thought to be a prostitute.
Status:	Available for fostering or adoption.
Remarks:	Abandoned in Holydene Hospital soon after birth and has since lived in Franmere Residential Nursery. A handsome, intelligent, happy child.

Welfare Officer in Charge: Miss L. Coney. North Central Area.

'It is recorded that his father was unknown, but there's some suggestion that he may have been a Serviceman.'

'We don't know for sure,' Miss Coney clasped her hands together, 'but I think the mother hinted to the hospital almoner that he was an American.'

'And the mother?' I said.

'Soon after the child was born she abandoned him in hospital. The hospital almoner got in touch with us and I went round to the address she had given, in Paddington – one of those old buildings now converted to rooming houses.

'She had just got out of bed – at eleven o'clock in the morning – and from the state of the room it was not too difficult to guess what she was up to. She claimed that she had been unwell, and promised to visit the child the following day – but she never turned up.

'I called again at the address in Paddington, but she had moved and we were unable to trace her. Even the police helped us in trying to find her, but without success. So, the child was removed to the

Children's Nursery, where he's been ever since. About two weeks ago she turned up here asking to see me, but I was away on leave, didn't get back till yesterday. Perhaps she'll come again.'

'Did she leave an address or telephone number?'

'Yes, here it is,' she consulted a pad on her desk, 'and would you believe it, it's the same place where she lived before.'

'Fine,' I said, 'I think I'll drop around there and have a chat with her.'

'That's if she's there. These fly-by-nights are always on the move, you know. I wonder what she wants. Pregnant again, perhaps.' Her lip curled in a fleeting expression of distaste.

I asked if there was any further information on the father. 'Nobody ever saw him,' Miss Coney replied. 'The mother told the hospital people that he was an American Serviceman and that's as much as we know. It may well be that she merely picked a man at random from the many she knew.'

'But in his file the child is referred to as half-Mexican.'

'Well, when you see Rodwell you will understand. I've been in this job for a long time and I can tell. It has to do with his colour and his hair and the shape of his nose and cheekbones. I know about these things.'

She smiled confidently, secure in knowing about 'those things'. I thought, 'You'd have a lovely old time in the West Indies or the United States trying to sort them out and label them . . . ' 'Has there been any attempt so far to find a foster home for him, or have him adopted?' I asked.

'Oh yes,' she replied brightly. 'I've been trying for the past three years to have him placed, ever since the Council became his legal guardians. But with coloured children it is not an easy thing. We have to think not only of today, but what will happen when the child grows older. Now and again people have expressed interest, but they've changed their minds when I've explained some of the problems they would have to cope with later on.'

'What problems?' I asked.

'Well, you know, there is the problem of placing him in a family where there might be girls. After all, the children won't always be young, and we must think of what could happen in adolescence or later.'

I looked at the woman aghast as the penny dropped, setting up its discordant clanging in my mind. Good Lord, under this neat, con-

trolled exterior there lurked all the frightening prejudices which so
often made us 'helpers' our own worst enemies, and baulked our best
efforts and intentions. Among her equipment was the huge crystal
ball of prejudice into which she looked for guidance every time a case
involved a coloured person. I could feel the sudden anger rising
inside me, making it difficult for me to be reasonable; but I had to be
reasonable, and even patient, so that I might learn how it was she
approached this case, and with what results. She seemed so nice, so
professional.

'I don't quite follow you,' I said, purposely not understanding.

'Well, you see, I've had a great many years' experience working
among coloured people, and there's not much I don't know about
them,' she said, calmly.

'Lucky you,' I thought. 'I'm one of them and I know damned little
about them.'

'I've had to work among Asians and Africans and West Indians in
London and before that in Cardiff, and I know how they feel about
things like sex, quite different from the way we English people feel.'

As she spoke I wondered where I fitted into this picture. Did the
same thing apply to me? Or did my status as a Welfare Officer somehow emasculate me and render me more acceptable?

'In this profession we need to be extremely careful,' she went on,
her voice cool and easy. 'You must forgive me for speaking so
frankly to you, Mr Braithwaite, but I think you know what I mean,
and considering Roddy's background and everything, we cannot
afford to take any chances.'

It all came out so smooth and plausible. She must have made up
her mind a long time ago about coloured people, and now the ideas
had jelled, hardened, ossified. Was there any hope at all of budging
her?

I couldn't resist trying. 'Well, Miss Coney, being coloured myself,
you're making me feel rather awkward in this situation.'

'Oh, no, Mr Braithwaite,' she exclaimed, her aplomb jarred
slightly off-centre, 'you're different. You're an educated man, and I
understand you've lived in England for many years. But . . .' with a
deft twist she had regained her assurance, 'thinking of Roddy, I'm
sure you will be able to do something for him. You might know some
nice coloured family who would be willing to have him so that he can
grow up in his natural background. I do hope you understand that I
have no prejudice of any kind. Some of my best friends are coloured

people, but at the same time one must be realistic about these things, and I'm sure you'll agree that the child would be far better off with people of his own kind.'

His own kind. The white part of his origin was not to be considered in this context. I was nettled, but hoping to find some tiny chink in the tight armour of her assurance, I said: 'But where do you suppose I shall find foster parents who have a half-Mexican, half-prostitute background?'

She laughed softly, unperturbed. 'Well we must have our little joke, mustn't we?' she replied. 'But I'm sure you'll find a place for him. And now I'm afraid I must throw you out, as I've piles and piles of stuff to get through.' She stood up and walked around her desk to show me to the door.

Well, that was that. The next step was to see the boy, Rodwell Clive Williams, half-Mexican, half-prostitute. Mix thoroughly for four and a half years. Result should be a cretinous gargoyle at worst, a problem child at best. What was all this talk about a handsome, intelligent, happy child? Maybe that was only the nymph stage and one day, as Miss Coney obliquely predicted, he would surely break through the camouflage and emerge as a fully-fledged sex-motivated problem.

LINDSAY BARRETT

Lindsay Barrett was born in Jamaica. He came to Europe in 1961 and went to Nigeria in 1966. He has lived in West Africa ever since, occasionally returning to London. He is a poet, novelist, journalist, playwright and scriptwriter, and his first novel, *Song for Mumu*, published in 1967, is an acknowledged classic text. His other novels include *Lipskybound* and *Veils of Vengeance Falling*. His collections of poetry include *The State of Black Desire, The Conflicting Eye* and *A Quality of Pain and Other Poems*.

'Age: The Night Air' is taken from *A Quality of Pain and Other Poems*.

Age: The Night Air

I

Grey steel, confident and buoyant
Brought us here
Where no one really wanted us.
They want your labour
They want your laugh,
They want your flesh, and
They want your arse!

II

Coming here to where hate stands
in a steep direction,
We have chosen to
go from knowledge.
Light is the father of darkness
where night is an instrument
of flight.

III

These seasons are youth's gifts:
we did not seek to know
what the sun explains in a silent hour
nor what the moon computes
beneath the skin.

IV

Children go sudden into manhood,
their eyes burnt and bent
Woods twist themselves into black shapes,
coalfires touch salt to the wound,
they cry about lost days.

V

False fear, and fiery years
come together in meaningless defiance
The hours have rusted
to a stiffness known to logs.
Now cannot be the time, they say,
and bow their heads in prayer . . .

THE OTHERS

One's neighbours are one's relations
YORUBA PROVERB

COLIN MACINNES

Colin MacInnes was one of the first white writers to locate his novels inside
the world being created by the new immigrants. His novels *City of Spades*,
Absolute Beginners and *Mr Love and Justice* take as their themes the birth of
new social forces, such as the teenage revolution and the emerging drug culture, that were to explode over an increasingly affluent Britain following the
drab and ration-hit postwar period.

City of Spades is about the new, exciting and slightly shabby London that is
being quietly but spectacularly transformed by the inflow of black immigrants from the colonies. Johnny Macdonald Fortune, a Nigerian rudeboy
from Lagos, hits town. On hand to meet and guide him in the ways of the
English is the new Assistant Welfare Officer of the Colonial Department,
Pew Montgomery. But increasingly it is Pew who is guided through the complex labyrinths of the evolving new London. In the extract below, starting his
first day in the Colonial Department, the untrained Johnny meets Pew.

from *City of Spades*
The Meeting of Jumble and Spade

Primed by my brief study of the welfare dossiers, I awaited, in my
office, the arrival of the first colonials. With some trepidation;
because for one who, like myself, has always felt great need of sober
counsel, to offer it to others – and to strangers, and to such exotic
strangers – seemed intimidating. Perhaps I should add, too, that I'm
not quite so old as I think I look: only twenty-six, Heaven be praised;
and certainly not so self-assured as my dry, drained, rarely perturb-
able countenance might suggest.

Picture my mild alarm, then, when there was a first polite knock
upon my door. Opening it, I beheld a handsomely ugly face, animal
and engaging, with beetling brow, squashed nose and full and gen-
erous lips, surmounted by a thatch of thick curly hair cut to a high
rising peak in front: a face wearing (it seemed to me) a sly, morose,
secretive look, until suddenly its mouth split open into a candid ivory
and coral smile.

'I'm Fortune,' said this creature, beaming as though his name was his very nature. 'Johnny Macdonald, Christian names, out of Lagos, checking to see what classes in meteorology you've fixed for me.'

'My name is Pew – Montgomery. Please do come over to these rather less uncomfortable leather chairs.'

I observed that he was attired in a white crocheted sweater with two crimson horizontal stripes, and with gold safety-pins stuck on the tips of each point of the emerging collar of a nylon shirt; in a sky-blue gaberdine jacket zipped down the front; and in even lighter blue linen slacks, full at the hips, tapering to the ankle, and falling delicately one half-inch above a pair of pale brown plaited casual shoes.

'Your curriculum,' I said, handing him a drab buff envelope, 'is outlined here. You begin next week, but it would be well to register within the next few days. Meanwhile I trust you're satisfied with your accommodation at the hostel?'

'Man, you should ask!'

'I beg your pardon?'

He gave me a repeat performance of the grin. 'It's like back in mission school at home. I shall make every haste to leave it as soon as I find myself a room.'

'In that case,' I said, departmentally severe, 'the rent would be appreciably higher.'

'I have loot – I can afford,' he told me. 'Have *you* ever lived inside that hostel, you yourself?'

'No.'

'Well, then!'

The interview was not taking the turn I thought appropriate. Equality between races – yes! But not between officials and the public.

'I should perhaps warn you at this juncture,' I informed him, 'that to secure outside accommodation sometimes presents certain difficulties.'

'You mean for an African to get a room?'

'Yes . . . We have however here a list of amiable landladies . . . '

'Why should it be difficult for an African to get a room?'

'There is, unfortunately, in certain cases, prejudice.'

'They fear we dirty the sheets with our dark skins?'

'Not precisely.'

'Then what? In Lagos, anyone will let *you* a room if you have good manners and the necessary loot . . . '

'It's kind of them, and I don't doubt your word. Here in England, though, some landladies have had unfortunate experiences.'

'Such as . . . ?'

'Well, for one thing – noise.'

'It's true we are not mice.'

'And introducing *friends* . . . '

'Why not?'

'I mean; to sleep – to live. Landladies don't wish three tenants for the price of one.'

'So long as the room is paid, what does it matter?'

'Ah – paid. Failure to pay is another chief complaint.'

'Don't Jumbles never skip their rent as well as Spades?'

'I *beg* your pardon once again?'

'Don't Jumbles . . . '

'Jumbles?'

'You're a Jumble, man.'

'I?'

'Yes. That's what we call you. You don't mind?'

'I hope I don't . . . It's not, I trust, an impolite expression?'

'You mean like nigger?'

I rose up.

'Now, please! This is the Colonial Department Welfare Office. That word is absolutely forbidden within these walls.'

'It should be outside them, too.'

'No doubt. I too deplore its use.'

'Well, relax, please, Mr Pew. And don't be so scared of Jumble. It's cheeky, perhaps, but not so very insulting.'

'May I enquire how it is spelt?'

'J-o-h-n-b-u-l-l.'

'Ah! But pronounced as you pronounce it?'

'Yes: Jumble.'

It struck me the ancient symbol, thus distorted, was strangely appropriate to the confusion of my mind.

'I see. And . . . ' (I hesitated) ' . . . spade?'

'Is us.'

'And that is not an objectionable term?'

'Is cheeky, too, of course, but not offending. In Lagos, on the waterfront, the boys sometimes called me the Ace of Spades.'

'Ah . . . ' He offered me, from an American pack, an extravagantly long fag.

'Let's not us worry, Mr Pew,' he said, 'about bad names. My Dad has taught me that in England some foolish man may call me sambo, darkie, boot or munt or nigger, even. Well, if he does – my fists!' (He clenched them: they were like knees.) 'Or,' he went on, 'as Dad would say, "First try rebuke by tongue, then fists".'

'Well, Mr Fortune,' I said to him, when he had at last unclenched them to rehitch the knife edge of his blue tapering slacks, 'I think with one of these good women on our list you'll have no trouble . . . '

'If I take lodgings, mister,' he replied, 'they must be Liberty Hall. No questions from the landlady, please. And me, when I give my rent, I'll have the politeness not to ask her what she spends it on.'

'That, my dear fellow, even for an Englishman, is *very* difficult to find in our sad country.'

'I'll find it.' He beetled at me, then, leaning forward said, 'And do you know why I think your landladies are scared of us?'

'I can but imagine . . . '

'Because of any brown babies that might appear.'

'In the nature of things,' I said, 'that may indeed well be.'

'An arrival of white babies they can somehow explain away. But if their daughter has a brown one, then neighbouring fingers start pointing.'

I silently shook my head.

'But why,' he cried, 'why not box up together, Jumble and Spade, like we let your folk do back home?'

I rose once more.

'Really, Mr Fortune. You cannot expect me to discuss these complex problems. I am – consider – an official.'

'Oh, yes . . . You have to earn your money, I suppose.'

I found this, of course, offensive. And moving with dignity to my desk, I took up the Warning Folder of People and Places to Avoid.

'Another little duty for which I'm *paid*,' I said to him, 'is to warn our newcomers against . . . well, to be frank, bad elements among their fellow countrymen.'

'Oh, yes, man. Shoot.'

'And,' I continued, looking at my list, 'particularly against visiting the Moorhen public house, the Cosmopolitan dance hall, or the Moonbeam club.'

'Just say those names again.'

To my horror, I saw he was jotting them on the back page of his passport.

'To visit these places,' I went on, reading aloud from the mimeographed sheet I held, 'has been, for many, the first step that leads to the shadow of the police courts.'

'Why? What goes in in them?'

I didn't, perhaps fortunately, yet know. 'I'm not at liberty to divulge it,' I replied.

'Ah well . . . '

He pocketed his passport and took me by the hand.

'Have you any further questions?' I enquired.

'Yes, Mr Pew. Excuse my familiar asking: but where can I get a shirt like that?'

'Like this?'

'Yes. It's hep. Jumble style, but hep.'

He reached out a long, long hand and fingered it.

'In Jermyn Street,' I said with some self-satisfaction, but asperity.

'Number?'

I told him.

'Thanks so very much,' said Johnny Macdonald Fortune. 'And now I must be on my way to Maida Vale.'

I watched him go out with an unexpected pang. And moving to the window, soon saw him walk across the courtyard and stop for a moment speaking to some others there. In the sunlight, his nylon shirt shone all the whiter against the smooth brown of his skin. His frame, from this distance, seemed shorter than it was, because of his broad shoulders – flat, though composed of two mounds of muscle arching from his spine. His buttocks sprang optimistically high up from the small of his back, and his long legs – a little bandy and with something of a backward curve – were supported by two very effective splayed-out feet; on which, just now, as he spoke, gesticulating too, he was executing a tracery of tentative dance steps to some soft inaudible music.

ELIZABETH TAYLOR

Elizabeth Taylor was born in 1912 and brought up in Reading in Berkshire. She published eleven novels and five volumes of short stories. She died in 1975.

'The Devastating Boys' is the title story of her most famous collection of short stories. A middle-aged, well-meaning Oxford professor and his anxious wife, Laura, decide to take in two unknown black boys from London's East End. What happens when Benny and Sep actually arrive surpasses all imagination and leaves them changed for ever.

The Devastating Boys

Laura was always too early; and this was as bad as being late, her husband, who was always late himself, told her. She sat in her car in the empty railway station approach, feeling very sick, from dread.

It was half-past eleven on a summer morning. The country station was almost spellbound in silence and there was, to Laura, a dreadful sense of self-absorption – in herself – in the stillness of the only porter standing on the platform, staring down the line: even – perhaps especially – in inanimate things; all were menacingly intent on being themselves, and separately themselves – the slanting shadow of railings across the platform, the glossiness of leaves, and the closed door of the office looking more closed, she thought, than any door she had ever seen.

She got out of the car and went into the station walking up and down the platform in a panic. It was a beautiful morning. If only the children weren't coming then she could have enjoyed it.

The children were coming from London. It was Harold's idea to have them, some time back, in March, when he read of a scheme to give London children a summer holiday in the country. This he might have read without interest, but the words 'Some of the children will be coloured' caught his eye. He seemed to find a slight tinge of warning in the phrase; the more he thought it over, the more he was convinced. He had made a long speech to Laura about children being the great equalizers, and that we should learn from them, that to insinuate the stale prejudices of their elders into their fresh, fair minds was such a sin that he could not think of a worse one.

He knew very little about children. His students had passed beyond the blessed age, and shades of the prison-house had closed about them. His own children were even older, grown up and gone away; but, while they were young, they had done nothing to destroy his faith in them, or blur the idea of them he had in his mind and his feeling of humility in their presence. They had been good children, carefully dealt with and easy to handle. There had scarcely been a cloud over their growing-up. Any little bothers Laura had hidden from him.

In March, the end of July was a long way away. Laura, who was lonely in middle age, seemed to herself to be frittering away her days, just waiting for her grandchildren to be born: she had agreed with Harold's suggestion. She would have agreed anyway, whatever it was, as it was her nature – and his – for her to do so. It would be rather exciting to have two children to stay – to have the beds in Imogen's and Lalage's room slept in again. 'We could have two boys, or two girls,' Harold said. 'No stipulation, but that they must be coloured.'

Now *he* was making differences, but Laura did not remark upon it. All she said was, 'What will they do all the time?'

'What our own children used to do – play in the garden, go for picnics . . . '

'On wet days?'

'Dress up,' he said at once.

She remembered Imogen and Lalage in her old hats and dresses, slopping about in her big shoes, seesawing on high heels, and she had to turn her head away, and there were tears in her eyes.

Her children had been her life, and her grandchildren one day would be; but here was an empty space. Life had fallen away from her. She had never been clever like the other professors' wives, or managed to have what they called 'outside interests'. Committees frightened her and good works made her feel embarrassed and clumsy.

She *was* a clumsy person – gentle, but clumsy. Pacing up and down the platform, she had an ungainly walk – legs stiffly apart, head a little poked forwards because she had poor sight. She was short and squarely-built and her clothes were never right; often she looked dishevelled, sometimes even battered.

This morning, she wore a label pinned to her breast, so that the children's escort would recognize her when the train drew in; but she felt self-conscious about it and covered it with her hand, though there was no one but the porter to see.

The signal dropped, as if a guillotine had come crashing down, and her heart seemed to crash down with it. Two boys! she thought. Somehow, she had imagined girls. She was used to girls, and shy of boys.

The printed form had come a day or two ago and had increased the panic which had gradually been gathering. Six-year-old boys, and she had pictured perhaps eight- or ten-year-old girls, whom she could teach to sew and make cakes for tea, and press wild flowers as she had taught Imogen and Lalage to do.

Flurried and anxious entertaining at home; interviewing headmistresses; once – shied away from failure – opening a sale-of-work in the village – these agonies to her diffident nature seemed nothing to the nervousness she felt now, as the train appeared round the bend. She simply wasn't good with children – only with her own. *Their* friends had frightened her, had been mouse-quiet and glum, or had got out of hand, and she herself had been too shy either to intrude or clamp down. When she met children – perhaps the small grandchildren of her acquaintances, she would only smile, perhaps awkwardly touch a cheek with her finger. If she were asked to hold a baby, she was fearful lest it should cry, and often it would, sensing lack of assurance in her clasp.

The train came in and slowed up. Suppose that I can't find them, she thought, and she went anxiously from window to window, her label uncovered now. And suppose they cry for their mothers and want to go home.

A tall, authoritative woman, also wearing a label, leaned out of a window, saw her and signalled curtly. She had a compartment full of little children in her charge to be delivered about Oxfordshire. Only two got out onto this platform, Laura's two, Septimus Smith and Benny Reece. They wore tickets, too, with their names printed on them.

Benny was much lighter in complexion than Septimus. He was obviously a half-caste and Laura hoped that this would count in Harold's eyes. It might even be one point up. They stood on the platform, looking about them, holding their little cardboard cases.

'My name is Laura,' she said. She stooped and clasped them to her in terror and kissed their cheeks. Sep's in particular, was extraordinarily soft, like the petal of a poppy. His big eyes stared up at her, without expression. He wore a dark, long-trousered suit, so that he was all over sombre and unchildlike. Benny had a mock-suede coat with a nylon-fur collar and a trilby hat with a feather. They did not speak. Not only was she, Laura, strange to them, but they were strange to one another. There had only been a short train-journey in which to sum up their chances of becoming friends.

She put them both into the back of the car, so that there should be no favouritism, and drove off, pointing out – to utter silence – places on the way. 'That's a café where we'll go for tea one day.' The silence was dreadful. 'A caff,' she amended. 'And there's the little cinema. Not very grand, I'm afraid. Not like London ones.'

They did not even glance about them.

'Are you going to be good friends to one another?' she asked.

After a pause, Sep said in a slow grave voice, 'Yeah, I'm going to be a good friend.'

'Is this the country?' Benny asked. He had a chirpy, perky Cockney voice and accent.

'Yeah, this is the countryside,' said Sep, in his rolling drawl, glancing indifferently at some trees.

Then he began to talk. It was in an aggrieved sing-song. 'I don't go on that train no more. I don't like that train, and I don't go on that again over my dead body. Some boy he say to me, "You don't sit in that corner seat. I sit there." I say, "You don't sit here. I sit here." "Yeah," I say, "You don't own this train, so I don't budge from here." Then he dash my comic down and tore it.'

'Yep, he tore his comic,' Benny said.

'"You tear my comic, you buy me another comic," I said. "Or else." "Or *else*," I said.' He suddenly broke off and looked at a wood they were passing. 'I don't go near those tall bushes. They full of snakes what sting you.'

'No, they ain't,' said Benny.

'My Mam said so. I don't go.'

'There aren't any snakes,' said Laura, in a light voice. She, too, had a terror of them, and was afraid to walk through bracken. 'Or only little harmless ones,' she added.

'I don't go,' Sep murmured to himself. Then, in a louder voice, he went on. 'He said, "I don't buy no comic for you, you nigger," he said.'

'He never said that,' Benny protested.

'Yes, "You dirty nigger," he said.'

'He never.'

There was something so puzzled in Benny's voice that Laura immediately believed him. The expression on his little monkey-face was open and impartial.

'I don't go on that train no more.'

'You've got to. When you go home,' Benny said.

'Maybe I don't go home.'

'We'll think about that later. You've only just arrived,' said Laura, smiling.

'No, I think about that right now.'

Along the narrow lane to the house, they were held up by the cows from the farm. A boy drove them along, whacking their messed rumps with a stick. Cowpats plopped onto the road and steamed there, zizzing with flies. Benny held his nose and Sep, glancing at him, at once did the same. 'I don't care for this smell of the country-side,' he complained in a pinched tone.

'No, the countryside stinks,' said Benny.

'Cows frighten me.'

'They don't frighten me.'

Sep cringed against the back of the seat, whimpering, but Benny wound his window right down, put his head a little out of it, and shouted, 'Get on, you dirty old sods, or else I'll show you.'

'Hush,' said Laura gently.

'He swore,' Sep pointed out.

They turned into Laura's gateway, up the short drive. In front of the house was a lawn and a cedar tree. From one of its lower branches hung the old swing, on chains, waiting for Laura's grandchildren.

The boys clambered out of the car and followed her into the hall, where they stood looking about them critically; then Benny dropped his case and shot like an arrow towards Harold's golf-bag and pulled out a club. His face was suddenly bright with excitement and Laura, darting forward to him, felt a stab of misery at having to begin the 'No's' so soon. 'I'm afraid Harold wouldn't like you to touch them,' she said. Benny stared her out, but after a moment or two gave up the club with all the unwillingness in the world. Meanwhile, Sep had taken an antique coaching-horn and was blowing a bubbly, uneven blast on it, his eyes stretched wide and his cheeks blown out. 'Nor that,' said Laura faintly, taking it away. 'Let's go upstairs and unpack.'

They appeared not at all overawed by the size of this fairly large house; in fact, rather unimpressed by it.

In the room where once, as little girls, Imogen and Lalage had slept together, they opened their cases. Sep put his clothes neatly and carefully into his drawer and Benny tipped the case into his – comics, clothes and shoes, and a scattering of peanuts. I'll tidy it later, Laura thought.

'Shall we toss up for who sleeps by the window?' she suggested.

'I don't sleep by no window,' said Sep. 'I sleep in *this* bed; with *him*.'

'I want to sleep by myself,' said Benny.

Sep began a babyish whimpering, which increased into an anguished keening. 'I don't like to sleep in the bed by myself. I'm scared to. I'm real scared to. I'm scared.'

This was entirely theatrical, Laura decided, and Benny seemed to think so, too; for he took no notice.

A fortnight! Laura thought. This day alone stretched endlessly before her, and she dared not think of any following ones. Already she felt ineffectual and had an inkling that they were going to despise her. And her brightness was false and not infectious. She longed for Harold to come home, as she had never longed before.

'I reckon I go and clean my teeth,' said Sep, who had broken off his dirge.

'Lunch is ready. Afterwards would be more sensible, surely?' Laura suggested.

But they paid no heed to her. Both took their toothbrushes, their new tubes of paste and rushed to find the bathroom. 'I'm going to bathe myself,' said Sep. 'I'm going to bathe all my skin, and wash my head.'

'Not *before* lunch,' Laura called out, hastening after them; but they did not hear her. Taps were running and steam clouding the window and Sep was tearing off his clothes.

'He's bathed three times already,' Laura told Harold.

She had just come downstairs and had done so as soon as she heard him slamming the front door.

Upstairs, Sep was sitting in the bath. She had made him a lacy vest of soap-froth, as once she had made them for Imogen and Lalage. It showed up much better on his grape-dark skin. He sat there, like a tribal warrior done up in war-paint.

Benny would not go near the bath. He washed at the basin, his sleeves rolled up: and he turned the cake of soap over and over uncertainly in his hands.

'It's probably a novelty,' Harold said, referring to Sep's bathing. 'Would you like a drink?'

'Later perhaps. I daren't sit down, for I'd never get up again.'

'I'll finish them off. I'll go and see to them. You just sit there and drink this.'

'Oh, Harold, how wonderfully good of you.'

She sank down on the arm of a chair, and sipped her drink, feeling stunned. From the echoing bathroom came shouts of laughter, and it was very good to hear them, especially from a distance. Harold was being a great success, and relief and gratitude filled her.

After a little rest, she got up and went weakly about the room, putting things back in their places. When this was done, the room still looked wrong. An unfamiliar dust seemed to have settled all over it, yet, running a finger over the piano, she found none. All the same, it was not the usual scene she set for Harold's homecoming in the evenings. It had taken a shaking-up.

Scampering footsteps now thundered along the landing. She waited a moment or two, then went upstairs. They were in bed, in separate beds; Benny by the window. Harold was pacing about the room, telling them a story: his hands flapped like huge ears at either side of his face; then he made an elephant's trunk with his arm. From the beds, the children's eyes stared unblinkingly at him. As Laura came into the room, only Benny's flickered in her direction, then back at once to the magic of Harold's performance. She blew a vague, unheeded kiss, and crept away.

'It's like seeing snow begin to fall,' Harold said at dinner. 'You know it's going to be a damned nuisance, but it makes a change.'

He sounded exhilarated; clashed the knife against the steel with vigour, and started to carve. He kept popping little titbits into his mouth. Carver's perks, he called them.

'Not much for me,' Laura said.

'What did they have for lunch?'

'Fishcakes.'

'Enjoy them?'

'Sep said, "I don't like that." He's very suspicious, and that makes Benny all the braver. Then he eats too much, showing off.'

'They'll settle down,' Harold said, settling down himself to his dinner. After a while, he said, 'The little Cockney one asked me just now if this were a private house. When I said "Yes", he said, "I thought it was, because you've got the sleeping upstairs and the talking downstairs." Didn't quite get the drift.'

'Pathetic,' Laura murmured.

'I suppose where they come from, it's all done in the same room.'

'Yes, it is.'

'Pathetic,' Harold said in his turn.

'It makes me feel ashamed.'

'Oh, come now.'

'And wonder if we're doing the right thing – perhaps unsettling them for what they have to go back to.'

'My dear girl,' he said. 'Damn it, those people who organize these things know what they're doing.'

'I suppose so.'

'They've been doing it for years.'

'Yes, I know.'

'Well, then . . . '

Suddenly she put down her knife and fork and rested her forehead in her hands.

'What's up, old thing?' Harold asked, with his mouth full.

'Only tired.'

'Well, they've dropped off all right. You can have a quiet evening.'

'I'm too tired to sit up straight any longer.' After a silence, lifting her face from her hands, she said, 'Thirteen more days! What shall I do with them all that time?'

'Take them for scrambles in the woods,' he began, sure that he had endless ideas.

'I tried. They won't walk a step. They both groaned and moaned so much that we turned back.'

'Well, they can play on the swing.'

'For how long, how *long*? They soon got tired of that. Anyhow, they quarrel about one having a longer turn than the other. In the end, I gave them the egg-timer.'

'That was a good idea.'

'They broke it.'

'Oh.'

'Please God, don't let it rain,' she said earnestly, staring out of the window. 'Not for the next fortnight anyway.'

*

The next day, it rained from early morning. After breakfast, when Harold had gone off, Laura settled the boys at the dining-room table with a snakes-and-ladders board. As they had never played it, she had to draw up a chair herself and join in. By some freakish chance, Benny threw one six after another, would, it seemed, never stop; and Sep's frustration and fury rose. He kept snatching the dice-cup away from Benny, peering into it, convinced of trickery. The game went badly for him and Laura, counting rapidly ahead, saw that he was due for the longest snake of all. His face was agonized, his dark hand, with its pale scars and scratches, hovered above the board; but he could not bring himself to draw the counter down the snake's horrid speckled length.

'I'll do it for you,' Laura said. He shuddered, and turned aside. Then he pushed his chair back from the table and lay face-down on the floor, silent with grief.

'And it's not yet ten o'clock,' thought Laura, and was relieved to see Mrs Milner, the help, coming up the path under her umbrella. It was a mercy that it was her morning.

She finished off the game with Benny and he won; but the true glory of victory had been taken from him by the vanquished, lying still and wounded on the hearth-rug. Laura was bright and cheerful about being beaten, trying to set an example; but she made no impression.

Presently, in exasperation, she asked, 'Don't you play games at school?'

There was no answer for a time, then Benny, knowing the question wasn't addressed to him, said, 'Yep, sometimes.'

'And what do you do if you lose?' Laura asked, glancing down at the hearth-rug. 'You can't win all the time.'

In a muffled voice, Sep at last said, 'I don't win any time. They won't let me win any time.'

'It's only luck.'

'No, they don't *let* me win. I just go and lie down and shut my eyes.'

'And are these our young visitors?' asked Mrs Milner, coming in with the vacuum cleaner. Benny stared at her; Sep lifted his head from his sleeve for a brief look and then returned to his sulking.

'What a nasty morning I've brought with me,' Mrs Milner said, after Laura had introduced them.

'You brought a nasty old morning all right,' Sep agreed, mumbling into his jersey.

'But,' she went on brightly, putting her hands into her overall pockets. 'I've also brought some lollies.'

Benny straightened his back in anticipation. Sep, peeping with one eye, stretched out an arm.

'That's if Madam says you may.'

'They call me "Laura".' It had been Harold's idea and Laura had foreseen this very difficulty.

Mrs Milner could not bring herself to say the name and she, too, could foresee awkwardnesses.

'No, Sep,' said Laura firmly. 'Either you get up properly and take it politely, or you go without.'

She wished that Benny hadn't at once scrambled to his feet and stood there at attention. Sep buried his head again and moaned. All the sufferings of his race were upon him at this moment.

Benny took his sweet and made a great appreciative fuss about it.

All the china had gone up a shelf or two, out of reach, Mrs Milner noted. It was like the old days, when Imogen's and Lalage's friends had come to tea.

'Now, there's a good lad,' she said, stepping over Sep, and plugging in the vacuum cleaner.

'Is that your sister?' Benny asked Laura, when Mrs Milner had brought in the pudding, gone out again, and closed the door.

'No, Mrs Milner comes to help me with the housework – every Tuesday and Friday.'

'She must be a very kind old lady,' Benny said.

'Do you like that?' Laura asked Sep, who was pushing jelly into his spoon with his fingers.

'Yeah, I like this fine.'

He had suddenly cheered up. He did not mention the lolly, which Mrs Milner had put back in her pocket. All the rest of the morning, they had played excitedly with the telephone – one upstairs, in Laura's bedroom; the other downstairs, in the hall – chattering and shouting to one another, and running to Laura to come to listen.

That evening, Harold was home earlier than usual and could not wait to complain that he had tried all day to telephone.

'I know, dear,' Laura said. 'I should have stopped them, but it gave me a rest.'

'You'll be making a rod for everybody's back, if you let them do just what they like all the time.'

'It's for such a short while – well, relatively speaking – and they haven't got telephones at home, so the question doesn't arise.'

'But other people might want to ring you up.'

'So few ever do, it's not worth considering.'

'Well, someone did today. Helena Western.'

'What on earth for?'

'There's no need to look frightened. She wants you to take the boys to tea.' Saying this, his voice was full of satisfaction, for he admired Helena's husband. Helena herself wrote what he referred to as 'clever-clever little novels'. He went on sarcastically, 'She saw you with them from the top of a bus, and asked me when I met her later in Blackwell's. She says she has absolutely *no* feelings about coloured people as some of her friends apparently have.' He was speaking in Helena's way of stresses and breathings. 'In fact,' he ended, 'she rather goes out of her way to be extra pleasant to them.'

'So she does have feelings,' Laura said.

She was terrified at the idea of taking the children to tea with Helena. She always felt dull and overawed in her company, and was afraid that the boys would misbehave and get out of her control, and then Helena would put it all into a novel. Already she had put Harold in one; but, luckily, he had not recognized his own transformation from professor of archaeology to barrister. Her simple trick worked, as far as he was concerned. To Harold, that character, with his vaguely left-wing opinions and opinionated turns of phrase, his quelling manner to his wife, his very appearance, could have nothing to do with him, since he had never taken silk. Everyone else had recognized and known and Laura, among them, knew they had.

'I'll ring her up,' she said; but she didn't stir from her chair, sat staring wearily in front of her, her hands on her knees – a very resigned old woman's attitude; Whistler's mother. 'I'm *too* old,' she thought. 'I'd be too old for my own grandchildren.' But she had never imagined *them* like the ones upstairs in bed. She had pictured biddable little children, like Lalage and Imogen.

'They're good at *night*,' she said to Harold, continuing her thoughts aloud. 'They lie there and talk quietly, once they're in bed. I wonder what they talk about. Us, perhaps.' It was an alarming idea.

In the night she woke and remembered that she had not telephoned Helena. 'I'll do it after breakfast,' she thought.

But she was still making toast when the telephone rang, and the boys left the table and raced to the hall ahead of her. Benny was first and, as he grabbed the receiver, Sep stood close by him, ready to shout some messages into the magical instrument. Laura hovered anxiously by, but Benny warned her off with staring eyes. 'Be polite,' she whispered imploringly.

'Yep, my name's Benny,' he was saying.

Then he listened, with a look of rapture. It was his first real telephone conversation and Sep was standing by, shivering with impatience and envy.

'Yep, that'll be OK,' said Benny, grinning. 'What day?'

Laura put out her hand, but he shrank back, clutching the receiver. 'I got the message,' he hissed at her. 'Yep, he's here,' he said, into the telephone. Sep smiled self-consciously and drew himself up as he took the receiver. 'Yeah, I am Septimus Alexander Smith.' He gave his high, bubbly chuckle. 'Sure I'll come there.' To prolong the conversation, he went on, 'Can my friend, Benny Reece come, too? Can Laura come?' Then he frowned, looking up at the ceiling, as if for inspiration. 'Can my father, Alexander Leroy Smith come?'

Laura made another darting movement.

'Well, no, he can't then,' Sep said, 'because he's dead.'

This doubled him up with mirth and it was a long time before he could bring himself to say goodbye. When he had done so, he quickly put the receiver down.

'Someone asked me to tea,' he told Laura. 'I said, "Yeah, sure I come."'

'And me,' said Benny.

'Who was it?' Laura asked, although she knew.

'I don't know,' said Sep. 'I don't know *who* that was.'

When later and secretly, Laura telephoned Helena, Helena said, 'Aren't they simply *devastating* boys?'

'How did the tea-party go?' Harold asked.

They had all arrived back home together – he, from a meeting; Laura and the boys from Helena's.

'They were good,' Laura said, which was all that mattered. She drew them to her, one on either side. It was her movement of gratitude towards them. They had not let her down. They had played quietly at a fishing game with real water and magnetized tin fish, had eaten unfamiliar things, such as anchovy toast and brandy-snaps without any expression of alarm or revulsion: they had helped carry the tea things indoors from the lawn. Helena had been surprisingly clever with them. She made them laugh, as seldom Laura could. She struck the right note from the beginning. When Benny picked up six-pence from the gravelled path, she thanked him casually and put it in her pocket. Laura was grateful to her for that and proud that Benny ran away at once so unconcernedly. When Helena had praised them for their good behaviour, Laura had blushed with pleasure, just as if they were her own children.

'She is really very nice,' Laura said later, thinking still of her suc-cessful afternoon with Helena.

'Yes, she talks too much, that's all.'

Harold was pleased with Laura for having got on well with his col-league's wife. It was so long since he had tried to urge Laura into academic circles, and for years he had given up trying. Now, sensing his pleasure, her own was enhanced.

'When we were coming away,' Laura said, 'Helena whispered to me, "Aren't they simply *dev*astating?"'

'You've exactly caught her tone.'

At that moment, they heard from the garden, Benny also exactly catching her tone.

'Let's have the bat, there's a little pet,' he mimicked, trying to snatch the old tennis racquet from Sep.

'You sod off,' drawled Sep.

'Oh, my dear, you shake me rigid.'

Sep began his doubling-up-with-laughter routine; first, in silence, bowed over, lifting one leg then another up to his chest, stamping the ground. It was like the start of a tribal dance, Laura thought, watching him from the window; then the pace quickened, he skipped about, and laughed, with his head head thrown back, and tears rolled down his face. Benny looked on, smirking a little, obviously proud that his wit should have had such an effect. Round and round went Sep, his loose limbs moving like pistons. 'Yeah, you shake me rigid,' he shouted. 'You shake me entirely rigid.' Benny, after hesitating, joined in. They circled the lawn, and disappeared into the shrubbery.

'She *did* say that. Helena,' Laura said, turning to Harold. 'When Benny was going on about something he'd done she said, "My dear, you shake me entirely rigid."' Then Laura added thoughtfully, 'I wonder if they are as good at imitating *us*, when they're lying up there in bed, talking.'

'A sobering thought,' said Harold, who could not believe he had any particular idiosyncrasies to be copied. 'Oh, God, someone's broken one of my sherds,' he suddenly cried, stooping to pick up two pieces of pottery from the floor. His agonized shout brought Sep to the french windows, and he stood there, bewildered.

As the pottery had been broken before, he hadn't bothered to pick it up, or confess. The day before, he had broken a whole cup and nothing had happened. Now this grown man was bowed over as if in pain, staring at the fragments in his hand. Sep crept back into the shrubbery.

The fortnight, miraculously, was passing. Laura could now say, 'This time next week.' She would do gardening, get her hair done, clean all the paint. Often, she wondered about the kind of homes the other children had gone to – those children she had glimpsed on the train; and she imagined them staying on farms, helping with the animals, looked after by buxom farmers'-wives – pale London children, growing gratifyingly brown, filling out, going home at last with roses in their cheeks. She could see no difference in Sep and Benny.

What they had really got from the holiday was one another. It touched her to see them going off into the shrubbery with arms about one another's shoulders, and to listen to their peaceful murmuring as they lay in bed, to hear their shared jokes. They quarrelled a great deal, over the tennis racquet or Harold's old cricket bat, and Sep was constantly casting himself down on the grass and weeping, if he were out at cricket, or could not get Benny out.

It was he who would sit for hours with his eyes fixed on Laura's face while she read to him. Benny would wander restlessly about, waiting for the story to be finished. If he interrupted, Sep would put his hand imploringly on Laura's arm, silently willing her to continue.

Benny liked her to play the piano. It was the only time she was admired. They would dance gravely about the room, with their bottles of Coca-Cola, sucking through straws, choking, heads bobbing up and down. Once, at the end of a concert of nursery rhymes, Laura played *God Save the Queen*, and Sep rushed at her, trying to shut the lid down on her hands. 'I don't like that,' he keened. 'My Mam don't like *God Save the Queen* neither. She say "God save *me*".'

'Get out,' said Benny, kicking him on the shin. 'You're shaking me entirely rigid.'

On the second Sunday, they decided that they must go to church.

They had a sudden curiosity about it, and a yearning to sing hymns.

'Well, take them,' said liberal-minded and agnostic Harold to Laura.

But it was almost time to put the sirloin into the oven. 'We did sign that form,' she said in a low voice. 'To say we'd take them if they wanted to go.'

'Do you *really* want to go?' Harold asked, turning to the boys, who were wanting to go more and more as the discussion went on. 'Oh, God!' he groaned – inappropriately, Laura thought.

'What religion are you, anyway?' he asked them.

'I am a Christian,' Sep said with great dignity.

'Me, too,' said Benny.

'What time does it begin?' Harold asked, turning his back to Laura.

'At eleven o'clock.'

'Isn't there some kids' service they can go to on their own?'

'Not in August, I'm afraid.'

'Oh, God!' he said again.

Laura watched them setting out; rather overawed, the two boys; it was the first time they had been out alone with him.

She had a quiet morning in the kitchen. Not long after twelve o'clock they returned. The boys at once raced for the cricket bat, and fought over it, while Harold poured himself out a glass of beer.

'How did it go?' asked Laura.

'Awful! Lord, I felt such a fool.'

'Did they misbehave, then?'

'Oh, no, they were perfectly good except that for some reason Benny kept holding his nose. But I knew so many people there. And the Vicar shook hands with me afterwards and said, "We are especially glad to see *you*." The embarrassment!'

'It must have shaken you entirely rigid,' Laura said, smiling as she basted the beef. Harold looked at her as if for the first time in years. She so seldom tried to be amusing.

At lunch, she asked the boys if they had enjoyed their morning.

'Church smelt nasty,' Benny said, making a face.

'Yeah,' agreed Sep. 'I prefer my own country. I prefer Christians.'

'Me, too,' Benny said. 'Give me Christians any day.'

'Has it been a success?' Laura asked Harold. 'For them, I mean.'

It was their last night – Sep's and Benny's – and she wondered if her feeling of being on the verge of tears was entirely from tiredness. For the past fortnight, she had reeled into bed, and slept without moving.

A success for *them*? She could not be quite sure; but it had been a success for her and for Harold. In the evenings, they had so much to talk about and Harold, basking in his popularity, had been genial and considerate.

Laura, the boys had treated as a piece of furniture, or a slave, and humbly she accepted her place in their minds. She was a woman who had never had any high opinions of herself.

'No more cricket,' she said. She had been made to play for hours – always wicket-keeper, running into the shrubs for lost balls while Sep and Benny rested full-length on the grass.

'He has a lovely action,' she had said to Harold one evening, watching Sep taking his long run up to bowl. 'He might be a great athlete one day.'

'It couldn't happen,' Harold said. 'Don't you see, he has rickets?'

One of her children with rickets, she had thought, stricken.

Now, on this last evening, the children were in bed. She and Harold were sitting by the drawing-room window, talking about them. There was a sudden scampering along the landing and Laura said, 'It's only one of them going to the toilet.'

'The *what*?'

'They ticked me off for saying "lavatory",' she said placidly. 'Benny said it was a bad word.'

She loved to make Harold laugh, and several times lately she had managed to amuse him, with stories she had to recount.

'I shan't like saying goodbye,' she said awkwardly.

'No,' said Harold. He got up and walked about the room, examined his shelves of pottery fragments. 'It's been a lot of work for you, Laura.'

She looked away shyly. There had been almost a note of praise in his voice. 'Tomorrow,' she thought. 'I hope I don't cry.'

At the station, it was Benny who cried. All the morning he had talked about his mother, how she would be waiting for him at Paddington station. Laura kept their thoughts fixed on the near future.

Now they sat on a bench on the sunny platform, wearing their name-labels, holding bunches of wilting flowers, and Laura looked at her watch and wished the minutes away. As usual, she was too early.

Then she saw Benny shut his eyes quickly, but not in time to stop two tears falling. She was surprised and dismayed. She began to talk brightly, but neither replied. Benny kept his head down, and Sep stared ahead. At last, to her relief, the signal fell, and soon the train came in. She handed them over to the escort, and they sat down in the compartment without a word. Benny gazed out of the further window, away from her, rebukingly; and Sep's face was expressionless.

As the train began to pull out, she stood waving and smiling; but they would not glance in her direction, though the escort was urging them to do so, and setting an example. When at last Laura moved away, her head and throat were aching, and she had such a sense of failure and fatigue that she hardly knew how to walk back to the car.

It was not Mrs Milner's morning, and the house was deadly quiet. Life, noise, laughter, bitter quarrelling had gone out of it. She picked up the cricket bat from the lawn and went inside. She walked about, listlessly tidying things, putting them back in their places. Then fetched a damp cloth and sat down at the piano and wiped the sticky, dirty keys.

She was sitting there, staring in front of her, clasping the cloth in her lap, when Harold came in.

'I'm taking the afternoon off,' he said. 'Let's drive out to Minster Lovell for lunch.'

She looked at him in astonishment. On his way across the room to fetch his tobacco pouch, he let his hand rest on her shoulder for a moment.

'Don't fret,' he said. 'I think we've got them for life now.'

'Benny cried.'

'Extraordinary thing. Shall we make tracks?'

She stood up and closed the lid of the keyboard. 'It was awfully nice of you to come back, Harold.' She paused, thinking she might say more; but he was puffing away, lighting his pipe with a great fuss, as if he were not listening. 'Well, I'll go and get ready,' she said.

ENOCH POWELL

J. Enoch Powell was a senior Conservative politician with a position in the Cabinet, before he was sacked by Prime Minister Edward Heath in 1968 for controversial and inflammatory comments he made about 'New Commonwealth' immigration. He was the leading mainstream politician actively to campaign against black immigration, making the issue an electric one which was to dominate and underlie discussions and policies around Britishness and identity. He eventually left the Conservative Party in 1974 over European policy, representing the Ulster Unionists until he lost his seat in 1987. He died in 1998.

Still to Decide brings together many of the speeches that Powell made around the three key issues that obsessed him: Who rules? On what principles? What sort of people?

from *Still to Decide*
Immigration

It often occurs in nature that an animal is fascinated or hypnotized by the danger which threatens it and thus fails either to escape or to defend itself while it still has the power. There is a weird parallel in the fate of nations: whole peoples will watch disaster approach until it engulfs them, apparently unable to stir out of a kind of horrified trance. It is not that action is impracticable, but that their will is paralysed and they cease to believe in the possibility of action. In such conditions individuals, when they speak at all about the approaching catastrophe, are heard saying: 'It is too late; nothing will be done; nothing can be done.'

You and I stand at such a place at such a time. All about me I hear it, as you do. In your town, in mine, in Wolverhampton, in Smethwick, in Birmingham, people see with their own eyes what they dread, the transformation during their own lifetime or, if they are already old, during their children's, of towns, cities and areas that they know into alien territory.

An Eerie Silence

The people who live about here, and in many another region of urban England, need no statistics to tell them; they know, because they see and because they think. Yet if statistics were needed, they are there. It is strange to recall the time only three years ago when statements falling far short of what is known were greeted with horrified ridicule everywhere but in the areas concerned. I can hardly believe how short a time it is since, as I dragged out one figure after another into the daylight, I had to endure those silly debates with academics and self-appointed experts explaining it was just a transitory scare. That babble of voices has fallen silent; but the silence is more eerie than the sound. As the demonstration is carried through, incapable of refutation, that a fifth, a quarter, a third of a whole generation is already coloured in places like Smethwick, Wolverhampton and Birmingham, people know what this portends in the future. It means a much larger ultimate proportion, because, leaving aside the further addition from outside (which continues) and leaving aside any difference whatsoever in birth rate, there is the fact of the centrifugal movement of the indigenous population outwards. In the face of this prospect, which only a few years ago would have seemed monstrous beyond imagination, those who gaze upon it maintain almost universal silence.

It is not that they are blind to the meaning, any more than to the magnitude, of the prospect. I have just used the words 'alien territory'. I used them in the most literal and factual sense – in all but the juridical sense.

Of the great multitude, numbering already two million, of West Indians and Asians in England, it is no more true to say that England is their country than it would be to say that the West Indies, or Pakistan, or India are our country. In these great numbers they are, and remain, alien here as we would be in Kingston or in Delhi; indeed, with the growth of concentrated numbers, the alienness grows, not by choice but by necessity. It is a human fact which good will, tolerance, comprehension and all the social virtues do not touch. The process is that of an invasion, not, of course, with the connotation either of violence or a premeditated campaign but in the sense that a people find themselves displaced, in the only country that is theirs, by those who do have another country and whose home will continue to be elsewhere for successive generations.

This is the process which hundreds of thousands of our fellow citizens watch day by day as they go about their business and live out their lives; and they say to themselves, as they watch: 'It is finished; there is no escape; this is our lot, and will be our children's lot.'

I suppose there can be circumstances in which a literally irremediable and unavoidable catastrophe overtakes a people; there are, I suppose, blind alleys of history, from which, once entered, there is no escape at the other end. What I do know is that this is not one. The prospect need not be realized, even now, if we will otherwise. Knowing this, I cannot choose but to declare it and to go on declaring it; for the appearance of inevitability is fallacious, as fallacious as were the denials and disclaimers of earlier days.

Let me, then, set up the model of what is happening and demonstrate to you with what apparently small leverage the momentum of events could not merely be altered but reversed. I will do so in simple terms and round figures. I am going to take the two populations of Great Britain, the coloured and the rest; and the term 'coloured' I use, as it is used officially, to mean New Commonwealth immigrants and their offspring. Each of these populations is increasing by about the same amount each year. The factors involved are, of course, natural increase (births minus deaths) and migration, namely, net immigration of coloured and net emigration of the rest. In 1969–70 the natural increase of coloured was on a conservative estimate about 50,000. This, with a net immigration of 43,000 gave a total addition of 93,000. The natural increase of the rest was 185,000, which, after deducting a net emigration of 105,000, gave a total addition of 80,000. Thus, the coloured population grew by 93,000 and the rest by only 80,000. Nor was there anything unusual about 1970: in 1969 the coloured population had grown by 103,000 and the rest by only 98,000.

These are vitally important facts. In the first place, it is not realized how dramatically a minority grows if the same addition is made to the minority and to the rest. For instance, a minority of two million out of 50 million, or 4 per cent, would be transformed, by the annual addition of 100,000 to each side, into 6 per cent after ten years, and nearly 8 per cent after twenty years. What is equally significant, however, about the simple facts I have put before you is the way they reveal the crucial importance of continuing immigration.

Immigration Rising

The idea that New Commonwealth immigration is diminishing and has already reached unimportant proportions is a prevalent and dangerous error. In fact, this mistaken belief is perhaps the chief cause of the prevailing apathy and sense of inevitable doom. Obviously current immigration is a controllable factor; the less important this is made to appear, the more intractable the future course of events must seem. No effort is spared to inculcate just that impression. Every month the propaganda machine at the Home Office lifts up its voice and announces yet another fall in immigration, faithfully echoed in the headlines of the newspapers which simply print the handout without thinking. It is not true. Immigration is not falling, rather it is rising. Immigration is not negligible; rather it is crucially significant.

It is now three and a half years since the greatest outburst of public attention and anxiety about New Commonwealth immigration occurred. In those three and a half years a further net immigration of 180,000 has been recorded – making no allowance at all for un-recorded entry. It was widely expected that a Conservative Government would reduce the rate at which immigration had been running under their predecessors; and certainly nothing was said (to put it mildly) to counteract that expectation. On the contrary net immigration in the first year of Conservative administration has been sub-stantially higher than in the last year of Socialist administration – over 17 per cent higher in fact. At 41,300 it was not far below the rate being recorded in the mid 1960s.

How, then, is the Home Office propaganda manufactured? Quite simply: they take only the figures of those admitted for permanent settlement immediately, and even in these they do not include the Asians from East Africa. Yet the men who put these statements out know perfectly well that many who are not admitted for settlement in the first place do in fact remain permanently. They also know per-fectly well that net immigration ('in' minus 'out') is the only relevant figure and is for that reason exclusively used by the Registrar-General himself in all computations and forecasts of coloured population. You may wonder who these men are who are determined to present a false picture, and what may be their motives.

I recur to the scale of current immigration. At over 40,000 a year it represents not far short of half the annual addition to the coloured population. If net immigration ceased, then the increase of the coloured population would be almost halved – if I may coin a phrase – 'at a stroke'.

Under the Immigration Bill due to become law this October (1971), there will no longer be any statutory obstacle: the Government will have the power to control immigration absolutely.* Surely no one could suggest that for Britain to terminate net immigration from the New Commonwealth would be unreasonable in the light of the admitted facts and prospects even on their most favourable interpretation. Most people, of all shades of opinion, would probably think this was long overdue – indeed, as I say, many of them have been cozened into supposing that it had virtually happened already. However that may be, no one surely can dispute that to attain nil net immigration is practicable.

We have therefore already exploded the bogey of inevitability so far as one of the two elements in the increase of the coloured population is concerned. Last year, for instance? If there had been no new immigration, the addition to the coloured population would have been only 80,000 as against the addition of 50,000 to the rest of the population. But that is not all.

The Immigration Act will for the first time contain powers to give assistance to immigrants and their families who wish to return home. This is in pursuance of an element of the Conservative Party's official policy since 1965: it is an element which the Prime Minister described as 'important'. There has been controversy, which in the nature of the case could not be conclusive, about the scale on which the provision of assistance could result in persons and families re-emigrating who would not otherwise do so. Clearly, the actual outcome must depend on all kinds of factors which are not yet known: the generosity of the terms, the spirit in which the scheme is publicized and operated, the economic situation and so on. Let us, however, make what must surely be a very modest estimate and suppose that no more than 5,000 families a year, who would not otherwise have departed, avail themselves of the scheme. Averaged at five persons – two parents and three children – this would represent a net annual reduction of 25,000 in the coloured population. Applied once again, by way of example, to 1970, this would have meant that the addition to the coloured population would have been no more than 25,000 as against 80,000 to the rest.

You will remember how, with 'level pegging', the 4 per cent minority grew to nearly 8 per cent in twenty years. At the new ratio which we have obtained by nil net immigration and a small assisted repatriation, the outcome is very different: the 4 per cent minority

---

* Amendments in the House of Lords restored the statutory obstacle.

has grown to no more than 5 per cent in the twenty years.

I repeat that the model which I have placed before you is a simplified one. In real life there are of course numerous qualifications and complications. For instance, the natural increase of the coloured population will no doubt continue to rise for a considerable time. Again, if voluntary repatriation attracted mainly individuals, the effect would be different from what it would be if it attracted mainly families. On the other hand, we have made no allowance for any fall in the emigration of the non-coloured population. At the present time no less than 150,000 British-born citizens are emigrating every year; and I know, from what many of them write to me and tell me, that the prospect of the future consequences of coloured immigration is one of the motives which impel them. If that prospect were substantially modified, it would not be unreasonable to suppose that fewer of our own people would wish to leave.

One could go on in this way, adding touches first to one side of the picture and then to the other. What I have proved beyond a peradventure is that our fate in the future is not yet signed and sealed, or reversible only by heroic and revolutionary or inhuman policies which it would be unrealistic to demand or to expect. On the contrary, the two measures which I have shown to produce a startling alteration in the outlook are measures which most ordinary people would regard as eminently reasonable: the cessation of further immigration for the foreseeable future and the offer of assistance to any who genuinely and voluntarily wish to go home or to go elsewhere.

Moreover, in assessing the latter I have deliberately estimated its scope much more modestly than my own observation and much other evidence would suggest is justified. The measures concerned are measures for which the way has been opened, in accordance with our Election promises, by the legislation of our first Parliamentary session. It now rests with the Government to take them, and upon the Government will rest the responsibility for all that will follow if they are not taken.

I have shown – and this was my purpose tonight – that belief in the inevitability of what I once described as 'many Washingtons in England' is mistaken. Those who say 'it is too late', those who say 'nothing can be done now', are not realists but the victims of propaganda. It is not too late; there is still time; but with every passing month and year the opportunity seeps away – forever. The Government cannot shift the burden on to the past. They themselves hold the future in their hands. They will be held to account by our children and our children's children – and not only they, but we. Let no one say: 'There's nothing that I can do.' There is. There is something that everyone can do. It is to give Parliament and Government no peace or quarter until those simple and available actions are taken which hold the balance between hope and despair. Us, too, our children will not forgive if out of fear or indolence or dejection we betray them.

ROY KERRIDGE

Roy Kerridge, writer and journalist, has written numerous books, including *Real Wicked, Guy – A View of Black Britain*. As a schoolboy in the early 1950s, Kerridge was thrust into the whirlpool of immigrant life following his mother's marriage to a West African.

The Storm is Passing Over: A Look at Black Churches in Britain, co-authored with Homer Sykes, explores the exhilarating ceremonies practised by these churches and their congregation. It also looks at their community-based identity, their worship through music and the similarities between their 'spiritual songs', passionate preaching and testimonies and those of the evangelical churches of America's Deep South.

from *The Storm is Passing Over: A Look at Black Churches in Britain*

The Wedding

It was a great day at the Mount Zion Spiritual Baptist Church when Teacher Jackie married the neat young pastor of a brother church. Guests and workmates of the couple, some of them white, swelled the usual number of worshippers. Twelve bridesmaids, dressed in pink or pale blue, eyed the door expectantly, for the bride was late. About their brows, they wore wreaths of dried flowers. Blue and yellow paper decorations hung from the ceiling. As for Bishop Noel and his wife, both were gorgeously attired, one in a huge gold bishop's hat, the other in a scarlet-painted royal crown. Half-hidden amongst all this finery, the town hall Registrar impassively awaited events.

Teacher Jackie the bride made a sensational entrance, a mass of white with a fifteen-foot gold train behind. Holding the Cloth of Gold was a tiny girl, dressed in a mass of pink ruffles. The groom, by contrast, wore a black suit and a scarlet bow tie. He was a nervous bespectacled man. Beaming, the bride made her way to the altar on the arm of her brother.

Bishop Noel began the ceremony with a sternness and rigour that would have done credit to St Paul. But as time went by his sense of humour got the better of him, and he ad-libbed his way through the wedding in fine form. Here are some highlights, spoken in a deep, throaty 'gospel voice'.

Now the groom is wishing he could get away, but the crowds are pressed too close! But why should he run away when his wife's so beautiful, he'd be mad, innit? . . . Now, groom, press the ring down firm on her finger, we do not want a divorce! You know, whoever pushes the ring furthest down is going to be the ruler! Better push it down together . . . When men see the woman's ring, they stop trying! Or maybe they don't . . . Now wife, be stern unto your husband – he needs it! Yet don't jump to conclusions. If he's out late, don't at once think it's another woman, there might be a good reason . . . Groom, if you don't say 'Yes' at this stage, I'll box your ears! And the bride too – I'll box *her* ears! Lord, guard them from all witchcraft, voodoo, black magic, scientists and socialism, Amen.

All this while, a hired camcorder man in a black-and-yellow zebra-patterned suit hopped around trying to film the event. A woman guest shrieked at her child who was playing outside the church, and this so upset her brother, a reluctant churchgoer, that the young man stormed from the building. Nothing could mar the great day, however, and we soon crossed the road to the Community Centre for the Reception.

Here a champagne buffet had been laid on, and we feasted royally on rhoti, a meat-and-chapati dish introduced to the Caribbean by Indian indentured labourers. There were speeches galore, and the bride embarrassed her new husband by saying, 'He kept asking me to marry him!'

Two rows of bridesmaids held bouquets aloft, forming an archway through which the bride and groom slowly waltzed to taped gospel music, seraphic expressions on their faces. Seizing a bouquet, the bride tossed it to an unarmed bridesmaid. Then the serious business of cake-cutting began.

The Funeral

In her little, dark, East End flat I found the Evangelist Steadman to be in a sombre mood. She was not dressed to match her mood, for she wore golden robes beneath a scarlet shawl and turban. But her words were full of omens. In order to cheer up her flat, where water streamed down the walls and cockroaches danced the night away, I had bought her a purplish potted plant in Stratford market.

'I am so pleased with that big-leaf plant,' she told me. 'It is a Croton, an' in Jamaica it grow as big as a tree. Back home, we uses the leaf for funeral wreath. But I am thinking there will be a funeral soon, Brother Roy.'

'Why is that?'

'Some time ago, I hear a knocking at me window pane. It a white dove knocking – somebody dies. Last week I was hill [ill] with neuralgia, I hear a bang by my side. The pain gone, and I know a soul has passed. Last night I dream I see a wooden house hung all over with meat for sale. White meat like pork – that's nothing but a funeral!'

She spoke on, about a 'vigion' [vision] she had seen of a white girl kneeling in her room.

'She look nice, so I was not afraid . . . '

'Are you talking about a dream or something real?' I asked in puzzlement, after a while.

'Is a *dream*, me tell you!' she spoke emphatically, her tone suggesting that dreams are real in a way the waking world can never be. Such an attitude is held in all the churches I describe. In Jamaica marriages take place in the Church of God if somebody dreams they saw Brother and Sister so-and-so getting wed. In England, dreams of marriages are often taken as prophecies, as are dreams that portend death. Is Heaven itself a never-ending happy dream we all can share?

A non-church-going Jamaican friend of mine claims he can tell dreams that are visions from dreams that are just dreams. Acting on the former kind of dream, he rushed from London to 'Birmingham' in time to call an ambulance for his ailing wife. I took the Evangelist's dreams to heart, and found that she wasn't wrong.

Pastor Spring is, in most ways, a model of everything a pastor should be. In winter, he goes to church at crack of dawn to light the paraffin fires so that members will enter a warm building. Always he impresses on his charges the need to love, respect and cherish old people. Most of them need no telling, for such attitudes are deeply instilled, even in the youngest. Oldest man in the church for some time was Brother Pullman, a tall, frail ninety-year-old. I had to listen to him carefully, for he spoke in deep 'patois'. He had never been to England before this lengthy visit. Pet of the church, to his obvious pleasure, he continued to write to the Brethren after his return to Jamaica.

His first letter caused some embarrassment to young Sister Dorothy who tried to read it to the Congregation.

'It's all written in Jamaican talk,' she appealed to the Pastor, who took over.

'Me feel like a pig with leg tied for market,' the Pastor read. 'Me struggle, but me can't go back to England.'

Everybody clapped when Pastor Spring had finished reading. After reminding the church once more of their duty to love and respect the old, the pastor mentioned the other side of the coin.

'Back home, as many brethren can tell you, grown-up men with wives and children still fear they parents an' get a lickin' from they Mum or Dad.'

Many an outwardly worldly and fashionable Jamaican in England refers to his Mum as 'Mummy' in awe and timidity.

With Brother Pullman away in Jamaica, the oldest member of the church now was Brother Hawkshaw. A stocky amiable bull-necked man, Brother Hawkshaw wore a tight waistcoat and black suit, and possessed a wonderful praying voice, hoarse and soulful. When he collected the offering and prayed over it, the church would first sing and then hum a chorus, timing it so that the soft soothing hum would act as a background to the spoken prayer. He and his best friend, silver-haired Brother Plummer, took turns at collecting offerings. Brother Plummer was a more relaxed person than sternly upright Brother Hawkshaw, but he too could give an offering a poetic blessing.

One Sunday, Pastor Spring called Brother Hawkshaw up to the front of the church to be honoured. The Spring daughters lined up beside him in their role as 'Heaven Harmonies' and prepared to sing.

'We all love Brother Hawkshaw, don't it?' the Pastor asked, to sounds of general agreement. 'We must love and honour him now, for he is old, and may not be with us always.'

In soft haunting voices, the Spring girls sang a repetitive chant: 'Death has a time – to carry you away.'

I could see that Brother Hawkshaw didn't like this very much, although he smirked and tried to look flattered. Sure enough, he was taken ill shortly afterwards, and was nursed at home by his devoted wife. Six months later, Brother Hawkshaw reappeared at church looking doleful. He had shrunk to skin and bone and his once-tight clothes hung about him. In happy surprise, Sister Dorothy congratulated him on losing weight. A week later, Sister Hawkshaw 'phoned the Pastor to say that her husband was dead.

Dismay met this announcement on Sunday, and Pastor Spring added that Sister Hawkshaw would welcome all church members to the Wake, to be held at her house. A traditional Jamaican Wake is known as a 'Nine Night', the ninth and last night of sitting up preceding the funeral. Like the bacchanalian Irish wakes of old, Nine Nights are growing less frequent, particularly in England. Songs and stories, often of an unusually bawdy nature, are told along with all-night hymn-singing and rum-drinking. There is a topsy-turvy atmosphere, for all the normal laws of life are suspended, an echo of Hallowe'en. The good self of the deceased will be presumed to be with God or awaiting judgement, but the bad self, a mischievous ghost called a 'duppie', might be present in the house and must be coaxed into leaving. Seeming irregularities in a Nine Night are for the naughty duppie's benefit. I have never been to a Nine Night, a custom renounced by Church of God members, who do not officially recognize the existence of duppies. However, I was to find that a little Nine Night topsy-turviness had rubbed off on the Hawkshaw Wake, even though it was only a Seven Night affair.

Near the narrow terraced house where the Hawkshaw family lived, fruit-laden stalls had been set up outside Indian shops. Lights blazed, their cables strung along makeshift awnings, and delicious sweet-meats sizzled over brazier-bucket fires, barbecued chunks of meat and roasted sweetcorn. Happy, excited faces beamed towards me from brightly dressed crowds who were celebrating the end of Ramadan. In the Hawkshaw home, when I eventually found it, festivities of another kind were taking place. Young 'unsaved' members of the family had prepared a banquet downstairs, where chicken, reggae and rum bottles greeted all-comers. Cars continually pulled up outside, as well-wishers queued to ring the doorbell.

'Sister Hawkshaw is upstairs,' I was told.

I had an awful premonition that Brother Hawkshaw himself would be laid out for all to see, but I was wrong. Instead, his widow sat up in bed, speaking on the 'phone to her sister in Jamaica. She seemed shaken, but pleased to have company.

'Don't worry 'bout me, the Pastor is right here now in this very room,' she assured her unseen relative.

She was right, for Pastor Spring and the church deacon were sitting on the end of the bed, roaring with laughter at a Lenny Henry film on television. The joke concerned a West Indian funeral, with the coffin falling all over the place. The Spring girls and other members of the church greeted me from various parts of the large eiderdown-covered bed on which they perched. Sister Hawkshaw looked up from her pillow and gave me a nod.

All of a sudden, a big man in a blue suit burst into the room as if in terror, and shouted out, 'The duppie come!'

Then he shook with laughter and said, 'Only me lickle joke, you know. I come straight from a night club, 'cos me not a yard man, me never go home! Hello, everybody! So the old man gone, eh? Too sorry, but it happen all the time. I just come to pay respects. Me children bring the message, or me stay out till 4 a.m. Pastor, excuse me lager can, I think it spill.'

He was welcomed to the gathering, and sat heavily on the bed, leaning over to prim Arlene Spring, who remained polite with seeming difficulty.

'I don't believe in all this God and Heaven business, do you?' he asked, then launched into a comic story in strong 'patois', using the word 'oonu', which means 'you-all'. Nobody seemed very offended by this behaviour. A yard man is a stay-at-home, since 'yard' in Jamaicanese means 'house and grounds'. I decided to leave for my own yard, and bade the company farewell. As I left, the company began to sing with pathos: 'Farther Along, We'll Know All About It.'

At the end of the week, I was summoned to the funeral by a grey card, and so presented myself at church amidst black-clad mourners. Everybody present had gone over to the English custom of wearing black for a funeral. In the Caribbean, however, white is frequently worn. My neighbour Sister Ruth had worn white for a family funeral, the veil hanging over her eyes, only a year or two ago. Young people have almost scoffed this custom out of existence.

When I reached the Church of God, I found that the service had already started. Two anxious young undertakers, black-clad with shoulder-length blond hair, at once turned to me to ask for help.

'Look, they made us put the coffin down at the front of the church, with the lid off,' one of them told me. 'We're s'posed to wait for the Pastor's nod, then go in and close it up. When's 'e likely to nod, d'you reckon? There's a programme on this card, but all the events are happening in the wrong order! Look, the choir is supposed to be singing, but they 'aven't even *got* here yet.'

'I think everyone here has to pay respects to the body,' I said doubtfully . 'The Pastor won't nod till then.'

So saying, I took my seat and mimed the words everyone was singing, 'When I've Gone the Last Mile of the Way'. Brother Hawkshaw had certainly walked his last mile. In his life, I had always been glad to meet him, but now I had to summon up all my courage for the long walk down the aisle to the open coffin.

Arlene Spring, immaculately dressed and coiffured, stood stiffly on the rostrum and solemnly read out a 'Eulogy' on Brother Hawkshaw. She had written this herself with a great deal of agonizing, and it sounded very impressive. Brother Hawkshaw had been born in 1911, he had worked for a sugar company in rural Jamaica, then emigrated to England in middle age. Details of his marriage, children, his work in transport and his loyalty to the Church followed. Sister Hawkshaw listened with bowed head. Prayers followed, then a sermon by a Bishop of the Church of God. Like all such bishops, he wore ordinary clothes and was addressed informally as 'Brother'. He knew Brother Hawkshaw well and made a sincere eulogy of his own.

Arriving in haste and slight disarray, the choir took their places and the band struck up a monotonous rhythm. Everyone rose and left their seats to walk around the large church and say goodbye to Brother Hawkshaw. Sister Hawkshaw, her children, her grandchildren and other relatives stood beside the coffin, all crying softly. The rest of the church filed past slowly.

Brother Hawkshaw had been smartly dressed for the occasion, but his body looked limp and empty. Plainly the real Brother Hawkshaw was not at home. Only in his face did a trace of spirit remain. More than a trace, in fact. His eyes were open, and he looked both shocked and angry at this thing that had happened to him. He had faced death with incredulity.

Before I reached my seat once more, I noticed a grizzled old man with white-flecked eyebrows and moustache, mournfully playing a harmonica. The Pastor gave his nod, and the coffin was sealed.

'We will sing the Closing Hymn from the memorial card, and then make our way to the Burying Ground,' announced the Bishop. Guitars and drums rang on a sharper note as the song began.

> To Canaan's land I'm on my way.
> Where the Soul of Man Never Dies!
> My darkest night will turn to day

> Where the Soul of Man Never Dies!
> No sad . . . farewells.
> No tear. . . dimmed eyes.
> Where all . . . is love.
> And the Soul of Man Never Dies!

This old 'country hymn', well-loved in the southern states of the USA, was once a favourite in Elvis Presley's circle. The gaps in the lines (which I have copied from the song card) accurately show the rhythm. As I left the church, I noticed a battered guitar propped in a corner.

At the 'Burying Ground', I soon found the Church of God party of mourners gathered around an open grave. Two young gravediggers, also West Indian, stood stripped to the waist, spades at the ready. A mountain of flowery wreaths, mostly white, lay nearby. Brother Hawkshaw was gently lowered down on canvas straps, and clods of earth and a few wreaths dropped upon him. Then the young men worked with ferocious energy, filling up the grave once more.

'You know there's unemployment, when young men have to take a job like this,' someone remarked. 'Once it was only old people who would work as gravediggers.'

'Me knew it would come to this – me see black washing hanging from line,' an old lady mourner observed.

When the grave was levelled, the flowers were heaped on top, all the mourners lending a hand. Hymns were sung from a songbook at first. To my surprise, the old, white-eyebrowed man I had seen earlier then took over the singing, which became traditional in character. He had fitted his harmonica on to a frame joined to the battered guitar, and danced from foot to foot as he played and sang in a style reminiscent of a mournful Jimmy Reed. Among the sombre, black-suited mourners, he wore an open-necked lumbershirt, and seemed a being from another age. This is the song he sang:

> No Grave Can Hold My Body Down!
> No Grave Can Hold My Body Down!
> When the trumpet shall sound
> And the dead in Christ shall rise.
> No grave! (No grave!) No grave!
> No Grave Can Hold My Body Down!

As the plaintive harmonies poured forth, Brother Plummer leaned forward, plunged his right hand into the mass of flowers, and made the motion of shaking an old friend's hand in parting.

'Goodbye, Brother Hawkshaw!' he exclaimed twice, very clearly.

Who wrote that haunting song, 'No Grave'? I have heard it sung by hillbillies in the Smoky Mountains of Tennessee. My mother, on an epic trip across the Kalahari Desert in 1990, heard the same song hoarsely whispered in English by her Tswana guide, George Lekaukau, as he fetched sticks for the fire that kept lions at bay. Jackals yelped and howled in the nearby darkness as if joining in the singing.

> I don't know when my death will come
> I don't know when my death will come.
> It may come in the night.
> It may come in the day.
> I don't know when my death will come!

LOVING, STRIFING AND PLEASURE

You know whom you love; you cannot
know who loves you
YORUBA PROVERB

JOHN AGARD

'Mouse in the Poetry Library' (taken from *A Stone's Throw from Embankment*) is inspired by a 'passing visitor' to the poetry library at the South Bank Centre, which celebrated its fortieth year during Agard's residence.

Mouse in the Poetry Library

(For Mary)

Was it fat?
Was it lean?
The mouse I mean –
        the one that ran out the word-processing machine
                in the poetry library.

Possibly in-between.
Certainly a quadruped.
Most definitely well-read
in twentieth-century prosody.

lt scampered across the screen
                without regard for scansion
loitered on the daisy wheel
              with some poetic licence
considered the automatic paper feed
              a rather fine place to breed
made a mockery of a computer's memory.
O that mouse had an intimate tour
of Canon's colour-coded keyboard
even contemplated leaving a load
              on the carbon copy mode.
Finally, it left a solitary dropping

like a punctuation mark
from e.e. cummings
and before you knew
had mousily sped
on its little haiku   legs.

Was this the mouse that fled
Christopher Smart's cat Jeoffrey
outmysteried T. S. Eliot's Macavity
outmelodied Stevie Smith's singing Kitty
and escaped the private bestiary
belonging to Ted Hughes?

What a plight
for librarian Mary Enright!
Should this mouse be filed
under stock to be renewed
or simply overdues?

E. A. MARKHAM

E. A. Markham was born in 1939 in Montserrat, and arrived in Britain in 1956. He studied at the University of Wales and taught in London in the 1960s. Since then he has worked and lived in the Caribbean, France and Papua New Guinea, where he worked as a media co-ordinator from 1983 to 1985. He has worked in the theatre, published two collections of short stories and has a novel forthcoming. Among his books of poetry are: *Living in Disguise*, *Towards the End of a Century*, *Letter from Ulster*, *The Hugo Poems* and *Misapprehensions*. He has also written a number of 'Lambchops' and 'Philpot' books under the pseudonym Paul St Vincent. He is now Professor of Creative Writing at Sheffield Hallam University.

'Two Haiku' is taken from *Living in Disguise*. 'On Another Field, an Ally' is taken from *Towards the End of a Century*.

Two Haiku

Third-World War

The beach, walking off
inland, dragging its bed of
sand. And look, no guns!

Food-Chain

The feeding over:
one eye hard and accusing –
fish out of water.

On Another Field, an Ally: A West Indian Batsman Talks Us Towards the Century

for Malcolm Marshall and Michael Holding, resting . . .

Into the nineties, into the nineties
Ten to go, ten runs, don't panic . . .
Think Bradman . . . never got out when into the nineties

Nerves of steel, drive them through legs
Beginning to buckle *think* the three W's *think* Clive Lloyd
Think Richards and all those ruling heads

On the coin of cricket. And relax. Now where am I?
Lost in the arms of voluptuous Anna. *Fin*
de siècle, recalling the days of immortal Kanhai

Hooking to the boundary from a prone position.
Cravats & decadence. Good ball. *Christ!*
Man in white coat weighing the decision

To point the finger, legalized gun
With power to run the 'Man of the Match'
Out of town. Not guilty. Not guilty, my old son

If I say it myself. A lapse
In concentration quickly repaired by nailing
The Will against any further collapse

This side of the century. Here behind the barricades
Stretching from 'Clifton' and Gordon 'Le Corbusier' Greenidge
Through 'homelier' architects of our days

Of glory – the team's Frank Lloyd Wrights –
Up against pollution, thinning ozone, treeless forests
In the tropics etc., each run lifts you to the heights

Of vertigo. And for you down there, Miss X, Mrs Patel
At the corner-shop, this wicket guarantees
Orgasms, guarantees that this last exile suits you well.

And damn it, I'm out. *Out?* There's no morality to this game.
Protesting genocide and burying your head
In sweet Anna's thighs, it's all the same.

The butcher of dreams, man in white coat
Offers no reprieve, his butchershop in Hounslow in need
Of more meat. Yet again I've missed the boat

Of the century. Breach in the wall.
Bowled through the gate. Marooned from the grand
Ocean liners: SS Sobers & Headley; not by formidable Wes Hall

Line of destroyers; no *chinaman* or finger-lickin' spin
To obscurity – just a *gift* with your name on it
Lacking spite, Physics or Philosophy, innocuous as sin.

Like I say, there's no morality in this game.
Protesting genocide or burying your head
In sweet Anna's thighs, it's all the same.

SAM SELVON

Ways of Sunlight contains Sam Selvon's characteristic vignettes of Caribbean and London life. From rural gossip and rivalry in Trinidad, to old Ma Procop protecting the fruit of her mango tree with magic, all are given the usual Selvon exuberance. In between the hard times and hustling for survival, *My Girl and the City* chronicles his love for London.

from *Ways of Sunlight*
My Girl and the City

All these words that I hope to write, I have written them already many times in my mind. I have had many beginnings, each as good or as bad as the other. Hurtling in the Underground from station to station, mind the doors, missed it!, there is no substitute for wool: waiting for a bus in Piccadilly Circus: walking across Waterloo bridge: watching the bed of the Thames when the tide is out – choose one, choose a time, a place, any time or any place, and take off, as if this were interrupted conversation, as if you and I were earnest friends and there is no need for a preliminary remark.

One day of any day it is like this. I wait for my girl on Waterloo bridge, and when she comes there is a mighty wind blowing across the river, and we lean against it and laugh, her skirt skylarking, her hair whipping across her face.

I wooed my girl, mostly on her way home from work, and I talked a great deal. Often, it was as if I had never spoken, I heard my words echo in deep caverns of thought, as if they hung about like cigarette smoke in a still room, missionless; or else they were lost for ever in the sounds of the city.

We used to wait for a 196 under the railway bridge across the Waterloo road. There were always long queues and it looked like we would never get a bus. Fidgeting in that line of impatient humanity I got in precious words edgeways, and a train would rumble and drown my words in thundering steel. Still, it was important to talk. In the crowded bus, as if I wooed three or four instead of one, I shot words over my shoulder, across seats; once past a bespectacled man reading the *Evening News* who lowered his paper and eyed me that I was mad. My words bumped against people's faces, on the glass window of the bus; they found passage between 'fares please' and once I got to writing things on a piece of paper and pushing my hand over two seats.

The journey ended there was urgent need to communicate before we parted.

All these things I say, I said, waving my hand in the air as if to catch the words floating about me and give them mission. I say them because I want you to know, I don't ever want to regret afterwards that I didn't say enough, I would rather say too much.

Take that Saturday evening, I am waiting for her in Victoria station. When she comes we take the Northern Line to Belsize Park (I know a way to the Heath from there, I said). When we get out of the lift and step outside there is a sudden downpour and everyone scampers back into the station. We wait a while, then go out in it. We get lost. I say, let us ask that fellow the way. But she says, no, fancy asking someone the way to the Heath on this rainy night, just find out how to get back to the tube station.

We go back, I get my bearings afresh, and we set off. She is hungry. Wait here, I say under a tree at the side of the road, and I go to a pub for some sandwiches. Water slips off me and makes puddles on the counter as I place my order. The man is taking a long time and I go to the door and wave to her across the street signifying I shan't be too long.

When I go out she has crossed the road and is sheltering in a doorway pouting. You leave me standing in the rain and stay such a long time, she says. I had to wait for the sandwiches, I say, what do you think, I was having a quick one? Yes, she says.

We walk on through the rain and we get to the Heath and the rain is falling slantways and carefree and miserable. For a minute we move around in an indecisive way as if we're looking for some particular spot. Then we see a tree which might offer some shelter and we go there and sit on a bench wet and bedraggled.

I am sorry for all this rain, I say, as if I were responsible I take off her raincoat and make her put on my quilted jacket. She takes off her soaking shoes and tucks her feet under her skirt on the bench. She tries to dry her hair with a handkerchief. I offer her the sandwiches and light a cigarette for myself. Go on, have one, she says. I take a half and munch it, and smoke.

It is cold there. The wind is raging in the leaves of the trees, and the rain is pelting. But abruptly it ceases, the clouds break up in the sky, and the moon shines. When the moon shines, it shines on her face, and I look at her, the beauty of her washed by rain, and I think many things.

Suddenly we are kissing and I wish I could die there and then and there's an end to everything, to all the Jesus Christ thoughts that make up every moment of my existence.

Writing all this now – and some weeks have gone by since I started – it is lifeless and insipid and useless. Only at the time, there was something, a thought that propelled me. Always, in looking back, there was something, and at the time I am aware of it, and the creation goes on and on in my mind while I look at all the faces around me in the tube, the restless rustle of newspapers, the hiss of air as the doors close, the enaction of life in a variety of form.

Once I told her and she said, as she was a stenographer, that she would come with me and we would ride the Inner Circle and I would just voice my thoughts and she would write them down, and that way we could make something of it. Once the train was crowded and she sat opposite to me and after a while I looked at her and she smiled and turned away. What is all this, what is the meaning of all these things that happen to people, the movement from one place to another, lighting a cigarette, slipping a coin into a slot and pulling a drawer for chocolate, buying a return ticket, waiting for a bus, working the crossword puzzle in the *Evening Standard*?

Sometimes you are in the underground and you have no idea what the weather is like, and the train shoots out of a tunnel and sunlight floods you, falls across your newspaper, makes the passengers squint and look up.

There is a face you have for sitting at home and talking, there is a face you have for working in the office, there is a face, a bearing, a demeanour for each time and place. There is above all a face for travelling, and when you have seen one you have seen all. In a rush hour, when we are breathing down each other's neck, we look at each other and glance quickly away. There is not a great deal to look at in the narrow confines of a carriage except people, and the faces of people, but no one deserves a glass of Hall's wine more than you do. We jostle in the subway from train to lift, we wait, shifting our feet.

When we are all herded inside we hear the footsteps of a straggler for whom the operator waits, and we try to figure out what sort of a footstep it is, if he feels the lift will wait for him; we are glad if he is left waiting while we shoot upwards. Out of the lift, down the street, up the road: in ten seconds flat it is over, and we have to begin again.

One morning I am coming into the city by the night bus 287 from Streatham. It is after one o'clock, I have been stranded again after seeing my girl home. When we get to Westminster Bridge the sky is marvellously clear with a few stray patches of beautiful cloud among which stars sparkle. The moon stands over Waterloo Bridge, above the Houses of Parliament sharply outlined, and it throws gold on the waters of the Thames. The Embankment is quiet, only a few people loiter around the public convenience near to the Charing Cross underground which is open all night. A man sleeps on a bench. His head is resting under headlines: Suez Deadlock.

Going back to that same spot about five o'clock in the evening, there was absolutely nothing to recall the atmosphere of the early morning hours. Life had taken over completely, and there was nothing but people. People waiting for buses, people hustling for trains.

I go to Waterloo Bridge and they come pouring out of the offices and they bob up and down as they walk across the bridge. From the station green trains come and go relentlessly. Motion mesmerizes me into immobility. There are lines of motion across the river, on the river.

Sometimes we sat on a bench near the river, and if the tide was out you could see the muddy bed of the river and the swans grubbing. Such spots, when found, are pleasant to loiter in. Sitting in one of those places – choose one, and choose a time – where it is possible to escape for a brief spell from Christ and the cup of tea, I have known a great frustration and weariness. All these things, said, have been said before, the river seen, the skirt pressed against the swelling thigh noted, the lunch hour eating apples in the sphinx's lap under Cleopatra's Needle observed and duly registered: even to talk of the frustration is a repetition. What am I to do, am I to take each circumstance, each thing seen, noted, and mill them in my mind and spit out something entirely different from the reality?

My girl is very real. She hated the city, I don't know why. It's like that sometimes, a person doesn't have to have a reason. A lot of people don't like London that way, you ask them why and they shrug, and a shrug is sometimes a powerful reply to a question.

She shrugged when I asked her why, and when she asked me why I loved London I too shrugged. But after a minute I thought I would try to explain, because too a shrug is an easy way out of a lot of things.

Falteringly, I told her how one night it was late and I found a fish and chips shop open in the East End and I bought and ate in the dark street walking; and of the cup of tea in an all-night café in Kensington one grim winter morning; and of the first time I ever queued in this country in 1950 to see the Swan Lake ballet, and the friend who was with me gave a busker two and six because he was playing Sentimental Journey on a mouth-organ.

But why do you love London, she said.

You can't talk about a thing like that, not really. Maybe I could have told her because one evening in the summer I was waiting for her, only it wasn't like summer at all. Rain had been falling all day, and a haze hung about the bridges across the river, and the water was muddy and brown, and there was a kind of wistfulness and sadness about the evening. The way St Paul's was, half-hidden in the rain, the motionless trees along the Embankment. But you say a thing like that and people don't understand at all. How sometimes a surge of greatness could sweep over you when you see something.

But even if I had said all that and much more, it would not have been what I meant. You could be lonely as hell in the city, then one day you look around you and you realize everybody else is lonely too, withdrawn, locked, rushing home out of the chaos: blank faces, unseeing eyes, millions and millions of them, up the Strand, down the Strand, jostling in Charing Cross for the 5.20: in Victoria station, a pretty continental girl wearing a light, becoming shade of lipstick stands away from the board on which the departure of trains appear and cocks her head sideways, hands thrust into pockets of a fawn raincoat.

I catch the eyes of this girl with my own: we each register sight, appreciation: we look away, our eyes pick up casual station activities: she turns to an automatic refreshment machine, hesitant, not sure if she would be able to operate it.

Things happen, and are finished with for ever: I did not talk to her, I did not look her way again, or even think of her.

I look on the wall of the station at the clock, it is after half-past eight, and my girl was to have met me since six o'clock. I feel in my pockets for pennies to telephone. I only have two. I ask change of a stander with the usual embarrassment: when I telephone, the line is engaged. I alternate between standing in the spot we have arranged to meet and telephoning, but each time the line is engaged. I call the exchange: they ascertain that something is wrong with the line.

At ten minutes to nine I am eating a corned-beef sandwich when she comes. Suddenly now nothing matters except that she is here. She never expected that I would still be waiting, but she came on the offchance. I never expected that she would come, but I waited on the offchance.

Now I have a different word for this thing that happened, an offchance, but that does not explain why it happens, and what it is that really happens. We go to St James's Park, we sit under a tree, we kiss, the moon can be seen between leaves.

Wooing my way towards, sometimes in our casual conversation we came near to great, fundamental truths, and it was a little frightening. It wasn't like wooing at all, it was more discussion of when will it end, and must it ever end, and how did it begin, and how go on from here? We scattered words on the green summer grass, under trees, on dry leaves in a wood of quivering aspens, and sometimes it was as if I was struck speechless with too much to say, and held my tongue between thoughts frightened of utterance.

Once again I am on a green train returning to the heart from the suburbs, and I look out of window into windows of private lives flashed on my brain. Bread being sliced, a man taking off a jacket, an old woman knitting. And all these things I see – the curve of a woman's arm, undressing, the blankets being tucked, and once a solitary figure staring at trains as I stared at windows. All the way into London Bridge – is falling down, is falling down, the wheels say: one must have a thought – where buildings and the shadows of them encroach on the railway tracks. Now the train crawls across the bridges, dark steel in the darkness: the thoughtful gloom of Waterloo: Charing Cross Bridge, Thames reflecting lights, and the silhouettes of city buildings against the sky of the night.

When I was in New York, many times I went into that city late at night after a sally to the outskirts, it lighted up with a million lights, but never a feeling as on entering London. Each return to the city is loaded with thought, so that by the time I take the Inner Circle I am as light as air.

At last I think I know what it is all about. I move around in a world of words. Everything that happens is words. But pure expression is nothing. One must build on the things that happen: it is insufficient to say I sat in the underground and the train hurtled through the darkness and someone isn't using Amplex. So what? So now I weave, I say there was an old man on whose face wrinkles rivered, whose hands were shapeful with arthritis but when he spoke, oddly enough, his voice was young and gay.

But there was no old man, there was nothing, and there is never ever anything.

My girl, she is beautiful to look at. I have seen her in sunlight and in moonlight, and her face carves an exquisite shape in darkness.

These things we talk, I burst out, why mustn't I say them? If I love you, why shouldn't I tell you so?

I love London, she said.

MERLE COLLINS

Merle Collins is Grenadian. She has studied at the University of the West Indies, Georgetown University in the United States, and at the London School of Economics and Political Science. Her published work includes: a volume of poems, *Because and Dawn Breaks*; a novel, *Angel*; *Watchers and Seekers: Creative Writing by Black Women in Britain* (coedited with Rhonda Cobham) and a volume of short stories, *Rain Darling*. She now lectures in the United States.

'The Sheep and the Goats' is taken from *Rotten Pomerack*, a collection of poems about people retracing the journey from the Caribbean to England.

The Sheep and the Goats

this is where you separate the sheep
from the goats

Sometimes
my mother's statements startle
with irrelevance
stay and tickle
disappear to appear again
some unlikely day

Standing in the queue
at the airport terminal
London
Heath-
row

I tried to decide
which were the sheep
and which
the goats

a sudden movement
a twitch
nervous toss of head
to shoulder
a forceful kicking
twitching leg
quick glance through the pages
of a pass-
port
taut tug
at the hand of a fearful child

and
on
the
other
side
the
sheep
serene

a few there
look like us
here
but this is clearly where
you separate the sheep
from the goats

at the desk
the officer's eyes
proclaim
a cold dislike of goats,
so throats are cleared
for bleating

this is where one begins
to learn
new speaking

when he stamped my pass
I looked down expecting to see
SHEEP

some goats who had tried to wear
sheep's clothing
had been discovered
un-masked
sat silent now along a wall
awaiting return to their pasture

this is where you
separate
the sheep
from the goats

tomorrow
I must write my mother.

C. L. R. JAMES

C. L. R. James, historian, novelist, cultural critic and political activist, was born in Port of Spain, Trinidad, in 1901. He came to Britain in 1932 to help his friend Learie Constantine write his autobiography. He became cricket correspondent of the *Manchester Guardian* and the *Glasgow Herald*. During this period, he was a central figure in the Pan-African movement. In 1958, he returned to Trinidad to take part in the preparations for colonial emancipation he had advocated for a quarter of a century. C.L.R. then returned to London where he died in 1989. He is the acknowledged grandfather of the Caribbean novel and critical writing, and his many extraordinary writings include his famous study of the Haitian revolution, *The Black Jacobins*, *Minty Alley*, *Nkrumah*, *The Ghana Revolution* and three volumes of selected writings – *The Future in the Present*, *Spheres of Existence* and *At the Rendezvous of Victory*.

Beyond a Boundary, from which the essay 'What is Art?' is taken, is generally perceived to be one of the greatest sport books ever written. C.L.R. used his love for and fascination with cricket to explore the wider political, cultural and social relationship between Empire and the West Indies.

from *Beyond a Boundary*
What is Art?

I have made great claims for cricket. As firmly as I am able and as is here possible, I have integrated it in the historical movement of the times. The question remains: what is it? Is it mere entertainment or is it an art? Mr Neville Cardus (whose work deserves a critical study) is here most illuminating, not as subject but as object. He will ask: 'Why do we deny the art of a cricketer, and rank it lower than a vocalist's or a fiddler's? If anybody tells me that R. H. Spooner did not compel a pleasure as aesthetic as any compelled by the most cultivated Italian tenor that ever lived I will write him down a purist and an ass.' He says the same in more than one place. More than any sententious declaration, all his work is eloquent with the aesthetic appeal of cricket. Yet he can write in his autobiography: 'I do not believe that anything fine in music or in anything else can be understood or truly felt by the crowd.' Into this he goes at length and puts the seal on it with 'I don't believe in the contemporary idea of taking the arts to the people: let them seek and work for them.' He himself notes that Neville Cardus, the writer on cricket, often introduces music into his cricket writing. Never once has Neville Cardus, the music critic, introduced cricket into his writing on music. He finds this 'a curious point'. It is much more than a point, it is not curious. Cardus is a victim of that categorization and specialization, that division of the human personality, which is the greatest curse of our time. Cricket has suffered, but not only cricket. The aestheticians have scorned to take notice of popular sports and games – to their own detriment. The aridity and confusion of which they so mournfully complain will continue until they include organized games *and the people who watch them* as an integral part of their data. Sir Donald Bradman's technical accomplishments are not on the same plane as those of Yehudi Menuhin. Sir John Gielgud in three hours can express adventures and shades in human personality which are not approached in three years of Denis Compton at the wicket. Yet cricket is an art, not a bastard or a poor relation, but a full member of the community.

The approach must be direct. Too long has it been impressionistic or apologetic, timid or defiant, always ready to take refuge in the mysticism of metaphor. It is a game and we have to compare it with other games. It is an art and we have to compare it with other arts.

Cricket is first and foremost a dramatic spectacle. It belongs with the theatre, ballet, opera and the dance.

In a superficial sense all games are dramatic. Two men boxing or running a race can exhibit skill, courage, endurance and sharp changes of fortune; can evoke hope and fear. They can even harrow the soul with laughter and tears, pity and terror. The state of the city, the nation or the world can invest a sporting event with dramatic intensity such as is reached in few theatres. When the democrat Joe Louis fought the Nazi Schmelling the bout became a focus of approaching world conflict. On the last morning of the 1953 Oval Test, when it was clear that England would win a rubber against Australia after twenty years, the nation stopped work to witness the consummation.

These possibilities cricket shares with other games in a greater or lesser degree. Its quality as drama is more specific. It is so organized that at all times it is compelled to reproduce the central action which characterizes all good drama from the days of the Greeks to our own: two individuals are pitted against each other in a conflict that is strictly personal but no less strictly representative of a social group. One individual batsman faces one individual bowler. But each represents his side. The personal achievement may be of the utmost competence or brilliance. Its ultimate value is whether it assists the side to victory or staves off defeat. This has nothing to do with morals. It is the organizational structure on which the whole spectacle is built. The dramatist, the novelist, the choreographer, must *strive* to make his individual character symbolical of a larger whole. He may or may not succeed. The runner in a relay race must take the plus or minus that his partner or partners give him. The soccer forward and the goalkeeper may at certain rare moments find themselves sole representatives of their sides. Even the baseball-batter, who most nearly approaches this particular aspect of cricket, may and often does find himself after a fine hit standing on one of the bases, where he is now dependent upon others. The batsman facing the ball does not merely represent his side. For that moment, to all intents and purposes, he is his side. This fundamental relation of the One and the Many, Individual and Social, Individual and Universal, leader and followers, representative and ranks, the part and the whole, is structurally imposed on the players of cricket. What other sports, games and arts have to aim at, the players are given to start with, they cannot depart from it. Thus the game is founded upon a dramatic, a human, relation which is universally recognized as the most objectively pervasive and psychologically stimulating in life and therefore in that artificial representation of it which is drama.

The second major consideration in all dramatic spectacles is the relation between event (or, if you prefer, contingency) and design, episode and continuity, diversity in unity, the battle and the campaign, the part and the whole. Here also cricket is structurally perfect. The total spectacle consists and must consist of a series of individual, isolated episodes, each in itself completely self-contained. Each has its beginning, the ball bowled; its middle, the stroke played; its end, runs, no runs, dismissal. Within the fluctuating interest of the rise or fall of the game as a whole, there is this unending series of events, each single one fraught with immense possibilities of expectation and realization. Here again the dramatist or movie director has to strive. In the very finest of soccer matches the ball for long periods is in places where it is impossible to expect any definite alteration in the relative position of the two sides. In lawn tennis the duration of the rally is entirely dependent upon the subjective skill of the players. In baseball alone does the encounter between the two representative protagonists approach the definitiveness of the individual series of episodes in cricket which together constitute the whole.

The structural enforcement of the fundamental appeals which all dramatic spectacle must have is of incalculable value to the spectator. The glorious uncertainty of the game is not anarchy. It would not be glorious if it were not so firmly anchored in the certainties which must attend all successful drama. That is why cricket is perhaps the only game in which the end result (except where national or local pride is at stake) is not of great importance. Appreciation of cricket has little to do with the end, and less still with what are called 'the finer points', of the game. What matters in cricket, as in all the arts, is not finer points but what everyone with some knowledge of the elements can see and feel. It is only within such a rigid structural frame that the individuality so characteristic of cricket can flourish. Two batsmen are in at the same time. Thus the position of representative of the side, though strictly independent, is interchangeable. In baseball one batter bats at a time. The isolated events of which both games consist is in baseball rigidly limited. The batter is allowed choice of three balls. He must hit the third or he is out. If he hits he must run. The batter's place in the batting order is fixed – it cannot be changed. The pitcher must pitch until he is taken off and when he is taken off he is finished for that game. (The Americans obviously prefer it that way.) In cricket the bowler bowls six balls (or eight). He can then be taken off and can be brought on again. He can bowl at the other end. The batting order is interchangeable. Thus while the principle of an individual representing the side at any given moment is maintained, the utmost possible change of personnel compatible with order is allowed. We tend to take these things for granted or not to notice them at all. In what other dramatic spectacle can they be found built-in? The greatness of the great batsman is not so much in his own skill as that he sets in motion all the immense possibilities that are contained in the game as structurally organized.

Cricket, of course, does not allow that representation or suggestion of specific relations as can be done by a play or even by ballet and dance. The players are always players trafficking in the elemental human activities, qualities and emotions – attack, defence, courage, gallantry, steadfastness, grandeur, ruse. This is no drawback. Punch and Judy, *Swan Lake*, pantomime, are even less particularized than cricket. They depend for their effect upon the technical skill and creative force with which their exponents make the ancient patterns live for their contemporaries. Some of the best beloved and finest music is created out of just such elemental sensations. We never grow out of them, of the need to renew them. Any art which by accident or design gets too far from them finds that it has to return or wither. They are the very stuff of human life. It is of this stuff that the drama of cricket is composed.

If the drama is very limited in range and intricacy there are advantages. These need not be called compensating, but they should not be ignored. The long hours (which so irritates those who crave continuous excitation), the measured ritualism and the varied and intensive physical activity which take place within it, these strip the players of conventional aspects, and human personality is on view long enough and in sufficiently varied form to register itself indelibly. I mention only a few – the lithe grace and elegance of Kardar leading his team on to the field; the unending flow of linear rhythm by which Evans accommodated himself to returns from the field; the dignity which radiates from every motion of Frank Worrell; the magnificence and magnanimity of Keith Miller. There are movie stars, world-famous and rightly so, who mumble words and go through motions which neither they nor their audience care very much about. Their appeal is themselves, how they walk, how they move, how they do anything or nothing, so long as they are themselves and their particular quality shines through. Here a Keith Miller met a Clark Gable on equal terms.

The dramatic content of cricket I have purposely pitched low – I am concerned not with degree but kind. In addition to being a dramatic, cricket is also a visual art. This I do not pitch low at all. The whole issue will be settled here.

The aestheticians of painting, especially the modern ones, are the great advocates of 'significant form', the movement of the line, the relations of colour and tone. Of these critics, the most consistent, the clearest (and the most widely accepted), that I know is the late Mr Bernard Berenson. Over sixty years ago in his studies of the Italian Renaissance painters he expounded his aesthetic with refreshing clarity. The merely accurate representation of an object, the blind imitation of nature, was not art, not even if that object was what would commonly be agreed upon as beautiful, for example a beautiful woman. There was another category of painter superior to the first. Such a one would not actually reproduce the object as it was. Being a man of vision and imagination, the object would stimulate in him impulses, thoughts, memories visually creative. These he would fuse into a whole and the result would be not so much the object as the totality of the visual image which the object had evoked in a superior mind. That, too, Mr Berenson excluded from the category of true art (and was by no means isolated in doing so): mere reproduction of 200 objects, whether actually in existence or the product of the sublimest imaginations, was 'literature' or 'illustration'. What then was the truly artistic? The truly artistic was a quality that existed in its own right, irrespective of the object represented. It was the line, the curve, its movement, the drama it embodied as painting, the linear design, the painterly tones and values taken as a whole: this constituted the specific quality of visual art. Mr Berenson did not rank colour very high; the head of a statue (with its human expression) he could usually dispense with. It was the form as such which was significant.

Mr Berenson was not at all cloudy or mystifying. He distinguished two qualities which could be said to constitute the significance of the form in its most emphatic manifestation.

The first he called 'tactile values'. The idea of tactile values could be most clearly grasped by observing the manner in which truly great artists rendered the nude human body. They so posed their figures, they manipulated, arranged, shortened, lengthened, foreshortened, they so articulated the movements of the joints that they stimulated the tactile consciousness of the viewer, his specially artistic sense. This significance in the form gave a higher coefficient of reality to the object represented. Not that such a painting looked more real, made the object more lifelike. That was not Mr Berenson's point. Significant form makes the painting life-giving, life-enhancing, *to the viewer*. Significant form, or 'decoration', to use his significant personal term, sets off physical processes in the spectator which give to him a far greater sense of the objective reality before him than would a literal representation, however accurate.* Mr Berenson does not

---

* If I do Mr Berenson any injustice it can be corrected in the reprint of his history, third edition, 1954, and his *Des Arts Visuels* (Esthétique et Histoire), Paris, 1953, where the original thesis is restated. (I am not being pedantic. In these metaphysical matters you can misplace a comma and be thereby liable to ten thousand words of aesthetic damnation.)

deny that an interesting subject skilfully presented in human terms can be interesting as illustration. He does not deny that such illustration can enhance significant form. But it is the form that matters. Mr John Berger of the *New Statesman*, ardent propagandist of socialist realism in art, claims that what is really significant in Michelangelo is his bounding line. The abstract artists get rid of the object altogether and represent only the abstract form, the line and relations of line. If I understand Mr Berger aright he claims that all the great representational paintings of the past live and have lived only to the degree that their form is significant – that, however, is merely to repeat Mr Berenson.

The second characteristic of significant form in Mr Berenson's aesthetic is the sense of 'movement'.

We have so far been wandering in chambers where as cricketers we are not usually guests. Fortunately, the aesthetic vision now focuses on territory not too far distant from ours. In his analysis of 'movement' Mr Berenson discussed the artistic possibilities and limitations of an athletic event, a wrestling match. His exposition seems designed for cricket and cricketers, and therefore must be reproduced in full.

> Although a wrestling match may, in fact, contain many genuinely artistic elements, our enjoyment of it can never be quite artistic: we are prevented from completely realizing it not only by our dramatic interest in the game, but also, granting the possibility of being devoid of dramatic interest, by the succession of movements being too rapid for us to realize each completely, and too fatiguing, even if realizable. Now if a way could be found of conveying to us the realization of movement without the confusion and the fatigue of the actuality, we should be getting out of the wrestlers more than they themselves can give us – the heightening of vitality which comes to us whenever we keenly realize life, such as the actuality itself would give us, *plus* the greater effectiveness of the heightening brought about by the clearer, intenser and less fatiguing realization.
>
> This is precisely what the artist who succeeds in representing movement achieves: making us realize it as we never can actually, he gives us a heightened sense of capacity, and whatever is in the actuality enjoyable, he allows us to enjoy at our leisure. In words already familiar to us, he *extracts the significance of*

movements, just as, in rendering tactile values, the artist extracts the corporal significance of objects. His task is, however, far more difficult, although less indispensable: it is not enough that he should extract the values of what at any given moment is an actuality, as is an object, but what at no moment really is – namely, movement. He can accomplish his task in only one way, and that is by so rendering the one particular movement that we shall be able to realize all other movements that the same figure may make. 'He is grappling with his enemy now,' I say of my wrestler. 'What a pleasure to be able to realize in my own muscles, on my own chest, with my own arms and legs, the life that is in him as he is making his supreme effort! What a pleasure, as I look away from the representation, to realize in the same manner, how after the contest his muscles will relax, and the rest trickle like a refreshing stream through his nerves!' All this I shall be made to enjoy by the artist who, in representing any one movement, can give me the logical sequence of visible strain and pressure in the parts and muscles.

Now here all of us, cricketers and aesthetics, are on familiar ground. I submit that cricket does in fact contain genuinely artistic elements, infinitely surpassing those to be found in wrestling matches. In fact it can be said to comprise most of those to be found in all other games.

I submit further that the abiding charm of cricket is that the game has been so organized that the realization of movement is completely conveyed despite the confusion and fatigue of actuality.

I submit finally that without the intervention of any artist the spectator at cricket extracts the significance of movement and of tactile values. He experiences the heightened sense of capacity. Furthermore, however the purely human element, the literature, the illustration, in cricket may enhance the purely artistic appeal, the significant form at its most unadulterated is permanently present. It is known, expected, recognized and enjoyed by tens of thousands of spectators. Cricketers call it style.

From the beginning of the modern game this quality of style has been abstracted and established in its own right, irrespective of results, human element, dramatic element, anything whatever except itself. It is, if you will, pure decoration. Thus we read of a player a hundred years ago that he was elegance, all elegance, fit to play before the Queen in her parlour. We read of another that he was not equal to W.G. except in style, where he surpassed The Champion. In *Wisden* of 1891 A. G. Steel, a great player, a great judge of the game and, like so many of those days, an excellent writer, leaves no loophole through which form can escape into literature:

> The last-named batsman, when the bowling was very accurate, was a slow scorer, but always a treat to watch. If the present generation of stone-wall cricketers, such as Scotton, Hall, Barlow, A. Bannerman, nay even Shrewsbury, possessed such beautiful ease of style the tens of thousands that used to frequent the beautiful Australian ground would still flock there, instead of the hundred or two patient gazers on feats of Job-like patience that now attend.

In 1926 H. L. Collins batted five hours for forty runs to save the Manchester Test and Richard Binns wrote a long essay to testify among much else that Collins was never dull because of his beautiful style. There is debate about style. Steel's definition clears away much cumbersome litter about left shoulder forward and straight bat: 'no flourish, but the maximum of power with the minimum of exertion'. If the free-swinging off-drive off the front foot has been challenged by the angular jerk through the covers off the back foot, this last is not at all alien to the generation which has experienced Cubism in posters and newspaper advertisements.

We are accustomed in cricket to speak of beauty. The critics of art are contemptuous of the word. Let us leave it aside and speak of the style that is common to the manifold motions of the great players, or most of them. There are few picture galleries in the world which effectively reproduce a fraction of them – I am sticking to form and eschewing literature and illustration. These motions are not caught and permanently fixed for us to make repeated visits to them. They are repeated often enough to become a permanent possession of the spectator which he can renew at will. And having held our own with the visitor from the higher spheres, I propose to take the offensive.

And I first meet Mr Berenson on his own ground, so to speak. Here is John Arlott, whose written descriptions of cricket matches I prefer to all others, describing the bowling action of Maurice Tate:

> You would hardly have called Maurice Tate's physique graceful, yet his bowling action remains – and not only for me – as

lovely a piece of movement as even cricket has ever produced. He had strong, but sloping shoulders; a deep chest, fairly long arms and – essential to the pace bowler – broad feet to take the jolt of the delivery stride and wide hips to cushion it. His run-in, eight accelerating and lengthening strides, had a hint of scramble about it at the beginning, but by the eighth stride and well before his final leap, it seemed as if his limbs were gathered together in one glorious wheeling unity. He hoisted his left arm until it was pointing straight upwards, while his right hand, holding the ball, seemed to counterpoise it at the opposite pole. Meanwhile, his body, edge-wise on to the batsman, had swung its weight back on to the right foot: his back curved so that, from the other end, you might see the side of his head jutting out, as it were, from behind his left arm. Then his bowling arm came over and his body turned; he released the ball at the top of his arm-swing, with a full flick of the wrist, and then plunged through, body bending into that earth-tearing, final stride and pulling away to the off side.

All these things the textbook will tell you to do: yet no one has ever achieved so perfectly a co-ordination and exploitation of wrist, shoulders, waist, legs and feet as Maurice Tate did. It was as if bowling had been implanted in him at birth, and came out – as the great arts come out – after due digestion, at that peak of greatness which is not created – but only confirmed – by instruction.

Because most people think always of batting when they think of cricket as a visual art another description of a bowler in action will help to correct the unbalance.

From two walking paces Lindwall glides into the thirteen running strides which have set the world a model for rhythmic gathering of momentum for speed-giving power. Watching him approach the wicket, Sir Pelham Warner was moved to murmur one word, 'Poetry!'

The poetry of motion assumes dramatic overtones in the last couple of strides. A high-lifted left elbow leads Lindwall to the line. The metal plate on his right toe-cap drags through the turf and across the bowling crease as his prancing left foot thrusts directly ahead of it, to land beyond the popping crease. This side-on stretch brings every ounce of his thirteen stone into play as his muscular body tows his arm over for the final fling that shakes his shirtsleeve out of its fold. In two more strides his wheeling follow-through has taken him well to the side of the pitch. Never had plunging force and science formed so deadly an alliance.

We may note in passing that the technique of watching critically, i.e. with a conception of all the factors that have contributed to the result, can be as highly developed and needs as many years of training in cricket as in the arts. But I do not want to emphasize that here.

What is to be emphasized is that whereas in the fine arts the image of tactile values and movement, however effective, however magnificent, is permanent, fixed, in cricket the spectator sees the image constantly re-created, and whether he is a cultivad spectator or not, has standards which he carries with him always. He can re-create them at will. He can go to see a game hoping and expecting to see the image re-created or even extended. You can stop an automobile to watch a casual game and see a batsman, for ever to be unknown, cutting in a manner that recalls the greatest exponents of one of the most difficult movements in cricket. Sometimes it is a total performance branching out in many directions by a single player who stamps all he does with the hallmark of an individual style – a century by Hutton or Compton or Sobers. It can be and often is a particular image – Hammond's drive through the covers. The image can be a single stroke, made on a certain day, which has been seen and never forgotten. There are some of these the writer has carried in his consciousness for over forty years, some in fact longer, as is described in the first pages of this book. On the business of setting off physical processes and evoking a sense of movement in the spectator, followers of Mr Berenson's classification would do well to investigate the responses of cricket spectators. The theory may be thereby enriched, or may be seen to need enrichment. To the eye of a cricketer it seems pretty thin.

It may seem that I am squeezing every drop out of a quite casual illustration extracted from Mr Berenson's more comprehensive argument. That is not so. Any acquaintances with his work will find that he lavishes his most enthusiastic praise on *Hercules Strangling Antaeus* by Pollaiuolo, and the same artist's *David Striding Over the Head of the Slain Goliath*. In more than one place *The Gods Shooting [arrows] at a Mark* and the *Hercules Struggling With a Lion*, drawings by

Michelangelo, are shown to be for him the ultimate yet reached in the presentation of tactile values and sense of movement, with the consequent life-giving and life-enhancing stimulation of the spectator. Mr Berenson, in the books I have mentioned, nowhere analyses this momentous fact: the enormous role that elemental physical action plays in the visual arts throughout the centuries, at least until our own. Why should he believe that Michelangelo's projected painting of the soldiers surprised when bathing would have produced the greatest masterpiece of figure art in modern times? I have been suggesting an answer by implication in describing what W.G. brought from pre-Victorian England to the modern age. I shall now state it plainly.

If we stick to cricket it is not because of any chauvinism. The analysis will apply to all games. After a thorough study of bull-fighting in Spain, Ernest Haas, the famous photographer, does not ignore the violence, the blood, the hovering presence of death, the illustration. Aided by his camera, his conclusion is: 'The bull fight is pure art. The spectacle is all motion . . . Motion, the perfection of motion, is what the people come to see. They come hoping that this bull-fight will produce the perfect flow of motion.' Another name for the perfect flow of motion is style, or, if you will, significant form.

Let us examine this motion, or, as Mr Berenson calls it, movement. Where the motive and directing force rests with the single human being, an immense variety of physical motion is embraced within four categories. A human being places himself physically in some relation of contact or avoidance (or both) with another human being, with an animal, an inanimate object, or two or more of these. He may extend the reach and force of his arms or feet with a tool or device of some kind. He propels a missile. He runs, skips, jumps, dives, to attain some objective which he has set himself or others have set for him. In sport there is not much else that he can do, and in our world human beings are on view for artistic enjoyment only on the field of sport or on the entertainment stage. In sport cricket leads the field. The motions of a batter in baseball, a player of lawn tennis, hockey, golf, all their motions added together do not attain the sum of a batsman's. The batsman can shape to hit practically round the points of the compass. He can play a dead bat, pat for a single, drive along the ground; he can skim the infielders; he can lift over their heads; he can clear the boundary. He can cut square with all the force of his wrists, arms and shoulders, or cut late with a touch as delicate as a feather. He can hit to long-leg with all his force or simply deflect with a single motion. He can do most of these off the front foot or the back. Many of them he can do with no or little departure from his original stance. The articulation of his limbs is often enough quite visible, as in the use of the wrists when cutting or hooking. What is not visible is received in the tactile consciousness of thousands who have themselves for years practised the same motion and know each muscle that is involved in each stroke. And all this infinite variety is from one base, stable and fixed, so that each motion in its constituent parts can be observed in its detail and in its entirety from start to finish.

The batsman propels a missile with a tool. The bowler does the same unaided. Within the narrow territory legally allowed to him there is, as Mr Arlott on Tate has shown, a surprising variety of appeal. He may bowl a slow curve or fast or medium, or he may at his pleasure use each in turn. There have been many bowlers whose method of delivery has seemed to spectators the perfection of form, irrespective of the fate which befell the balls bowled. Here, far more than in batting, the repetition conveys the realization of movement despite the actuality. Confusion is excluded by the very structure of the game.

As for the fieldsmen, there is no limit whatever to their possibilities of running, diving, leaping, falling forward, backwards, sideways, with all their energies concentrated on a specific objective, the whole completely realizable by the alert spectator. The spontaneous outburst of thousands at a fierce hook or a dazzling slip-catch, the ripple of recognition at a long-awaited leg-glance, are as genuine and deeply felt expressions of artistic emotion as any I know.

You will have noted that the four works of art chosen by Mr Berenson to illustrate movement all deal with some physical action of the athletic kind. Mr Berenson calls the physical process of response mystical.* There I refuse to go along any further, not even for the

---

* Mr Berenson's aesthetics do not by any means exhaust the subject. Mr Adrian Stokes, for example, on Michelangelo, is suggestive of much that is stimulating to any enquiry into the less obvious origins of a game like cricket. Further I find it strange that (as far as I know) so ardent an apostle of mass culture and non-representational art as Sir Herbert Read has never probed into the question whether the physical modes so beloved by Michelangelo and the physical movements of popular sports and games so beloved by millions do not appeal to the 'collective unconscious' more powerfully than the esoteric forms of, for example, Mr Henry Moore. The difficulty here, it seems to me, is not merely the habit of categorizing into higher and lower. The aesthetics of cricket demand first that you master the game, and, preferably, have played it, if not well, at least in good company. And that is not the easy acquisition outsiders think it to be.

purpose of discussion. The mystical is the last refuge, if refuge it is. Cricket, in fact any ball game, to the visual image adds the sense of physical co-ordination, of harmonious action, of timing. The visual image of a diving fieldsman is a frame for his rhythmic contact with the flying ball. Here two art forms meet.

I believe that the examination of the stroke, the brilliant piece of fielding, will take us through mysticism to far more fundamental considerations than mere life-enhancing. We respond to physical action or vivid representation of it, dead or alive, because we are made that way. For unknown centuries survival for us, like all other animals, depended upon competent and effective physical activity. This played its part in developing the brain. The particular nature which became ours did not rest satisfied with this. If it had it could never have become human. The use of the hand, the extension of its powers by the tool, the propulsion of a missile at some objective and the accompanying refinements of the mechanics of judgment, these marked us off from the animals. Language may have come at the same time. The evolution may have been slow or rapid. The end result was a new species which preserved the continuity of its characteristics and its way of life. Sputnik can be seen as no more than a missile made and projected through tools by the developed hand.

Similarly the eye for the line which is today one of the marks of ultimate aesthetic refinement is not new. It is old. The artists of the caves of Altamira had it. So did the bushmen. They had it to such a degree that they could reproduce it or, rather, represent it with unsurpassed force. Admitting this, Mr Berenson confines the qualities of this primitive art to animal energy and an exasperated vitality. That, even if true, is totally subordinate to the fact that among these primitive peoples the sense of form existed to the degree that it could be consciously and repeatedly reproduced. It is not a gift of high civilization, the last achievement of noble minds. It is exactly the opposite. The use of sculpture and design among primitive peoples indicates that the significance of the form is a common possession. Children have it. There is no need to adduce further evidence for the presupposition that the faculty or faculties by which we recognize significant form in elemental physical action is native to us, a part of the process by which we have become and remain human. It is neither more nor less mystical than any other of our faculties of apprehension. Neither do I see an 'exasperated vitality' in the work of the primitive artists. The impression I get is that the line was an integral part of co-ordinated physical activity, functional perhaps, but highly refined in that upon it food or immediate self-preservation might depend.

Innate faculty though it might be, the progress of civilization can leave it unused, suppress its use, can remove us from the circumstance in which it is associated with animal energy. Developing civilization can surround us with circumstances and conditions in which our original faculties are debased or refined, made more simple or more complicated. They may seem to disappear altogether. They remain part of our human endowment. The basic motions of cricket represent physical action which has been the basis not only of primitive but of civilized life for countless centuries. In work and in play they were the motions by which men lived and without which they would perish. The Industrial Revolution transformed our existence. Our fundamental characteristic as human beings it did not and could not alter. The bushmen reproduced in one medium not merely animals but the line, the curve, the movement. It supplied in the form they needed a vision of the life they lived. The Hambledon men who made modern cricket did the same. The bushmen's motive was perhaps religious, Hambledon's entertainment. One form was fixed, the other had to be constantly re-created. The contrasts can be multiplied. That will not affect the underlying identity. Each fed the need to satisfy the visual artistic sense. The emphasis on style in cricket proves that without a shadow of doubt; whether the impulse was literature and the artistic quality the result, or vice-versa, does not matter. If the Hambledon form was infinitely more complicated it rose out of a more complicated society, the result of a long historical development. Satisfying the same needs as bushmen and Hambledon, the industrial age took over cricket and made it into what it has become. The whole tortured history of modern Spain explains why it is in the cruelty of the bull-ring that they seek the perfect flow of motion. That flow, however, men since they have been men have always sought and always will. It is an unspeakable impertinence to arrogate the term 'fine art' to one small section of this quest and declare it to be culture. Luckily, the people refuse to be bothered. This does not alter the gross falsification of history and the perversion of values which is the result.

Lucian's Solon tells what the Olympic Games meant to the Greeks. The human drama, the literature, was as important to them as to us. No less so was the line, the curve, the movement of the athletes which inspired one of the greatest artistic creations we have ever known – Greek sculpture. To this day certain statues baffle the experts: are they statues of Apollo or are they statues of athletes? The games and sculpture were 'good' arts and popular. The newly fledged democracy found them insufficient. The contrast between life under an ancient landed aristocracy and an ancient democratic regime was enormous. It can be guessed at by what the democracy actually achieved. The democracy did not neglect the games or sculpture. To the contrary. The birth of democracy saw the birth of individualism in sculpture. Immense new passions and immense new forces had been released. New relations between the individual and society, between individual and individual, launched life on new, exciting and dangerous ways. Out of this came the tragic drama. After a long look at how the creation of the Hambledon men became the cornerstone of Victorian education and entertainment, I can no longer accept that Peisistratus encouraged the dramatic festival as a means of satisfying or appeasing or distracting the urban masses on their way to democracy. That would be equivalent to saying that the rulers of Victorian England encouraged cricket to satisfy or appease or distract the urban masses on their way to democracy. The Victorian experience with cricket suggests a line of investigation on the alert for signs both more subtle and more tortuous. It may be fruitful to investigate whether Peisistratus and his fellow rulers did not need the drama for themselves before it became a national festival. That at any rate is what happened to the Victorians.

The elements which were transformed into Greek drama may have existed in primitive form, quite apart from religious ceremonial – there is even a tradition that peasants played primitive dramas. However that may be, the newly fledged Greek democrat found his need for a fuller existence fulfilled in the tragic drama. He had no spate of books to give him distilled, concentrated and ordered views of life. The old myths no longer sufficed. The drama recast them to satisfy the expanded personality. The end of democracy is a more complete existence. Voting and political parties are only a means. The expanded personality and needs of the Victorian aspiring to democracy did not need drama. The stage, books, newspapers, were part of his inheritance. The production of these for democracy had already begun. What he needed was the further expansion of his aesthetic sense. Print had long made church walls and public monuments obsolescent as a means of social communication. Photography would complete the rout of painting and sculpture, promoting them upstairs. The need was filled by organized games.

Cricket was fortunate in that for their own purposes the British ruling classes took it over and endowed it with money and prestige. On it men of gifts which would have been remarkable in any sphere expended their powers – the late C. B. Fry was a notable example. Yet even he submitted to the prevailing aesthetic categories and circumscribed cricket as a 'physical' fine art. There is no need so to limit it. It is limited in variety of range, of subject-matter. It cannot express the emotions of an age on the nature of the last judgement or the wiping out of a population by bombing. It must repeat. But what it repeats is the original stuff out of which everything visually or otherwise artistic is quarried. The popular democracy of Greece, sitting for days in the sun watching *The Oresteia*; the popular democracy of our day, sitting similarly, watching Miller and Lindwall bowl to Hutton and Compton – each in its own way grasps at a more complete human existence. We may some day be able to answer Tolstoy's exasperated and exasperating question: 'What is art?' – but only when we learn to integrate our vision of Walcott on the back foot through the covers with the outstretched arm of the Olympic Apollo.

GRACE NICHOLS

Grace Nichols was born and educated in Georgetown, Guyana, but has lived in Britain since 1977. She won the Commonwealth Poetry Prize in 1983 with her first collection of poems, *I is a Long-memoried Woman*. Since then she has read and performed her poetry widely, as well as published a number of other books, including *The Fat Black Woman's Poems*, *Lazy Thoughts of a Lazy Woman*, and her first novel, *Whole of a Morning Sky*. She lives in Sussex.

'Wings' is taken from *Sunris*, her latest collection of poems, which spans continents and histories.

Wings

(For John Figueroa, Jamaican poet.

Inspired by his comment that as Caribbean people we're preoccupied with Roots, when maybe we should be signifying ourselves by Wings – 'Out of the Margins Festival', South Bank, London 1993)

Consigned to earth
we thought it fitting
to worship only
the sustenance of our roots,
so that when uprootment came
in its many guises
we moved around like
bereaving trees, constantly touching
our sawn-off places.

And though we pretended to be
bright migrant birds
it was always an inward yearning
for the compelling earth

of our roots – lost Africas, Indias,
then the love-tugging land
of our immediate birthmothers.
Past more poignant
than any future.

Root-lovers
Root-grounders
Root-worshippers,
We've been
old hoarding mourners,
constantly counting
our sea-chest of losses,
forgetting the other end
of our green extremis –
the imperishable gift of our wings.

But wasn't it wings
that made our ancestors
climb the airy staircase
whenever they contemplated
rock and a hard place?

And isn't it wings, our own wilful wings,
still taking us into migratory-pull
still taking us into homing-instinct,
beating up the winds
to find our respective heavens?

And even if we stay
blissfully or unblissfully still,
in sun-eye or snowflake-kiss
it's still wings taking us back
to the bigger presence of wings.

Wings over women
beating clothes on stones
resting faith on river-water
and the soapless transfiguration
of clothes.

Wings over my sacred village road,
dust bringing sandflies,
candleflies
and Jordanites,
dark as their robes were white,
religious man-moths, hobnobbing
around scriptures by gaslight.

Wings over my mother
who leaned on light
who could make a meal
from love alone in no time

Wings over the unpainted little shack
of my nextdoor neighbour,
shaking with music and laughter
on the christening of his baby daughter,
the amplifiers and loudspeaker
he's erected outside, proclaiming him King,
everything threatening to take off
in tradewind.

Wings over my hardpressed sister,
who, when I went back home,
flew around, gathering a get-together,
a flocking of family, friends, neighbours,
food, singing, all determined
to send me (wet-eyed grateful sinner)
flying high 'wid dih gift of dih holy fire'

And wings over you, John,
for your white-bearded
and timely reminder
of our wings.

BUCHI EMECHETA

Buchi Emecheta was born in 1944 in Lagos, Nigeria, of Ibusa parentage. A graduate in sociology from London University, she has been a teacher, librarian and community worker. She has written many novels, including *In the Ditch*, *The Bride Price*, *The Slave Girl* and *The Joys of Motherhood*. She also writes poetry, plays, essays and books for children. Since 1962, Buchi has lived in London with her five children.

Second-Class Citizen follows young and clever Adah, who leaves her cushy librarian job to come to London to join her husband, Francis, who is already studying there. But Francis turns out to be cold and cruel, offering little support and sapping her confidence. She rapidly gives birth to a brood of children, as she struggles to work and provide for them and her husband, who sits one unsuccessful exam after another. At her lowest ebb, she discovers her voice through writing and begins the long walk back to independence. In the following extract, Adah describes her friendship with Janet and her struggle to find reliable childcare provision.

from *Second-Class Citizen*

At about this time she met and became friendly with a Cockney girl called Janet.

Janet was Mr Babalola's wife. Her story was not only remarkable, but startling as well.

Mr Babalola had come to England, just like Francis and Adah, to study, but, unlike Adah and Francis, he had been single, and had a Northern Nigerian Scholarship. This meant that he had more money to spend, because the Northerners, unlike the over-educated Southerners, would do anything to encourage the men to really get educated so that they could come home and obtain the jobs in the North which were then going to the Southerners. Mr Babalola was, therefore, a very rich student.

Rumour had it that he had a glossy flat and was always entertaining. This was no surprise to anyone who knew the Northerners. They liked to spend their money, to really enjoy what they had, and to them what they had was theirs only today, not tomorrow or the day after. Allah would take care of the future. That was certainly Babalola's philosophy of life.

For some reason, however, the money for Mr Babalola stopped coming, no one knew why. One thing was sure, he was not doing any studying, though he had come originally to read journalism. Word went round that he was getting poor. He could not maintain his old level of entertainment, so his friends of the happier days took to their heels. They stopped coming and Babalola moved to a much more modest area – Ashdown Street in Kentish Town.

It was at this time, when his funds were running low and he was desperately trying to convince his government that, given another opportunity, he would do well, that he met Janet.

He was waiting impatiently at a telephone kiosk to make a call to one of his now elusive friends. He waited for what seemed ages, but the young woman already in the kiosk seemed to clutch at the receiver for hours. Many others came, got tired of waiting and left, grumbling. But Babalola waited. He was going to make his call, even if it took him all day. It started to drizzle and he was getting soaked to the skin, so he banged on the kiosk door, and shook his fist at the girl to frighten her. Then he looked closer, and saw that the girl was not phoning anybody, she was asleep, standing up.

Babalola's first reaction was fear. Was she dead, he wondered? Then he banged harder and the girl woke. He was so sorry for her that he took her home.

Janet was pregnant. The father of her baby was a nameless West Indian. Her stepfather would not take her in unless she promised to give the child away. Her mother had died a year before, leaving her stepfather seven young children to look after. Janet was the oldest, so she had been turned out of the house. She would not go to any social worker; all he would do would be to convince her that, at the age of sixteen, she was too young to keep her baby. But Janet wanted her baby.

This story awakened the communal African spirit in Babalola. It never occurred to him that he was doing anything illegal, taking in a sixteen-year-old girl. On the contrary, Babalola started to entertain his few remaining friends with Janet. It never occurred to him that he might fall in love with her, that he might want to protect her, to make her his wife; at that time, Janet was being offered to any black man who wanted to know how a white woman looked undressed. Most of

Adah's neighbours had had their sexual adventures with Janet. But soon all that changed.

Babalola realized that Janet could get dole money for herself and her child, enough to pay the rent. Janet, not knowing where else to go and also, like Adah, coming to terms with Babalola's weaknesses, complied. Soon Babalola started to monopolize Janet.

'You are not thinking of going straight with that thing you picked up at a kiosk?' his friends asked, astonished.

Babalola said nothing, but gave orders to Janet to stop being liberal with his friends any more. Janet, feeling wanted at last, glowed. Soon after her first baby, she became pregnant with her second, Babalola's.

It was at this time that Adah arrived. They became friends straight away. Adah found Janet very intelligent and realized that the rumours about her sleeping around were not true. She only wanted a roof over her head so that she could bring up her little boy, Tony. He was then a noisy eighteen-month-old baby who was a good playmate for Titi.

Adah told Janet about her troubles and Janet confided in Adah. She suggested that Adah should look for a daily minder for her children until the nursery had vacancies for them. Even Babalola was willing to help – by now he had become unpopular with his friends because he refused to hand his 'fish and chips' girl around. The search was really depressing. It reached a point where Adah had started knocking on door after door. Things got even worse for her when Francis failed his summer examinations. He blamed it all on her. If she had not brought her children and saddled him with them, if she had allowed them to be fostered, if she had not become pregnant so soon after her arrival, he would have passed.

Francis forgot that it had taken him five attempts to pass the first part, that he did not attend any lectures because he felt he could do better on his own, that he was always reluctant to get up early enough in the mornings.

Luckily for Adah, Babalola heard of Trudy. She had two children of her own and agreed to look after Adah's two as well. Francis praised Trudy to the skies. She was clean, well dressed and very friendly. Adah had not seen her yet, because she usually worked late in the library, coming home at eight o'clock most evenings.

She would dress the children, and Francis wheeled them to Trudy's, which was just a block away, and collected them at six, after Trudy had washed them and given them tea. That, at least, was the arrangement.

After a few weeks, Adah noticed that Titi stopped talking altogether. This surprised Adah because Titi was a real chatterbox. She wondered what was happening and decided to take the children to Trudy herself. After all, she had carried them for nine months, not Francis. Francis was happy about this because he claimed that his friends laughed at him when they saw him with the children in a pushchair.

What struck Adah first was the fact that Trudy's milkman delivered only two pints every morning even though she was given Adah's children's milk coupon. But Trudy told her that Adah's children took three pints a day and that her milkman delivered not the two Adah saw, but five pints every day.

Adah said nothing, but started giving her children cereal before leaving for work. This meant extra work, but she would do all she could to bring Titi back to her old self again.

Still uneasy, she started paying Trudy visits on her half-days. She did not like what she saw. Trudy's house, like all the houses in that area, was a slum. A house that had been condemned ages ago. The back yard was filled with rubbish, broken furniture, and very near an uncovered dustbin was the toilet, the old type of toilet with faulty plumbing, smelly and damp.

On the first day that Adah went, she saw Trudy's two little girls playing in the front garden. They both had red slacks and blue pullovers. Their long brown hair was tied with well-pressed red ribbons. They were laughing and looked very happy. They swung something in the air and Adah realized that Trudy's girls were playing with the spades and buckets that she had bought for her own children. Her heart burned with anger, but she told herself to stop behaving like the little Ibo tigress. After all she had not stayed five good years at the Methodist Girls' High School for nothing. At least she had been taught to tame her emotions. Maybe her children were having a nap or something.

She walked in and entered the sitting room. She saw Trudy, a plump woman with too much make up. Her lips were scarlet and so were her nails. The colour of her hair was too black to be natural. Maybe it was originally brown like those of her little girls – but the jet black dye gave her whole personality a sort of vulgarity. She was laughing loudly at a joke she was sharing with a man who was holding her at a funny angle. Adah closed her eyes. The laughter stopped abruptly when they noticed her.

'Why aren't you at work?' Trudy gasped.

'I was going to the clinic at Malden Road, so I thought I'd look in and see how you were getting on with Titi and Vicky.'

There was a pause, during which Adah could hear her heartbeat racing. She was finding it more and more difficult to control her temper. She remembered her mother. Ma would have torn the fatty tissues of this woman into shreds if she had been in this situation. Well, she was not Ma, but she was Ma's daughter, and, come what may, she was still an Ibo. She screamed.

'Where are my children? You pro—' She stopped herself. She was about to call Trudy a prostitute, but was not sure whether the man watching them, with his flies open, was her husband or not. The man quickly excused himself though, and Adah blamed herself for not completing her sentence. The man was not Trudy's husband. He was a lover; a customer or a boyfriend, or maybe a mixture of both. Adah did not care. She wanted to see her children.

Trudy pointed towards the door. Adah's eyes followed the pointing finger to the back yard. Yes, Adah could hear the faint voice of Vicky, babbling something in his own special language. She ran out and saw her children. She stood there, her knees shaking and burst into tears.

Vicky was busy pulling rubbish out of the bin and Titi was washing her hands and face with the water leaking from the toilet. When they saw her, they ran to her, and Adah noticed that Vicky had no nappy on.

'They won't talk to us. The other day I gave an ice-cream to Titi and she did not know what to do with it. They wet themselves all the time.' Trudy went on and on like a woman possessed, talking non-stop.

Adah bundled the children into their pushchair and took them to the children's officer at Malden Road. After all, Trudy was a registered baby-minder, whatever that was supposed to mean.

The children's officer tut-tutted a great deal. Adah was given a cup of tea and told not to worry too much. After all, the children were all right, weren't they?

While they were still talking, Trudy arrived in floods of tears. She protested that she had only allowed them into the back yard that day because she had a stinking visitor who would not go. Had Adah not seen him? He wouldn't leave her alone. Of course the children had wandered into the back yard. She wouldn't have the heart to put a dog there, to say nothing of little 'angels' like Adah's kids. She was a registered daily-minder. Registered by the Borough of Camden. If her standards had been low, she would not have been registered in the first place. Adah should ask Miss Stirling.

Miss Stirling was the children's officer. She wore a red dress and rimless spectacles, the type academics in old photographs usually wore. She blinked a great deal. She was blinking now, as her name was mentioned. But she could not get a sword in, Trudy was making all the running.

As for Adah, she listened to Trudy destroying forever one of the myths she had been brought up to believe: that the white man never lied.

JEAN BINTA BREEZE

Jean Binta Breeze is a Jamaican dub poet and storyteller who has performed throughout the world, including South East Asia, Africa, Europe, America and the Caribbean. An actress, dancer, choreographer and film writer, she has released three poetry collections, *Riddym Ravings*, *Spring Cleaning* and *On the Edge of an Island*. She also has several record releases to her name. She now divides her time between Jamaica and London.

'Homegrown' is taken from *On the Edge of an Island*, a collection of prose and poetry dealing with English and Jamaican themes.

Homegrown

I
homegrown
never had full strength
but always there
stix
to tide you over

homegrown

didn't crash your brain
more like a gentle lover

homegrown
no hybrid grown
on dung
to make you run
for cover

homegrown
no transplanted tongue

selling out
over and over

homegrown
heads cut off
our native flower

homegrown
gift from a friend
homegrown
a whisper in the wind
homegrown
like a long lost limb
homegrown
searching the skies
for star-eyed children

II

in her mound
shaped like a rising
to a god
she gently pushes
stick
casts a dark eye
on the sun
and shutting one side
for rain
asks for bread

while cassavas sprout
her quick spear
through water
brings her
fish

now
in shingle
on the cast out shores
of cities

one last crippled note
inside her hand
she reaches over the counter
for wheat she does not grow
and fish
from Newfoundland

while
in the mountains
yam drums beat
down the soil to
cane sticks
bending backs to toil

her eyes search
the horizon
picturing greener
bucks
on the other side

but the canoe's days are over
this coast
will suck you in

a nervous spirit
trapped
between mountain and sea

cannot run fluid
across the sand
cannot catch crabs now
running
from the lobster legs
broiling in the sun

> *'No more black bench*
> *up front*
> *to de edge of de bump*
> *up front*
> *to de edge of de bump.'*

gone to wind
this spirit
gone to wind
under a heavier pounding

dusts from mortar rises
settling into clay

rise again
peaceful arawak
rise again

these drums of rage and fire
need a continent

III

that night
a star cried
and a baby
fell.

TENSION, CRISIS AND IDENTITY

A crossroads with seven roads intersecting
terrifies a stranger
WEST AFRICAN PROVERB

STUART HALL

The Formation of a Diasporic Intellectual III

KHC: Getting back to the question of the diaspora. Some of the diasporic intellectuals I know of have exercised their power, for better or worse, back home, but you have not. And some of them are trying to move back, in whatever way. So, in that sense, you are peculiar.

SH: Yes. But remember, the diaspora came to me. I turned out to be in the first wave of a diaspora over here. When I came to Britain, the only blacks here were students; and all the black students wanted to go back after college. Gradually, during my postgraduate and early New Left days, a working black population settled here, and this became the diaspora of a diaspora. The Caribbean is already the diaspora of Africa, Europe, China, Asia, India and this diaspora re-diasporized itself here. So that's why more of my recent work is not just about the postcolonial, but has to be with black photographers, black film-makers, with black people in the theatre, it's with the third generation black British.

KHC: But you never tried to exercise your intellectual power back home.

SH: There have been moments when I have intervened in my home parts. At a certain point, before 1968, I was engaged in dialogue with the people I knew in that generation, principally to try to resolve the difference between a black marxist grouping and a black nationalist tendency. I said, you ought to be talking to one another. The black marxists were looking for the Jamaican proletariat, but there were no heavy industries in Jamaica; and they were not listening to the cultural revolutionary thrust of the black nationalists, and Rastafarians, who were developing a more persuasive cultural, or subjective language.

But essentially I never tried to play a major political role there. It's partly because the break in the politics there – the cultural revolution that made Jamaica a 'black' society for the first time in the 1970s – coincided with a break in my own life. I would have gone back, had the Caribbean Federation lasted, and tried to play a role there. That dream was over at the moment in the 1950s when I decided to stay, and to open a 'conversation' with what became the New Left. The possibility of the scenario in which I might have been politically active in the Caribbean closed at the very moment when personally I found a new kind of political space here. After that, once I decided I was going to live here rather than there, once Catherine and I got married, the possibility of rerun became more difficult. Catherine was an English social historian, a feminist; her politics were here. Of course, paradoxically, she is now working on Jamaica, and the imperial relationship, and now she knows more Jamaican history than I do, and she loves being there. But in the 1960s, it was very difficult for a white British feminist to feel anything but an outsider, in relation to Jamaican politics. My 'reconnection' with the Caribbean happened because of the formation of a Black diasporic population here. I began to write about it again in the context of the studies of ethnicity and racism for UNESCO, then I wrote about it in *Policing the Crisis*,* focusing on race and racism, and their internal relation to the crisis of British society, and now I write very much in terms of cultural identities.

KHC: So diaspora is defined by the historical conjunctures both personally and structurally, and the creative energies and power of the diaspora come, in part, from these unresolvable tensions?

SH: Yes, but it is very specific and it never loses its specificities. That is the reason why the way in which I'm trying to think questions of identity is not fixed, it's always hybrid. But this is precisely because it comes out of very specific historical formations, out of the very specific histories and cultural repertoires of enunciation, that it can constitute a 'positionality', which we call, provisionally, identity. It's not just anything. So each of those identity-stories is inscribed in the positions we take up and identify with, and we have to live this ensemble of identity-positions in all its specificities.

* Stuart Hall, Chas Critcher, Tony Jefferson, John Clarke, Brian Robert, *Policing the Crisis: Mugging, the State, and Law and Order*, Macmillan, 1978.

ANDREW SALKEY

Andrew Salkey was part of the first generation of Caribbean writers to arrive in Britain in the 1950s. Working for the BBC, he was a strong advocate of the writing that emerged from the region, editing many anthologies about the creative output of the area. His first novel was *A Quality of Violence*. He wrote several other novels and was an accomplished travel and children's writer. He left Britain to lecture in the United States in the late 1970s, where he died in 1995.

Come Home, Malcolm Heartland explores the anguish of going home when there is no longer a home. Lawyer Malcolm Heartland is in exile, severed from his West Indian roots. He feels washed up and marginalized in London – neither wanting to become part of the deadening hopelessness of black politics or the mimicry offered by integration. Jamaica, he believes, holds his personal salvation. But others are out to stop him going. In the extract below, Malcolm Heartland is confronted by a cynical reporter about his reasons for going home.

from *Come Home, Malcolm Heartland*
The Interview

Reporter: I think it's reasonable to assume that the very first question, which our *Carib News* readers, in the Caribbean, would want me to put to you, is: what made you decide to return home after living for so many years, here, in London? I'm sure they'd like me to ask that, right at the beginning.

Malcolm Heartland: I can't see why they should be interested. I can't see why *Carib News* thinks they should be. I honestly can't see why. And it isn't pretended modesty on my part. I simply can't see why. Anyway, for what it's worth, I'm going back to Jamaica, really, because I want to do so. That's it.

Reporter: Why now? And why so suddenly?

Malcolm Heartland: 'Suddenly' can be any time, I suppose. 'Now', simply because I've chosen to leave at this point in time.

Reporter: But, why?

Malcolm Heartland: Because the time is right.

Reporter: What makes now the right time to return?

Malcolm Heartland: That's my business. It can't possibly be any concern of yours or your readers.

Reporter: Our readers are interested in news about people and events that affect our communities overseas, here, in Britain, and in America and Canada. In fact, you've been a part of the Black radical scene in London for quite some time. You've been involved in the 'Black Revolutionary Movement', as the scene is referred to by the Brothers in the so-called vanguard of the new consciousness. You haven't been in the leadership, vague and undeclared as that is, but you've been loosely associated with it, and you've attended meetings, demonstrations and so on. Your actions, though limited, have shown some kind of evidence of political commitment. Don't you think that by leaving, at this moment, you could be said to be deserting the 'Revolution', in a sense?

Malcolm Heartland: No.

Reporter: You seem certain of that.

Malcolm Heartland: I am.

Reporter: You're a barrister. You haven't practised for some time. In fact, you haven't had much work as a barrister. Perhaps none at all. Will you practise in Jamaica?

Malcolm Heartland: I don't know. I shouldn't think so.

Reporter: What do you hope to do, when you get back?

Malcolm Heartland: Look around, and find my bearings. I'd imagine.

Reporter: Only for a week or two. But what will you work at?

Malcolm Heartland: Your guess is as good as mine.

Reporter: Politics?

Malcolm Heartland: No.

Reporter: You aren't giving anything away, are you?

Malcolm Heartland: Can't see why I should. And not to *Carib News*. Not to anybody, in fact.

Reporter: It's said that you're apprehensive about returning home. You're uncertain about Black Power politics in Jamaica. You're disappointed by Black Power, here, and even more pessimistic about it, in the Caribbean. It's also said that you're out on a limb politically. The lack of unity within the Caribbean radical groups, together with the constant feuding and splitting up among the revolutionary aspirants, is something that's caused you to be disillusioned about the black scene, here and at home. Is that right? Would you like to comment?

Malcolm Heartland: Yes. What you've just said sounds extremely interesting, but where I'm concerned, it's wholly fictional. I'm not pessimistic. I like to believe I'm a private person. As such, I'm always hopeful.

Reporter: You haven't answered my question.

Malcolm Heartland: You asked for my comment. I gave it.

Reporter: Caribbean intellectuals are usually evasive when their backs are to the wall. Black Power can drive them into that position. Is that the case with you?

Malcolm Heartland: No.

Reporter: The Brothers in the ghetto consider Caribbean intellectuals to be the original cowards. Rewards-seekers. Sell-outs. Any comments?

Malcolm Heartland: The Brothers are right in thinking that. There's more than ample evidence, both here and in the Caribbean. Yes.

Reporter: So, you agree with that condemnation?

Malcolm Heartland: Why shouldn't I? Yes, I do.

Reporter: They say you're a coward. You're running away. You're opting out, and going after the soft middle-class rewards, at home.

Malcolm Heartland: D'you want me to comment on that, too?

Reporter: Are you running away?

Malcolm Heartland: Yes. And no. And of course, you know you can run by standing quite still; you can appear on the scene, as you put it, and be miles away from it.

Reporter: They say you're running away, because you loathe the futility of the black situation. They say the intellectuals think the whole thing self-defeating and dangerous. The aimless, sporadic protest almost totally negative; the impetus, false; the public demonstrations, sloppily organized and really set up for the self-regarding leadership, a handful of elite figures seeking desperately after recognition and very little else. You're embarrassed. You're put off by everything the Brothers are trying to do. That's why people like you are going back home.

Malcolm Heartland: I'm going back for entirely different reasons. Most of us who're returning or thinking of doing so, surely, make the move back for reasons which have nothing to do with the ups and downs of black radicalism. The spur to return usually comes from the other side of your so-called scene. You should know that. And, by the way, I hope you've actually met the 'They' you keep on throwing at me, and correctly assessed what they're supposed to be saying? D'you really know them? Been in touch with them? You quoting them accurately?

Reporter: I think so. The 'They' I've been talking about definitely exist, and they're saying things which you may not want to believe they're capable of saying. I know it's difficult for some of us to admit that there's a community of black people, in this country, a thinking community, critical of itself, and very critical of the attitudes and conduct of individuals like yourself.

Malcolm Heartland: I think I know that.

Reporter: Well, then, they also say that you're afraid of what you call the failure and nothingness of the struggle. Intellectuals hate failure, public failure. You all gathered in London in the early fifties, mainly for metropolitan approval and recognition. The approval 'thing' is finished now, and so is the recognition 'bit'. Malcolm, Stokely, Rap, the Panthers and the others broke the back of that. The young Brothers, here, stepped good and hard on the pieces. That's left the intellectuals without aim and purpose. So, it's home where the grass is greener and the old embarrassment at a minimum.

Malcolm Heartland: What am I to say about that?

Reporter: Do you agree?

Malcolm Heartland: Seems extreme. Overstated. Dramatic.

Reporter: Does it apply to you?

Malcolm Heartland: No. Nor to anybody I know. In fact, I can't think of anybody it applies to. Sounds just a little like an inspired journalist's concoction.

Reporter: But, you're going?

Malcolm Heartland: Yes. For my own reasons. And not for those thought up by *Carib News* or by some of the embattled young Brothers whom you may well be misquoting. But simply for my own private reasons. I can't say more than that.

Reporter: Playing *Anancy* to the last, eh?

Malcolm Heartland: That, too, if you like. And for your editor and your interested readers, perhaps?

LINTON KWESI JOHNSON

Linton Kwesi Johnson has been a pioneering figure in black poetry and music. He caught the rage and anger of the second generation of British-born black people, and popularized the use of 'native language' and music, in the fusion he called reggae poetry. He has published a number of books of poetry, including *Voices of the Living and Dead, Dread Beat An' Blood*, and *Inglan Is a Bitch*. He has also released six dub albums.

'Inglan Is a Bitch' is included in a collection of poems, *Tings an Times*, which charts the progress of his career, and includes pieces about the collapse of communist totalitarianism in Eastern Europe.

Inglan Is a Bitch

w'en mi jus' come to Landan toun
mi use to work pan di andahgroun
but workin' pan di andahgroun
y'u don't get fi know your way aroun'

Inglan is a bitch
dere's no escapin' it
Inglan is a bitch
dere's no runnin' whey fram it

mi get a lickle jab in a big 'otell
an' awftah a while, mi woz doin' quite well
dem staat mi aaf as a dish-washah
but w'en mi tek a stack, mi noh tun clack-watchah!

Inglan is a bitch
dere's no escapin it
Inglan is a bitch
noh baddah try fi hide fram it

w'en dem gi' yu di lickle wage packit
fus dem rab it wid dem big tax racket
y'u haffi struggle fi mek en's meet
an' w'en y'u goh a y'u bed y'u jus' cant sleep

Inglan is a bitch
dere's no escapin' it
Inglan is a bitch fi true
a noh lie mi a tell, a true

mi use to work dig ditch w'en it cowl noh bitch
mi did strang like a mule, but, bwoy, mi did fool
den awftah a while mi jus' stap dhu ovahtime
den awftah a while mi jus' phu dung mi tool

Inglan is a bitch
dere's no escapin' it
Inglan is a bitch
y'u haffi know how fi suvvive in it

well mi dhu day wok an' mi dhu nite wok
mi dhu clean wok an' mi dhu dutty wok
dem seh dat black man is very lazy
but if y'u si how mi wok y'u woulda seh mi crazy

Inglan is a bitch
dere's no escapin' it
Inglan is a bitch
y'u bettah face up to it

dem have a lickle facktri up inna Brackly
inna disya facktri all dem dhu is pack crackry
fi di laas fifteen years dem get mi laybah
now awftah fifteen years mi fall out a fayvah

Inglan is a bitch
dere's no escapin' it
Inglan is a bitch
dere's no runnin' whey fram it

mi know dem have work, work in abundant
yet still, dem mek mi redundant
now, at fifty-five mi gettin' quite ol'
yet still, dem sen' mi fi goh draw dole

Inglan is a bitch
dere's no escapin' it
Inglan is a bitch fi true
is whey wi a goh dhu 'bout it?

BERYL GILROY

Beryl Gilroy was born in Guyana and came to England in 1951. Though an experienced teacher, she was forced to take jobs as a clerk and a domestic, including a spell in an old people's home – before being able to resume her career in education. This has involved teaching, researching, lecturing and the headship of a London primary school. She now works as a Counselling Psychologist, and holds a doctorate in that discipline. She began writing a series of children's books in 1970, and in 1976 published *Black Teacher*, which recounted her experiences as the first black headmistress in her London Borough. This was followed by *In For a Penny* and *Frangipani House*, which won the GLC Black Literature Competition.

'Boy-Sandwich' is black Londoner Tyrone, whose cosy and protected world begins to fragment when his grandparents are evicted to an institution. Despite his pledge to look after them, his own sense of identity is under threat. He feels he has to travel back to the island of his parents and grandparents for some answers. In the extract below, Tyrone drives away his grandparents to their new home.

from *Boy-Sandwich*

That morning stubborn clouds hung low and brought feelings I could describe only as irregular. It seemed as if time itself was being agitated, the echoes of the past colliding with the voices of the present, creating moments that boiled and swirled and pushed. I drove fast, much too fast for that time of day. Speed, I thought, was the answer to the turbulence and frustration inside me.

A road sweeper, struggling to subdue the chaotic borders of debris, leaned on his broom and crossed himself as I drove by. I imagined myself pursuing a point of moving light imprisoned in a tunnel. It challenged me and compelled me to move forward, unconcerned for my own safety or for that of my parents, who sat tense and nervous in the back seat of my car.

'Don't drive so crazy,' snapped my mother. 'We want to arrive in one piece.' Ignoring her remark, I turned into Selwyn Avenue where my grandparents had lived for many years.

The house in that once unsavoury part of London was theirs. For years they had tended it and cared for the garden with a love that was deep and eloquent. The kind of love one gave to a helpless child. Now the developers had won their way. The old couple were being forced to accept the pittance offered for their home so that it could lawfully be demolished, along with others, to make room for town houses which only the rich could afford. My grandparents had held out for as long as they could but time had run out. The day for eviction had arrived and they were about to embark on the journey which some old folk sometimes must make – the journey to the limbo of a sheltered home.

As we approached my grandparents' house the silence suddenly snapped. The house itself had lost its well-cared-for look and dust from the rubble of the surrounding construction work had formed a film on the windows; but my grandparents could be seen from the outside like two ghostly figures. Voices of idle onlookers seeking early-morning distraction rose and fell, while rent-a-mob racists stood around.

Clutching their Union Jacks, they thumped their chests as they chanted, 'Nigs out!', 'Schwartzers out!' We stopped close to the front door. The racists booed and held their flags high. My grandparents, dressed and waiting, had heard it all before. Those days would never return but they would always live in memory.

My grandpa hurried to the lavatory and then, hand in hand, he and my grandmother walked regally round the room, stroking and caressing the walls in a final goodbye. There was an upsurge of chanting as they opened the front door but the rumble of the bulldozers getting into position drowned out the voices. Our few supporters could only stare helplessly at those faces so welcoming of the chaos around them.

The police arrived, crossed the road and reprimanded the racists. It made things worse. Sergeant Keeler, whom I knew, walked round the garden. He recognized me. When I was twelve, and he a policeman on the beat, he used to sus-search* me every single day just for fun.

'No more wogs! Out! Out! Out!' came lovelessly to our ears. A brief smile played round the sergeant's lips as the racists yelled. The whole performance was funny enough for tears.

---

* *sus-search*: search on suspicion

'You must leave, Mr Grainger,' said the sergeant. 'You've made your point. You're an old man.'

'Tell those racist cowards!' shouted my father. 'Not us! The old people are where they belong!'

'You may not like what they're saying but free speech is what we British are all about,' he replied. 'I would advise you to help your parents and conclude this unpleasant business.'

'Harassment!' yelled my mother. 'Injustice!' It did not take much to whip up a storm inside her.

'Persecution in de name of de Union Jack,' Grandma chimed in. 'Ever seen such a t'ing!'

More chants of 'Nigs out!' 'Schwartzers out!' came at us like bricks.

'Mr Grainger,' said another policeman. 'Please, sir, let's go. It's the best thing to do.' He curled an arm round Grandpa's shoulder. 'This is a building site now, sir.'

'Don't touch him!' yelled my mother. 'He's not a person in your world! Get off him!'

As I looked out, I could see a priest trying to reason with the racists.

'Calm and peace,' said my grandpa. 'De Lord save Daniel from de jaws of death. God will protect us.'

'Make sure you have everything,' I said. 'This is the point of no return. These are people, not lions. A small part of a large population.'

We walked cautiously out of the house and entered the car, but before we could drive off a small group of militants encircled us, banging on the roof and rocking the car. Grandpa wet himself. My dad began to wheeze. The police waded in, using their truncheons liberally. My mum screamed. Grandma became hysterical.

'Don't hit us!' the mob yelled. 'Hit them!'

The police, still wielding truncheons, cleared a path for us and I accelerated to safety. A few yards away I stopped the car and re-assured my family. Some of our supporters had followed us to offer help.

My grandparents were softly crying – it was as if they were singing a very sad song about their fears and the noises that now echoed in their heads.

'Don't cry,' I said. 'Everything will be OK. Racists hunt in packs – like wolves.'

I talked to them, the way my mum had often talked to me. Grandpa nodded. He stared out of the window as if his eyes were making contact with something unrelated to the present. He tried to talk but the words he wanted to speak had been swallowed. We changed his trousers in the car and he didn't like that kind of invasion of his privacy at all. After several more stops for reassurance we arrived at the sheltered accommodation which the social worker had recommended. The Birches offered communal facilities, allowed personal possessions and admitted people of all races. We were not entirely happy to leave my grandparents but I reckoned I would be around to see fair play. I promised myself that, come what may, the year before my university course began was theirs. I was going to live to be a hundred. What was one single year in a giant lifespan like that?

JOAN RILEY

Joan Riley was born in St Mary, Jamaica. She was educated at Sussex and London universities, where she gained a master's degree, and has since worked for a drugs advisory agency. She has written a number of novels, including *Waiting in the Twilight* and *Romance*, which have dealt with various themes surrounding black British women. *The Unbelonging* was her début novel.

The Unbelonging is the story of Hyacinth, who, at eleven, is summoned to England by a father she has never known. She leaves her Jamaican idyll for the gloom of inner-city life and being the only black face in a sea of hostile white faces at school. At home, she faces violence and indifference from her father, and escapes into dreams of her homeland. But reality constantly intrudes.

from *The Unbelonging*

She sat up with a start, a feeling of dread following her through layers of sleep into a reality of clammy wetness. The damp nightdress clung to her in increasingly cold folds every time she shifted. Her mind grappled with the problem. Rejected it. She told herself it was perspiration, that the nights were warmer and she was sweating in her sleep. Filled with dread, mingled with hope, her fingers groped, found and recoiled from a soggy wetness that no amount of perspiration could have brought. A shiver shook her as her nose gradually became aware of the smell of fresh urine all around her. She could imagine it seeping through the bed, penetrating the mattress till it gradually dripped into a pool on the worn carpet underneath, as it had done the last few times. Fear crawled in her belly as she thought of the morning, and she wondered what time it was. Eyes strained to pick up signs of telltale lightness in the impenetrable darkness of the room.

She prayed that night would never end, and that when she woke tomorrow it would be a dream and the bed would be dry – anything but that she would have to face another stinging beating on her already tender back. Her heartbeat increased with the anticipation of what was to come, but she pushed it to the back of her mind, and slid down into the bed, curling round to avoid as much of the wet as possible. The more she tried to relax, the more her heart raced, while anticipation and fear made her mouth dry; but finally she slept, a restless sleep full of terrifying, nightmare images.

Morning found her waiting in fearful anticipation, unable to move, filled with horror at what must come. He was working nights that week, and the ritual of bed-checking would come soon. The sound of a key in the front door brought a wave of shaking to her limbs, and she lay there, unable to move, sweat breaking out all over her body. A few moments later, the bottom but one stair groaned as a weight was lowered onto it. She squeezed her eyelids closer together, breathing deeply as she had been taught in PE, hoping that this would slow her racing heart. Her mind followed the ritual up the stairs without thought. First to come off would be the large brown boots, laces carefully loosened. Then the socks. Then would come the sound of the stair settling as the weight was lifted from it. His coat would come off next, followed by the railway jacket he was so proud of. Last the red railway tie would be loosened, and the top two buttons of the grey shirt undone.

Now mind-image merged with reality and the stairs creaked slowly, each one nearer, each bringing a fresh wave of fear shaking through her body. She did not dare look up as the door was pushed open, but stumbled to her feet as he came into the room.

'This room stinks,' he said mildly, a humourless smile on his face. 'Did you wet the bed again?'

Hyacinth nodded, keeping her eyes averted from him, not trusting herself to speak. He walked over to the narrow bed, pulling down the blanket with a quick tug, exposing the brown-edged stain she had hidden in her shame.

'Why did you wet the bed?' The words mingled in her ears with the painful pumping of blood and ragged breathing. She kept her head bent, ears straining desperately, as if to pick up the blow before it landed.

'I don't know,' she said faintly, pleadingly.

'Don't know was made to know,' he said ominously.

Hyacinth felt the desperation bubbling up inside. How could she tell him how it was? How could she explain the dream, the dream that had haunted her for so long? He would never understand how it felt to get up in the middle of the night, to creep down the stairs, along the dark corridor, the glimmer of the street light casting long, monstrous shadows in her way as she darted through the kitchen, the strange wailing of the congregating cats the only sound to be heard. He could never understand what it was like to sit on the toilet, hands braced against the seat, feet pressed hard against the cold lino. Then came the straining, the pushing to get it over quickly, all the time holding back the fear that lapped at the dark corners of her mind, and lurked in anticipation somewhere out of sight, somewhere along the route she had come. It had always been like this. Fear driving her to hum songs to God, to mutter 'Get thee behind me Satan', in a hushed and frightened voice. Aunt Joyce had always understood, but he never could. He would never understand her panic as it started to rise in warm wetness around her thighs, to run in rivulets down her legs. She could never explain the suffocating fear of waking to a freshly wet bed.

A stinging slap brought her sharply out of her thoughts, head lifting fearfully.

'I ask you if you don't have no shame.' His eyes had narrowed to slits, the smile replaced by a frown which multiplied the lines on his forehead, bringing a fresh wave of fear. She felt helpless in the face of the question. To say yes would be insolent, no, arrogant. Jumbled, half-formed sentences raced through her mind, mingling with her pounding heartbeat which seemed to echo there.

'This dumb insolence has got to stop,' he said ominously and Hyacinth tensed in readiness for the next blow. Time seemed to drag, agonizing seconds in which she dared not look at him, wished she had the courage to run, or at least to fight back.

'Strip the bed and tell Maureen you are to have a cold bath.'

Hyacinth hid her surprise, keeping her head averted; he was going to let her off. Yet the hope just born was short-lived as he continued, 'And when you finish, I want to see you in the front. And Hyacinth,' – he had been walking towards the door, but now he stopped – 'don't let me have to come for you.'

It was later, the numbness of the cold bath still deep in her fingers and toes, that she pushed open the dull pink door to the lounge. Down in her stomach she could feel the beginnings of the shaking he always inspired and, as she closed the door, she felt it spread. She had to clench her teeth to prevent them chattering as she stood stiffly in front of his chair, knowing from experience that to betray fear was to invite early punishment. He was drinking barley wine this early, and a wave of hate and disgust made her clamp her teeth together harder. Two

years she had watched him drink that stinking brew, two years of
beatings and mistreatment, and she was sure that same barley wine
had been the cause of some of it. She had read somewhere that you
couldn't drink so much without becoming violent.

'I am not going to beat you today.'

Hyacinth blinked in surprise. Her mind had been painstakingly
avoiding acceptance of the beating to come, and now she found she
was safe after all.

'I am going to take you to the doctor,' he continued. 'Something
must be wrong with you, for you to keep bed-wetting like this.'

Hyacinth nodded eagerly, fear pushed to the back of her mind in
the sudden relief. Why hadn't she thought of that? Of course something was wrong with her. Nobody wet the bed, not at her age. She
wondered if she would have to go into hospital, have an operation
maybe. It would be nice to get away from him, especially as a girl at
school who went there once said that all the nurses were Jamaican.

'If the doctor say nothing wrong with you, God help you!' he
warned. She didn't care about that, she knew there was something
wrong with her, that the doctor would say as much. At least now the
beatings wouldn't be so frequent. There would be less excuses to find
for curious schoolmates and prying teachers asking about the raised
red weals and broken skin on her legs, arms and back. Then she was
free to go and, as she closed the door, relief flooded her. She took the
stairs two at a time, not noticing the skinny woman at the top until she
almost collided with her.

'Your father he never beat you, eh?' There was malice in her eyes
as she reached out to give Hyacinth a vicious pinch. 'You think he
like you, make you get away with it? Well you do anything and see if
he going to let you off so easy.'

Hyacinth shrugged off the bony hand, pushing impatiently past the
woman. 'Why don't you get lost, you big-eyed toad,' she said in sudden anger, as the other reached out and cuffed her.

'What did you say?' the woman asked angrily, eyes glittering with
spite. 'Say that again and see if I don't tell your father how you insult
me. Then is he you will have to deal with.'

'Tell him what you want,' Hyacinth said indifferently, walking
away with head held high, not even trying to hide the smile on her
face. She knew he hated Maureen as much as he hated her. After
all, why else would he beat her, and in front of his friends too?
The only thing he would punish her for was hitting the woman. What

she said to her was their business.

She had not always been so bold with Maureen, of course. Once she had been almost as afraid of her as she was of him. At first when stung to respond, she had waited with pounding heart for him to hear of it. Yet nothing had come of it. She soon realized that as long as she was not rude to Maureen in front of him, he didn't care what she did. Sometimes, when her conscience troubled her about her disrespect, she would remind herself how much the woman hated her. Maureen had made her hatred known from the start, had announced her intention of getting Hyacinth out from the day the girl walked through the door.

Hyacinth remembered those first days with bitterness, remembered Maureen telling her that her two children were the only children of the house, and she, Hyacinth, only there on sufferance. God, if they only knew how much she wanted to leave that bleak, unhappy house. How much she longed for the sun-bleached cheerfulness of the grey wood shack that had been her home for the first eleven years of her life. How different it had been from this peeling, black-painted house full of fear and hate. Now her whole life seemed to be one endless round of work and fear, cleaning, cooking, beating and bed-wetting. It had been so nice with Aunt Joyce, who had always understood, had never treated her badly. She had been popular, with lots of friends. No one had teased her, taunted her. Now her only happiness was sleep, for that was when she could go home again and take up her interrupted life.

It was peaceful in the brown-carpeted surgery, most of the hard grey chairs empty in the silent waiting-room. Hyacinth sat quietly beside her father, hardly daring to move for fear of attracting his attention, willing her knees to stop shaking. She couldn't understand it. How was it that her knees shook even when he was not about to beat her? Straining her eyes to try and pick out the words from the murmur of voices coming from the partially open door of the doctor's surgery, she tried to judge how long the fat woman who had just gone in would be. It was her turn next, and she couldn't wait to escape from his company. It seemed like forever, but finally she found herself being ushered into the room by a large, white-coated nurse, her father following close on her heels.

'Hyacinth Williams,' the woman announced as she opened the door, and she walked in on a wave of importance, her father temporarily forgotten in the thrill of hearing her name called so officially.

'What can I do for you?' the doctor asked, when father and

daughter were both seated on chairs facing his desk. To Hyacinth's surprise, her father took off his cap, looked servile.

'Hyacinth keep wetting the bed,' he said respectfully. 'This two year since she come to England, she wet the bed non-stop.'

The doctor looked at the notes on the desk in front of him, but made no comment.

'She is thirteen last birthday,' Mr Williams continued awkwardly after the pause had stretched on for some time, 'and I feel something wrong with her.'

'Have you taken her to a doctor before?'

Mr Williams shifted uncomfortably. 'No, I thought she would grow out of it,' he said defensively. 'Is only 'cause she getting worse that I decided to come.'

Hyacinth squirmed in the seat beside him, feeling the prickly heat of shame rise in her face, sting on her back, cause her scalp to itch, as the doctor turned his gaze on her.

'What happens when you wet the bed?' the doctor asked, his voice reassuring.

'I don't know,' she mumbled.

'Speak up when the doctor speak to you!' The voice, like the crack of a whip, caused her to jump and fresh shaking to start in her body. She had not expected that from him, here.

'Mr Williams, perhaps it would be better if you waited outside,' the doctor suggested quietly.

'I don't think so, doctor, you don't know her like I do. Hyacinth is a liar,' Mr Williams blustered. 'She refuses to tell the truth and I have to watch her.'

Hyacinth felt the sting of tears and she stared hard at her hands, trying to force the tears back, not wanting the white man to see her cry; not daring to do so anyway, with her father there.

'I am sure I can detect lies from truth,' the doctor said coldly, dismissively.

'But you don't know her, sir. You wouldn't be able to tell, she so good at it,' Mr Williams persisted, and Hyacinth curled her toes in her shoes in shame.

'Nevertheless, I would still like you to wait outside,' came the reply.

Once he had gone, Hyacinth felt herself relax, some of the tension leaving her.

'Are you afraid of your father?' the doctor asked suddenly.

Hyacinth stiffened, mingled pride and fear warring with a sudden hope. 'No,' she mumbled finally, reluctantly, eyes sliding away from him. She would never dare tell him that her father had warned her about white people – how they hated black people, how they would trick them and kill them. Even at school she saw that – how the black kids were treated, how she was treated and, if she needed more evidence, look how afraid he had been of this man. No, she mustn't tell him anything.

'Does he hit you when you wet the bed?'

'No.' She shifted uncomfortably as she repeated the lie.

'In that case, why were you trembling when he was here?'

She could not answer that, could not bring herself to admit the truth, not to this man, not to anyone. They would take her away, kill her, and then no one would ever know. The doctor changed tack. 'Did you wet the bed before you came to England?' She shook her head vigorously. After all, one or two accidents could hardly be called wetting the bed.

'What caused you to do it here? Are you afraid of the dark? Is that it?'

'It's not that . . . ' she said, trailing off. Then, taking a deep breath, she plunged on before she could think about what she was saying. 'If I knew it was going to happen, I would never let it,' she blurted out.

'So how does it happen?'

'Sometimes when I wake up the bed is wet, and sometimes I really think I am on the toilet. I sit on the toilet and it doesn't seem to stop coming down. Then when I wake up the bed is wet.

The doctor thought for a while. 'Do you wet yourself in the day-time?' he asked gently.

Hyacinth looked shocked. 'No!'

'Do you think there might be something wrong with you?' he persisted.

She raised her shoulders uncertainly, not quite sure what to say. 'I think maybe there is,' she said finally.

'Are you homesick? Would you like to go back to . . . Jamaica?'

Hyacinth nodded eagerly, heart leaping with sudden excitement, sudden hope. No wonder he was asking questions about Jamaica. She was glad she had told him now. Perhaps he would suggest that the only way for her to stop wetting the bed was to go back to Jamaica. Maybe he would say she was sick because she had to leave her aunt. Oh boy! she couldn't wait. She would be home soon. Home and safe.

E. A. MARKHAM

'This England?' is taken from *Towards the End of a Century*.

This England?

... guests at midnight
                    stopping
outside the house. The one
without the gun demands

her name and (through
an interpreter) tells Mammie

she's got nothing to fear
if she's legal.

MERLE COLLINS

'When Britain Had Its GREAT' is taken from *Rotten Pomerack*.

When Britain Had Its GREAT

Some people yearn for simple things
Like
Putting the GREAT back into Britain
They cannot hear the strangled haunting voices
of infant sisters
and brothers
who died
because enslaved mothers loved too much
to watch them grow to mate, unloved, unloving
to build GREAT Britain's greatness

Put the GREAT back into Britain
and my GREAT GREAT GREAT grandmother
groans
and churns her graveyard ocean
at the memory of Britain with its GREAT

Put the GREAT back into Britain
and can't you feel the shivering shake
of a great dead sister
turning to mourn within a canefield grave
dug by Britain with its Great

Put the GREAT back into Britain
and my GREAT GREAT GREAT grandparents'
ghostly hands
touch my face

and ghost faces claim my restless
roving eyes
to whisper

And you
would you, then,
be part of the GREAT British nation, too,
when Britain regains its GREAT?

DERVLA MURPHY

Dervla Murphy was born in Ireland, and specializes in travel writing. She has cycled around Europe and India and worked with Tibetan refugees. The two latter journeys resulted in the books *Full Tilt: Ireland to India with a Bicycle* and the *The Waiting Land: A Spell in Nepal*. Other travel books include: *In Ethiopia with a Mule, On a Shoestring to Coorg: An Experience of South India, A Place Apart: Northern Ireland, Muddling Through in Madagascar, The Ukimwi Road, Where the Indus is Young: A Winter in Baltistan* and *South from the Limpopo*. She has also published *Wheels Within Wheels: Autobiography*.

Tales from Two Cities is an account of time spent travelling amongst the Pakistani community in Bradford and in multi-racial Handsworth in Birmingham. In Bradford she reports on the 'Honeyford Affair', where a local headmaster, Ray Honeyford, was being boycotted by Pakistani parents following an article in the right-wing *Salisbury Review*, in which he made unflattering comments about Pakistan and criticized the cultural relativism behind multi-culturalism. She arrived in Birmingham at a time of great tension between the police and black youths. In the extract below she describes the riot that exploded as a result.

From *Tales from Two Cities*

On the afternoon of Saturday 7 September, as I was walking up Heathfield Avenue – a very short road just round the corner from my pad – a tall young Rasta overtook me, twisted my right arm violently, pushed me against the wall, trod hard on my left foot, repeated my other enemy's 'police informer' accusations and told me to get out of Handsworth. Then he raced off round the corner into Radnor Road. That was a more painful but much less frightening episode than the first.

Twenty-four hours later, I stood outside No. 45 watching the Carnival procession passing down Heathfield Road. Handsworth's annual Afro-Caribbean Carnival is perceived by many Blacks (not just Rastas) as Babylon-organized propaganda to show the outside world how well community policing has worked in Handsworth. The smallish crowd following the floats and steel bands was almost entirely Black and the occasion seemed to lack verve. A fortnight earlier I had gone to the Notting Hill Carnival with a group from the Marcus Garvey Foundation and had enjoyed eighteen hours of gaiety – including the bus journeys to and from London. It would be absurd to expect anything similar in Handsworth, yet an infusion of both Rasta and MGF high spirits could have done a lot, I felt, for the 1985 event. Observing the professionally matey community police in the procession, I wondered how they were *really* feeling . . . At that stage I still assumed the police must be aware of where the needle was on the tension-graph – despite Superintendent Love's evident unawareness at the Residents' meeting. On 29 August I had lunched with two senior police officers; but being a semi-trusted Villa Cross regular inhibited me from any explicit reporting of Rasta words and deeds. Had I realized how completely out of touch with local feeling the police then were, and had I been able to foresee the near future, I might have felt a duty to overcome my inhibitions. But the lack of second-sight spared me that nightmare writer's dilemma.

At about 5.10 p.m. on Monday 9 September I went out to post a letter, in which I mentioned my relief that Rachel had left Handsworth because 'things are getting rough around here'. They were in fact getting so rough that I never reached the post office. Instead, I returned to my pad at 5.40 p.m. and wrote in my journal:

Crossing the front line just now, saw three traffic-cops with motorbikes (*not* local police) arguing with a driver who'd parked his car – and had no excise licence – on a double yellow line outside the Acapulco. Stood by the car and watched, scarcely able to credit what I was seeing. Given the atmospherics, for the fuzz to challenge and try to arrest! – any Black today, in the heartland of Rasta territory, seemed an act of criminal stupidity. The cops soon realized their mistake and went white with fear beneath their huge helmets as about sixty Rastas crowded round, gesticulating and shouting the sort of gross insults to which I've recently become accustomed. The fuzz did *nothing* to provoke violence – apart from the initial error of trying to make an arrest at that spot! – yet within moments the first punch had been thrown and the action was on. Already the nearby shops had swiftly barred their doors and pulled down their steel shutters. Then a dozen local police arrived in Pandas, including two young women PCs who walked into the middle of it all looking less scared than the males. At least the traffic cops were wearing heavy jackets and helmets; the locals were all in shirtsleeves (today seems this summer's *hottest* in Brum) and looked alarmingly vulnerable as bricks and bottles flew from every direction – supplies are kept handy for such occasions – and litterbins were torn from their moorings and used as weapons. I sheltered in the Acapulco doorway, able to watch every move in safety. For some reason one traffic-cop tried to mount his machine and ride away. A Rasta rushed out and kicked him off it, sending him sprawling across the road. Groups of police and Blacks fought and several police vehicles were attacked. Inevitably there was a traffic-jam; the Villa Road carries heavy through traffic. A stupid bus-driver tried to edge forward – I suppose to try to get his vehicle out of range of flying missiles – just as a cop rolled half-under the bus in the course of a scuffle. For one ghastly moment I thought his torso was going to be squashed by the back wheels; then the driver heard a warning yell and stopped. It wasn't my impression that the Blacks deliberately pushed the cop under the bus; it simply happened that way. Only the senior officer was 'armed', with a pathetic short stick like quarter of a *lathi*. Wisely, he didn't use it, even when two cops were being rolled on the ground. Had he done so, we might have had a *real* riot. He left it to other PCs to join in the fray, on equal fisticuff terms, and rescue their mates. Clever. I noticed again what's struck me before: the Rastas' bark is often worse than their bite. The cops were outnumbered by about five to one and could have been overwhelmed and mashed up. An interesting though not unusual feature was the violence of two Black women who joined in the swearing, punching and bottle-throwing as vigorously as any male. To an extent these confrontations seem like a game and both sides know how they're going to end. There's a ritualistic quality about the abusive language, missile-throwing, kicking and vandalizing police vehicles and (relatively) mildly assaulting cops. Then comes the arrest of a few Blacks (two this time) and suddenly the party's over ... As the last Panda drove off, with two cops in the back literally sitting on an amiable (in my experience) Rasta, the brute who so frightened me last week came over and said, 'Fuck off now, you dirty White c***! You've had a good time, right? Watching your bloodclot friends winning, right?' So I fucked off, to write down every detail while fresh. Writing easy today: arm much better. I feel I've long since ceased to 'study' Race Relations; now I'm just hanging in *surviving* Race Relations . . . No wonder poor R. thought Handsworth's vibes 'rather unsettling'. But possibly this violence may, paradoxically, lower the tension – as action often does. To the Villa Cross now, to get Rasta reactions.

I didn't have to go even as far as the Villa Cross to get Rasta reactions. While writing the last few sentences I had smelt smoke but thought nothing of it; the season of garden bonfires was beginning. But when I stepped out of No. 45 at 7.25 p.m. I saw three fire-engines arriving outside the bingo hall beside the Acapulco. It was immediately apparent that this would be no routine fire-quelling operation; the atmosphere was electric, with Rastas yelling abuse at the firemen. (For some entirely inexplicable reason, firemen are regarded as allies of the police and so part of Babylon and 'legitimate targets', as the Provos would put it.) For a few moments I stood beside the engines, watching the hoses being unrolled. Then the bricks and bottles started flying and I moved, for the second time that day, to the shelter of the Acapulco doorway. This was two hours after the end of the last incident and there wasn't a policeman in sight. When a fireman was knocked unconscious by a brick one fire-engine sped him away to hospital. Another went around to Radnor Road, entered the bingo hall from the back and soon put out the small fire; no flames were ever visible from outside. As the third crew hastily rolled up its hoses the first petrol bombs were thrown from the Villa Cross forecourt. When petrol ignited on the pavement three yards away from me I reckoned it might be healthier to be behind rather than in front of the bombers. So I circled around them – they had a milk-crate full of petrol bombs behind the wall – and entered the pub as eight unprotected police officers arrived from Thornhill Road in a Ford Transit van (also unprotected) which was at once rained with petrol bombs and other missiles and forced to withdraw to await reinforcements.

Kevin looked ashen – defeated. As he drew my pint of cider he said, 'You'd better drink up quickly, we'll have to close soon.' There were only three others in the bar; two Black youths still playing pool, ostentatiously ignoring the drama, and a very tall Rasta who stood by a window observing developments. The pub stands where the Villa Road ends and the Heathfield and Lozells Roads form the arms of a Y. I joined the Rasta as another police vehicle arrived; its windscreen was instantly smashed but a line of a dozen or so officers – with shields but without protective clothing – formed across the end of the Villa Road and held their ground while being petrol-bombed by about 200 Blacks.

At that point I had to accept the shocking fact that the police were not prepared for trouble at the Villa Cross – or even half-prepared. It later emerged in the Chief Constable's Report that at this time (8 p.m.) there were only *thirty-three* officers available, many of whom had to be used to prevent pedestrians or traffic from entering the riot area. However, if we are talking simply of courage, the West Midlands police covered themselves in glory that night. Their bravery was astounding. There is no other country in the world (except my own) where so few officers would be expected to face such appalling danger with such meagre equipment.

When another small group of police arrived – some protected, though inadequately – the rioters moved back slightly to the top of Lozells Road, directly opposite the Villa Cross windows. Thus they drew the fuzz into a position which left them vulnerable to being attacked also from the rear from Barker Street. I crossed to a window overlooking this battlesite where the police were to be held, helpless, for the next two hours. Even to a sheltered non-participant, the scene was terrifying. So few policemen, so many Blacks hurling a variety of missiles – and all the time blazing bottles curving through the darkness and spurts of flame illuminating the ground around the fuzz. Very soon the *unprotected* officers were forced to withdraw: it would have been suicidal to do otherwise. Already a protected officer had been knocked to the ground by the sheer force behind one missile. I suddenly vividly remembered one Rasta-friend's words, spoken in the Villa Cross on the evening of 10 July, after the raid on the Acapulco – 'If the lid comes off while you're still around . . . ' For three months I had been exposed to the Rastas' resentment, frustration, despair, rage and irrational hatred of the fuzz – as representing the very *essence* of Babylon. It didn't surprise me that one thrown missile could fell a policeman. I had listened often enough to verbal expressions of the energies that propelled that missile. The very tall Rasta was standing beside me as I silently surveyed the sort of scene that doesn't seem real when it's happening almost literally in your front garden. He said quietly, but with the joy of triumph in his voice – 'Man, you ain't seen nuthin' yet! Wait till we've got our mortar bombs!'

Kevin shouted at us – 'For Christ's sake get away from the windows!' It was the first time I had ever heard him raising his voice or using profane language. Most of the bar lights were switched off then and the Rasta left; the oblivious pool-playing youths had already been sent home. I helped to draw heavy curtains across all the pub's windows. 'Otherwise we could be a target,' Kevin explained. 'It wouldn't make sense, but there's no sense left out there.' He wanted me to spend the night in the Villa Cross. 'You can't go out now,' he insisted. 'It's got too bad – they're taking over.' He hurried off then, to attend to a woman who had become hysterical (clinically hysterical) somewhere in the background. I gulped the rest of my pint, said goodbye to the barmaids and at 8.20 p.m. was the last customer to leave the Villa Cross before it closed – for ever.

I left through a normally unused door on the quiet Heathfield Road side and sprinted to the first turning on the right – Mayfield Road – which took me back on to Lozells Road. There I paused for a moment. About 100 yards away on my right the Blacks were still holding their position outside the pub: by now dense smoke from their heavy petrol-bombing marked the spot. Much closer, on my left, two large vans had been overturned and set alight at the Finch Road/Burbury Street junction; between that junction and the pub, the Lozells Road is mainly residential. Dozens of Blacks and a few Brown youths were racing towards the main shopping area beyond the fiercely burning vehicles. As I trotted after them two ferocious-looking but normally amiable Rastas sped past me – then recognized their regular drinking companion and paused to shout kindly, 'Get home you stupid bitch!'

I shouted back, 'Thanks, but I'm on duty!' Human beings are peculiar. Where is the logic in being scared rigid when nothing is happening – as I was during the previous week – yet dead cool when everything is happening? Once the action starts the tension is over and adrenalin flows and away one dashes without a care in the world – very odd!

A fire-engine had just come onto the Lozells Road through side-streets and its crew was bravely attempting to deal with the burning vehicles; but they were savagely attacked and forced to withdraw quickly. No more fire-engines were seen anywhere in the area until about 10.30 p.m. It would have been futile for them to try to intervene without police protection.

Beyond the blazing vans I saw several other vehicles being set alight at strategic junctions. At first this looked like nothing more than anarchic destructiveness. Being rather slow-witted, I didn't realize until a little later that a looting area was thus being efficiently isolated from law-and-order interference. But by midnight my observations had convinced me that considerable pre-planning was involved.

The next ninety minutes felt so weirdly unreal I could scarcely believe it was all happening. During that extraordinary interlude I watched the Have-nots running riot, systematically looting and burning shops without any apparent risk of police intervention. Although started by Blacks, this was certainly no race-riot. Within a quarter of an hour many Browns and Whites had zestfully joined in the plundering, some hurrying from nearby areas when the local media newsflashed: 'RIOTING IN HANDSWORTH!' Prim and proper White women from little terrace houses off the Lozells Road – houses with sparkling windows and neatly pruned roses in their front garden patches – came rushing to load up prams, baby-buggies and wheelbarrows. Motor vans and car boots were being frenziedly stuffed with goodies. And the Blacks were in a sharing mood. I saw many come leaping out of smashed shop windows to throw armfuls of loot on the street – or lay it on the street, in cases of delicate electronic equipment – while inviting all and sundry to help themselves. It was quite clear at this early stage that many looters regarded the operation as something more than a conventional criminal exercise in 'gain for me'. I have a most vivid memory of one elated Black youth, his face coppercoloured in the glow of flames, inviting a White woman to choose from his pile of shoe-boxes – while the emptied shoe-shop blazed in the background. 'What do you need?' he asked her – shouting above the roar of the new fire. Has anyone seriously heeded this aspect of Handsworth's riot – *'What do you need?'* – and recognized its implications for the future?

Another memory is of laughing looters being cheered by onlookers as they pushed heaped supermarket trolleys down the middle of the road between high sheets of flame: I couldn't have believed those trolleys were capable of such speed. The atmosphere was totally free of any threat of inter-personal violence, racial or otherwise; it was not even a quarrelsome – far less a 'murderous' – night. Aggro was confined to the Rasta versus fuzz battle, still in progress outside the Villa Cross. There was of course a slight risk of injury from the combustible environment as car-engines, petrol-pumps and domestic gas-cylinders in the burning buildings exploded – and some of the buildings themselves began to collapse. Yet during those chaotic twelve hours only *seven* civilians were injured: a figure which tells more about the nature of the riot than any number of 'Reports'.

To compound the unreality one pub – the Lozells Arms – stayed open while the shops all around it were going up in flames. Outside the door stood a group of Black, White and Brown men, calmly swigging their pints and viewing the riot as though it were some form of street entertainment. Another pint of cider was just what I needed but had not, in the circumstances, expected to find. Half a dozen customers still sat in the pub; as the barman drew my pint I suggested that it might be time to clear the place. Then I joined the drinkers on the pavement.

In a bizarre way the feeling was of a perverted lunatic carnival rather than a riot. But the heat was intense; now all the multi-racial looters looked the same copper colour in the glow of towering flames. And still more shops, having been swiftly stripped of their stock, were being set alight with manic glee. Providentially the evening was windless. One felt sick with fear to think of the consequences should a breeze spring up and take the flames down the many little nearby streets of crowded houses.

At about nine o'clock I had passed Lozells Post Office; the adjacent buildings were ablaze but it seemed undamaged. Some fifteen minutes later I came running back, to get away from a burning garage, and saw it in flames. A Pakistani youth told me – 'People are inside!' But I didn't believe him; by then it seemed incredible that anyone would have stayed in any building along Lozells Road.

By 10 p.m. there wasn't much left of the Lozells shopping area; some £16 million worth of property was burning. In harrowing contrast to the carnival spirit of the looters was the dazed, incredulous grief of the traders – the majority Brown. Most were as yet too shocked to be angry; rage came later. At the end of Lozells Road I found a group sitting on the edge of the pavement near an expanse of wasteland, opposite their burning premises, weeping like little children. An elderly Pakistani man stood alone, slightly apart from the rest, sobbing and repeatedly mopping his tears with his shirt-sleeve. A passing Black youth – empty-handed – paused and crossed the road to put an arm around the trader's shoulder. Then he offered him a cigarette and a moment later they walked away together, round the corner into Wheeler Street – where shortly before I had seen the Midland Bank being ransacked.

I was amidst a maze of side-streets, where I saw more petrol bombs being made in the grounds of Holte School, during the first police advance – in a fully protected van – down Lozells Road. Vehicles were being overturned and set alight in the side-streets by smallish gangs of youths – mainly Black, but supported by a few Browns. However, some protected police were at last visible, being sporadically attacked by yelling youths as they tried to cordon off the approaches to the main riot area. I returned circuitously to that area and reached the corner of Malthouse Gardens in time to see a phalanx of police, still under heavy attack from missiles and petrol bombs, slowly fighting their way through the by now almost intolerable heat of the Lozells Road. An elderly White couple were also watching. 'They're risking their lives!' said the husband. 'And what use are they now? There's not much left to loot! Why didn't they come two hours ago? They got 'phone calls by the dozen – they knew well what was going on . . . Why did they give those Black bastards *two hours* to help themselves? And do *this* to Lozells!' As he spoke his wife suddenly burst into tears – and then a policeman appeared beside us and said the area might have to be evacuated because of the risk of a massive garage explosion in nearby Berner Street.

During the rest of the night – while firemen were coping with the inferno and police were protecting firemen from rioters and residents from fire – I wandered about talking to people of all colours. In retrospect I realized that by then we were all – even those least personally affected – in a state of shock. And it was shock at two levels. To see a large part of one's neighbourhood destroyed by fire within ninety minutes would be traumatic even if the blaze were accidental. But for most the greater shock was the knowledge that it had been destroyed because the police could not (or, as many believed that night, *would not*) protect it. To the average citizen that was more profoundly frightening than the potential danger should a wind suddenly spring up before the firemen gained control.

While the riot was at its most dramatic I had been shaken to observe several elderly Blacks, whom I knew to be devout church-goers, encouraging the looting and burning – though not of course taking part in it. As I toured the side-streets during the small hours many other 'good citizen' Blacks refused to condemn the rioters, as most of their White and Brown neighbours were then doing – even some who had, a few hours earlier, taken advantage of the disorder to 'stock up'. Instead, these pillars of Pentecostalism were openly identifying with the 'activists' and sharing in the general Black euphoria. I kept in touch with these individuals and within forty-eight hours their 'un-respectable' emotions had been suppressed and law-abiding attitudes were again prevailing; most of them later attended an interfaith two-hour service of reconciliation in a Methodist Church on the Lozells Road almost opposite the Villa Cross – a symbolic site. Yet what they revealed that night seemed to me at least as genuine as their 'respectable' aspect: and possibly more so. It felt as though a vast reservoir of repressed resentment of White racialism had suddenly burst its dam. Most 'immigrant-generation' Blacks may choose to ignore the manifold disadvantages of being Black in Britain. But that does not mean they are insensitive to their second-class-citizen status, or indifferent to the impotent anguish of the younger generation. So perhaps after all it is true to say that at the deepest level this *was* a race-riot – Blacks versus The Rest – but with multi-racial crosscurrents of Have-nots versus Haves and an increasing infusion of common criminality as more and more professional criminals from other areas arrived to take advantage of this unprecedented breakdown in law-and-order. I encountered no muggers or robbers during the night, but heard numerous reports of their activities. Significantly, of the first batch of rioters brought to court, forty-nine out of sixty-six did *not* come from Handsworth.

At about 7 a.m. I was devastated to hear that firemen had found two bodies in the Post Office. The Moledina brothers had been immensely kind and helpful to me – among the most welcoming Browns in Handsworth when I was a newcomer.

That was a most dreadful dawn, made inexpressibly more so by groups of jubilant Blacks celebrating their 'achievement' – their destruction of an area of Babylon – by singing and dancing in the streets while dazed Brown traders (many of whom lived elsewhere) arrived to face the negation of decades of hard work and sobbed in each other's arms. At that stage it felt very like a Black versus Brown race-riot. One could understand why so much media instant comment misinterpreted it as such, yet there had been many Brown looters and some of the Lozells Road's few Black business premises were also destroyed.

At 7.45 a.m. I rang my closest London friends from a Berners Street telephone kiosk. Its glass sides had half-melted in the heat, to become all opaque and wavy, yet the telephone was still working – which seemed part of the general unreality, since most Handsworth telephones do not work in normal times. Then I went home for a quick mug of coffee; usually breakfast is my main meal but I was too churned up to eat – a widespread reaction, I later discovered, among those involved in the night's events. The 9 a.m. news included a supremely fatuous police statement – 'This trouble came as a complete surprise. A happy Carnival, opened by the Chief Constable, has just taken place, with police and West Indians dancing together in the streets.'

In several media interviews during the next few days, and subsequently in his official Riot Report, Mr Geoffrey Dear made much of the fact that, 'The riots took place on a Monday afternoon after a weekend on which a successful Carnival had been held in the streets.' Yet the minority of Blacks who help to organize a police-sponsored Carnival have no connection with that other minority who help to organize a riot. A police force that prides itself on its 'community policing' should know better than to regard the 'West Indians' as a homogeneous group. The claim that the riot 'came as a complete surprise' infuriated Handsworth's Browns. Mr Jaswant Sohal, secretary of the Handsworth Traders' Association and a member of the local police Consultative Committee, said: 'Six Asian shops on the Soho Road were vandalized and looted by West Indians on Sunday night. It was no ordinary act of theft. I immediately contacted the police to warn them that this was likely to be the start of something bigger. I cannot believe it when the police say they were not prepared for something. They had been told, but they just did not heed the warning.'

By 9.45 a.m. I was back on the Lozells Road, where hundreds of media people and sightseers had gathered. Soon after, the BBC reported that Mr Hurd, the Home Secretary, was heading our way. (His Handsworth nickname can be left to my readers' imagination.) I could scarcely credit this official piling of stupidity on stupidity. Among both Blacks and Browns the Home Secretary (*any* Home Secretary) is at the best of times the most hated Government Minister – for obvious reasons. To have let Mr Hurd loose on the Lozells Road on that Tuesday afternoon seemed grotesquely irresponsible to every resident of Handsworth, whatever their other differences. We all knew beforehand exactly what would happen; by noon I had chosen which garden wall to lie behind while observing the farce. But it seems the police did *not* know. Although then present in vast numbers, up and down the Lozells Road, they had somehow failed to notice what was going on all morning, from about 8 a.m., as local Black militants, who wanted the rioting to be resumed at dusk, incited gangs of youths to more violence. There was nothing furtive about this rabble-rousing; the speakers stood on garden walls, only yards away from lines of policemen, while spouting revolution to increasingly emotional gatherings of Black youths. And yet the Home Secretary was allowed into that area to mingle with those youths – a novelist who invented such an implausible episode wouldn't be published. It was indeed brave of Mr Hurd to venture into the war-zone, but one can feel only modified admiration for that sort of bravery – based on total ignorance of and insensitivity to the feelings of a community. He was lucky to escape without injury (except to his dignity). But when he had been rescued by the police, and bundled rump-up into a prison-van, Handsworth was left to take the consequences of Home Office misjudgement and police obtuseness. As the rescue vehicle sped away, missiles flew thick as a flock of starlings and several journalists were attacked and burning car tanks exploded – including an overturned police van, close to my garden wall, which was looted before being set on fire. Then the disorder spread over a wide area of Handsworth and many more shops were looted and vehicles burned. Afterwards a black (no pun intended) joke circulated in police circles: 'When we got him in the van we beat nine shades of stuffing out of him – just habit – before we saw who he was!' It would please me if that story were true, but I fear it isn't.

It was another hot sunny day, which seemed to emphasize the tragedy of the still smouldering Lozells Road. While sitting with Black friends – a middle-aged couple – on the doorstep of their terrace house in a nearby street, I listened to Mrs Thatcher setting the tone for Tory reaction to the riot. Having condemned it as 'utterly appalling', and emphasized that it was in no way connected with unemployment or inner-city deprivation, she rejected any criticism of the police and added: 'We shall need all the leaders of the local community to make sure it doesn't happen again.' My friends switched off their transistor and looked at me despairingly. The husband slowly rubbed a hand to and fro across his forehead and said, 'That frightens me. That's scary – specially the bit about community leaders. So this country's Prime Minister knows nothing – understands nothing – about our problems. How many more riots before she learns?' Immediately, 'Utterly Appalling!' became a Handsworth catch-phrase; for days one heard it being chanted with derision up and down the back-streets.

Watching media people at work deepened my post-riot depression. They are set an impossible task on such occasions – flung into a complex crisis, without any background knowledge, yet required to deliver their 'piece' by a deadline. On that Tuesday morning various bemused-looking characters wandered up to me with pencils poised over notebooks and asked, 'Do you live around here? Can you say *why* this riot happened – in just a few words?'

I gazed at them with genuine sympathy and replied, 'I do live around here, but no comment – certainly not in less than ten thousand words.' No wonder they produced so much drivel during the next few days, while trying to explain a riot in 'a few words'. It was disquieting to observe them being manipulated by publicity-seeking politicians, ambitious local councillors, devious so-called 'community leaders' – ninety per cent of whom are wildly unrepresentative of their communities – and eloquent Black zealots who fed them packs of lies about police aggro during the 'sparking off' incident outside the Acapulco. Much of the press coverage was as usual malicious/hysterical/racialist. And unfortunately coverage of such an event only has to be *incompetent* to do more damage to community relations than the event itself.

Even more damaging than the press are television interviews, which make cruel demands in times of stress on people in authority. On that Tuesday morning the Chief Constable was expected to do his bit before the cameras after a sleepless night. When asked, 'Do you think this trouble was Blacks against Asians?' he emphatically said 'Yes'. That monosyllable considerably heightened tension, in complicated ways, throughout the rest of the day. In one sense brief television interviews and cobbled-together newspaper articles are ephemeral as the dew and each media excitement seems to blot out the last riot/spy drama/earthquake/sex scandal. Yet given a Handsworth-type situation the most apparently trivial 'error in communication' can have malign long-term effects among people predisposed to misinterpret or take umbrage at any statement from those in authority.

By agreement with the police, all our local pubs remained closed on 10 September: a sensible move, though it punished the innocent as well as the guilty. Throughout that day the atmosphere was very much nastier than it had been during the night. Post-Hurd, rioting was resumed for a few hours – this time on Heathfield Road. Many windows of private houses were smashed; cars were overturned and a few set on fire; I saw several groups of Rastas rushing around with more petrol bombs and about 150 Black youths erected a barrier at the junction of Heathfield and Westminster Roads. Again the police were excluded from an area for long enough to permit the looting of most Heathfield Road shops and the burning of one set of premises. A Pakistani greengrocer-cum-tobacconist had a flash of inspiration and put up a notice saying – ALL GOODS FREE TODAY. Most of the looters passed him by and when I entered in search of cigars the shop was deserted and more or less intact. I went upstairs but Ali refused to take any money. 'Help yourself!' he said. 'That notice is genuine!' As there was no other shop open within a three-mile radius, and my frayed nerves needed nicotine, I did help myself; but later I righted that wrong.

Heathfield Road remained so long unprotected because at this stage the police were alarmingly over-extended. Many had to remain on the Lozells Road, to keep the public out of the danger area of collapsing buildings. And simultaneously gangs had gone into action just beyond Handsworth, in Perry Barr, where there was much looting, burning, robbing at knife-point and stoning of cars on the A34 trunk road.

When I passed Heathfield Primary School at 2 p.m. all gates into the playground were locked and the staff had requested police protection for their 300 pupils. Groups of tense parents stood about on the pavement debating what to do for the best. Should they take their children home, or would they be safer in the school building? Emotions were tangled. When large groups of Black youths raced purposefully past us, towards the barricade at the end of the road, fear of their violence was palpable – as it had not been during the night. Yet mingled with that fear, on the faces and in the voices of some young mothers, was admiration for their continuing defiance of the fuzz.

'They've got the cops on the run!' exclaimed one Black woman, holding her year-old baby tightly in her arms. 'They'll take the Soho Road tonight – there's no way anyone can stop them now!'

Her companion shivered and said, '*I* don't want no more burning! It'll be houses next – our homes – anything – they've gone mad, they're just criminals. What *good*'s it doing us?'

An older Black woman, red-eyed and dishevelled, had come to collect a grandchild. She said, 'We were evacuated last night – Berner Street, the garage, it was like a war-film! I've a crippled husband, I thought he'd be burnt in his bed – he's gone now to his sister in Coventry, anything could happen tonight and he couldn't take no more.' Then she threw back her head and folded her arms and looked directly at me. 'You think we're all savages?' she asked rhetorically. 'OK – *I* think we're savages. But maybe we have to be, see? Remember the States? *I* remember! "Burn, Baby, Burn!" And *then* something happened . . . It's bad when you're in the middle of it – like us, now, here, on the Heathfield Road and we don't know will it still be here tomorrow. And those kids are just gone crazy with excitement – it breaks the monotony, see? And maybe it has to be like this – like this and worse than this, all over Britain, wherever there's Blacks . . . And *then* maybe something happens, see?'

A very young White mother was listening; she had a pale, thin, drawn face – one of those heart-breaking inner-city faces that look old at twenty. Now she thrust out her hand to the Black granny. 'Shake!' she said. 'You're talking for us, too! Handsworth isn't having a race-riot – *no way!*'

Violence spread rapidly throughout that grim afternoon. All Handsworth's criminals, joined by scores from other areas, seemed to be on the rampage. Six Soho Road shops, including two jewellers, were looted and one petrol-bombed. Shops and offices on Rookery Road, Grove Lane and Oxhill Road were ransacked. Anyone who tried to defend property or cash was threatened – and several people were attacked – with knives acquired the night before along the Lozells Road. The police couldn't cope and terrified Brown traders were complaining that they had been abandoned to the mercilessness of the Blacks. Earlier the police had stupidly announced that they were treating the Moledina brothers' deaths as murder. Several newspapers had printed fictitious accounts – under 'BLOODLUST!' or 'KILLING!' or 'MURDER!' headlines – of the brothers having been beaten and stabbed by a Black gang who then set the post office alight and left them to roast to death. Anyone who had been near the post office at the time found these accounts incredible; the Lozells rioters were not, as the Chief Constable later admitted in his report, person-threatening. And many months later a twenty-year-old *White* man was convicted of the brothers' *manslaughter*. But post-riot the shockingly irresponsible media image of *Blacks murdering Browns* added immeasurably to the terror and despair felt by Brown traders when Black gangs invaded their premises and there wasn't a policeman in sight.

By dusk the windows of most shops, pubs, post offices, banks and offices had been boarded up and the siege atmosphere was strong. Happily several pubs along the Soho Road were accessible at that stage though not open; by knocking on a side-door, and identifying oneself, it was possible to gain admission. About 200 young Blacks gathered at the Soho Road–Villa Road junction soon after dark; a similar group at the Boulton Road junction petrol-bombed a police Traffic Control van. Gangs of youths – Black, Brown and White – were roaming the surrounding streets and I roamed too. At irregular intervals police-gang confrontations took place but I was then sufficiently familiar with Handsworth's back streets and alleyways to move from trouble spot to trouble spot without getting too involved.

PAUL GILROY

Paul Gilroy is Professor of Sociology and Cultural Studies at Goldsmith's College, London University. He has taught at the South Bank Polytechnic and the University of Essex, and been a regular visitor in the programme for African and African-American studies at Yale. He is the author of *Ain't No Black in the Union Jack* and *The Black Atlantic*, and co-author of *The Empire Strikes Back*.

Small Acts is a collection of essays that meditate on the emergence of a distinctive black British culture, and its connections to the wider diasporas which it feeds off. It contains essays on rap music, Spike Lee, black British art, photography and film, the artist Turner, and on nationalism, ethnicity, and history. The extract below considers the significance of Frank Bruno, arguably the most popular black British personality there has ever been. A shorter version of this chapter was published in the *New Statesman* in 1990.

from *Small Acts*
Frank Bruno or Salman Rushdie?

Frank Bruno has become a significant public figure, an unlikely but nonetheless important symbol of the future of blacks in this country. His defeat by Mike Tyson drew no serious comment from cultural critics or commentators. Yet over 14 million Britons watched the first showing of that contest which turned out to be the most popular sporting event of the decade. The adulation heaped on Frank is unprecedented for a black athlete, unmatched even by the praise showered on Daley Thompson at the peak of his career or on Tessa Sanderson before she fell foul of her rival Fatima Whitbread. In tasting defeat, Frank found a triumph which had considerable significance beyond the sporting sub-culture in which it originated. This came across in the extraordinary way that Frank Bruno instantly became 'our Frank': a broad English oak, standing sluggish not firm, amidst the unwholesome tornado of Tyson's Bedford Stuyvesant atavism.

England's other pre-eminent black sportsman, John Barnes, provides an interesting comparison. Barnes retains a Jamaican passport and remains an enigmatic and peripheral figure, drifting aimlessly on the wing of national life. His role in the team mirrors the problems of his public personality and, in spite of his heroic and dignified behaviour in the aftermath of the Hillsborough tragedy, he seems unlikely ever to get stuck into the hard graft involved in being British. In contrast, Frank's sincere patriotism and cultural authenticity are self-evident. His canonization was particularly important because it happened at a time when racism regularly constructed blackness and Britishness as mutually exclusive social and cultural categories. The key to comprehending his special significance lies first in his obvious Englishness – an attribute which has been noted by several commentators but not explored. He was, for example, casually compared to St George by one writer and ridiculed by another who suggested that it would have been more appropriate for him to have fought the all-conquering world champion wearing a red nose. These sniggery responses, which view Frank as a kind of Gary Wilmot in Lonsdale trimmings, typify a peculiar malaise that takes hold of English critical thinking where race is concerned. An additional symptom of this is the inability to appreciate how both racialized subjectivity and the national identity that nourishes it have been crucially shaped by the discourses of sporting achievement in popular culture and beyond. It is hard to avoid the conclusion that the inability to see Frank as a significant symbol, or indeed, to see Frank at all, is a striking illustration of the remoteness and introspection that characterize so much commentary on popular culture.

If the radicals and the anti-racists either ignored or ridiculed Frank, those who did notice him – on the right and in the tabloid press – elected to celebrate his performance, seeing in it a deep cultural affiliation to the British national community. It was his predictable failure that cogently expressed all that community's sterling masculine qualities. Failure became heroic rather than disappointing and was rapidly annexed by the 'Eddie the Eagle' syndrome whereby English losers are able to transcend the indignity of defeat and acquire special status. You can just imagine the over-wordy, red, white and blue T-shirts 'Two world wars, one World Cup and eight failed attempts at the World Heavyweight Championship'.

The broader resonance of Frank's heroism of the vanquished and conspicuous 'trans-racial' popularity for the cultural dimensions of racism and nationalism in this country should have been obvious at any time. But coming in the midst of the Rushdie affair, its important lessons have appeared all the more striking. Frank's physical accomplishment, however meagre beside Tyson's own, conveys a clear message that *some* representatives of the ethnic minorities in this country *are* capable and willing to make the cultural and social adaptations demanded of them in the wake of *The Satanic Verses*. For a while, Frank's muscular black English masculinity became a counterpart to the esoteric and scholastic image of Rushdie – the middle-class intellectual *immigrant* – so remote from the world of ordinary folk that he was able to misjudge it so tragically.

For two weeks the two stories were articulated directly together. They fed off each other, echoing, replying and reworking the same range of visceral themes: belonging and exclusion, sameness and assimilation, the difficulty of escaping from the racial cultures which now more than ever appeared to constitute an absolute division in history and humanity.

It is tempting to suggest that the inability to perceive the connection between these two narratives of black cultural development itself portrays the weakness of the left/liberal line within the *Satanic Verses* debate. Alongside the lofty principles and abstract aesthetic excellence invoked by Rushdie's supporters in the nation's literary elite, Frank's triumph must appear trivial and base. But, every bit as much as the responses to Rushdie's book, Frank's five stumbling rounds in Vegas offered a means to clarify contemporary British identity and values. The image of each man stood as a convenient emblem for one of Britain's black settler communities, marking out their respective rates of progress towards integration. Each image increased its symbolic power through implicit references to the other – its precise inversion. The same complex interplay was to be repeated exactly one year later when Frank's wedding to his long-time sweetheart coincided with the anniversary of Ayatollah Khomeini's fatwa.

The different ways in which the class and the masculinity of both men worked to portray wider ideas of race and national identity needs to be located in the context of the historic folk grammar of British racism. This in turn requires consideration of what has been called the 'Goldilocks-and-the-three-bears theory of racial culture and identity'. This common-sense perspective specifies that animal blacks enjoy an excess of brute physicality and wily oriental gentlemen conversely display a surfeit of cerebral power, while only the authentic Anglo-Brit is able to luxuriate in the perfect equilibrium of body and mind.

The right, of course, had no difficulty in recognizing the manner in which Bruno had become important or the obvious relationship between the parallel ordeals of Bruno and Rushdie. This tale of two immigrants was immediately perceived as one epic account of the progress of Britain's black settlers. In the *Sunday Telegraph* Walter Ellis outlined the peculiar mechanisms whereby, in losing his big fight, Big Frank had ironically won the hearts of the nation:

> What we admire about him is his defiant dignity in the face of impending calamity . . . When Frank turned up in a Savile Row suit for a prefight news conference and Tyson appeared in what looked like an outsize babygrow, the writing was already on the wall . . .

In a direct comparison with Rushdie, Ellis concluded that being British was what Big Frank did best: 'In the area of Englishness he is tops, the champ, the number one man.' Frank's well-publicized depression at having let the British public down was the cherry on a patriotic cake.

The black prizefighter has a long and noble history in this country and an almost unbroken line of black pugilists connects Frank's recent modest efforts to the brave strivings of Joe Leashley in 1791. Pierce Egan's *Boxiana*, first published in 1812, is replete with tales of Frank's nineteenth-century antecedents. Though probably more nimble than Bruno, the most famous of these men, Bill Richmond, was similarly well-dressed and smart. Richmond was landlord of the Horse and Dolphin pub near Leicester Square and is probably best remembered for having taught William Hazlitt to use his fists. Comparing Richmond to Othello, Egan continues: 'we cannot omit stating of our hero that he is intelligent, communicative, and well behaved'. We are also informed that, notwithstanding a defect in one of his knees, Mr Richmond excelled as a cricketer.

It becomes necessary to ask how the long-overdue entry of a black boxer into the mystical communion of authentic British nationality has been achieved. The obvious answer lies in the nature of the sport in which 'our Frank' has chosen to earn his corn. The heavyweight division is absolutely unmatched as a location for putting masculine aggression on display. But, apart from the simple fact that he is a boxer, Frank has considerable charm and can be witty, even if his 'suntan' gag has been seriously overused. He toys cleverly with the white audience's expectation that he is nothing more than a punch-drunk buffoon. He wears his Savile Row suits with grace and a genuine humility shines like a beacon through the hype that surrounds him. It is only half a joke to say that Frank has been given a halo. In him, the gentle giant and the noble savage fuse to form a black man who cares so little for his beefcake profile that he cries in public – no wonder Iron Mike walked all over him.

Frank's class, and particularly his South London working-class speech, is another powerful factor. It provides a clue to the construction of his own ethnicity in the circuitous route from Wandsworth to Essex via the Old Kent Road. At the most basic level, his class tells us that he is one of the boys. His definition of manliness works through the imagery and symbols of class as well as those of race. What makes him heroic works both in spite of his blackness *and* because of it. The extraordinary detail with which his personal history has been revealed in the media is a further means to place him. We now know, for example, that a kindly school-dinner lady gave him extra puddings to help him on his way. We know that his mother sits in the toilet rather than watch her boy in combat. We know how his sister Angela was mistakenly manhandled by security guards. We know above all about Frank's partner, Laura, and their two daughters, Nicola (6) and Rachel (2) – the two tiny knockouts who wait to welcome him home to Hornchurch. It is not only that the issue of whether Frank would finally make an honest woman of Laura generated a mini soap opera in its own right. The means to comprehend Frank's transfiguration into a genuine or at least an honorary Brit lies with the representation of the Bruno family – nuclear and extended.

Laura is white, but Frank does not menace her white femininity; he complements it. Nobody makes cracks about Beauty and the beast when they are around. Laura's declaration of love for the Big Man was the pivot of the TV spectacle. 'Tyson hasn't got what Frank's got,' she intoned, suddenly looking serious, and somehow made the adoration of all Frank's fans an extension of her own personal passion for him. What exactly has Frank got that Tyson lacks? Laura? A British passport? A stable and orthodox domestic set-up?

Contemporary British racism deals in cultural difference rather than crude biological hierarchy. It asserts not that blacks are inferior but that we are different, so different that our distinctive mode of being is at odds with residence in this country. Roughly speaking, black settlers of 'Afro-Caribbean' descent are deemed to be incapable of subscribing to the designated standards of acceptable cultural conduct, whereas comparable 'Asians', even if they possess the potential to meet these standards, lack the requisite inclination. The Goldilocks-and-the-three-bears theory affirms that this too is a matter of simple common sense. The cultural character of this form of racism differentiates it from earlier forms but it is important for at least two other reasons. First, it aligns race and nation very closely together, and second, the family is identified as the primary means through which the inappropriate, deviant and incompatible cultures of resident blacks are illegitimately reproduced to form the oxymoronic 'second-generation immigrant'. 'Afro-Caribbean' families are weak and disorganized, while their 'Asian' equivalents are equally damned for being excessively durable and much too scrupulous in the tasks of cultural transmission.

As the post-war idea of the British Commonwealth as a family of nations began to date and fade, a more sinister vision of the British race as a nation of neatly symmetrical families began to replace it. Against this background, even before they acquired a marriage certificate, Frank's immediate family was cast in the image of the acceptable majority rather than the deviant Caribbean alternative. His partner's whiteness redeemed him from the curse of his ethnicity and provided a means to escape the fortifications of cultural alterity. The fundamental image of domestic harmony which surrounds Frank, Laura and their daughters enables the national community to be presented as an extension of the Bruno clan – one big, happy family. Frank himself compensates for the absence of his own father through the force of his own devotion to that role. We have already met his mother and for most public purposes his manager, Terry Lawless, operates as an authoritative father surrogate. Harry Carpenter made his own bid for the part in a post-fight *Mirror* article where he confided his secret wish that the saintly Frank could have been *his* son. Carpenter would be a prominent figure in media accounts of Bruno's eventual marriage.

The cultural character of today's racism also accentuates ethnic differences *within* the black communities. Some of what were once black communities are now happily shrugging off that label. The precarious political grouping, which for a brief, precious moment during the late 1970s allowed settlers from all the corners of the Empire to find some meaning in an open definition of the term 'black', has been all but destroyed. Today, polite 'anti-racist' orthodoxies demand an alternative formulation – 'black and Asian'. This involves the sacrifice of significant political advantages but is presented as a step forward, a means to remind ourselves that by invoking the term 'black', we are not 'Africanizing' our struggles or declaring everybody to be the same.

Like the activities of his *alter ego*, Lenny Henry, whose own domicile with a white woman was recently attacked by racists, Frank's rise is a significant index of the fragmentation of this older black politics. It is no accident that it was Lenny's appropriation of Frank's linguistic signature 'Know what I mean, Harry?' which triggered the boxer's meteoric ascent into the public eye. Frank, like Lenny's sometime principal character Delbert Wilkins, occasionally threatens to become an embarrassment. But his assertive and provocative occupation of the contested space between blackness and Englishness merits cautious support. The story of his sporting defeat and domestic triumph offers a rich perspective on new patterns of racial realignment. However, the clamour of calls for black and white to unite and fight for the World Heavyweight Championship cannot conceal a new political problem. What do we say when the political and cultural gains of the emergent black Brits go hand in hand with a further marginalization of 'Asians' in general and Muslims in particular?

SALMAN RUSHDIE

Salman Rushdie was born in Bombay in India, and was educated in Britain. He was working as an advertising copywriter when he wrote his first novel, *Grimus*. He won the Booker Prize with his second, the epic *Midnight's Children*. This was followed by *Shame* and *The Satanic Verses*, the latter leading to death threats against him and the issuing of a fatwa by the Iranian leader, Ayatollah Khomeini, for blasphemy against the Koran. He has spent the years since the publication of *The Satanic Verses* in hiding, campaigning vigorously for the right of freedom of expression. He has continued to write, producing another major novel, *The Moor's Last Sigh*, as well as a collection of children's stories, *Haroun and the Sea of Stories*.

'Imaginary Homelands', first published in 1982, is the opening piece in *Imaginary Homelands, Essays and Criticism 1981–1991*, Salman Rushdie's collection of non-fiction pieces written for various publications. The collection contains reviews on other authors, pieces on India, Pakistan, black British culture and on the controversy provoked by *The Satanic Verses*. In 'Imaginary Homelands' he brings together many of these themes as he meditates on the writing of *Midnight's Children* and the role of the writer.

Imaginary Homelands

An old photograph in a cheap frame hangs on a wall of the room where I work. It's a picture dating from 1946 of a house into which, at the time of its taking, I had not yet been born. The house is rather peculiar – a three-storeyed gabled affair with tiled roofs and round towers in two corners, each wearing a pointy tiled hat. 'The past is a foreign country,' goes the famous opening sentence of L. P. Hartley's novel *The Go-Between*, 'they do things differently there.' But the photograph tells me to invert this idea; it reminds me that it's my present that is foreign, and that the past is home, albeit a lost home in a lost city in the mists of lost time.

A few years ago I revisited Bombay, which is my lost city, after an absence of something like half my life. Shortly after arriving, acting on an impulse, I opened the telephone directory and looked for my father's name. And, amazingly, there it was; his name, our old address, the unchanged telephone number, as if we had never gone away to the unmentionable country across the border. It was an eerie discovery. I felt as if I were being claimed, or informed that the facts of my faraway life were illusions, and that this continuity was the reality. Then I went to visit the house in the photograph and stood outside it, neither daring nor wishing to announce myself to its new owners. (I didn't want to see how they'd ruined the interior.) I was overwhelmed. The photograph had naturally been taken in black and white; and my memory, feeding on such images as this, had begun to see my childhood in the same way, monochromatically. The colours of my history had seeped out of my mind's eye; now my other two eyes were assaulted by colours, by the vividness of the red tiles, the yellow-edged green of cactus-leaves, the brilliance of bougainvillaea creeper. It is probably not too romantic to say that that was when my novel *Midnight's Children* was really born; when I realized how much I wanted to restore the past to myself, not in the faded greys of old family-album snapshots, but whole, in CinemaScope and glorious Technicolor.

Bombay is a city built by foreigners upon reclaimed land; I, who had been away so long that I almost qualified for the title, was gripped by the conviction that I, too, had a city and a history to reclaim.

It may be that writers in my position, exiles or emigrants or expatriates, are haunted by some sense of loss, some urge to reclaim, to look back, even at the risk of being mutated into pillars of salt. But if we do look back, we must also do so in the knowledge – which gives rise to profound uncertainties – that our physical alienation from India almost inevitably means that we will not be capable of reclaiming precisely the thing that was lost; that we will, in short, create fictions, not actual cities or villages, but invisible ones, imaginary homelands, Indias of the mind.

Writing my book in North London, looking out through my window on to a city scene totally unlike the ones I was imagining on to paper, I was constantly plagued by this problem, until I felt obliged to face it in the text, to make clear that (in spite of my original and I suppose somewhat Proustian ambition to unlock the gates of lost time so that the past reappeared as it actually had been, unaffected by the distortions of memory) what I was actually doing was a novel of memory and about memory, so that my India was just that: 'my' India, a version and no more than one version of all the hundreds of millions of possible versions. I tried to make it as imaginatively true as I could, but imaginative truth is simultaneously honourable and suspect, and I knew that my India may only have been one to which I (who am no longer what I was, and who by quitting Bombay never became what perhaps I was meant to be) was, let us say, willing to admit I belonged.

This is why I made my narrator, Saleem, suspect in his narration; his mistakes are the mistakes of a fallible memory compounded by quirks of character and of circumstance, and his vision is fragmentary. It may be that when the Indian writer who writes from outside India tries to reflect that world, he is obliged to deal in broken mirrors, some of whose fragments have been irretrievably lost.

But there is a paradox here. The broken mirror may actually be as valuable as the one which is supposedly unflawed. Let me again try and explain this from my own experience. Before beginning *Midnight's Children*, I spent many months trying simply to recall as much of the Bombay of the 1950s and 1960s as I could; and not only Bombay – Kashmir, too, and Delhi and Aligarh, which, in my book, I've moved to Agra to heighten a certain joke about the Taj Mahal. I was genuinely amazed by how much came back to me. I found myself remembering what clothes people had worn on certain days, and school scenes, and whole passages of Bombay dialogue verbatim, or so it seemed; I even remembered advertisements, film-posters, the neon Jeep sign on Marine Drive, toothpaste ads for Binaca and for Kolynos, and a footbridge over the local railway line which bore, on one side, the legend 'Esso puts a tiger in your tank' and, on the other, the curiously contradictory admonition: 'Drive like Hell and you will get there.' Old songs came back to me from nowhere: a street entertainer's version of 'Good Night, Ladies', and, from the film *Mr 420* (a very appropriate source for my narrator to have used), the hit number 'Mera Joota Hai Japani',* which could almost be Saleem's theme song.

* *Mera joota hai Japani*
  Yé patloon Inglistani
  Sar pé lal topi Rusi –
  Phir bhi dil hai Hindustani
  – which translates roughly as:
  O, my shoes are Japanese
  These trousers English, if you please
  On my head, red Russian hat –
  My heart's Indian for all that.
[This is also the song sung by Gibreel Farishta as he tumbles from the heavens at the beginning of *The Satanic Verses*.]

I knew that I had tapped a rich seam; but the point I want to make is that of course I'm not gifted with total recall, and it was precisely the partial nature of these memories, their fragmentation, that made them so evocative for me. The shards of memory acquired greater status, greater resonance, because they were *remains*; fragmentation made trivial things seem like symbols, and the mundane acquired numinous qualities. There is an obvious parallel here with archaeology. The broken pots of antiquity, from which the past can sometimes, but always provisionally, be reconstructed, are exciting to discover, even if they are pieces of the most quotidian objects.

It may be argued that the past is a country from which we have all emigrated, that its loss is part of our common humanity. Which seems to me self-evidently true; but I suggest that the writer who is out-of-country and even out-of-language may experience this loss in an intensified form. It is made more concrete for him by the physical fact of discontinuity, of his present being in a different place from his past, of his being 'elsewhere'. This may enable him to speak properly and concretely on a subject of universal significance and appeal.

But let me go further. The broken glass is not merely a mirror of nostalgia. It is also, I believe, a useful tool with which to work in the present.

John Fowles begins *Daniel Martin* with the words: 'Whole sight: or all the rest is desolation.' But human beings do not perceive things whole; we are not gods but wounded creatures, cracked lenses, capable only of fractured perceptions. Partial beings, in all the senses of that phrase. Meaning is a shaky edifice we build out of scraps, dogmas, childhood injuries, newspaper articles, chance remarks, old films, small victories, people hated, people loved; perhaps it is because our sense of what is the case is constructed from such inadequate materials that we defend it so fiercely, even to the death. The Fowles position seems to me a way of succumbing to the guruillusion. Writers are no longer sages, dispensing the wisdom of the centuries. And those of us who have been forced by cultural displacement to accept the provisional nature of all truths, all certainties, have perhaps had modernism forced upon us. We can't lay claim to Olympus, and are thus released to describe our worlds in the way in which all of us, whether writers or not, perceive it from day to day.

In *Midnight's Children*, my narrator Saleem uses, at one point, the metaphor of a cinema screen to discuss this business of perception: 'Suppose yourself in a large cinema, sitting at first in the back row,

and gradually moving up, . . . until your nose is almost pressed
against the screen. Gradually the stars' faces dissolve into dancing
grain; tiny details assume grotesque proportions; . . . it becomes clear
that the illusion itself is reality.' The movement towards the cinema
screen is a metaphor for the narrative's movement through time
towards the present, and the book itself, as it nears contemporary
events, quite deliberately loses deep perspective, becomes more 'partial'. I wasn't trying to write about (for instance) the Emergency in
the same way as I wrote about events half a century earlier. I felt it
would be dishonest to pretend, when writing about the day before
yesterday, that it was possible to see the whole picture. I showed certain blobs and slabs of the scene.

I once took part in a conference on modern writing at New College,
Oxford. Various novelists, myself included, were talking earnestly of
such matters as the need for new ways of describing the world. Then
the playwright Howard Brenton suggested that this might be a somewhat limited aim: does literature seek to do no more than to describe?
Flustered, all the novelists at once began talking about politics.

Let me apply Brenton's question to the specific case of Indian
writers, in England, writing about India. Can they do no more than
describe, from a distance, the world that they have left? Or does the
distance open any other doors?

These are of course political questions, and must be answered at
least partly in political terms. I must say first of all that description is
itself a political act. The black American writer Richard Wright once
wrote that black and white Americans were engaged in a war over the
nature of reality. Their descriptions were incompatible. So it is clear
that redescribing a world is the necessary first step towards changing
it. And particularly at times when the State takes reality into its own
hands, and sets about distorting it, altering the past to fit its present
needs, then the making of the alternative realities of art, including the
novel of memory, becomes politicized. 'The struggle of man against
power,' Milan Kundera has written, 'is the struggle of memory against
forgetting.' Writers and politicians are natural rivals. Both groups
try to make the world in their own images; they fight for the same
territory. And the novel is one way of denying the official, politicians'
version of truth.

The 'State truth' about the war in Bangladesh, for instance, is that
no atrocities were committed by the Pakistani army in what was then

the East Wing. This version is sanctified by many persons who would describe themselves as intellectuals. And the official version of the Emergency in India was well expressed by Mrs Gandhi in a recent BBC interview. She said that there were some people around who claimed that bad things had happened during the Emergency, forced sterilizations, things like that; but, she stated, this was all false. Nothing of this type had ever occurred. The interviewer, Mr Robert Kee, did not probe this statement at all. Instead he told Mrs Gandhi and the *Panorama* audience that she had proved, many times over, her right to be called a democrat.

So literature can, and perhaps must, give the lie to official facts. But is this a proper function of those of us who write from outside India? Or are we just dilettantes in such affairs, because we are not involved in their day-to-day unfolding, because by speaking out we take no risks, because our personal safety is not threatened? What right do we have to speak at all?

My answer is very simple. Literature is self-validating. That is to say, a book is not justified by its author's worthiness to write it, but by the quality of what has been written. There are terrible books that arise directly out of experience, and extraordinary imaginative feats dealing with themes which the author has been obliged to approach from the outside.

Literature is not in the business of copyrighting certain themes for certain groups. And as for risk: the real risks of any artist are taken in the work, in pushing the work to the limits of what is possible, in the attempt to increase the sum of what it is possible to think. Books become good when they go to this edge and risk falling over it – when they endanger the artist by reason of what he has, or has not, *artistically* dared.

So if I am to speak for Indian writers in England I would say this, paraphrasing G. V. Desani's H. Hatterr: The migrations of the fifties and sixties happened. 'We are. We are here.' And we are not willing to be excluded from any part of our heritage; which heritage includes both a Bradford-born Indian kid's right to be treated as a full member of British society, and also the right of any member of this post-diaspora community to draw on its roots for its art, just as all the world's community of displaced writers has always done. (I'm thinking, for instance, of Gras 's Danzig-become-Gdansk, of Joyce's abandoned Dublin, of Isaac E shevis Singer and Maxine Hong Kingston and Milan Kundera and many others. It's a long list.)

Let me override at once the faintly defensive note that has crept into these last few remarks. The Indian writer, looking back at India, does so through guilt-tinted spectacles. (I am of course, once more, talking about myself.) I am speaking now of those of us who emigrated . . . and I suspect that there are times when the move seems wrong to us all, when we seem, to ourselves, post-lapsarian men and women. We are Hindus who have crossed the black water; we are Muslims who eat pork. And as a result – as my use of the Christian notion of the Fall indicates – we are now partly of the West. Our identity is at once plural and partial. Sometimes we feel that we straddle two cultures; at other times, that we fall between two stools. But however ambiguous and shifting this ground may be, it is not an infertile territory for a writer to occupy. If literature is in part the business of finding new angles at which to enter reality, then once again our distance, our long geographical perspective, may provide us with such angles. Or it may be that that is simply what we must think in order to do our work.

Midnight's Children enters its subject from the point of view of a secular man. I am a member of that generation of Indians who were sold the secular ideal. One of the things I liked, and still like, about India is that it is based on a non-sectarian philosophy. I was not raised in a narrowly Muslim environment; I do not consider Hindu culture to be either alien from me or more important than the Islamic heritage. I believe this has something to do with the nature of Bombay, a metropolis in which the multiplicity of commingled faiths and cultures curiously creates a remarkably secular ambience. Saleem Sinai makes use, eclectically, of whatever elements from whatever sources he chooses. It may have been easier for his author to do this from outside modern India than inside it.

I want to make one last point about the description of India that *Midnight's Children* attempts. It is a point about pessimism. The book has been criticized in India for its allegedly despairing tone. And the despair of the writer-from-outside may indeed look a little easy, a little pat. But I do not see the book as despairing or nihilistic. The point of view of the narrator is not entirely that of the author. What I tried to do was to set up a tension in the text, a paradoxical opposition between the form and content of the narrative. The story of Saleem does indeed lead him to despair. But the story is told in a manner designed to echo, as closely as my abilities allowed, the Indian talent for non-stop self-regeneration. This is why the narrative constantly throws up new stories, why it 'teems'. The form – multitudinous, hinting at the infinite possibilities of the country – is the optimistic counterweight to Saleem's personal tragedy. I do not think that a book written in such a manner can really be called a despairing work.

England's Indian writers are by no means all the same type of animal. Some of us, for instance, are Pakistani. Others Bangladeshi. Others West, or East, or even South African. And V. S. Naipaul, by now, is something else entirely. This word 'Indian' is getting to be a pretty scattered concept. Indian writers in England include political exiles, first-generation migrants, affluent expatriates whose residence here is frequently temporary, naturalized Britons, and people born here who may never have laid eyes on the subcontinent. Clearly, nothing that I say can apply across all these categories. But one of the interesting things about this diverse community is that, as far as Indo-British fiction is concerned, its existence changes the ball game, because that fiction is in future going to come as much from addresses in London, Birmingham and Yorkshire as from Delhi or Bombay.

One of the changes has to do with attitudes towards the use of English. Many have referred to the argument about the appropriateness of this language to Indian themes. And I hope all of us share the view that we can't simply use the language in the way the British did; that it needs remaking for our own purposes. Those of us who do use English do so in spite of our ambiguity towards it, or perhaps because of that, perhaps because we can find in that linguistic struggle a reflection of other struggles taking place in the real world, struggles between the cultures within ourselves and the influences at work upon our societies. To conquer English may be to complete the process of making ourselves free.

But the British Indian writer simply does not have the option of rejecting English, anyway. His children, her children, will grow up speaking it, probably as a first language; and in the forging of a British Indian identity the English language is of central importance. It must, in spite of everything, be embraced. (The word 'translation' comes, etymologically, from the Latin for 'bearing across'. Having been borne across the world, we are translated men. It is normally supposed that something always gets lost in translation; I cling, obstinately, to the notion that something can also be gained.)

To be an Indian writer in this society is to face, every day, problems of definition. What does it mean to be 'Indian' outside India? How can culture be preserved without becoming ossified? How should we discuss the need for change within ourselves and our community without seeming to play into the hands of our racial enemies? What are the consequences, both spiritual and practical, of refusing to make any concessions to Western ideas and practices? What are the consequences of embracing those ideas and practices and turning away from the ones that came here with us? These questions are all a single, existential question: How are we to live in the world?

I do not propose to offer, prescriptively, any answers to these questions; only to state that these are some of the issues with which each of us will have to come to terms.

To turn my eyes outwards now, and to say a little about the relationship between the Indian writer and the majority white culture in whose midst he lives, and with which his work will sooner or later have to deal:

In common with many Bombay-raised middle-class children of my generation, I grew up with an intimate knowledge of, and even sense of friendship with, a certain kind of England: a dream-England composed of Test Matches at Lord's presided over by the voice of John Arlott, at which Freddie Trueman bowled unceasingly and without success at Polly Umrigar; of Enid Blyton and Billy Bunter, in which we were even prepared to smile indulgently at portraits such as 'Hurree Jamset Ram Singh', 'the dusky nabob of Bhanipur'. I wanted to come to England. I couldn't wait. And to be fair, England has done all right by me; but I find it a little difficult to be properly grateful. I can't escape the view that my relatively easy ride is not the result of the dream-England's famous sense of tolerance and fair play, but of my social class, my freak fair skin and my 'English' English accent. Take away any of these, and the story would have been very different. Because of course the dream-England is no more than a dream.

Sadly, it's a dream from which too many white Britons refuse to awake. Recently, on a live radio programme, a professional humorist asked me, in all seriousness, why I objected to being called a wog. He said he had always thought it a rather charming word, a term of endearment. 'I was at the zoo the other day,' he revealed, 'and a zoo keeper told me that the wogs were best with the animals; they stuck their fingers in their ears and wiggled them about and the animals felt at home.' The ghost of Hurree Jamset Ram Singh walks among us still.

As Richard Wright found long ago in America, black and white descriptions of society are no longer compatible. Fantasy, or the mingling of fantasy and naturalism, is one way of dealing with these problems. It offers a way of echoing in the form of our work the issues faced by all of us: how to build a new, 'modern' world out of an old, legend-haunted civilization, an old culture which we have brought into the heart of a newer one. But whatever technical solutions we may find, Indian writers in these islands, like others who have migrated into the north from the south, are capable of writing from a kind of double perspective: because they, we, are at one and the same time insiders and outsiders in this society. This stereoscopic vision is perhaps what we can offer in place of 'whole sight'.

There is one last idea that I should like to explore, even though it may, on first hearing, seem to contradict much of what I've so far said. It is this: of all the many elephant traps lying ahead of us, the largest and most dangerous pitfall would be the adoption of a ghetto mentality. To forget that there is a world beyond the community to which we belong, to confine ourselves within narrowly defined cultural frontiers, would be, I believe, to go voluntarily into that form of internal exile which in South Africa is called the 'homeland'. We must guard against creating, for the most virtuous of reasons, British-Indian literary equivalents of Bophuthatswana or the Transkei.

This raises immediately the question of whom one is writing 'for'. My own, short, answer is that I have never had a reader in mind. I have ideas, people, events, shapes, and I write 'for' those things, and hope that the completed work will be of interest to others. But which others? In the case of *Midnight's Children* I certainly felt that if its subcontinental readers had rejected the work, I should have thought it a failure, no matter what the reaction in the West. So I would say that I write 'for' people who feel part of the things I write 'about', but also for everyone else whom I can reach. In this I am of the same opinion as the black American writer Ralph Ellison, who, in his collection of essays *Shadow and Act*, says that he finds something precious in being black in America at this time; but that he is also reaching for more than that. 'I was taken very early,' he writes, 'with a passion to link together all I loved within the Negro community and all those things I felt in the world which lay beyond.'

Art is a passion of the mind. And the imagination works best when it is most free. Western writers have always felt free to be eclectic in their selection of theme, setting, form; Western visual artists have, in this century, been happily raiding the visual storehouses of Africa, Asia, the Philippines. I am sure that we must grant ourselves an equal freedom.

Let me suggest that Indian writers in England have access to a second tradition, quite apart from their own racial history. It is the culture and political history of the phenomenon of migration, displacement, life in a minority group. We can quite legitimately claim as our ancestors the Huguenots, the Irish, the Jews; the past to which we belong is an English past, the history of immigrant Britain. Swift, Conrad, Marx are as much our literary forebears as Tagore or Ram Mohan Roy. America, a nation of immigrants, has created great literature out of the phenomenon of cultural transplantation, out of examining the ways in which people cope with a new world; it may be that by discovering what we have in common with those who preceded us into this country, we can begin to do the same.

I stress this is only one of many possible strategies. But we are inescapably international writers at a time when the novel has never been a more international form (a writer like Borges speaks of the influence of Robert Louis Stevenson on his work; Heinrich Böll acknowledges the influence of Irish literature; cross-pollination is everywhere); and it is perhaps one of the more pleasant freedoms of the literary migrant to be able to choose his parents. My own – selected half consciously, half not – include Gogol, Cervantes, Kafka, Melville, Machado de Assis; a polyglot family tree, against which I measure myself, and to which I would be honoured to belong.

There's a beautiful image in Saul Bellow's latest novel, *The Dean's December*. The central character, the Dean, Corde, hears a dog barking wildly somewhere. He imagines that the barking is the dog's protest against the limit of dog experience. 'For God's sake,' the dog is saying, 'open the universe a little more!' And because Bellow is, of course, not really talking about dogs, or not only about dogs, I have the feeling that the dog's rage, and its desire, is also mine, ours, everyone's. 'For God's sake, open the universe a little more!'

1982

LOOKING BACK IN ANGER

The person digging the ground is the one burying the
dead; the one weeping is only making a noise

YORUBA PROVERB

BEN OKRI

Ben Okri is a Nigerian writer resident in London. He was educated in Nigeria and at the University of Essex. He has published seven novels and two volumes of stories, *Incidents at the Shrine* and *Stars of the New Curfew*. Ben Okri has won several prizes, including the Paris Review Aga Khan Prize, and the Booker Prize for his novel *The Famished Road*.

'Laughter Beneath the Bridge', taken from *Incidents at the Shrine*, concerns a young boy's account of the tragic outbreak of a civil war. As his family flee back to their tribal heartland, others from the secessionist group are trapped on the wrong side, and in the way of advancing government troops.

Laughter Beneath the Bridge

Those were long days as we lay pressed to the prickly grass waiting for the bombs to fall. The civil war broke out before mid-term and the boarding school emptied fast. Teachers disappeared; the English headmaster was rumoured to have flown home; and the entire kitchen staff fled before the first planes went past overhead. At the earliest sign of trouble in the country parents appeared and secreted away their children. Three of us were left behind. We all hoped someone would turn up to collect us. We were silent most of the time.

Vultures showed up in the sky. They circled the school campus for a few days and then settled on the watch-night's shed. In the evenings we watched as some religious maniacs roamed the empty school compound screaming about the end of the world and then as a wild bunch of people from the city scattered through searching for those of the rebel tribe. They broke doors and they looted the chapel of its icons, statuaries and velvet drapes; they took the large vivid painting of the agony of Christ. In the morning we saw the Irish priest riding furiously away from town on his Raleigh bicycle. After he left, ghosts flitted through the chapel and rattled the roof. One night we heard the altar fall. The next day we saw lizards nodding on the chapel walls.

We stayed on in the dormitories. We rooted for food in the vegetable field. We stole the wine of tapsters at the foot of palm trees. We broke into the kitchen and raided the store of baked beans, sardines and stale bread. In the daytime we waited at the school gate, pressed to the grass, watching out for our parents. Sometimes we went to town to forage. We talked about the bombings in the country whispered to us from the fields. One day, after having stolen bread from the only bakery open in town, we got to the dormitory and found the lizards there. They were under the double-decked beds and on the cupboards, in such great numbers, in such relaxed occupation, that we couldn't bear to sleep there any more. All through the days we waited for the bombs to fall. And all through that time it was Monica I thought about.

She was a little girl when I learned how to piss straight. When I learned how to cover my nakedness she developed long legs and a pert behind and took to moving round our town like a wild and beautiful cat. She became famous for causing havoc at the barbers' shops, the bukkas, pool offices. She nearly drowned once trying to outswim the other boys across our town's river, which was said to like young girls. I watched them dragging her through the muddied water: her face was pale, she looked as though she had taken a long journey from her body. After that she took to going around with Egunguns, brandishing a whip, tugging the masked figure, abusing the masquerade for not dancing well enough. That was a time indeed when she broke our sexual taboos and began dancing our street's Egungun round town, fooling all the men. She danced so well that we got coins from the stingiest dressmakers, the meanest pool-shop owners. I remember waking up one night during the holidays to go out and ease myself at the backyard. I saw her bathing near the shrub of hibiscus; and there was a moon out. I dreamed of her new-formed breasts when the lizards chased us from the dormitories, and when the noise of fighter planes drove us to the forests.

I remember it as a beautiful time: I don't know how. Sirens and fire engines made it seem like there was an insane feast going on somewhere in the country. In town we saw a man set upon by a mob: they beat him up in a riot of vengeance, they broke sticks and bottles on his head. So much blood came from him. Maybe it seemed like a beautiful time because we often sat in the school field, staring at the seven hills that were like pilings of verdigris in the distance: and because none of us cried. We were returning from a search for food one day when we saw someone standing like a scarecrow in the middle of the field. We drew closer. The figure stayed still. It was mother. She looked at us a long time and she didn't recognize me. Fear makes people so stiff. When she finally recognized me she held all three of us together like we were a family.

'Can't take your friends,' mother said, after we had all been given something to eat.

'I'm not a wicked person to leave behind children who are stranded,' mother said, her face bony, 'but how will I rest in my grave if the soldiers we meet hold them, because of me?'

I didn't understand. I began to say a prayer for my friends.

'You will have to wait for your parents, or both of you go with the first parent that turns up. Can you manage?' mother asked them. They nodded. She looked at them for a long time and then cried.

Mother left them some money and all the food she brought. She took off two of her three wrappers for them to cover themselves with in the cold winds of the night. I felt sad at having to leave them behind. Mother prayed for them and I tried not to think of them as we walked the long distance to the garage. I tried not to see both of them in the empty fields as we struggled to catch a bus in the garage. Then the commotion of revving lorries, wheezing buses, the convulsion of people running home to their villages, women weeping, children bawling, soldiers everywhere in battle-dress and camouflage helmets, their guns stiff and strange, the whole infernal commotion simply wiped my two friends from my mind. After several hours we finally caught a lorry that could take us home. Then afterwards I tried to think only of Monica.

The lorry we caught was old and slow. It had an enduring, asthmatic engine. The driver was very talkative and boastful. There were all kinds of cupboards and long brooms and things in sacks strapped to its roof. As we fought to clamber in, I caught a glimpse of the legend painted on the old wooden bodywork. It read: THE YOUNG SHALL GROW.

There was absolutely no space in the lorry to move because most of the passengers had brought with them as many of the acquisitions of their lives in the city as they could carry. We sat on wooden benches and all about us were buckets, sewing machines, mattresses, calabashes, mats, clothes, ropes, pots, blackened pans, machetes. Even those with household jujus could not hide them: and we stared at the strange things they worshipped. It was so uncomfortable and airless in the lorry that I nodded in and out of sleep, the only relief.

That was a long journey indeed. The road seemed to have no end. The leaves of the trees and bushes were covered with dust. There were a hundred checkpoints. The soldiers at every one of them seemed possessed of a belligerent vitality. They stopped every vehicle, searched all nooks and crannies, emptied every bag and sack, dug their guns in our behinds, barked a thousand questions. We passed stretches of forest and saw numerous corpses along the road. We saw whole families trudging along the empty wastes, children straggling behind, weeping without the possibility of consolation.

I was asleep when mother woke me up. It was another checkpoint. There were many soldiers around, all shouting and barking orders at the same time. There was a barricade across the road. There was a pit not far from the barricade. The bodies of three grown men lay bundled in the pit. One of them had been shot through the teeth. Another one was punctured with gunshots and his face was so contorted it seemed he had died from too much laughing.

The soldiers shouted that we should all jump down. It would begin all over again: unpacking the entire lorry, unstrapping the load at the top, being subjected to a thorough and leisurely search. Then we would wait for one or two who couldn't prove they were not of the rebel tribe, sometimes being made to leave without them.

'Come down, all of you! Jump down now!' shouted the soldiers. We all tramped down. They lined us up along the road. Evening was approaching and the sun had that ripe, insistent burn. The forest was riotous with insects. Many of the soldiers had their fingers on the triggers. As they searched the lorry, one of the soldiers kept blowing his nose, covering the lemon-grass with snot. They questioned the driver, who shivered in servility. They took us aside, into the bush, one by one, to be questioned. I stood there beneath the mature burning sun, starving, bored, and thinking of Monica. Occasionally I heard one of the women burst into crying. I heard the butt of a gun crash on someone's head. I didn't hear them cry out.

They searched and questioned us a long time. The sun turned from ripe, blazing red to dull orange. I blew my nose on the lemon-grass, thinking of Monica. The soldier who had also been blowing his nose came over to me.

'You dey crase?' he shouted at me.

I didn't know what he was talking about so he cracked me across the head. I saw one of Monica's masks in the stars.

'Are you mad?' he shouted at me again.

I still didn't know what he was talking about. He whacked me harder, with the back of his hand, and sent me flying into the cluster of yellowing lemon-grass. Mother screamed at him, dived for his eyes, and he pushed her so hard that she landed near me. She picked herself up, snot drooling from the back of her wrapper; her wig had fallen into the pit. I lay on the lemon-grass and refused to get up. My head hurt. Behind me another soldier was knocking a woman about in the bushes. The soldier who had hit me came over to where I lay. His gun pointed at me from the hip. Mother, who feared guns, cowered behind him. Someone called to the soldier.

'Frank O'Nero,' the voice said, 'leave the poor boy alone now, ah ah.'

Frank O'Nero turned to the voice, swinging the gun in its direction, then swinging back to me. His eyes were raw. I was afraid that he was mad.

'All you children of rich men. You think because you go to school you can behave anyhow you want? Don't you know this is war? Goat! Small goat!'

Mother, in a weak voice, said: 'Leave my son alone, you hear. God didn't give me many of them.'

Frank O'Nero looked at her, then at me. He turned with a swagger and went to the bush where they were questioning the passengers. They called us next.

Behind the bushes three soldiers smoked marijuana. Half-screened, a short way up, two soldiers struggled with a light-complexioned woman. The soldiers smoking marijuana asked mother questions and I never heard her answers because I was fascinated with what the soldiers a short way up were doing. The soldiers asked mother where she came from in the country and I thought of Monica as the soldiers, a short way up, struggled with and finally subdued the woman. They shouted to mother to recite the paternoster in the language of the place she claimed to come from: and mother hesitated as the woman's legs were forced apart. Then mother recited the paternoster fluently in father's language. She was of the rebel tribe but father had long ago forced her to master his language. Mother could tell that the interpreter who was supposed to check on the language didn't know it too well: so she extended the prayer, went deeper into idiom, abusing their mothers and fathers, cursing the suppurating vaginas that must have shat them out in their wickedness, swearing at the rotten pricks that dug up the maggoty entrails of their mothers – and the soldiers half-screened by the bushes rode the woman furiously till the sun started its slow climb into your eyes, Monica. The soldiers listened to mother's recitation with some satisfaction. Then they turned to me and asked me to recite the Hail Mary. The soldier in the bush had finished wrecking his manhood on the woman and was cleaning himself with leaves. I told the soldier interrogating me that I couldn't speak our language that well.

'Why not?' he asked, his voice thundering.

I heard the question but couldn't find an answer. The woman on the floor in the bush was silent: her face was contorted, she was covered in a foam of sweat.

'I'm talking to you! Idiot!' he shouted. 'If you don't speak your language you're not going with your mother, you hear?'

I nodded. Their marijuana smoke was beginning to tickle me. Mother came in quickly and explained that I hadn't grown up at home. The woman on the ground began to wail tonelessly. Mother turned on me, pinched me, hit my head, urged me to speak the language of my father, gave me hints of children's songs, the beginnings of stories. I couldn't at that moment remember a word: it had all simply vanished from my head. Besides, I was suddenly overcome with the desire to laugh.

It was partly the interrogator's fault. He said: 'If he can't speak a word of your language then he can't be your son.'

I burst out laughing and not even mother's pincerous fingernails, nor the growing fury of the soldiers, could stop me. I soon found myself being dragged deep into the forest by Frank O'Nero. Mother wailed a dirge, her hair all scattered. The woman on the ground made inhuman noises. Fear overcame me and I shouted the oldest word I knew and mother seized on it, screaming, the boy has spoken, he has just said that he wants to shit. Frank O'Nero stopped, his fingers like steel round my wrists. He looked at the other soldiers; then at mother, and me. Then he completely surprised, and scared, me with the rough sound that came from his throat. Mother wasted no time rushing to me, pushing me towards the lorry. The soldiers passed the joke all the way round the barricade. In the lorry, we waited for the others to prove they were not of the enemy. The woman on the ground was obscured from view, but I could still hear her wailing. The sky was darkening when we pulled away. We were forced to leave without her.

Mother never stopped chastising me. They shoot people who can't speak their language, she said. As she chastised me, I thought about Monica, who did only what she wanted. I wondered if she would have long enough to say a word when they came for her.

The rest of the journey was not peaceful either. The faces of war leapt up from the tarmac, shimmering illusions in my drowsiness. Armoured trucks, camouflaged with burr, thundered up and down the roads. Planes roared overhead. From time to time a frenzy seized the driver: he would suddenly stop the lorry in the middle of the road and dive for the bushes. Sometimes it took a while to convince him to come out, that we were safe.

'I'm never going to drive again in this madness,' he kept saying.

The taste of madness like the water of potent springs, the laughter of war: that is perhaps why I remember it as a beautiful time. And because in the lorry, with corpses drifting past along the road and soldiers noisy in their jeeps, we were all silent. The weight of our silence was enormous. When we finally arrived I felt like I had seen several lifetimes go past.

Loud cheering and hooting broke out as our lorry swung into the town's garage. People rushed to us from all the silent houses. Children ran with them, cheering and not knowing why. We came down and were thronged by people who wanted to know how the war was doing, how many dead bodies we saw. The driver told them all the stories they wanted to hear.

Mother didn't like the bicycle taxis, which were the only taxis in operation, so she made us walk home. There were soldiers everywhere. Hysteria blew along the streets, breathed over the buildings and huts.

When father saw us coming up the street I heard him shout that the chicken should be caught. It turned out to be an unruly little chicken with a red cloth tied to its leg, one that had been bought expensively and saved up during that time of food shortage. We had been expected for some time and father was afraid something bad had happened. They had all grown a little fond of the chicken. Father opened a bottle of Ogogoro and made profuse libations to our ancestors, thanking them for allowing our safe passage home. Father made me bathe in herbal water, to wash the bad things of the journey off me. Then the chicken was killed and cooked and served with Portuguese sardines, boiled cassava, little green tomatoes and some yam.

And then I started looking out of our window, stirring as I looked, down our street, past the yellowing leaves of the guava tree and the orange tree, with its mottled trunk, that was planted the year I was born, past the cluster of hibiscus and passion plants, looking at the house which was really a squat bungalow, where she lived with her family, ten in all, in one room. And with a small part of my mind I heard the old ones in the sitting-room, their voices cracked by the searing alcohol, as they talked in undertones about the occupation of the town, about the ones who had died, or gone mad, or the ones who had joined the army and promised good things and turned in the heat of battle and fired at their own men.

When mother came to urge me to sleep, I asked, as though it were her responsibility:

'Where's Monica?'

'Why are you asking me? Haven't we both just come from a journey?'

'Where is she?'

Mother sighed.

'How would I know? Before I left she was staying with us. The townspeople pursued them from their house and the family are scattered in the forests. They killed her brother.'

'Which one?'

'Ugo.'

I felt sick.

'So where is she then?'

'What sort of question is that? Nobody in the house knows where Monica is. Sometimes she comes back to the house to eat and then she disappears for several days and then she comes back again. You know how stubborn she is. The day before I came to collect you she went to the market and got into some trouble with a soldier. The soldier nearly shot her. It was your father's good name which saved her.'

I wanted to go out, to find her.

'We are thinking of sending her to the village. The way she is behaving they will kill her before the war is over. You always liked her. When she comes back, talk to her. You will soon be a man, you know.'

Flattered by the last thing she said, for I was only ten, I got up.

As I went out through the door, father said: 'Don't go far-o! There's a curfew. This is not a holiday, you hear?'

At the backyard the other kids said they hadn't seen her all day. I went to the town's market, which sprawled along the length of the main road all the way to the bridge. Couldn't find her. I went round all the empty stalls of the butchers, where she sometimes went to collect offal, which she had a talent for cooking. Couldn't find her. I went to the record shop that overlooked an abattoir of cow and sheep bones. Went to the palm wine bars where she sometimes sold wine to the hungry bachelors and old men of the town: they were now full of soldiers. I went from one rubber plantation to another, walking through tracts of forest sizzling with insects, listening to the rubber pods explode through tangles of branches and crash on the ground. Still couldn't find her.

When I got home father was in a furious temper. Monica stood by the door, her head drooping, staring mulishly at the floor. Father shouted that he didn't want to be responsible for anyone's death, that this was a war, and so on. Father finished shouting at her and she rushed out and went and stood beneath the mango tree, scratching herself, slapping at mosquitoes. It was getting dark. The fragrance of mango fruit was on the wind.

'Monica!' I called.

'Get away!' she screamed at me.

'Where have you been? I've been looking every—'

'Get away from here!' she screamed even louder. I went away, up the street. I walked past the post office and came back. She was still leaning against the tree, her eyes hard. I went on into the sitting-room, where I slept at night on a mat on the floor. Later she tapped on the window with a mango branch. I opened the window and she climbed in.

'Let's go out,' she whispered. She saw father's Ogogoro bottle and took a swig of the alcohol.

'Get away!'

'Let's go out,' she said again.

'Where were you today? I searched for you all over town.'

'Look at your big nose,' she said, 'full of pimples.'

'Leave my nose alone.'

She always had such a peppery mouth. She went on abusing me.

'Your head like a bullet,' she said. 'You no tall, you no short, you be like Hausa dagger.'

'What about you? Anyway, where have you been that no one can find you?'

'You're such a fool,' she whispered.

Then she went quiet. She seemed to travel away from her body a little bit and then she came back. All that time I had been telling her about our journey and the soldiers and the lizards. She sort of looked at me with strange eyes and I wanted to draw close to her, to hold her, wrestle with her.

But she said: 'Let's go out.'

'Where?'

'I won't tell you.'

'What about the curfew?'

'What about it?'

'What about the soldiers?'

'What about them?' she asked, taking another swig, the alcohol dripping down her mouth on to her lap. She coughed and her eyes reddened.

'I'm not going. I'm sleepy. They are killing people, you know!'

'So you are afraid of them?'

'No, I'm not.'

'You are a fool.'

She looked me up and down. She pouted her lips. She climbed back out of the window. And I followed.

There was a moon coming over the mango tree.

She went out of the compound and up the street and then turned into another compound. I got there and found a group of kids standing beneath a hedge of hibiscus. Two of them carried great wads of raffia trailings. One of them held a big and ugly mask. Another had little drums surrounding him.

I felt left out.

'Who's building an Egungun?' I asked in as big a voice as I could muster.

'Why do you want to know?' came from, of all people, Monica.

'I want to dance the Egungun. I have not danced it for a long time.'

'Why don't you go and build your own?'

I ignored her and went to the other kids and tried to rough them up a little. None of them said anything. There was a long silence and I listened to the wind moaning underneath the moon. I watched the kids as they went on building the Egungun, sticking raffia trailings to the mask. They strung threads through the corals, which would eventually become bracelets and anklets and make joyous cackles when dancing. The drummer tapped on one of the drums. He got a little

carried away. Someone opened a window and shouted at us to stop
making noise. One of the boys tried on the mask and shook around. I
tried to snatch it from him and Monica said: 'Don't do that. You
know you're not allowed to take off an Egungun's mask. You'll die if
you do.'

'It's an ugly mask, anyway,' I said, going out from the compound
and walking up the street towards the main road. There were a few
bicyclists around, furtively looking out for passengers. The moon
was big and clear. I heard footsteps. Monica was coming behind me.
Two other kids from the group were behind her: ragged companions.
I could hear them talking about running away from home to join the
army. I suddenly had a vision of my two friends at school, standing in
the expanse of fields, surrounded by lizards. I said a prayer for them.

We walked alongside the market. Its arcade of rusted zinc roofing
was totally dark underneath: but above it was bright with the moon.
The piles of refuse continued all the way past the market.

In the moonlight we could see that there was a roadblock just after
the bridge. Mosquitoes were madly whining. Soldiers sat around on
metal chairs, smoking intensely in the dark. Their armoured truck, a
solitary bulk, covered the road. The other two kids said they were
going back, that their parents would be worried about them. I wanted
to go back too. I didn't like the way the soldiers smoked their cigarettes. I didn't like the sound of the laughter that came from around
the truck.

But Monica was determined to go past them.

The other kids stopped and said they were going to improve on the
Egungun. They didn't look too happy about going back. They turned
and went sadly alongside the dark and empty market. I looked for
Monica and found that she was already over the bridge. I had to run
and catch up with her before she got to the soldiers.

They stopped us as we went past.

'Where do you think you are going?'

'Our father sent us a message,' Monica said.

The soldier who had spoken got up from the metal chair. Then he
sat down again.

'What message? What message? Is your father mad? Doesn't he
know we are fighting a war? Does he think that killing Biafrans is a
small thing? Is he mad?'

Monica fidgeted with her toes on the asphalt. The other soldiers
smoked stolidly in the dark, taking a mild interest in us. The soldier

who had been shouting asked us to move closer. We did. He was a stocky man with an ill-fitting uniform. He had bulging cheeks and a paunch. He looked at Monica in a funny way. He looked at her breasts and then at her neck.

He said: 'Come closer.'

'Who? Me?' I asked.

'Shut up!' he said. Then to Monica: 'I said, come closer.'

Monica moved backwards.

The soldier stood up suddenly and his rifle fell from his lap and clattered on the road. I ducked, half expecting it to fire. He scooped it up angrily and, to Monica, said: 'You be Yamarin?'

Monica stiffened.

'We're from this town,' I said haltingly, in our language.

The soldier looked at me as though I had just stepped in from the darkness.

'Who is your father?'

'The District Commissioner,' I said, lying.

He eyed Monica, stared at her legs. He scratched his nose, fingered his gun, and pulled his sagging military pants all the way up his paunch. He looked as though he was confronted with the biggest temptation of his adult life. Then he touched her. On the shoulder. Monica stepped back, pulled me by my shirt sleeve, urged us to hurry. Soon Monica was in front and her buttocks moved in a manner I hadn't noticed before. We turned and went down the bank of reeds alongside the stream. We sat under a tree and soon a terrible smell came from the water and it stayed a long time and after a while I didn't notice it.

Monica was restless. I had an amazing sense of inevitability. The last time I tried something on Monica she swiped me viciously on the head. Blooming had the effect of making her go around with an exaggerated sense of herself. She always believed she'd marry a prince.

She said: 'I feel like going to war.'

'As what?'

'A soldier. I want to carry a gun. Shoot. Fire.'

'Shut up.'

She was quiet for a moment.

'You know they killed Ugo?'

I nodded. Her eyes were very bright. I had this feeling that she had been changed into something strange: I looked at her face and it seemed to elude me. The moon was in her eyes.

'This is where they dumped his body. It's floated away now.'

She was crying.

'Shoot a few people. Fire. Shoot,' she said. Then she got up and tried to climb the gnarled trunk of the iroko tree. Couldn't do it. She stopped trying to climb and then stood staring at the stream. The soldiers were laughing above the bridge, their boots occasionally crunching the gravel. I went to Monica and she pushed me away. I went to her again and she shoved me away so hard that I fell. I lay down and watched her.

'This is where I've been. All day I sit here and think.'

I went to her and held her round the waist and she didn't do anything. I could smell her armpit, a new smell to me. Above on the bridge, one of the soldiers laughed so hard he had to cough and spit at the end of it.

'Do you see the stream?' she asked me, in a new voice.

'Yes.'

'What do you see?'

'I see the stream with the moonlight on the rubbish.'

'Is that all?'

'Yes.'

'Look. Look. That's where Ugo was. I measured the place with this tree.'

Then something shifted in my eyes. The things on the water suddenly looked different, transformed. The moment I saw them as they were I left her and ran up the bank. The stream was full of corpses that had swollen, huge massive bodies with enormous eyes and bloated cheeks. They were humped along on the top of the water. The bridge was all clogged up underneath with waterweeds and old engines and vegetable waste from the market.

'Monica!'

She was silent. The smell from the stream got terrible again.

'Monica!'

Then she started to laugh. I had never heard that sort of twisted laughter before. After a while I couldn't see her clearly and I called her and she laughed and then I thought it was all the swollen corpses that were laughing.

'Monica! I am going home-o!'

One of the soldiers fired a shot into the air. I rushed down and grabbed Monica. She was shivering. Her mouth poured with saliva, her face was wet. I held her close as we passed the armoured truck.

She was jabbering away and I had to cover her mouth with my palm. We didn't look at the soldiers. I could smell their sweat. When we got home we both came down with a fever.

By Saturday the town had begun to smell. All the time I lay in bed, feverish and weak, the other kids brought me stories of what was happening. They said that at night swollen ghosts with large eyes clanked over the bridge. They said the soldiers had to move from the bridge because the smell of the stream got too strong for them.

I saw very little of Monica. It seemed she recovered faster than I did. When I saw her again she looked very thin and her eyes were mad. There was a lot more talk of sending her to the village. I learnt that in the bungalow behind the hibiscus hedge they were building a mighty Egungun – one that would dwarf even the one with which ja-ja johnny walked over the River Niger, long ago before the world came to be like this. I asked who would ride the Egungun and the others still wouldn't say. On Saturday afternoon I was just strong enough to go and see this new masquerade for myself. The town stank. It was true: the boys had built this wonderful Egungun with a grotesque laughing mask. The mask had been broken – they say Monica's temper was responsible – but it was gummed back together.

In my loudest voice I said: 'I will dance the Egungun.'

They stared at me and then fled, as though they had seen another spirit.

How could it have been a beautiful time when that afternoon the smell got so strong that gas masks and wooden poles had to be distributed to respectable and proven citizens of the town so that they could prod the bodies and clear the rubbish to enable the corpses to flow away beneath the bridge? We saw these respectable citizens marching down our street. They were doctors, civil servants, businessmen, police constables. Their pot-bellies wobbled as they marched. They had the gas masks on. Mother spat when they passed us. The kids in the street jeered at them.

When they had gone I went to the building-place of the Egungun and found that the group was ready to dance along the market and all the way round town. Two small Egunguns warmed up and shook their feet while they waited for the main one. Then we heard a flourish of drums from the backyard and the main Egungun came dancing vigorously towards us. We cheered. Too weak to do anything else, I ended up getting a rope that controlled the main one.

We danced up the street and down the market road. The drumming was strong. The masquerade danced with a wild frenzy, the bracelets and anklets contributing to the rough music. Occasionally the Egungun tore away from my grip and the others blamed me and I had to run and catch the rope and restrain its ferocity. We shouldered bicyclists from the road, danced round old men and women, rattling the castanets made out of Bournvita cans and bird-seeds. When we got to the empty market the spirit of Egunguns entered us. As we danced round the stalls, in the mud of rotting vegetables and meat, we were suddenly confronted by a group of big huge spirits. They were tall, their heads reached the top of the zinc roofing. They had long faces and big eyes. We ran, screaming, and regrouped outside the market. We went towards the bridge.

The Egungun didn't want to cross the bridge. The small ones were dancing over and we were beating our drums across and singing new songs and we turned and found the main Egungun still behind, refusing to come with us. We went back and flogged it and pulled and pushed; but it didn't want to go. The other boys suggested we stone the Egungun. I suggested that we drown it. Then finally the Egungun turned round and we followed, singing ja-ja johnny to the ground, hitting the drums, beating the castanets on our thighs. We danced past the shop of the only tailor in town, whose sign read: TRAINED IN LONDON; and the barber's shed that bore the legend: NO JUSTICE IN THIS WORLD; and past the painter of signboards (who had all sorts of contradictory legends nailed round his shed). We bobbed in front of the houses of the town that were built with the hope that they would, at least, be better than their neighbours. Nobody threw us any coins. None of the grown-ups liked us dancing at that time and they drove us away and abused us. We danced our way back up town again. At the market we saw a confusion of several other Egunguns. We didn't know where they had sprung from. They rattled tin castanets, beat drums, brandished whips.

We clashed with them. We fought and whipped one another under the blazing sun. We toppled stalls and threw stones and spat and cursed, sending a wild clamour through the market. The drummers went completely mad competing amongst themselves. We fought and the commotion increased till some soldiers ran over from the bridge and shouted at us. When we heard the soldiers we took cover behind the fallen stalls. Only our Egungun – an insane laughing mask split in the middle of the face – went on as if nothing had happened. It danced round the stalls, provocatively shaking its buttocks, uttering its possessed language, defying the soldiers.

'Stop dancing! Stop dancing!' one of them thundered. Our Egungun seemed only to derive more frenzy from the order. Then one of the soldiers stepped forward, tore the mask off the Egungun's face, and slapped Monica so hard that I felt the sound. Then suddenly her eyes grew large as a mango and her eyelids kept twitching.

'Speak your language!' the soldier shouted, as her thighs quivered. 'Speak your language!' he screamed, as she urinated down her thighs and shivered in her own puddle. She wailed. Then she jabbered. In her language.

There was a terrible silence. Nobody moved. The soldiers dragged Monica towards the bridge and on to the back of a jeep. When the jeep sped off, raising dust in its rear, there was a burst of agitation and wailing and everybody began to mutter and curse at once and the spirits in the market were talking too, incoherently and in feverish accents. I ran home to tell father what had happened. He rushed out in a very bad temper and I didn't hear what abuse he came out with because when we got to the market a cry of exultation from the men in gas masks told us that the stream had been cleared. The rubbish had gone.

Father rushed on angrily to the army barracks. We passed the bridge and I saw the great swollen bodies as they flowed reluctantly down the narrow stream. I never saw Monica again. The young shall grow.

JAN CAREW

Jan R. Carew was born in Guyana, South America, in 1920. He was educated at the Berbice High School in Guyana, Howard and Western Reserve universities in the United States, Charles University in Czechoslovakia, and the Sorbonne in Paris.

In 1987, he was named Emeritus Professor of African-American and Third World Studies at Northwestern University, following a long tenure during which time he set up and directed the Department of African-American Studies. Recently, he retired from a three-year stint at Lincoln University where he served as the Director of the Center for the Comparative Study of the Humanities and a Distinguished Research Professor. He has also served as an adviser to heads of state of numerous nations on the African continent and in the Caribbean.

Professor Carew is the author of numerous publications, including: *Black Midas* (1958), *The Wild Coast* (1958), *The Last Barbarian* (1962), *Moscow is Not My Mecca* (1965), *The Third Gift* (1975), *Children of the Sun* (1980), *Sea Drums in My Blood* (1981), *Rape of Paradise* (1994) and *Ghosts in our Blood: With Malcolm X in Africa, England and the Caribbean* (1994).

'The Caribbean Writer and Exile' is taken from the collection of essays contained in *Fulcrums of Change*, which was awarded the Pushcart Prize. It is a passionate re-statement of the Caribbean past, the mythologies and ideas – Indian, African and European – that have shaped it, and voices hope that its writers will finally, out of these myriad influences, locate the region's own centre – and theirs.

The Caribbean Writer and Exile

There was a traditional format in the classical Akan theatre around which all drama – comedy, tragedy, farce – evolved. The important features of this drama were these: there was an archetypal middle-man and on either side of him were powerful spirits opposing one another. The figure in the middle often stood between malevolent and benign spirits of the ancestral dead, and a host of other spirits that were urbane or demonic, creative or destructive, compassionate or cruel, surrogates of the living or the dead, ethereal or earthy, part saint, part trickster. These spirits were involved in eternal conflicts which could only be resolved if the human being periodically renewed contact with communal wellsprings of rhythm, creation and life.

The Caribbean writer today is a creature balanced between limbo and nothingness, exile abroad and homelessness at home, between the people on the one hand and the colonizer on the other. Exile can be voluntary or it can be imposed by stress of circumstances; it can be a punishment or a pleasure. The exile can leave home for a short time or he can be expelled forever. The colonizing zeal of the European made indigenous peoples exiles in their own countries – Prospero made Caliban an exile in his. The Caribbean writer by going abroad is in fact searching for an end to exile.

This, at first, appears to be a contradiction until one lays bare some of the truths of Caribbean life. The Caribbean person is subjected to successive waves of cultural alienation from birth – a process that has its origins embedded in a mosaic of cultural fragments – Amerindian, African, European, Asian. The European fragment is brought into sharper focus than the others, but it remains a fragment. Hiding behind the screen of this European cultural fragment the Caribbean writer oscillates in and out of sunlight and shadows, exile abroad and homelessness at home. At home, he is what C. L. R. James described very aptly as a 'twentieth century man living in a seventeenth century economy' while abroad he is a performer in a circus of civilization.

There are times when he claims that he is a nomad, but this is one of his clever evasions. The irony of it all is that he can only become a nomad when his place in the sun, the speck on the globe that is his home is freed from the economic, psychological and political clutches of usurpers who had seized it since the beginning of the Columbian era. The spaces that the nomad's imagination encompass exist within a circumference of seasons, and national borders have no meaning for him.

For the Caribbean writer, therefore, to become a true nomad his feet must traverse a territory that his imagination encompasses without let or hindrance. In his country, however, the land, the air-space, the water, the minerals under the earth are owned from abroad and administered by local surrogates; the rights of passage are overtly or covertly restricted. Every new trespass, therefore, for the male and female writer alike, is a kind of reckless lurch into a wider indifference.

The term Caribbean in this essay describes the island archipelago, the countries on the Caribbean littoral and Guyana, Surinam and Cayenne. Cuba is the exception that proves the rule. Cuba belongs to the Cubans. In Cuba, the north-eastern sheet anchor of the Caribbean archipelago, the pre-revolutionary economic relationship between expatriate owners, local surrogates and the majority of people, no longer exists. Cuba is, therefore, a point of reference for us, a living example of how in less than two decades, age-old problems of economic and cultural alienation, race and color, caste, class and identity, can be looked at afresh and in many instances successfully dealt with.

In order to deal with our heritage of exile today one must return to the beginnings of the Columbian era. Marx had said that history always repeats itself, the first time is tragedy and the next time farce. In the Caribbean we often appear to be like sleep-walkers reliving the history and repeating the farce.

The early accounts written by European colonizers, about their apocalyptic intrusion into the Amerindian domains, are characterized, with few exceptions, by romantic evasions of truth and voluminous omissions. Have we ever really examined the images that these historical fictions have created of us? If we do so empirically, then we can begin to understand this question of the writer's exile abroad and homelessness at home.

After Columbus and his sailors were discovered by the Arawakian Lucayos on their beaches in 1492, the Americas of the colonizer came into being as part of both a literary exercise and one of the most appalling acts of ethnocide in recorded history. First, there were Columbus's diaries (the first literary offering of the interlopers), which told us more about the man himself than about the islands he had stumbled upon; and the man revealed to us was a schizoid being, a Janus astride two worlds, one medieval, the other of the Renaissance. These diaries are a blend of fantasies fed by writings from the Middle Ages; obsessive ramblings about a new crusade to recapture Jerusalem from the infidel Turks; special pleadings to the sovereigns of Castile; a precise sailor's log and useful observations about the flora, fauna and topography of the Caribbean island he had touched upon through good luck, fanatical persistence and blind faith in his Enterprise of the Indies. This instinctive interest in plants, animals and landscapes inadvertently betrayed his village artisan-farmer-fisherman origins which he tried to deny with a studied mendacity for most of his life. He had left the countryside around Genoa in his early youth and the land had etched images on the palimpsest of his mind that no amount of self-deception could erase. On the other hand accounts of the native peoples he encountered are contradictory, inaccurate and biased, and in the midst of pious declarations about converting 'natives' to Christianity, sprinkled with asides of racial arrogance and a lust for gold.

Columbus led an early life that was very similar to the one that Caribbean artists, vagabonds, sailors, writers and immigrants would lead centuries later. In his journey from the land to a nameless street in Genoa, and then his quantum leap to the Portuguese and Spanish courts and everlasting fame, he had to cross not only distances in land and seascapes, but centuries in time. Son of a wool carder, he began his trespass into the fifteenth and sixteenth centuries with little more than great expectations; his whole life, indeed, would become a journey to new illusions. He had had to cross not only distances in time and space, but the almost immeasurable gulf between the peasant-artisan and the nobility. Having made this impossible leap he carried with him a multitude of insecurities and a persistent fear of looking back and acknowledging his lowly beginnings.

On his first journey across the Atlantic, Columbus became prey to the medieval fantasies nurtured like fungus on his narrow Genoese street with its gloomy doorways yawning like entrances to minotaur caves, its shuttered windows and its persistent odors of decay which the sea breezes even now do not seem to dispel completely. As he became more and more convinced that he would survive the Atlantic crossing, his mind was filled with dreams of golden-roofed palaces on the one hand, and on the other, a bestiary inhabited by griffins and by other fabulous creatures, some of which ate human flesh, had human bodies and the snouts of dogs. When he did not find the monsters that medieval writers had dreamed up, Columbus invented a monstrous racial slander, he declared that the Caribs were cannibals.

What we can prove about the Caribs is that they fought with surpassing courage and skill against the European intruders, and that this became the basis for a new kind of ideological arrangement. Those who welcomed the colonizers were praised, enslaved and exterminated, and those who resisted were damned. The contumely heaped upon the heads of the Caribs by Columbus led to interesting lexical and literary aberrations – from Carib derived the word cannibal and from cannibal Shakespeare gave us Caliban. The institutionalization of racism and colonialism begins with the Carib-cannibal-Caliban slander, which has persisted for five centuries. In the Caribbean, school children are still being taught from texts, some of which have ostensibly been written by eminent Caribbean historians, that the Caribs ate human flesh. Richard Moore, the Barbadian historian refuted this calumny in a brilliant booklet, and a very well-researched one, entitled *Caribs, Cannibals and Human Relations*.

The Carib cannibal, the African and other Third World species are fruit from the same tree of racism. Every time a Caribbean child reads about the ancestral cannibal it becomes an unconscious act of psychological self-mutilation. 'Do we not know', Jose Martí had written, 'that the same blow that paralyzes the Indian, cripples us?' But our children neither read the works of Martí nor know who he is. They are still taught to idolize the colonizer and in so doing hate themselves.

On his second voyage, Columbus found human bones, relics of ancestor worship, in Carib huts in Dominica. He used this as evidence to prove his racial slander. Had a group of Caribs 'discovered' Rome and visited the catacombs, they too would have found certain Catholic Orders preserving human bones, and by the same curious logic that Columbus used, could have assumed that the Pope and his followers were cannibals.

If the Admiral of the Ocean Sea had remained in Genoa he would most likely have been a part-time sailor and a worker in wool. His family had for generations been clothmakers. They took sheep's wool, spun it into thread and wove the thread into cloth which they finally sold. Since ancient times, the Genoese youth, particularly those who were artisan apprentices, fishermen or small traders, had gone to sea in search of fame and fortune. For, if they were ambitious, it would be clear as bells of the Angelus that for them their society was one of many dogs and few bones. So the urge to seasons of adventure was not entirely a romantic one. During the Renaissance the challenge of conquering the seemingly infinite spaces of the Atlantic beyond the Pillars of Hercules began to excite the imaginations of those young Genoese as it had never done before. Many of them migrated to Portugal, the unrivalled center of the nautical sciences in fifteenth-century Europe. There were so many Genoese in

Portugal in 1481 that the Cortes petitioned the King to exclude them from his dominions.

Columbus arrived in Portugal when he was about thirty years old. He is a man with whom we should be well acquainted, for he had heaped so much suffering upon our ancestors that we would be betraying their dreams of freedom for all mankind, if we did not mark him well. We should know not only the mythical Columbus, but also the real one. And, since knowing is not just an abstract concept for us, we would be able to divine clearly what he looked like. His son Ferdinand said of him:

> The Admiral was a well built man of more than medium structure, long visaged with cheeks somewhat high, but neither fat nor thin. He had an aquiline nose and his eyes were light in color; his complexion too was light, but kindling to a vivid red. In youth his hair was blond, but when he came to his thirtieth year it all turned white.

Bartolomé de Las Casas, the Dominican monk, amplifies this description telling us that:

> He was more than middling tall; face long and giving an air of authority; aquiline nose, blue eyes, complexion light and tending to bright red; beard and hair bright red when young but very soon turned gray from his labours . . .

While Ferdinand, the Admiral's son, was writing his father's biography, he was receiving the revenue from six hundred African slaves in Hispaniola. It would be interesting to discover how many generations of the Columbus family subsequently rode on the backs of sweating and anonymous Africans.

But, let us return to the impoverished Columbus setting himself up in Portugal. He did not remain in penury for long, because he soon married a noble, wealthy and well-connected lady, Beatriz Enriquez de Harana, and he was eventually able to plead for royal sponsorship of what he himself described as La Empresa de las Indias, the Enterprise of the Indies.

The King of Portugal turned him down, but nine years later Ferdinand and Isabella, the rulers of Castile, became his patrons. Certain that he could sail to India and China via the Western Seas, he surprised the Indians on their island beaches in the Bahamas, though he believed for a while that these islands were in the Bay of Bengal.

Alberigo Vespucci (and I deliberately use his authentic Christian name), a Florentine dilettante and rascal, corrected Columbus's error, if error it really was, because Columbus and Vespucci remained on very close and friendly terms until the former's death in 1506. Vespucci, having sailed to the American mainland, declared that what Columbus had indeed stumbled upon was a New World – a surprising declaration about twin continents which had already been inhabited for over two hundred millenniums! Having returned from his travels, Vespucci wrote a number of letters to the Duc de Medici in Paris, using a lively and entertaining prose style, and causing a great stir when these letters were published.

Columbus's writings are intense, humorless, turgid and occasionally poetic. The intensity of his passions seemed to burn through the dense prose and illuminate it for moments, until once again it becomes uneven, repetitive and dense – the cumulative effect of what is left of his writings (most of the originals have been lost) is like fists drumming against one's brain.

Vespucci, on the other hand, composing his *Quatuor Navigationes* (c. 1504–1505) in Portugal, did not write in the white heat of his experiences. He gave us an elegant, retrospective and very persuasive view, and he was never averse to plagiarism if the accounts of other people's voyages could enhance his own. Vespucci invented a colonizer's America, and the reality that is ours never recovered from this literary assault and the distortions he inflicted upon it. The fiction of a 'virgin land' inhabited by savages, at once a racist one and a contradiction, remains with us to this day.

Alberigo was undoubtedly a Florentine dilettante, but he was also an extraordinarily clever one. Why would he otherwise have changed his Christian name after his voyages to the Americas? There is a mountain range in Nicaragua called the Sierra Amerrique, and a group of Indians called Los Amerriques. These mountains stretch between Juigalpa and Libertad in the province of Chontales, and they separate Lake Nicaragua from the Mosquito Coast. The Amerriques had, since pre-Columbian times, always been in contact with the area around Cape Garcia a Dios, and the whole length of the Mosquito Coast. In 1502, Columbus visited this coast at Carriai and Carambaru. In 1497, Vespucci landed at Cape Garcia a Dios, and, in 1505, sailed along the Mosquito Coast. Both navigators must certainly have heard the word 'Amerrique' from the Indians over and over again during those voyages.

After the initial greetings and the limping exchange of pleasantries, it was a tradition with explorers like Columbus and Vespucci (they confirm this repeatedly in their writings), to ask the Indians where gold could be found. For, as Cortes confessed, they all suffered from a disease that only gold could cure. The alluvial gravels of the Sierra Amerrique had yielded gold for the Indians from time immemorial. They used gold, the sun's sweat, to create objects of surpassing beauty. It was a good metal for sculpture. Beyond that it had little value in itself until it was touched by man's creative genius. By capturing light on the burnished surfaces that metal workers and sculptors created through the use of fire, gold could link people to the sun, moon and stars, and both the act of creative labor and the object created became touched by magic, mystery and beauty. Sometimes they indented pieces of raw gold, and putting them in a sack full of sand, allowed the sea or a running stream to sculpt and polish them, and so through these processes the objects, man, Nature and the gods could become one.

For the colonizer gold meant money, personal and national aggrandizement and power over others. In their burgeoning capitalist system, gold could buy a place in the very Throne Room of the Kingdom of Heaven for the most despicable sinner. And in particular, once this sinner made the right propitiatory noises to the Almighty and gave generously to the Church, he could be assured of absolution from any crime committed against the colonized. 'I came for gold, not to till the land,' Cortes had declared. He was noted for his occasional outbursts of brutal frankness about himself and his countrymen. Their lust for gold was such that the Indians declared that the colonizer would even rape the sun to rob it of its miraculous sweat.

For Columbus and Vespucci, therefore, the words 'Amerrique' and 'gold' had become synonymous. After his visits to the Mosquito Coast (he made the last one in 1505), Vespucci changed his Christian name from Alberigo to Amerigo. In the archives of Toledo, a letter from Vespucci to the Cardinal dated December 9, 1508, is signed Amerrigo with the double 'r' as in the Indian Amerrique. And between 1508 and 1512, the year in which Vespucci died, at least two other signatures with the Christian name Amerrigo were recorded.

Robbing peoples and countries of their indigenous names was one of the cruel games that colonizers played with the colonized.

Names are like magic markers in the long and labyrinthine streams of racial memory, for racial memories are rivers leading to the sea where the memory of mankind is stored. To rob people or countries of their names is to set in motion a psychic disturbance which can in turn create a permanent crisis of identity. As if to underline this fact, the theft of an important place name from the heartland of the Americas and the claim that it was a dilettante's Christian name robs the original name of its elemental meaning. Dr A. Le Plongeon, a nineteenth-century scholar from Merida (Yucatan), in a letter to the French Professor Jules Marcou dated December 10th, 1881, wrote:

> The name AMERICA or AMERRIQUE in the Mayan language means, a country of perpetually strong wind, or the Land of the Wind, and sometimes the suffix '-ique', '-ik' and '-ika' can mean not only wind or air but also a spirit that breathes, life itself.

We must, therefore, reclaim the name of our America and give it once again its primordial meaning, land of the wind, the fountainhead of life and movement.

In the Mayan genesis myth, the *Popol Vuh*, Wind stands at the center of creation. As the story unfolds, we are told that it was manifested to the gods:

> That at dawn man should appear. So they decided on the creation and the growth of trees and bees and the birth of life and the creation of man. This was resolved in the darkness and in the night by the Heart of Heaven called Hurricane.

On the rocky eastern slopes of the Sierra Amerrique the wind pounds like giant fists upon the gates of time demanding to be recognized. M. Asturias's novel *Strong Wind* (1968) resurrects this symbol of the wind in a Guatemalan setting that is near to the Sierra Amerrique. In this novel, Hurricane, the Heart of Heaven, the Mayan and Carib god, unleashed its avenging wrath upon the huge banana plantations owned by an overseas concern that was remarkably like the United Fruit Company. Other Caribbean writers, English speaking ones, had written about hurricanes. There was John Hearne and Edgar Mittelholzer; but their hurricanes had no roots in America's mythological archetypes; the British did not encourage this kind of thing in their stultified colonial educational systems. Hearne can be excused. The Jamaican indigenous connection was absolutely

severed by ethnocide, but Mittelholzer came from a country where
the Amerindian still lives in the forests of the Guyana hinterland
and in the forests of our flesh and blood. In *Strong Wind*, Asturias
reunites myth, magic, man, creative labor and the elements. His
American characters with the exception of Stoner, the hero, are
slightly unreal; Stoner is real because he became indigenized. He
fought with and for the people and in the process became their
brother and no longer their master. So, by the time Stoner and
his wife were killed, it was a death outside the pale of the Judaeo-
Christian tradition; rather it was one that the god Hurricane
demanded so that an act of expiation could be immortalized.
Hearne's and Mittelholzer's hurricanes are depicted with a kind of
clinical detachment. Their strong wind seems anglicized when compared to Asturias's Amerindian-ized one.

The similarity between Columbus's life and that of the colonials
he ultimately helped to bring into being, ends the moment he himself
became a colonizer. The Atlantic crossing created profound psychological changes in those who made it. If all the cultural baggage
dumped in the Middle Passage during the five centuries of the
Columbian era were to be dredged up, it would need a new planet to
house it.

Having survived the crossing, Columbus and his sailors announced to their Indian hosts that they had come 'from Heaven'. It
was something of a contradiction, Las Casas remarked cryptically,
to have come from Heaven and to be so overcome with a lust for
gold. As a dying Cuban Cacique was to reveal, the colonizer gave
Heaven a bad name in the eyes of the colonized. In 1509, the self-
proclaimed 'men from Heaven' had turned their attention to the
beautiful island of Cuba. One of the principal Caciques there, hearing in advance of their coming, carried out a propitiatory ceremony
of drowning all the gold he and his subjects possessed. He was
convinced that since gold was the only real god the Spanish worshipped, if this god was thrown away, perhaps he and his people
would be spared. The invaders incensed by this act of sacrilege had
the cacique burnt alive. When he was in the midst of the flames a
Franciscan Friar of great piety, holding a cross before him, promised
the cacique eternal life if he would embrace the Christian faith and
hell and damnation if he didn't. With the fire burning slowly to
prolong the torture, the Friar, as best as he could, tried to explain
some half a hundred doctrines of the Christian faith. The cacique, in

the midst of his discomfort, enquired if Heaven was open to all Spaniards:

'Some who were good can hope to be admitted there,' the Friar replied. 'Then', declared the cacique, 'since I would prefer not to share Heaven with such cruel company, if you'd swear that none of your people will go to hell, hell would be the perfect place for me.'

We are, in fact, re-examining the roots of our Columbian exile because as an Amerindian proverb says, those who forget the ancestral past will re-live it again and again. If we neglect this task of re-examination, then the contradictions between our psychological and actual exile, an induced state of intellectual amnesia and a conscious awareness of what was, what is, and what is to be done, is liable to lead us into a labyrinth of metaphysics. For our intention must be not merely to analyze the world, our world, but to change it. Only by changing our world can we inherit it, and only by inheriting it can we end our internal and external exile.

The first European settlement in the Americas was established in Marien, one of the five Kingdoms on the island of Bohio which the Spaniards renamed Hispañola. The settlement was called La Navidad. Guacanagari, the ruler of Marien, had treated the Spaniards with great hospitality on their arrival. When the *Santa Maria* was wrecked on Christmas Day 1492, because Juan de la Costa and a group of Basque shipmates had disobeyed Columbus's orders and tried to save their own skins, the Admiral himself wrote that at sunrise on December 26, this same Guacanagari came aboard the *Niña*:

and said that he would give him all that he had, and that he had given the Christians who were ashore two very big houses, and would give more if necessary . . . 'To such extent' says the Admiral, 'are they loyal and without greed for the property of others, and that King was virtuous above all.'

Las Casas revealed the fate that befell Guacanagari barely a decade later:

The Spaniards pursued this Chief with peculiar bitterness and forced him to abandon his Kingdom . . . he died of fatigue and sorrow. Those of his people who were not fortunate enough to be killed suffered countless pains in slavery.

After a warm and hospitable reception, Columbus repaid his Amerindian hosts by enslaving them hardly a year later. The Atlantic Slave Trade began when under Columbus's sponsorship, a shipload of five hundred Indians was dispatched to Spain in 1493. The absence of greed for the property of others is definitely not a quality that has surfaced in the hearts of colonizers during the five centuries of the Columbian era.

After the five Kingdoms of Hispañola and their estimated three million inhabitants were erased, the peoples of Jamaica and Puerto Rico were next in line for their journey to oblivion. By 1540, these two islands which between them had a population of six hundred thousand, could boast of having hardly 200 of their original inhabitants alive. The population figures are those of Las Casas and, naturally, apologists for the colonizer have often warned us that his figures should be doubted. But who should be believed, the initiators, sponsors and apologists of ethnocide, or one who fought for its victims for sixty-eight of his ninety-two years? The silences and the empty spaces which remained in the wake of this early example of a final solution, bore eloquent testimony to the enormity of the crime. Even if the figures are incorrect we might well ask where then are the indigenous peoples of the Caribbean today? Why don't they come forward and speak for themselves? I have penetrated into those profound silences which remain in the aftermath of ethnocide, for it is not only a crime of past centuries, it lives on today. In vast areas of the Guyana highlands west of the Pakaraimas and south of the Akarai, the Amerindian peoples are still being exterminated and their land is still being violated by usurpers. There are islands of silence in those vast spaces which leave a more terrible impression on the mind than screams of the dying. In those profound silences, the Mayan *Popol Vuh* is no longer a genesis myth, but a prophecy, for it began like this:

> This is the story of how everything was in suspense, everything becalmed, wrapped in silence, everything immobile, silent and empty in the vastness of the sky.

As one penetrates into those brooding spaces, one feels the pain and suffering of the dead Amerindian hosts and at that moment one begins to realize that the real dead are the sowers of death, not its victims; at that moment one understands the unwritten histories of the victims intuitively and enters into the heart of their suffering. One feels their anguish in the same way that an amputee feels a persistent ache in the limb he has lost; and at that moment one also becomes the inheritor of the dauntless courage and the humanity of the victims, and at that moment suffering is no longer suffering and death is no longer death. Perhaps it is at that moment too, that one sees the beginning of the end of exile. But before one deals with the cure one must diagnose the ailment. The history of our exile is a dismal one of ethnocide, slavery, indentured labor, racism, colonialism and more recently neo-colonialism. Everywhere that we touch the earth in this hemisphere and seek to establish roots, the roots are bound to invade the graves of the innocent dead. For, after the Indian was sent on his journey to oblivion, the colonizer established new colonies of the dead – slaves from Africa, indentured labor from India, China, Java, Madeira and once again Africa, and along with these the permanent human flotsam in Capitalism's Kingdom of Chance, the unemployed, the hungry, the sick who belong to no special race, color or creed, but are numbers in statistical tables, raw material for academics to pontificate upon. To define this situation today in simplistic clichés about black, brown or white power is to induce a kind of intellectual euphoria in which the mind becomes anesthetized with half-truths. One has to excavate the answers from the abyss of one's self and one's mutilated society.

I had pointed out earlier that the Caribbean writer was poised between limbo and nothingness, like the middle-man in Akan classical drama, but we, in fact, Caribbean-ized the role and became not so much a figure in the middle of Furies and benign spirits, but an honorary marginal person. The writer is, therefore, islanded in the midst of marginal tides of sorrow, despair, hope, whirlpools of anxiety, cataracts of rage. He is the most articulate member of the marginal class, articulate, that is, with the written word. There are others of his class who speak to the mind's ear with music – the calypso, reggae, the folk-song – and who speak with immediacy and a sensuous ease to a much vaster audience. The marginal class is a creation of the 'system' in the Caribbean. The system sustained itself for centuries, by ensuring that at all times there would be a large reservoir of cheap labour. Expatriate manipulators, while controlling vast acreages of land, brought only a fraction of what they controlled into productive use; they also exercised absolute controls over all other important means of production, distribution and exchange by an economic and cosmetic sleight-of-hand, which makes it appear as if the local surrogates were the real bosses, which they never were, and, under the present system, will never become. The economic base of the marginal class is, therefore, like mud on the Guyana coast. The tides carpet beaches with this mud for a season and then roll it up and move it elsewhere.

After centuries in the wilderness, the first law of the marginals is that of survival. To the middle class, which has only recently left the shiftless and insecure world of marginality, the marginal class appears to be truly menacing, a breeding ground for symbols of terror.

The middle class, and particularly the most recent recruits to its ranks, haunted by the spectre of the marginal class, tries almost in a fury to shut itself behind ramparts of self-deception and iron bars. A regular job, a bicycle and a collar and tie used to be the symbols of emancipation from the marginals, but now the symbols have become more expensive and they are a shirtjack, a car, and the third symbol which is optional, is what Andrew Salkey described as 'a waggon-wheel Afro.' When the Black Power gesticulation promised to be safe, social and definitely not socialist, the most unlikely people began to decorate themselves with its exotic accoutrements. But, as soon as it began to crystallize into a class struggle, the middle class abandoned it and hitched their wagon-wheels once more to old tried-and-true neo-colonialist symbols. Naipaul, one of our distinguished literary colleagues, made the profound pontifical declaration that it lacked intellectual content. But the Caribbean writer, whether he likes it or not, is an honorary marginal person, and it is from the constantly shifting islands of marginality that he makes his sallies into the world, into the wider indifference of Britain, the United States, Canada, France or wherever the rumor-gram noises it abroad, that the pastures are greener.

When the colonizer exterminated the indigenous inhabitants in many regions of the Americas, they severed connections with a vast network of secret tributaries that led into the mainstream of the memory of mankind. The total reservoir of memory was seriously impoverished by this loss. The colonizer, reaching into the cultural reserves he believed he had brought with him, discovered that these were soon exhausted, leaving him with psychic voids that could not be filled. The cultural baggage he had dumped in the Middle Passage could not be salvaged. In any event, it was mostly the culturally deprived who immigrated to the Americas, so that from the start they had set out with depleted stocks. Of all the major groups that came to the Americas during the initial three hundred years of the Columbian era, the African alone understood the profound need to create a fusion of his culture with that of his Indian host:

> The African brought with him, regardless of the mosaic of cultural groups from which he derived, a built-in ethic which bound him first, as a stranger in a strange land, to study and respect the host culture before he established elements of his own. This gave the children of the African diaspora a means of surviving anywhere in the human world and they did not need guns and superior weapons in order to do this. When the African arrived in the New World, he knew that the colonizer who had brought him there was a usurper who had seized the land of the Indians, desecrated the graves and the altars of their ancestors, and sent countless of the ones who had welcomed them to the Forest of the Long Night. It was clear to the slave from Africa, that in order to escape the terrible retribution that was certain to overtake their masters, they had to make peace with both the living and the dead in this new land . . . The African had to recreate his vision of himself in the universe often being violently uprooted . . . to have seen himself only through his master's eyes and to have even appeared to be an accomplice in his obnoxious deeds, would have left him with a permanent heritage of self-hatred, distorted self images and guilt. In order to reconstruct his ontological system, the African was compelled by the logic of his own cultural past, to establish relations with his Indian host independent of the white man.

It was fortunate for us all in this hemisphere that the African began once more to make his appearance in the New World from around 1502. It was also a matter of profound cultural significance that Africans had come to the Americas in pre-Columbian times. But within two decades of his arrival in the Columbian era, there were rebellions in Hispañola, Puerto Rico, Cuba, Jamaica and Mexico, in which Africans and Indians joined forces against a common enemy.

Herrera tells us that the Wolofs of San Juan de Puerto Rico 'walked rebelliously through the land,' and that no sooner had they set foot in the Indies, than they 'began to disaffect the Indians.' The Wolofs could, thereafter, only move from one island to another with special permission from the Viceroy.

The humane and civilized African example of cultural accommodation which runs counter to the bigotry of the white settler mentality, has largely been ignored by both our historians and the colonizers. And yet in dealing with questions of cultural roots, alienation and identity in the Americas, it is an example that cannot be overlooked.

At a time when independence – that is, an anthem, a flag and a color on the map – brings into sharper focus questions of national identity and liberation, the Caribbean writer is faced with harsh choices. The end of his marginal status is now in sight. As an honorary member of the marginal class, he has both consciously and unconsciously internalized the mounting chaos that is pushing this class inexorably, not into revolution but revolutionary situations. Their ranks have been swelled by unemployed graduates from high-schools and universities, by preachers of cults and fads, by crooks, pushers, choke-and-rob practitioners, political touts and bouncers, by instant prophets and Transatlantic Gurus. Their dress, their speech, their music, the mumbo-jumbo they invent and discard seasonally are all imaginative forms of protest. They are often unsure of what they are for, but are absolutely certain of what they're against: the corrupt, bullying, pompous, dishonest, cruel, incompetent and often mindless regimes under which they live.

Elements from the marginal class have taken to the streets again and again during the past decade. Their most dramatic street scenes were acted out in Trinidad in 1969. 'The revolution has started!' some of the more naive had cried out. These street demonstrations could best be described by two lines from a Robert Burns poem – for they were 'like the Borealis race, that flits e'er you can point its place ... '

Yet, one should not dismiss the street demonstrations of the marginals lightly. In every instance they attracted elements from the working class and a minority of the intelligentsia. These elements went back to bear the brunt of the repression that followed, to become more politicized and to move the struggle to a higher level.

The Caribbean writer, during this period, played the role of the middle-man in the Akan Classical theatre to such perfection that scholars researching African survivals would have been delighted.

Some went into hiding, others wore gaudy costumes and transformed the slogans into academic canons. If occasionally their denunciations of white imperialism sounded too emotional, they ended by declaring that Marx was irrelevant, long live Fanon. Others played a cunning counter-revolutionary role. The honorary marginal is a supreme mimic and in addition to this quality can perform a literary ventriloquism. He can imitate his colonial master so perfectly that the master hears himself speaking through the servant. This servant has a phonal apparatus inside his head that those who behold it marvel at its sensitivity.

The colonial intellectual passes through three stages – at the first stage, he is an imitator, devoted to the idea of showing the colonizer that he has learnt all his cultural catechisms well and is ready to be accepted as an honorary white man. He is a creature who lives as though he were constantly under the scrutiny of a disapproving colonizer's eye. He is even careful about the way in which he talks in his sleep. At the second stage, our colonial has grown bold enough to be disgruntled. He has grown cunning enough to understand that Uncle Toming from the heart is no longer in fashion; he, therefore, assumes postures of protest. The language that he has come to know better than the colonizer himself is used like a stick to beat the man, but the beating is handed out guardedly. The intention is more to make noise than to inflict pain. It is, in essence, a protest inspired by petulance, a signal to the colonizer, a plea for recognition, a cry from the emptiness of the marginal's soul which says: accept me as an honorary white man and I will commit new and unspeakable treacheries against my own.

The third stage is one of unequivocal adherence to the cause of liberation, one that challenges the Caribbean writer to take sides with the sufferers and not their exploiters, local or expatriate, with the have-nots, not the have-gots, with the scorned, the rejected, not those lapping the fat of the years. Once the writer has made the choice he is on the road to the end of exile, the road to hope, the Freedom road, the road to the new day where:

> with morning bursting
> like pale lightnings from our eyes
> together side by side
> we'll burst asunder
> pale ramparts of Heaven
> with bare hands and bare feet
> to pluck wild orchids
> of ultimate release.

The Caribbean writer is a person from the sun. 'Sun's in my blood today' Seymour writes in his very fine poem, unconsciously entering into regions of African myth which tell of how Nyankopon, the Sky-God, shoots a particle of the sun's fire into the bloodstream of the child, thus bringing the blood to life. In the Caribbean world-view, the sun is a dialectical entity: it is creative and destructive, it gives life and takes it away. Anancy, the West African folk archetype in whose name all fables were told, is shaped like a *gadwal,** a sun-wheel, a mathematically perfect calendar. Anancy was also the victim of an encounter with the Wax Girl. The story goes that Anancy lost his perfect shape after this encounter.

Among the Hausas, the rainbow was called the spider's bow. This shows how close Anancy was to the divinities from heaven. And his bow which had the shape of a snake was called the god of rains and storms.

In the Caribbean, Anancy lost his contacts with divinities and is known exclusively as a trickster.

The European, settling in the tropical world in the Columbian era brought Medieval fantasies with him, of the equatorial region being a land of fire, and when this turned out to be untrue, he invented the myth that only dark-skinned peoples could do strenuous manual labor in the sun. White workers in Cuba, and those thousands of miles away in tropical Australia, and white peasants in the Caribbean have proved this to be the fiction that it is, but the myth persists; and the myth is now embraced not only by its originators but also by its victims. The creoles will still declare unblushingly that their constitutions are too delicate for them to attempt strenuous manual labor in the sun; that only blacks or coolies are fit for that kind of thing. Exile from the sun, therefore, begins in the creole mind. It is the result of a plot hatched by parents who are mesmerized by colonial fantasies of class and color escape. These parents begin telling children as soon as the amniotic fluid is washed from their eyes, that the only hope for them is to go abroad, away from the sun. The sun, in this sick marginal imagination, must always be avoided at all cost. The sun's furious glare darkens the complexion and threatens to hurl this rootless creature back into the ranks of the blacks and coolies which he had only recently abandoned.

The title of Sam Selvon's novel *A Brighter Sun* (1954) suggests an

* Arabic word, meaning a talismanic sign written in columns or circular pieces of stone

unconscious desire to move closer to his peasant origins, not to the distant lands of pale sunlight, but to the regions where it is brightest. Going away from the tropics, one loses one's place in the sun. What follows is a psychic imbalance from which one seldom recovers.

But creating distances between oneself and the tropical sun was not only a question of removing one's physical presence from an equatorial to a temperate region; the colonized could also do it as part of a conditioned psychological reflex. The colonial person rooted in the parasitic economic relationships and the schizoid cultural ones he had had with the mother country could, in his imagination, be at home and overseas, in the furnace heat of his brighter sun and in pale winter sunshine at the same time. The arch colonial still locks himself up in warm, heavy clothing in the equatorial sun and will swear that he feels no discomfort; on certain ceremonial occasions, the neo-colonial ladies and gentlemen even wear gloves. But the marginal, from the beginning of his emergence as a peripheral-man in the Columbian era, while seeking to distance himself from the field slave was always treated with a contemptuous disregard by the master upon whom he fawned. But this did not lessen his zeal to sever his connections with the dark hinterlands under the sun. His real and imagined journeys were forever outward bound ones, towards the 'superior' culture of the colonizer and away from the 'inferior' one of the colonized. The very communication networks that vein neo-colonial territories are like tracings from the marginal's mind and the psyche of the colonized: all roads lead outwards towards overseas cultural and spiritual meccas. The situation, though, remains a dialectical one at its core. There have always been important, living cultural and spiritual bases outside the ethos of the marginal's facile borrowings and spurious imitations. But an indestructible rockpool of peasants, workers and committed intellectuals who were rejected by the colonizer and the marginal alike, continued throughout the Columbian era to incorporate rich and enduring cultural survivals into the fabric of their daily lives transforming these fragments and bequeathing to them a new life and fresh meaning.

The Caribbean writer and artist, if he must end his exile, is compelled by the exigencies of history to move back and forth from the heart of those cultural survivals into whatever regions of the twentieth century, the island, the continent or the cosmos, his imagination encompasses; and, in roaming across the ages of man in this blood-stained hemisphere, he must penetrate into the unfathomable silences where a part of the Amerindian past is entombed, he must gnaw at the bones of universal griefs, and the reservoir of compassion in his heart for the dispossessed must be limitless.

An Acewayo *droger** once told me of the journeys he took in and out of the regions of his mind. The band across his forehead, and the harness strapped under his armpits distributed the hundred and twenty-five pounds he carried in his *wareshi*† so that by thrusting his head forward he could walk at a steady, rhythmic shuffle from dayclean‡ to sunset. We were averaging twenty-five miles a day in the mountainous Potaro district.

'How do you manage?' I asked, thinking of the thirty pounds I was carrying and the way it seemed to double itself after every ten miles. After a long pause he replied, 'It's like this, skipper, most of the time you see me walking here, carrying this big load, I'm not here at all . . . is only a shadow here, the substance is back home in Aquero, hunting agouti or deer or labba, playing with my children, catching a gaff, listening to the Old Ones speak, talking to the Ancestors or to God. You can ask me how come I can be two places at the same time, I will tell you the secret: the pressure of this wareshi on my brain makes it easy for me to send my mind away. . . At the start I feel like a drunken man, there's a singing inside my head, my body feels heavy and the wareshi feels like a mountain on my back. Then all of a sudden everything gets lighter and lighter until I feel like a silk-cotton blossom floating on wind. Once I reach this stage, I can walk from here to the Forest of the Long Night without feeling any weariness.'

The Acewayo droger had remained for most of his life outside the awful grinding inevitability of linear time that the Columbian era had imposed upon his people. The Amerindian induction into the remorseless cycles of time on the European calendar had been traumatic. In 1493, Columbus ordered that every able-bodied Amerindian in Marien should, within a specified time, pay the Spanish Crown a tribute of a hawk's bell full of gold. Those who failed were enslaved, mutilated or put to death. This was also the Amerindian's introduction to a cruel system in which forced labor of the colonized would produce wealth for the colonizer. Labor and the colonizer's timeclock became the totems heralding a new age for the Amerindian and the

---

* A porter in the interior of Guyana
† An Amerindian backpack with a harness around the forehead and shoulders
‡ A Caribbean creole word for dawn

African. For both of these peoples, time had been something one felt like a pulse or a heartbeat. Time for them was finite. In their cosmologies, past time went back as far as the genesis of their races; it was a link between the living and their ancestors; present time merely spanned the seasons of each day, while future time covered the shortest span of all, it was restricted to the inevitable future and little else. This was how it had always been with the black and brown Men of Corn – one could live in the midst of infinities of stasis, of no time – and when one chose, one could then generate new time. In order to turn the Men of Corn into Natives of Capitalism the colonizer committed unspeakable atrocities of ethnocide and the enslavement of millions. He then attempted to remove all traces of his crime. He did it with the same cunning the authorities had used after the massacre of workers in the public square in Márquez's novel *One Hundred Years of Solitude* (1970). In the ghoulish silence and the emptiness that came in the wake of the massacre, even the stones could not speak after they were washed clean of the bloodstains.

Having shattered forever the Afro-Amerindian concepts of time, the colonizer created a new time which he chained inexorably to his own future expectations, and time became money.

In order to illuminate the dialectic of pre-Columbian time and time in the Columbian era a few Caribbean writers had to unlock secrets of lost centuries. They used rivers as the symbol of their journeys into the past.

In *Black Midas*, Aron Smart had said about his grandparents that, 'they felt time like a river in their blood.'

An early Wilson Harris poem had described the journey of one of his mythical characters:

> Down Rivers of his Night
> Where he must drown to banish fear.

This orphic journey was re-enacted later in the search for the *Palace of the Peacock*.

In Alejo Carpentier's *The Lost Steps* (1956), the hero travels into primordial hinterlands up one of the great rivers of South America, traversing millenniums in his profoundly symbolical journey. Carpentier went far afield from his island home to find a setting for his hero's wanderings. He needed a continent.

Edouard Glissant chose a river in Martinique as the symbol of his search for roots and a genuine identity in his novel *La Lézarde* (1959).

What was interesting about the droger's psychological escape route is that it led inwards. It never occurred to him to move beyond the frontiers of home and the forest. Glissant's river '*la lézarde*', however, takes us inland to its source and from the secret spring where it rises to the sea. For on an island your cosmos of the imagination begins with the sea.

In the search for an identity, one of the major themes in Caribbean writing, the impulse is either to move inwards towards some undiscovered heartland as in Carpentier's *The Lost Steps*, Glissant's *La Lézarde*, Reid's *New Day* (1970), Asturias's *Hombres de Maiz* (1957), Harris's *Palace of the Peacock*, my own *Black Midas* (1958); or outwards towards the meccas of the colonizer as in Lamming's *The Emigrants* (1955), *Natives of My Person* (1972), Clarke's *Survivors of the Crossing* (1965), *The Meeting Point* (1967). These novels are works I have chosen from what has now become an impressive array. They are, therefore, by no means the only ones that illustrate the dichotomy of the inward and the outward vision in Caribbean writing.

Salkey's *Come Home Malcolm Heartland* (1976) is a novel about a Caribbean exile preparing to return home. Having explored the outward vision to its utmost limits, the hero is escaping the wide indifference of decades abroad to return to a spiritual Sleepy Hollow.

The hero of Carpentier's *The Lost Steps* is a Euro-American musicologist and composer. In his search for an identity he first goes to Europe but does not find the illusory Europe that his father had brought him up to revere. His disillusionment is complete when he realizes that a psychic uprootment had taken place when his ancestors abandoned the Old Country. But in America as a white settler, he also has to seek out and find the inner sanctuaries of a spiritual heartland that racist fantasies, a strident and spurious nationalism, and a spate of colonizer's myths had unconsciously prevented him from exploring. And he is also an artist surrounded by dilettantes and colonial cultists of art with a capital 'A'. After a chance encounter with the curator of a museum, he sets out from New York on an expedition to find the first musical instruments that man created in the Americas. He is delayed for a while in a South American city where, from the relative safety of a tourist hotel, he watches a palace revolt flare up only to be extinguished. His journey continues over mountains as close to heaven as man can hope to be without leaving the earth. A steep descent brings him to tropical lowlands, the main setting of his search for an American and a human identity. In a few weeks he journeys to the upper reaches of the great river, and, in the millenniums he traverses during this small span of time, his journey becomes one of self-discovery – the discovery of a new American self which was hidden in primordial rain forests: the roots of the Amerindian psyche and the Amerindian person; the inner spiritual sanctum of the Men of Corn; the point from which they began their migrations outwards. In this remote world where linear time as he knew it had become meaningless, the hero is, he believes at first, reborn. But this was a romantic illusion. He goes back to the world of the twentieth century, his spirit refurbished, the scales scraped away from his eyes; when he tries to return to the Eden he thought he had rediscovered, the steps are lost. Yet, he had gathered unto himself an immense creative power in that trespass into pre-history and back. He returned to the sisyphian tasks of the artist, chastened and reformed, knowing that he had to cross not only past centuries but to venture into future ones. In Glissant's *La Lézarde* the search for an identity follows the course of a river to its source, and the spring from which it rises is enclosed by an old colonial stone house. The river takes us into the heartland of a country. Glissant introduces us to a journey of discovery with a poem:

> 'What is this country?' he asked
> And the answer was:
> 'First weigh every word,
> make the acquaintance of every sorrow.'

The author's 'Lézarde' is really a river of life which runs through both a physical and spiritual landscape. As the river makes its way to the sea, one can feel the people stirring, the land awakening and the people, the land, the river, the sky coming together in a miraculous unity. And during the long season of a people's consciousness ripening, the author poses a question that goes to the heart of the dream to end the feeling of homelessness at home. 'Can we,' he asks, 'give a name to any parcel of earth before the man and woman who inhabits it has arisen?'

La Lézarde illuminates the psychological landscape it traverses like flashes of lightning. Its symbols are revealed to us like the vast array of different species of flora and fauna secreted away in a rain forest. The river brings clarity to the apparent chaos; it is linked to geological time; it existed before man did; it flows into an expectation of countless seasons. It is like Alegria's *The Golden Serpent* (1947), a

Peruvian river that threads its way through the life of a people and one
that becomes a timeless symbol of a people's fight for freedom. The
river is a perfect symbol of man's seminal connection with life and
being. Similarly the interior landscapes of Harris's novels are veined
with dreaming rivers of life, death and seasons of eternity.

Pia and Makunaima, the Children of the Sun, are the oldest and
most universal culture heroes in this hemisphere. From Patagonia to
the edge of the Canadian Barens, the same story was told by the
Amerindians from time immemorial. It is the story of how these
twins were born and how their two greatest feats were to bring fire to
man, and to tame the rivers by placing gigantic rocks and boulders
across them. An Amerindian poem sings about:

> The white sun
> raping dark rivers
> the white sun
> biting like a Vaquero's ship
> the white sun singing, singing
> singing the songs of the dead
> the white sun a
> burning requiem
> but the cool night must come.

In this song-poem the seminal anthropomorphic symbols, the sun,
the dark interior river, the songs of the dead, the night, are united. The
river rises in hinterlands of silence and flows to the clamorous sea
and on the way its tributaries reach into the flesh of the land like so
many capillaries. The river can be the symbol of the exile journeying
outwards or the exile coming home.

'All men return to the hills finally' the Roger Mais poem declared.
His hills, both real and symbolical, were an oasis where the writer
and artist went to gather strength, to heal the wounds inflicted by the
philistines at home and racists abroad. From the hills one moves
outwards, towards the sea. Both the consciousness of the sea and the
absence of this consciousness are interesting psychological phen-
omena in the Caribbean. The dream that emerges in Caribbean
writing is one of crossing the sea or of contemplating its moods,
never of conquering it. The Caribs and the Europeans were con-
querors of the sea, creators of sagas; their imaginations were forever
encompassing new horizons of turbulent water. But for the new
Caribbean man the sea was a capricious and often dangerous moat

between stepping stones of islands and continents. The sea, which Lamming describes in great detail in *Natives of My Person*, is perceived as though from a great distance; it is something, not only separating continents and islands, but suspended between them. It is a weightless, static sea, like the one described in the Mayan genesis myth, the *Popol Vuh*, rather than a heaving turbulent reality.

In an earlier novel, Lamming's emigrants cross the Atlantic and are barely aware of this ocean's existence. But in their conversations it is clear that they're carrying enduring memories of the smell of their earth and the dreams of their people with them. The journey by sea is an interlude between home and the Caribbean communities islanded abroad. Clarke's *Survivors of the Crossing* (1965) also erase the reality of the ocean they crossed from their minds. In his *The Meeting Point* the emigrants have moved to air travel and are more at ease. Perhaps we all carry deep in our unconscious minds the traumatic memory of the ancestral crossing in the Columbian and slave era. In Salkey's *Come Home Malcolm Heartland* the Caribbean Janus astride two worlds is about to abandon one of the two and return home regardless of the philistines, the areas of mindlessness that he must invade and conquer, the malice waiting to ambush him and the deep awareness that a part of him had died during the decades abroad in the emptiness, the racial scorn, the endless encounters with real and imagined acts of discrimination he had had to endure. Malcolm Heartland also knows that the home to which he is returning is innocent of many social and political resonances for which he had developed an inner ear. Heartland dies both in a real and symbolical death before he takes the plunge. But there are Heartlands at home who survived both crossings, the one to the meccas of the colonizer and the other home to the secret heartlands where the waters of the River of Life began their flow. Perhaps the finest evocation of this return home to slowly awakening Sleepy Hollows perched on top of the people's volcanic discontents can be found in Mervyn Morris's poetry. This poetry is uncompromisingly honest, sensitive and it penetrates the heart of the discontents centuries of cultural alienation gave birth to.

'All people have a right to share the waters of the River of Life and to drink with their own cups, but our cups have been broken,' laments the Carib poem-hymn. The writer, artist, musician is directly involved in the creative process of reshaping the broken cups. But as an Asian writer had said from a Republic perched on the Roof of the

World in the Soviet Far East, 'Art and literature are like lightning, and lightning can never be timid.'

Therefore, while we shape exquisite new cups, we must, side by side with the disinherited millions of the Third World, confront those who would deny us our fair share of the Waters of the River of Life, for it was at the source of those waters that the exile of the Caribbean writer began and it is there that his exile will end.

A. SIVANANDAN

A. Sivanandan came to Britain from Ceylon (now Sri Lanka) in the wake of the race-riots of 1958. Since then he has lectured and written extensively on Black and Third World issues. His two collections of essays, *A Different Hunger* and *Communities of Resistance*, were landmark books, providing deep insights and coherence to the political struggles engaged in by Britain's Black community. He was the founder of the journal *Race & Class*, which he continues to edit, and he is Director of the Institute of Race Relations.

When Memory Dies is a sprawling three-generational saga of a Sri Lankan family's search for coherence and continuity, following the interregnum of colonial occupation. It moves from the days of the *hartal* in 1920, through independence in 1948, to the fractures of the 1980s when the country disintegrated into communal violence.

from *When Memory Dies*

Tissa was in love again. With a Muslim girl this time, he confided to Saha, and this time it was serious.

She lived in the tenements across the road from the union offices. Of course they had not spoken to each other yet, but their eyes had met and talked many times. Even this morning, when she was putting out the rubbish. In fact, this morning had been different: they had exchanged smiles. He had crossed the road on his way to work just in time to catch her at close quarters, and she had smiled, lowered her head shyly and smiled, at him.

Tomorrow he would speak to her, now that he had got the timing right. The only trouble was that there were people about at that hour of morning, and her father or one of her brothers might see him accosting her. Oh yes, she had three or four brothers, and he didn't want to get her into trouble because of him. They seemed to be strict Muslims. But he had an idea.

'What is that, then?' asked Sahadevan.

'You come with me.'

'*Whaat?*'

Tissa let his friend get over his surprise before repeating the request.

'To do what?' Sahadevan protested.

'We can go on union business. Find out where the men work, and talk to them about joining the union.'

'So why do you need me?'

'My Tamil isn't very good, and they may not speak Sinhalese. And there's always the chance that I might get to talk to her while you keep them busy.'

'Her? Oh, her!'

Reluctantly Sahadevan agreed. He thought the whole scheme too wild, but there was no budging Tissa. He either went along with the plan or forfeited Tissa's friendship, for a month at least. He had been in these situations before with Tissa, but nothing so outlandish. Generally it was a cousin here or the sister of a friend there, somebody within reach. But this was straying into unknown territory. You couldn't go messing around with Muslim girls without getting into trouble, and tenement people at that. They were very protective of their women, and Tissa would be lucky to get off with a thrashing.

But that only seemed to give an edge to Tissa's excitement. He did not care if he got beaten, he said with a sweep of his hand. She was worth it. Her eyes . . . once Saha had looked into those eyes he would know she was worth it. And her face, her face, was like a . . . like a lotus. So open, so fresh. Saha had simply no idea what it was to be in love: he was so bloody old-fashioned and staid.

'Hmm,' murmured Sahadevan, remembering Rani, his first great love. It had never come to anything. What would have happened, he wondered, if Rani had turned up at the palmyrah grove that night? They would have been caught, of course, and he would have got thrown out of the house, out of the village. His father would have been disgraced and his mother could never have looked anybody in the eye after that, and his sister never found a husband.

Rani was sixteen at the time and he not much older. He had just returned from Colombo to look after the farm. He had seen Rani before, of course, when as a young girl she used to come to their house to do menial jobs for his mother. But suddenly, in the two years he had been away, she had grown into a woman. And he had hardly recognized her when, returning from his bath at the well one morning, he saw her in the kitchen compound, pounding rice. Transfixed, he stood behind the clump of plantain trees watching the music of her movements as she raised and dropped the long wooden pestle into a mortar that came up to her knees, her body swaying and bending, gently, rhythmically, with the movement of her arms. Every so often her hair would come undone, shedding the jasmine she had placed there, and cascade around her shoulders – and impatiently she would knot it up again, nestling the pestle between her breasts the while. Or she would pause between strokes and remain quite still, resting her face against the pestle, her raised hands gripping it above, pulling her breasts tight against the coarse cloth of her blouse. He moved closer, sidling along the wall of the kitchen. She saw him and quickly returned to her work. He hurried into the house.

He took his bath at the same time every morning thereafter, and every morning, he stood by the banana grove to gaze at her. She knew he was there, and let him know she knew it, so that he could gaze at her at will. And that made him more brazen still, till he fetched up by the kitchen window, just fifteen paces from her. She lowered her eyes, would not look at him, and he remembered then that she was an untouchable: he could only take her with his looks. He wanted more, to get closer, talk to her. He began to tend the kitchen garden, pottering around the aubergines and the *bandakka*, till his mother shooed him off to work. He tried to speak to Rani from behind the bitter gourd creeper, making faces at her, and at last she smiled a huge smile and went back to her pounding. Her smile killed him, it was as giving as her mouth, the lower lip so rounded out and sensual that he wanted to suck on it till he lost his senses.

He could bear no more. He had to touch her, feel her, smell her. He stopped her in the lane one evening, on her way home. She fled, limping. She was lame. He turned back, sadly. But the next evening, following her at a discreet distance, waiting for a lonely stretch of the lane to speak to her, he watched her buttocks rise and fall to the rhythm of her limp, and joyed in it. Suddenly she left the lane and turned into a thicket of palmyrah trees, and he was hard-pressed to follow her. When he emerged from the wood, she was gone, but before him lay the mudhouses of the *nalava* settlement. He could go no further. He turned back home.

The following day, he put a note in her hand. He could not pretend to tend the kitchen garden any more. His mother was becoming suspicious. But he had found a ventilation hole in the shrine room which overlooked the kitchen compound and from there he watched his Rani pound and winnow, rest and dream (and dream him into her dreams?), till he felt his excitement grow and sing and die in his hand.

He put another note in her hand, and another. She smiled and shook her head: she could not read. But she secreted them, like a vow, in her bosom, and gazed longingly back at him.

Desperate, he trapped her in a bend in the lane at dusk one evening, and held her wordlessly in his arms, crushing the world out of her that kept him out. And for a moment, caressing his mouth with her lips, she gave herself up to him, lost herself in him. But a dog barked, and she broke away, but not before he had made her promise to meet him in the palmyrah grove that night.

She never came, not to the grove that night, or to work for his mother, thereafter. She was taken sick, they said. And he never saw her again. But the scent of goat-dung and jasmine haunted his senses still.

GRACE NICHOLS

'Against the Planet' is taken from *Sunris*.

Against the Planet

The ones whose
small hands
once played in our blood

Regard us coldly.
But not so cold to go it alone
on the skien of science,

So up they haul us,
irritated as Jesus
was with his earthly mother;

The way her eyes would fall back
from the greatest works
of his heavenly father

To dwell more wonderingly
upon the infant-hymn
peacefully sleeping

In her lap's shadow.
The ten little stars
of his human toes.

EMPIRE REVISITED

The time will come when, with elation,
you will greet yourself arriving
at your own door, in your mirror,
and each will smile at the other's welcome
DEREK WALCOTT, 'Love After Love'

S. I. MARTIN

S. I. Martin was born in Bedford. At various times he has been a postman, clerk and factory worker. As a journalist he has contributed to *The Voice* and *The Bulletin*. He lives in South London and organizes walking tours around historical black London (now supported by the London Tourist Board). *Incomparable World* was his first novel.

Incomparable World describes the years just after the American Revolution, when London was awash with thousands of Black-American refugees who had fought for the British. The teeming back-streets of London, home to these 'Blackbirds', are powerfully evoked in this historical thriller. The central protagonist, Buckram, and his cronies may have escaped the overseers' lash but on the streets of London, poverty and destitution await with equal cruelty. Unable to find regular work, they are forced into a life of crime. To escape and allow themselves the possibility of redefining themselves, they plan an incredible and daring robbery. In the extract below, posh Charlotte, Buckram's unusual, educated black friend, has a surprise for him.

from *Incomparable World*

London, 28 July 1786

He was sandwiched in a bouncing post-chaise between Charlotte and the ever-present Mrs Brookes. Buckram ignored the catcalls and oaths that their presence elicited from the poxy Westminster pedestrians and sat out the journey to the waterfront in rueful reflection. *Very special people.* He shuddered at the thought. It could mean one of many, terrible things. Was he doomed to spend the rest of his life enduring Charlotte's ingenuous taste in people and places? It was as William had warned: she was not of their caste. She was happiest surrounded by the flotsam of the black beaumonde; timidly proffering the lowest bids at Christie's Auction Rooms, singing aloud in the Opera House (over-embellishing half-understood arias), or huddled with a knot of radicals in the draughty back room of some Fleet Street alehouse, firing up their seditious fantasies with genteel sips of bland liqueurs. Not his idea of fun. No.

'Here we are. Thameside, my good friends!' bawled the cabbie. They alighted near the cathedral by a long, high wall beside some stone steps which led to the river. Buckram paid the driver with the money Charlotte had forced on him before they left the house.

'Oh, look,' trilled Mrs Brookes. 'There's that grouchy egg-woman from Berwick Street Market. Remember her, Charlie?'

'Oh yes,' Charlotte stated flatly.

Buckram stared at the shifty, beetle-browed harridan on the steps. She was selling rotten vegetables, bad eggs and old bones at tuppence a bag. 'All yer bad stuff, ladies 'n' gents! All yer bad, ready for the river! Chuck it or shuck it! Two pennies a sack! Get all yer bad stuff here.'

Charlotte sighed, exasperated. 'I suppose we should take some for the crossing. It is a custom, after all.' She purchased a mixed bag of lamb's skulls and greening potatoes.

'You'll need 'em 'n' all out there, you lot,' barked the muck-vendor, making the sign of the cross.

'Dare say we will,' retorted Mrs Brookes. 'Dare say we will.'

The river was at low tide. Its brown water sparkled prettily where wavelets caught the sunlight. Buckram guided the two women past the teams of novice pickpockets working the slippery stairs.

Very special people. Buckram saw them now, an odd party of three women and two men gossiping on the riverbank by a small ferry. He kissed his teeth on noticing the tallest member of the group. It was Lizzie, Charlotte's noisiest and nosiest friend. She sweltered in a pink riding costume. Her companions were a pair of middle-aged couples dressed in clean, unfashionable styles, and one of the women was white. Not Charlotte's usual crowd at all.

'Hellooo!' screamed Charlotte. 'Hellooo! Praise be, you've finally made it!' She hitched up her skirts and scampered over the wet sand, leaving Buckram and Mrs Brookes behind her.

'What's all this now?' grumbled Buckram discomfited by his beloved's hysteria.

Mrs Brookes flashed him a cruel grin. '*On verra*,' she sang.

They batted their way through the curtains of flies buzzing about the party. Like Charlotte, the others had bought bags of rubbish on their way down. Charlotte was wiping tears from her eyes and wallowing in the fussy embraces of the black couple. Dismissing Lizzie's chortled greeting, Buckram strode up to the cuddling threesome.

'Oh, Buckram,' she said, catching his arm and dragging him to the centre of attention. 'Buckram, I'd like you to meet my parents.'

His jaw dropped. His solar plexus see-sawed. *Parents?*

'Pleased to make your acquaintance, young man.' The kind-faced, grey-whiskered man offered Buckram his hand.

Buckram was paralysed. This was something he could never have imagined: seeing a black adult in the company of their parents. It was as much as he could do to gasp and take the older man's hand.

'Charlotte's told us all about you.'

'The pleasure's all mine,' blurted Buckram nonsensically. He wondered how any black man living in England could radiate such open warmth as Mr Tell.

'And this is my lady wife, Anne.'

'Ma'am.' Buckram tipped his hat and bowed to the tiny woman with tired features. She emitted a squeak and returned the bow with more of a wince than a smile. Her eyes were like Charlotte's, though harder and more contained: she was unable to cloud the caution and dismay swimming in them.

'Oh, do hurry up!' implored Lizzie. 'The boatmen can't wait all day.' She flashed the pilot and oarsmen a toothy, apologetic smile.

The ferry was called *Wheeler's Right.*

'Are we to embark, or no, father?' asked Charlotte, sounding just like a five-year-old.

'One moment, daughter.' He was still beaming at Buckram. 'Our introductions are unfinished. Mr Buckram, allow me to introduce our dear friends and neighbours, the Barbers, Francis and Betsy. They travelled down with us from Lichfield.'

'Ah-hah, so you're our Charlotte's intended, are ye?' asked Mr Barber.

Buckram stuttered.

'I'm joshing you, lad. Take no notice. Francis Barber, you may've heard my name mentioned in these parts.'

Buckram shook his head, wondering why this man had adopted the mannerisms of a country squire. He slapped Buckram on the shoulder and wrung his hand too fiercely, as if to hide some private disappointment.

The Barbers were a short, good-looking couple in their late forties or early fifties. Mrs Barber curtsied and grimaced sweetly. She had the face of a white woman who has lived for two years in the heart of the English countryside with her outspoken black husband of ten years: she looked absolutely terrified.

'Oi! You crossin', or what?' growled an oarsman. His fellow rower was lying asleep under the seats.

'To the Pleasure Gardens, then, my good man,' shouted Francis. 'Let's to Vauxhall.'

As the ferry wobbled in the water, steadying itself for the first stroke, Charlotte blurted, 'This is making me seasick!' She meant it. 'I've got to get off. Tell them to turn back!' Crouching on all fours, she felt her way to the side of the boat.

'Gentlemen, row on,' ordered Francis. 'Ladies, restrain your sister.'

Lizzie and Mrs Brookes immediately shifted apart to create a new place for Charlotte. They held her carefully, but warily, as if she was a leper with a fortune.

The ferry pulled out, rocking sharply as the oars cut against the current.

'That's not like her at all,' said Mr Tell, watching his daughter gulp and convulse. 'My girl has never been a soft one; I blame this bad air. How can a man live within it? Is this not an accursed city?'

His wife looked at him as if he was insane.

'London,' boomed Francis – Buckram thought he'd been too quiet for too long, 'London, Queen of cities, all. Best place for a young man, let me tell you.' He stood upright in the boat and (to his wife's ill-concealed dismay) began to recite:

> Assemblies, parks, coarse feasts in city-halls,
> Lectures and trials, plays, committees, balls,
> Wells, Bedlams, executions, Smithfield scenes,
> And fortune-tellers' caves and lions' dens,
> Taverns, Exchanges, Bridewells, drawing-rooms,
> Instalments, pillories, coronations, tombs,
> Tumblers and funerals, puppet-shows, reviews,
> Sales, races, rabbits and (still stranger) pews.

There was tolerant applause. The boatmen cackled. Buckram had never heard anything like it. The only part of the verse he could relate to was 'Bridewells'. Now that Francis had their attention he began to bore them with accounts of his perambulations and excesses in the company of 'The Good Doctor Johnson'.

Buckram felt relaxed enough with Mr Tell to pose a quiet question: how did he and Francis Barber come to be friends?

'Young man,' he whispered, barely audible above the oar-teased water. 'Lichfield's a small place. My wife apart, his is the only black face I see.' He scratched his ear and hunched his shoulders. 'Can't always choose your friends, eh?'

'Indeed not, Mr Tell,' concurred Buckram. 'Indeed not.' This was the first time he had ever unmockingly addressed another black man as Mr.

'Oh, oh,' said Mr Tell, pointing at Betsy with her head over the side by the prow. 'Not another sick woman, I pray?'

'I doubt it,' said Buckram, checking the horizon and the bag between his feet.

Betsy had obtained a clear view upstream. Buckram saw how her muscles locked as another ferry rounded the river by Lambeth Palace. This ferry was full of bare-chested men with their hats turned back to front.

'Oh, Jesus, what new torment?' whimpered Charlotte's mother as the other ferry changed course to draw up alongside *Wheeler's Right*.

'This, good woman,' Francis declared excitedly, 'is your famous London river josh. Great sport wouldn't you say, pilot?'

The pilot was completely uninterested.

'Let the ark-ruffians make the first move,' Buckram said aloud, reluctantly acknowledging his role as the ablest-bodied male passenger.

'Ahoy there,' hailed a river ragamuffin. 'You ugly black sons-of-bitches! Your mothers are all bawds and your women are tupp'ney tups!' Much laughter.

'Ah well,' Buckram sighed. 'Let's get it over with.' He stood up and cleared his throat. 'Talk to me like that! You chicken-stinking cockless white bastard! Go bend for Satan and sear your mouthpiece!' With the exception of Mrs Tell, the passengers and crew of *Wheeler's Right* cheered loudly.

'Talk to me like that!' came the reply, 'I'll run a rusty needle through my ol' mare's doo 'n' sew up yer fat black lips!'

Buckram cleared his throat again. Someone patted his back. 'Allow me,' said Francis, eager to join the exchange. He stood. 'You lousy crew of grey-bellied rats! The only clap you've clapped is your mothers! Talk to me like th . . . !'

A soggy onion flew across the water and caught him square on the nose.

'Oooh, that's it!' squealed Lizzie, pulling up her bag of muck.

'Here we go! Have at them!' She hurled two rotten eggs at the onion-thrower. They missed him, but one splattered neatly against the opposing pilot's neck.

The air was soon thick with malodorous missiles flying between boats. Charlotte discreetly emptied her stomach over the port side as the battle raged.

Mrs Brookes screamed. A heavy, pungent projectile had exploded on her apron. 'Dung!' she gasped. 'They've got dung! That's not fair. They're using dung!'

Buckram was holding his last lamb's skull and Betsy was taking aim with baby carrots. Lizzie chucked a handful of compacted maggots. More manure was coming on board. It wasn't looking good.

The pilot of *Wheeler's Right* tugged a fat sack from the stern and tipped out its contents. 'Here, use this.' Great chunks of coal littered the deck around him. 'And look lively! Won't get *your* hands dirty, will it?'

They pounced on the new ammunition and commenced a judiciously aimed barrage against the gong-wielders. Two of their crew fell immediately. The river rats had run out of things to throw. The volleys of coal grew heavier, became demented, in fact. Even Mrs Tell was up and lobbing. Buckram heard her laugh, k-k-k-k-k-k . . .

The enemy pilot pulled down his breeches and mooned at the black people. He singled out Betsy for a final piece of abuse, 'Aaah, you dirty sow, better you marry a pig than a monkey. May dogs defile your unborn litter! Bugger the lot o' you!'

Francis bunged a last lump of coal, but it fell short and splashed dead in the wake of the departing ferry. 'The swine,' he fumed. 'Listen to them!'

The scoundrels sang as they sculled out of reach:

> The Blackies have taken my sweetheart away,
> The Blackies have taken my sweetheart away,
> The Blackies have taken my sweetheart away,
> Turra-lie,
> Turra-lee,
> Turra-lay . . . O.

Visitors were arriving at the Pleasure Gardens in flotillas of small ferries and wherries, lik elves floating in nutshells. Bands of mud-larks, equipped with bru: es, waited on the steps to clean up the new arrivals.

Francis elected himself as guide, but before they entered the park he insisted on having his shoes cleaned, and he insisted that Betsy should watch him. While the bootblack set to work with his slop of egg-white and lamp soot, the rest of the party dawdled at a liquor parlour which had been decorated as a Moorish harem.

Buckram settled Charlotte on a bench beside a table lined with vases of tulips and minute glasses of syrupy beverages. He plucked a flower and rubbed it softly under her nostrils.

'For all that we have, and for all that's to come,' he uttered. He kissed the flower and placed it in her bag.

'Thank you. It's lovely,' she said, absently. She was staring at a mewling doxy and her cull lost in a deep canoodle on a giant silk cushion.

Buckram drew up a stool and straddled it. 'How d'you feel?' Charlotte's face had that deathly, washed-out pallor, unique to beautiful, ailing women.

'I'm fine. It's nothing. Nothing grave.' She nudged Buckram's elbow, prompting him towards her beckoning father.

'What do you drink, young man?' Mr Tell passed a hand over the table. 'There's arrack, punch, ratafia, orange brandy, a world of it. Civilization, or no? What do you want?'

Four jars of scurvy-grass, thought Buckram. He settled for orange brandy. It was the smallest serving of the brightest colour.

'You must let Charlotte bring you up to Lichfield, one day,' announced Mr Tell.

'That sir,' Buckram raised his glass, 'would be my greatest pleasure.' He let the orange brandy wet his upper lip, then set it down again.

Mrs Tell was lecturing Lizzie and Mrs Brookes on the writings of Samuel Johnson, Francis Barber's deceased benefactor.

'So it's all Dr Johnson's money, then?' asked Mrs Brookes, awestruck. 'They've none of their own, Francis and Betsy?'

Mrs Tell nodded and shook her head at the same time.

'Why, that's terrible,' clucked Lizzie. 'A man of his age, with children, too. *Quelle horreur*! What do you think, Buckram? Shouldn't a man, by honest toil alone, support his own family?'

'That's as it should be,' said Buckram, barely registering her comments. He was busy scanning the gardens, ticking off points of potential conflict; the plain-clothed, freelance pressmen slowly counting through the gagglers under the hot-air balloon, the ecstatic, primal gasps from the nearby labyrinth of arboured walks, the long line of tense men standing silent by the Hairy Woman's tent, and the same at the White Negress's. Gravel paths were everywhere: a noiseless flight would be impossible. A pair of sword-jugglers, a fire-eater, the bear-pit . . . 'Mmmm, that's the way it is,' he replied to whatever Lizzie had been preaching.

The women fell silent as the subject of their gossip appeared in the pavilion .

'Look what I've found!' Francis came strutting up from his shoe-shine. His right hand pulled a toddler of mixed race. She had short, clumpy hair, torn up in places by someone's combing. Her face was a nest of worm eggs.

Huge, open sores wept down her neck and chest. A soft, happy spark twinkled from deep-sunken eyes.

'Found her kneeling by the river bank, lapping Thames water like a foal,' Francis explained. 'Seems to have taken a shine to me, the little urchin.' He chucked her under the chin. 'Truly it's as the poet said: "From the strangest admixtures the greatest beauties grow".' He glanced at his wife who was pursing her lips.

'Whaddye' say, we take her for a swing ride and a feed of pease pottage?' he proposed.

Mrs Brookes sniffed. 'I was rather hoping to hear the operetta over a dish of oysters and cold collations.'

The girl staggered up to Charlotte. 'Mama,' she cried, 'MAMA!' Betsy sighed with ill-concealed relief.

'Awhhh, she thinks I'm her mother, poor thing.' Charlotte smoothed her skirts down between her knees and let the thumb-sucking youngster burrow. 'Poor thing,' she murmured, dusting bugs from the child's head. 'Poor thing, poor little thing.'

A shower of rude laughter was moving through the Pleasure Gardens. It trickled across the Italianate rotundas, it swept through the grottoes and beer lodges, it gathered over the dicers and the sharps in the pagoda, and coursed down to the riverside to splash viciously about the pavilion.

A massive woman was striding through the crowd as if it was invisible. She reeked of soused herring and wore a patched mob cap, a patched dress, and a patch over one eye. She was barefoot, breath-less and quite white beneath her dirt-caked face. Rotting lungs rattled against her ribs every time she inhaled. She stamped across to the pavilion, looked left, then looked right.

'How now, my sweet?' She addressed the infant at Charlotte's waist. 'Found favour in a new family, have yer!'

Her voice almost jolted Buckram from his seat. She bulked straight towards Charlotte and scooped up the child between her fleshy arms. She snarled chuckles at the horrified black women and shook the toddler at them.

'Mine!' she yelled in a broad Northern accent. 'Not yours, she's mine. She is mine!'

Buckram felt his gonads shrivelling far too rapidly. She turned to the massing sightseers who had followed her through the park. 'Mine, mine, yes, mine!' she declared defiantly.

She turned to Francis and to Betsy. 'This girl is mine. This is my daughter. Right?'

She turned to Buckram.

He wet himself.

Strangely enough, she was much bigger than before. Those shoulders, once full and straight, bowed and sloped under the weight of her enormous, dangling breasts. Nipples, thick as otter's snouts, stood out against the fabric on either side of her navel. Now face to face, he noticed her split nose and her many missing teeth. Her single eye, now voided of gleam, was compacted and bloodshot as a Smithfield gutter. It dilated, as did her nostrils, and was welling in recognition of the man before her, who echoed her petrification.

Her voice was unaltered and the lips hadn't changed. That was the very mouth that had once worked for him. It was fighting to find words.

'You . . . you . . . you . . . *bastard*!' shrieked Harriet. She shook her daughter at him. 'You evil, black bastard!' The suffocating child warbled a wail.

Hullside Harriet pushed the wretched, snivelling infant in Buckram's face. 'For all that we have, and for all that's to come.' She blew a sneer through clenched teeth, bathing Buckram's head in gin fumes. 'That's what you said. You lyin' black arsehole. You're all the same, you dark men. Fook 'em 'n' forget 'em. Look at her! You don't even know your own fookin' kid!'

The little girl struggled to escape her mother's mighty forearms, as if to swim the air to another's embrace.

'Mine?' Buckram choked.

'Look at you, a-quaffing in your fancy threads with your gang o' Sanchos, and your own blood penniless and two years starvin'.' The strumpet bared her gums and tossed the bawling child into his lap. The little girl pinched him. He *wasn't* dreaming.

'Your dadda,' seethed Harriet. She nodded savouring ancient, well-brewed hatred. 'This is yer fookin' black sire, Cary-lass. Give 'im a good bite 'fore yer ol' ma gets one.'

Harriet lunged, all teeth and nails, at her old lover's freshly soiled breeches.

Buckram said, 'Urrrrgh!' and toppled backwards off his stool. He said it again as the girl fell from his arms and bounced one and a half times, knocking her head and hands against the pavilion's hard granite floor.

Harriet moved with unearthly speed, snatching wildly at Buckram's flailing ankles. He twitched frantically on the ground, like a terrier in a rat-pit, between the bawling babe on one side and Harriet looming on the other, like a lunar eclipse darkening his future.

The crowd in the pavilion was now afoot and staring at them. Beloved Charlotte, her mother and father and friends, were shocked speechless, aghast and gawping.

Harriet was standing over him, trying to kick his face.

'Buckram?' Charlotte, with a parent clutching each arm, was straining towards Harriet. 'Buckram?' Her voice was high and trembling, like a rope-walker's toes more than halfway across. 'Do you know this dishclout?' she cried. 'What is she saying? Who is she? *Who is she?*'

Onlookers cheered as Harriet's huge, hardened heel connected with Buckram's jaw.

Buckram pulled himself onto his knees and elbows. He closed his eyes, covered his head and let himself be kicked, once or twice like an untrained cur.

How many more times . . . ? he wonders. *How many more . . . ?*

Everyone on earth will die before they die. Lives will be lost many times, in many ways. And the boundless, private voids – where one's momentum is the only measure – must be haunted anew with fresh hope and new suspicion. Here is Buckram now, falling yet again, from nowhere to nowhere else, plummeting through the banked-up years of failure, strewn with the husks of his ever dwindling selves. And the single truth he now perceives, the last imploring memory from his fast-fading history is an intonation, once uttered by Neville, 'The land of desire is like the kingdom of the dead: there is always room for more.' And once more, this awful abyss must be re-peopled, but Buckram has no real science, he has no fast religion: he has to learn, just one more time, how to be a human he could love.

There was nothing he could say or do. Nothing now. Nothing new. The child was theirs, his and Harriet's, he knew it in his blood, that blood that pulsed thick-veined across the infant's African eyes. He was the father of Carol (feeling the name stick in his mind, he knew it in his throat), an English girl, a white woman's child, and Charlotte, through her tears, could see his promises and his past, now torn and corrupted, for the living lies they were.

Beadles were approaching, press-gangs converged, Mrs Tell had fainted. Buckram had no purpose here. He was a victim, a target: object of the world's derision and subject to his own, errant will.

He fled through the pleasure garden, punching a path through officials and bystanders, gaining comfort from his desperation now the world had re-drawn his goal. He was running to freedom. Running away, running to freedom, running from Charlotte, running from family. Running alone. back to the wished-for brotherhood of men; the innocent, undemanding planet of play, where unjudged, he could wallow in his unrealized destinies, and unwanted, he could flounder and nurse his wounded pride.

Four trained hares, with drumsticks strapped to their paws, sounded his newest retreat from reality with their rhythmless beat on an old kettle drum.

His last memory: Harriet lumbering up behind him with a tulip-chewing girl-child under one arm, and from somewhere behind them, the unmistakable racket of a Punch-and-Judy show.

CARYL PHILLIPS

Caryl Phillips was born in St Kitts in the West Indies and was brought up in England. He began writing for the theatre, before publishing his first novel, *The Final Passage*. Other novels include: *A State of Independence*, *Higher Ground*, *Crossing the River* and *The Nature of Blood*. *Crossing the River* was shortlisted for the Booker Prize, and won the James Tait Black Memorial Prize. His other awards include: the Martin Luther King Memorial Prize and a Guggenheim Fellowship. He is Henry R. Luce Professor of Migration and Social Order at Barnard College, Columbia University. He also writes for TV, radio and film.

Cambridge is set in the uneasy time between the abolition of the slave trade and the freeing of black slaves. Emily Cartwright, a young English-woman, is sent to her father's West Indian plantation, before her marriage. Like Cambridge, an educated and Christianized slave, she struggles to maintain her own sense of dignity in the face of the barbarism of the planta-tion system. In the extract below, as the system begins to unravel from its own hypocrisies and contradictions, she finds her status and sense of self are challenged.

from *Cambridge*

Without rank and order any society, no matter how sophisticated, is doomed to admit the worst kind of anarchy. In this West Indian sphere there is amongst the white people too little attention paid to differences of class. A white skin would appear passport enough to a life of privilege, without due regard to the grade of individuals within the range of that standing. The only exception I have so far observed was the modesty displayed by the book-keeper who first conveyed me here. However, sensible to propriety, he has subsequently main-tained his distance. The other men, perhaps because I am a woman, have shown little courtesy in affording the attentions proper to my rank. They converse with me as freely and as openly as they wish. This is barely tolerable amongst the whites, but when I find the blacks hereabouts behaving in the same manner I cannot abide it, and see no reason why I should accommodate myself to the lack of decorum which characterizes this local practice.

Today I arrived at the luncheon table and yet again found Mr Brown's strange and haughty black woman, Christiania, seated opposite me. I ordered her to retire from the table, for I am not accustomed to eating my meal in the company of slaves. Further, I informed this coal-black *ape-woman* that I desired her to put on a serving gown and take up a role among my attendants, male and female, who properly circled the table to wait upon their mistress. On a property belonging to Christian owners, this was her rightful place. Unfortunately, she seemed to display a total lack of concern at my words, and showed no sign of quitting her chair, so I asked her again if she would kindly remove her person in order that I might commence my luncheon. The wench cast on me a look of intense passion that indeed appeared unhinged, her eyes blazing with a malice the source of which I imagined to reside deep in her bosom, springing from some other hurt than that which I had inflicted upon her. Her manner becoming frivolous, she then tossed her head in seeming annoyance. 'Massa say I can eat at table. Why missy not like me?' This, as you might imagine, only served to compound the insult of her presence. That she was asking after me an explanation of my behaviour caused my blood to overheat, and I began to tremble with indignation.

Again, this time in a more uncompromising voice, I ordered her to rise and leave my table. When it became clear that she was set on her stubborn course I turned to the chief butler, a slight-looking fellow greying around the temples who, it must be admitted, appeared at least as outraged as I by this woman's display of intransigence. I ordered this black retainer to escort the negress from my table. He immediately set down his burnished silver platter and approached her, whereupon she began to scream in the most reckless and foul-spoken manner, spitting out words whose meaning I dared not imagine. It proved sufficient to cause the butler to back away. The unfortunate lackey turned to me, pleading for clemency. 'Missy, she too dangerous, altogether too dangerous.' For a third time, now beside myself with fury, I shouted my commands at the black woman, but her lungs were better fitted for the occasion than mine, as she loosed her invective upon me, howling and hurling abuse like some sooty witch from *Macbeth*. At this juncture, I am sorry to admit, my cue was to flee into the sanctuary of my bed-chamber where I concealed both my tear-stained face and my impotent rage.

I had determined to isolate myself in my soft and feminine chamber, uncharacteristic of the Great House, until the merciful day of my departure, which I knew I would welcome much as a prisoner might greet the end of his hated sentence. It was then that I heard a knock upon the door, and the quiet voice of my companion Stella. I drew back the bolt and admitted her to my chamber, whereupon I noted that she seemed equally afflicted by the events that I had recently been compelled to endure. Further, she appeared distressed that she had not been in attendance to offer me support both moral and practical. Quickly I shut in the door and bade her rest in a large basket-chair, while I reclined upon the Holland sheet. 'Missy,' she began, 'Christiania is obeah woman, but massa do like she and that is enough.' Well, this was information too rich for me to comprehend at once, so I asked her to explain.

According to Stella's testimony, the negro belief in obeah involves the possession of a variety of strange objects which are used for incantations: cats' ears, the feet of various animals, human hair, fish bones, etc., all of which make their vital contribution to the practice of the magical art. One skilled in the practice of obeah is able to both deliver persons to, and retrieve them from the clutches of their enemies. Such practitioners hold great sway over their fellow blacks, and they sell medicines and charms in profusion, thus acquiring a status unsurpassed within the community. It would appear that this traffic in charms and remedies is the business of Christiania, which manifestly explained the reluctance of my other slaves to cross the woman, but assuredly did not explain Mr Brown's desire to have her share his table.

Putting aside all modesty, I felt it only proper that I investigate further. I asked if the black Christiania was indeed a slave and the property of my family. 'Yes, missy. She in your service.' *But what is her role on the estate?* 'Missy, she just in the house. She don't have no use as such.' I began to grow impatient. I asked if she was something to Mr Brown, but Stella professed ignorance of what I was suggesting. I informed Stella that I had been sufficiently alert to realize that it is sometimes the custom for white men to retain what they term *housekeepers*. These swarthy dependants elevate their status by prostrating themselves. Stella was vociferous, in defence of whom I am not sure. She spoke against these liaisons with such force that I recalled the proverbial saw that 'the lady doth protest too much'. I did not think that I imagined a conspiracy of black womanhood against white, but I knew that I would find this difficult to prove. Therefore I thought it best to reveal to Stella my awareness of such *amours*, in the hope that she would realize that by speaking frankly, she was unlikely to cause me grief.

Apparently such illicit relationships came about because comparatively few wives journey out to the tropics, and those that do are often distinguished by the meagreness of their conversation with their husbands. As a result concubinage appears to have become universal. I revealed to Stella that I was also aware that the highest position on which a sable damsel could set her sights was to become the mistress of a white man. They seek such unions with planters, overseers, book-keepers, doctors, merchants and lawyers, and when their beauties fail, they seek similar positions for their daughters, knowing that success will assure them of a life of ease and prestige among their own people. This much I have gleaned from my brief perusal of the tawdry newspapers, from conversation, and from a knowledge of human conduct observed not only in these parts but in England also. Naturally, the children of such unions receive the status of the slave mother, unless manumitted by their fathers. They seldom achieve recognition as full heirs, and rarely rise above the skills of the artisan. These hybrid people, who hold themselves above the black, but below the white, abound throughout these island possessions as physical evidence of moral corruption.

All of this I conveyed to Stella in the hope that she might be persuaded to share her knowledge with me, but I succeeded only in arousing her ire. It appeared that she took offence at the manner in which I portrayed the ambitions of black womanhood, but she manifested her rage not by overt onslaught, but by covert smouldering. I asked her if it were not true that young black wenches are inclined to lay themselves out for white lovers, and hence bring forth a spurious and degenerate breed, neither fit for the field nor for any work that the true-bred negro would relish. She would not answer. I asked her if it was not entirely understandable that such women would become licentious and insolent past all bearing because of their privileged position? Again, she would say nothing in response. I informed her that I have even heard intelligence that if a mulatto child threatens to interrupt a black woman's pleasure, or become a troublesome heir, there are certain herbs and medicines, including the juice of the cassava plant, which seldom fail to free the mother from this inconvenience. At this point Stella seemed ready to quit my chamber. Her insolence fired me, and I resolved to cast my accusatory stone where it properly belonged. I demanded that Stella immediately conduct me to Mr Brown. At this Stella protested that it was the height of the aftenoon, and that I should not be exposed to the vertical rays from on high, but I insisted. The arrogance of the inky wench, who had dared publicly to preside at my table, still burned within me. I wished to quiz Mr Brown as to her status.

Indeed the sun was high. I had but stepped ten paces from the Great House before I knew that I ought not to be so exposed. Stella was correct. We were attended by Hazard and Androcles, two inferior lackeys who carried our parasols and sauntered along with an air which belongs to creatures unfettered by those responsibilities which are the familiar burden of rational humanity. Stella carried herself with comical self-assurance, quite as if she were a white. I can remember little of the walk to the fields, where according to *fair* Stella our Mr Brown was supervising his drivers, but I do recall that on more than one occasion I felt sure that I should expire before we reached our destination. Inwardly I cursed myself for even attempting such a journey, but after what seemed an eternity Stella finally pointed out Mr Brown. As we approached, a flight of birds rose in the air and cast a shadow like that of a cloud, causing the sun to darken for a few seconds. I found new resolution, and stormed ingloriously across the field, leaving instructions that Stella was not to follow.

The slaves ceased their Sisyphean labours and inclined their heads towards the wild Englishwoman charging across the denuded cane-piece. Noticing this, Mr Brown understood that something was amiss. He too turned and watched, waiting, hands upon hips and whip in hand, for my approach. 'Mr Brown,' I demanded, 'what is the meaning of this black woman sharing my dining table?' Mr Brown stared at me as though I had finally taken leave of my senses in this inhospitable climate. 'I will not tolerate such a vile and offensive perversion of good taste,' I cried. 'I demand your assurance that she will never again be allowed to disgrace my table.' Mr Brown raised a hand to block the sun from his face. He seemed rather confused by my performance, and he nodded as though uncertain of why he was doing so. For some time we stood, toe to toe, two solitary white people under the powerful sun, casting off our garments of white decorum before the black hordes, each vying for supremacy over the other.

I played my final card. 'Mr Brown, if you do not display more consideration for my position, immediately upon my return I shall have you replaced.' Mr Brown, with no discernible movement of his body, and certainly without taking his eyes from my face, called to his trustee, Fox. He ordered this black man to bear me back to the Great House. Fox, a somewhat docile but evidently sturdy negro, positioned himself before me. I repeated my threat, but Mr Brown simply uttered the word 'Fox', at which point the nigger laid his black hands upon my body, at which I screamed and felt my stomach turn in revulsion, at which its contents emptied upon the ground. Despite the heat of the day, I felt a cold shudder through my body, and I tried desperately to keep back a sob of distress. Thereafter, I have to confess that my memory remains blank until I regained consciousness in the coolness of my chamber with my Stella in attendance on me.

I judged from the sounds of nature without, and the darkness within, that the later hours of the evening were upon us. I was pleased to see the loyal Stella hover over me with concern writ large and bold across her sooty face. How far she has come in matching the loyalty of the dearly departed Isabella! Although sadly lacking the natural advantages of my former companion, and incapable of mastering even the most elementary intellectual science of the alphabet, my sable companion has virtue still. Her smiling ebony face and broadly grinning lips, which display to good advantage her two rows of ivory, offer a greeting that has helped make tolerable my sojourn on this small island in the Americas. I have been thinking seriously of taking her back with me to England, but my fear is that she may be mocked as an exotic, as are the other blacks who congregate about the parish of St Giles and in divers parts of our kingdom. However, when the time is ripe I will suggest to her that she might wish to meet with her master in his own country, the prospect of which, I am sure, will delight her. I cannot believe that any West Indian negro would spurn the opportunity of serving their master a quart of ale and a tossed tea-cake on a wintry English night.

THE NEW BRITAIN

If you love the land, nourish it
For the land provides for those who nourish it
IGBO PROVERB

What we know in our heads, our children will know
in their hearts, our generations in their souls
ARTHUR FLOWERS

MERLE COLLINS

'A Journey' is taken from *Rotten Pomerack*.

A Journey

a journey, perhaps, in search of my soul?
of the power behind my sunday-school self?

God, they told me then
made me
in his own image and likeness.

Almost.

I have the words of the language
they gave me for God's
but the goddess inside changed the music.
I learnt the gestures and movements
they told me were God's
but the goddess inside keeps revolting

and the Goddess grows stronger
Sunday-school voices are fainter
and perhaps this painful dying
this constant questioning
is really a recreation of self

or do i just linger here
as i lingered there
because it's seductive
and i'm seeking an answer
that doesn't exist?

DIRAN ADEBAYO

Diran Adebayo was born in London to Nigerian parents. He studied at Oxford University and went on to work as a print and television journalist. His debut novel, *Some Kind of Black*, won the first Saga Prize.

Set in London in the 1980s, *Some Kind of Black* is a coming-of-age story about Dele, a young student, and his sister, Dapo, a sickle cell sufferer. It's the London of Nubians, Afro-bohos, the 'Love Has No Colour' brigade, nationalist politics, violence and intrigue. It's a place that reinvents itself on a daily basis; a place where the codes of various street languages, like walls and fences, work as much to keep insiders in as to keep outsiders at bay. In the following extract, we meet Dele in his last days at Oxford before he returns to immerse himself in the 'vibes' of Black London.

from *Some Kind of Black*

The games that white folk play on blacks are straightforward enough and well documented; the games that black folk play on whites are equally obvious. But the games that black folk play on one another! Well, that's something else again.

Dele had some knowledge of the first and scant purchase on the third. But, come the second now, and our man was a connoisseur. Nearly three years in Oxford town had honed those skills. So it was with something of the world-weariness of the dab old hand that Dele strolled to the stereo situated at the back of Tabitha's cavernous sitting-room. The Motown selection had just played out and the punters parted and smiled expectantly at the brother as he moved through the crowd to exercise his inalienable prerogative. He shook his head in avuncular but firm fashion when a guy, with due deference, held out some doomy Nick Cave and The Bad Seeds vinyl for his inspection. 'Nah, man. That can't work. This is a dance, not a wake!' Dele sighed. He dug deep into his baggy pockets and unearthed a clutch of tapes. Rule number one, he thought, if you're going to a student's rave, always bring your own sounds.

'Hey!' squealed an approaching voice.

'Easy, Tabitha.'

Tabitha, with her freshly scrubbed, Enid Blyton Five-Go-On-Frolics face, pecked Dele on both cheeks. 'Thanks for taking over, sweetie. What are you putting on? How about The Godfather Funkmaster? That'll get them dancing.'

'Please! Enough already with James Brown. If I hear "Sex Machine" one more time it'll be too many. We want something with an up-to-date '93 lick. Trust me,' Dele soothed, pointing to a tape marked *Breaking-Up at the Basement*, 'this is pure west London sounds.'

The Basement was a club that played to a Love Has No Colour crowd in London's Ladbroke Grove. The Basement was Tabitha's spiritual home although, hailing from Tewkesbury, she had never been there. 'That sounds wild, Delboy.' Her face was patchily ruddy; a combination of the liquor and the fall-out from the first sunny day of the year. 'We're over there.' She pointed to a little stage erected in the back garden, where a small group was showboating to the tunes. 'Your presence is required!'

'OK. Very soon.' Dele smiled. The bogus Basement label worked every time. In fact, the tape sticker was a cover for tunes altogether more hardcore and X-rated but this way you could slip them on and no one would complain. His task completed, Dele found a vacant piece of wall, settled himself down with a shot of peppered vodka, savoured its flavoured hit, pulled out some Rizla papers to build the customary five-sheeter, and took a predatory look around.

Tabitha's jamboree for the talented and beautiful was now in full swing; posh people, clubbers, budding journalists and actors, all were milling around her north Oxford place. Tabitha was neither talented nor beautiful, so she was forever having to host raves for the bright young things to keep her hand in. Dele wasn't necessarily talented or beautiful either, but up here there just wasn't a big enough supply of brothers to go round. Well, there were the bloods who laboured at the British Leyland plant and lived on the big estates down Cowley way, on the east side, but they didn't count in the student scheme of things. Up here, Dele was what you'd call a Mr Mention. A player. X amount of invites to events and launches littered his college pigeon-hole.

After three years of sharing his sensi and flexing across the city, Dele was now the undisputed number one negro. For sure, there had been some competition along the way, like that guy Tetteh, whom he could glimpse now in a side room, tinkling a Scott Joplin rag on Tabitha's piano to a little crowd. Tetteh was stocky, strong, cobalt-dark, with unnerving obsidian discs for eyes. With Ghana's Minister for Transport as his old man, his long-time mixing in English 'Society', and his weekend trips to Paris and Geneva for exclusive parties, Tetteh was the living Supernegro. Entering college straight from Harrow public school, Tetteh had arrived with a reputation and a crew of school chums already in place – a big advantage. Then there was Deidre, the busty coffee-coloured thing profiling her chest, on the stage with Tabitha and the others. Deidre was a permanent fixture on the scene. No one quite knew how long she'd been around, how old she was, or where she was from – sometimes she said Ivory Coast, sometimes Gambia – or indeed what she was doing in town at all. Rumour was that she'd studied at the poly or a secretarial college back in the day. Certainly, she wasn't leaving town until she'd persuaded one of her rich part-time lovers to slip a ring on her finger. Or Colin, of Bajan natural parentage but adopted by a liberal English couple. Hitherto lumbered with a nondescript mid-Afro, Colin had gone AWOL and returned only today sporting long, braided extensions. He was shaking his funky locks around and twirling a canapé by the food table. But still, with his Home Counties burr, his cords and his brogues, Colin was coming like an English gentleman of the old school.

This was the problem with his rivals, Dele reflected as he pulled on his smoke. They were all too speaky-spoky, as Oxford as yards of ale. But most students didn't want to hear that. No, sir! Be they Chelsea girls or strident left-wingers, they wanted danger, they wanted to play away just once in their lives. It was best to homey the hell out of them, indulge their romance of the real nigga!

Dele hadn't always been like this. He had arrived here to begin his history degree nearly three years ago open-minded, totally up for these new runnings. He had embraced new musics, styles and fashions. But various things had led him to review the situation. The first problem, he'd have to confess, was there were precious few checks in it. And even those few were with these grungey types. And second, there was the celebrated occasion when Dele had been rucking violently to a twangy-guitared Smiths song at a college bop and cannoned into Jonathan, a languages student from another college, standing in a corner. Now Jonathan was about the only person around who had had anything like a similar background to Dele's own –

West African descent, inner-city (albeit Liverpool), elevated post-GCSEs to a state grammar school – and Dele was keen for them to get better acquainted. So it had bothered him slightly when he had smashed into Jonathan at the dance and soul-man Jonathan had stared at him with a kind of pitying astonishment.

Shortly afterwards, when they bumped into each other on Holywell Street, Jonathan had let on by immediately launching into a reworking of the chorus of 'This Charming Man', an old Smiths hit:

> I would go out tonight
> but I haven't got a stitch to wear
> My name is Dele
> and I may be black
> but I don't care-aa-are!

Jonathan had sung mockingly, his bare arms clenched above his head, rucking and rotating around like some Nubian New-Age Traveller.

A joke thing then, if still with a sting. But they had become friends and Dele had been at his right hand when Jonathan had set up an informal Black Students Discussion Group in their second year. The problem was that people came – those who came at all – with different agendas. Deidre said why did we need to have our own discussion group anyway, and it was inverse racism. Tetteh said look, let's be realistic, there really aren't any problems for us, are there? And he was right, in a way. For Tetteh, with free flights to Accra when he wanted and prosperous dual futures ahead, there was no problem. And Ruby, the ferociously militant mixed-race girl, she was for severe, separatist action. Only nobody took her seriously, as she was known to fling down the cream of European manhood behind closed doors.

It was funny, though. There was a certain wanky air of self-satisfaction bubbling under the surface at these Black Chats. Folk felt that whatever the problems had been out there, *they* had overcome them, they must be the *crème de la crème*. As an evening wore on and tongues got loose, some would invoke hoary myths of the integrity of strong African cultures and contrast that with the Caribs' lack of a coherent identity to explain their minuscule representation there. But when he checked it, Dele could barely find a person in the room, himself included, who was truly sorted. Most of them were unreconciled either to their families or to their role here, if any. Their heads were mash-up, frankly. It was quite possible that the only thing they were really sorted about, were good for, was taking exams. But you couldn't linger over thoughts like that. The implications were too troublesome.

It was after that group foundered that Dele lost the thread a little. In some barely acknowledged way, he lost commitment to the place, took it less seriously, and began donning different hats to see how they fitted. Oh, there he would be at a dinner party with liberal friends, and wait until the second course had been served and chat was free and comfortable, then hush the room in an instant with some choice Race facts. And the smiles would be replaced with flurries of worry and concern, and they would say, 'Gosh, Del! Is that really how it is? I can't believe black cabs think they can get away with that! You should write to the papers . . . ' But, truth say, he didn't really feel that a history of slavery and low-level grief around town made him a bona fide candidate for Black Rage.

He had grown tired of this game, tired of sitting with his peers, worthy and curious, and explaining to them bits of experience that he knew about already. So he had started moving with a less right-on crowd, and here Dele had developed a range of broader comic roles. He'd been a fool, he'd made few close friends, he could see that. He was unhappy although he was having a nice time. But he felt that he was on the case and was fond of telling Dapo of his imminent return to purity. The trouble was that he endlessly deferred.

The night's event has been hyped as the last great blowout for the student hip set before they settled down to prepare for their final exams. Like a dictator of the thirties, Tabitha engaged in a tireless quest for *lebensraum*. She and her empire of kissy-kissy friends were set to graduate and keen to seal contacts for life. The five-year plan was to recreate the same scene in west London's Notting Hill. Her place had the usual nods in the direction of downward mobility that no cool posh girl these days could do without: a Student Loans Company policy plastered prominently on the kitchen wall, a 'Can't Pay/Won't Pay' sticker defiantly underneath, and guests in their polished Doc Martens and lumber jackets. All this jarred slightly with the glassy clink of cherry, lemon, and peppered Polish vodkas and champagne being iced in the bath, the boiled quails eggs, and tomatoes stuffed with roe all ripe on the table, but who gave a shit? Not Dele. That wasn't what he was invited for.

Scoping the vibe, he was assailed by a growing sense of detachment from proceedings. He didn't know why. These sights and sounds that he had waded into knee deep were now beginning to defamiliarize themselves. These same old shapes – greys clad in Levis that their flat-jack backsides could not properly fill out – reasserted their difference. No rumps and no lips, never mind a stiff upper one. How did they build an empire?

Dele's reflections were interrupted when the bars of a popular tune started up and the company on the podium by the open French windows shouted for him to 'Stop hiding yourself down there!' He grimaced at this loud, long-distance acknowledgement of his role as court entertainer and sauntered over to do his stint.

As he found a few free square yards for his self on the stage, Dele was dimly aware of Tabitha and this guy he recognized with a dark-brown mop of hair, looking at him and giggling loudly, 'How much do you think he's worth then? Five, fifteen . . . I reckon he's worth thirty if he's worth a penny.' But Dele's attention had been distracted by the first sight of a potential chirpsee.

She was fairly tall, five feet six or seven, auburn hair tied in a French bun, black polo neck under the check jacket, black flimsy elephant pantaloons rounded off with a pair of black leather boots. She leant gracefully against a table. Twice she had looked up at him and smiled. The first, a too-ready open beam, Dele had read as a 'I don't have any problems with black wood!' smile. The second, just as borderless and full but more focused, was a 'So who are you? I might be interested.' But just as he was mulling over some lyrics, four or five pairs of hands grabbed and blindfolded him, knocked him off his feet and carried him off the stage to the back of the garden. There were cheers and he could hear Tabitha singing 'Surprise, surprise!'

Dele steeled himself for a practical joke. Why were these people distressing a perfectly nice do with these silly japes? But the full ugliness was only revealed when a hand slipped the blindfold off and Dele found his shirt-crumpled self in front of a sniggering throng and standing opposite the nerdy Grant Knowles, Tabitha's college union president.

Grant was wearing a judge's robe and pince-nez with the executioner's black cloth perched on his head. To his left, behind a long table, stood his lieutenant, the union treasurer, suited and booted, with a gavel. A blackboard was mounted on the grass, and Dele's name was up there, above a number of others, with starting-price pound signs by their names. A length of rope cordoned off a section of the garden where four members of the university rugby team sat shackled together. Among them, grinning inanely, was John Omiteru, star rugby winger and Supernegro. And Deidre, now clad in a low-cut leopard-skin number, scuttled seductively around them, cracking her whip to keep them in line.

Damn, Dele was thinking, it must be the rag-week's slave auction. A yearly ritual of obscure origins, it involved auctioning off participants as 'slaves for the day' to the highest bidder. Sometimes the bidder was a group, sometimes the slaves were a group. If you were a lucky guy, you might get four fit young ladies to hire you for a day and strap you to their four-poster bed. But no one had ever been lucky. 'Look, Tabitha. I'm not doing this. No way,' he muttered quietly to her.

'Oh Delboy! Relax. It's all for charity, you know—'

'Fuck charity, Tabitha! It's not my bag. You shoulda told me you were planning this. It's so out of order—'

'You shouldn't take yourself so seriously. We're not dunking you in the water tank or anything.'

The girl he liked had wandered down to the scene. She looked amused. Not you too, thought Dele.

'Really, Del!' huffed a friend of Tabitha's. 'It's not as if Deidre and John aren't joining in.'

'So what do they have to do with it? They're not my business.'

'Oh why are we wai-ting?' sang Grant, with mock impatience. Then he turned to the crowd and said, 'Time to start early bids for this lot. What do you say, Ladies and Gentlemen, to this real live black person?'

'And why did you even let that ignorant fool in here in the first place!' said Dele sharply.

Until then, all the exchanges had taken place within the accepted cut and thrust of slave-auction foreplay, but this last remark chilled the temperature. Dele sucked loudly on his teeth and stomped back inside. He felt to walk out altogether, but then people would notice and think he was making a big deal out of the incident. So he propped himself up by a speaker and tried to look relaxed while his mind ticked away. Boy! John and Deidre, the shame of it! Is that really how he's been coming these past three years for Tabitha to think she could run that slave fuckrey past him? Is that what everyone thinks? Funny how he thought it was he who was taking the piss . . .

BERNARDINE EVARISTO

Bernardine Evaristo was born in England to a Nigerian father and an English mother. She trained as an actress and spent many years working in the theatre as a writer and actress. Her work has appeared in many anthologies and her first collection of poetry, *Island of Abraham*, was published in 1994 by Peepal Tree Books. *Lara*, a novel in verse, was published in 1997 by Angela Royal Publishing.

A lyrical and epic tale, *Lara* is the story of a new Britain and its origins. Through a kaleidoscope of voices, we trace two disparate families through succeeding generations to one girl-child: Lara. It is a rich but painful heritage: of proud Yorubas enslaved in Brazil, free in Nigeria and hopeful in England; of Irish Catholics leaving behind them generations of poverty, ascending to a rigid middle class in England – and of the universal requirement to conform at all costs, in the 'Motherland'. In the following extract, as she begins to discover her black identity, Lara meets her first black boyfriend, Josh.

from *Lara*
1981

I began to dip into my skin like a wet suit,
toes first, warily, wriggled about, then legs all in,
by summer 81 I'd zipped up and dived head first,
that year I started art school, Landscape of the Souls
I called my anarchic blood and black vortexes,
I loved exploding the energy of colours, being bold.
Summer heat choked my city's horizon, sluggish clouds
of fumes were mountains of dirt way up in the ether.
Tourists homed in on Piccadilly like brain-damaged fish,
I barged, my large portfolio an aggressive advance guard,
boarded the bus to Camden Town, my squat room,
all purple walls, pampass grass and mexican mats.
Nights steamed my pores in the 100 Club where
pupil-swimming arousal came in the countenance of Josh.
Under his pillar-propping gaze, I tried to dance cool, slyly
studied the Dreads in corners with towels round necks,
trainers, shiny tracksuits – red, gold and green striped,
confidently shuffling, moving just off the beat.
'Go slower, syncopate, less movement, more weight,'
we exchanged numbers like French kisses, at 2 a.m.
my creamed knickers rode the night bus home.

Josh, your limbs were waves. I swam.
Your myriad hands smooth licked me. The sea.
Flesh. Breath. Flesh. Your tongue swelled in me.
Juiced, me. You, carefully, entered, sensing your
way in, alert to my every whimper, responding.
Kiss. Kissed my hips, like water, every secreted crevice,
seduced, and only when I cried out first, did you go
for the shoot, the spawn game, tadpoles into the pond.
At last, on safe ground, at last, I was, on safe ground.
'Hey Princess, let's take the tube-train into darkness.'
Your public school tones joked, open Ibo vowels
squeezed into nasal tubes, staccato consonants.
Years before I'd made my teenage foray into Brixton,
awed by the vivacious tableaux of Atlantic faces. I was
born into whiteness, this was the moon, I was elated.
'Ssssss!' The Atlantic pub, Coldharbour Lane 'Ssssss!
Yuh look nice, gyal.' Red eyes and Tennants extra.
I wore my grandmother's stiff back, her deaf ear.
'Tcha! She favour pork!' I panicked to the station.
With you I merged into Tottenham, the Bush, the Grove,
jostled in markets, pubs under arches, basement clubs.
You squeezed my hand, I was six years old, Daddy?
I poached your easy slope, excited, I was, exalted.
Summer 81 I was touched by the sun.

I was jelly, you were my mould, yet
I could not set, would freeze or throw a wobbly,
criticized your arrogance, your African-at-Eton act.
'You can talk!' you retaliated, easing your motorway legs
onto my cul-de-sac. 'You're as rootsy as the driven snow.'
You rolled onto me, into me, my anger drifted
downriver like a log while I became an unplugged dam.
You loved your skin, polished with cocoa butter,
advised I do the same or I'd 'flake to dust like a relief
in an Egyptian tomb.' You'd coo over my complexion.
'Do you like me or my light-skinned factor?' I challenged.
'Both, and at least I'm honest before you throw one.
You know, I suggest you pursue an academic career.
Paint as a hobby. You have a trunkful of O's and A's.
I only ever had three choices: law, medicine, finance.
Well, you know how we Nigerians are.' 'Yes,' I lied,
then flared up. 'So why are you trying to change me?'
'Because I want to lick your chocolate button nippies.'
You twirled and stroked yourself, 1 laughed, coalesced,
but felt my summer of passion waning.

'You'll not marry a Nigerian if you can't obey me.'
I shook my head slowly. 'You are such a wanker!'
'Ditto, Lara, ditto!' G & T in hand he rolled off
the mattress, loped his gorgeousness to the bookshelf,
leaned provocatively, crisp sinews, a little pot belly.
'Marriage! Hah!' I flung my head back. 'Marriage?
I love the F-word too much, you know . . . freedom!'
'Just as well, because you don't even know what
Jollof rice is, let alone how to cook it. You're strictly
a fish fingers and mash girl. You'll make a sorry wife.'
He sniffed, smugly sipped his drink, crossed his legs.
'Why don't you put me down, Bertie Wooster, you know
for a change, and who says I only like Nigerian men?'
'It's obvious, you hope some of it will rub off on you.'
'Oh fuck off, you idiot! Shithead! Tampon dick!'
Then he melted, vulnerable in his contrived pose,
the sweet Josh, two years old and thumb sucking,
it was so easy to oust the monster, to get at his ego.
I softened, 'Sorry, Josh. Cuddle?' 'Yes,' he pouted,
'A treatie for Wole the Wonder will do the trick.'
I crawled towards him, took his pitiful dejection
in my mouth, chomped, left a shiny oozing Bounty Bar.
Such a failsafe method of resuscitation.

Lautrec posters, blue lamps, Portobello pub,
candlewax bubbles over baroque holders, hedgehog
barmaids have stapled noses, safety-pinned flesh.
I hover in a dungeon alcove, nurse my port, insecure,
wish I'd been born a Holland Park babe, was a funky
half-caste dahling, a Cleo Laine jazztress with a voice
that sails, seducing the crowd. My kohl-eyed cohorts –
Hampstead, Chelsea and Fulham have tunnelled
salt up their nostrils. 'Is that not your Josh?'
Emma exclaims, glimmering. Hickory, dickory, dock.
Stop. Time clocks. Incongruous in blazer and loafers,
he confidently guides a young Shirley Bassey in sassy
zippy leather to the bar, all kissy-kissy, gooey-gooey.
Yuk! I kamikaze my port, emerge bloodened, dazed,
confront him outside. O to serrate beer bottles!
Scarify his cologned cheeks! Kung Fu his dim sums!
'You like the F-word, remember. We're not wed, Lara.'
My alphabet tumbles, jumbles into a 3 yr old's bawl.
You . . . you . . . ,' I barely whimper, a dissolving asprin.
Verbals! I need verbals! Please! I want my verbals!
'A hungry gerbil up your hairy arse!' I muster, he snaps,
'Oh do grow up, Lara! Welcome to the real world.'

Fury rode me. A wild buckjumper,
I scalped myself, sacked Josh, speared my nose,
my little Afro ears coiled a C of silver earrings,
I barricaded myself into an army surplus trench coat
and fronted a permanent Desperate Dan scowl,
nuggets of disease erupted on my surface, squidgy
pus-filled hillocks splattered my bathroom mirror,
I denounced my patriarchal father, deconstructed
my childhood, regurgitated appropriated ideas
like closing-time vomit, I flirted with sensi, swooped
on trendy markets for cowries, batiks and sculptures,
I was a walking irradiated automated diatribe, saw
the rapist in every homme, worms in every phallus,
the bigot in all whites, the victim in every black
woman, London was my war zone, I sautéed
my speech with expletives, detonated explosives
under the custard arses of those who dared detour
from my arty political dictates, I divorced my honky
mother, rubbished the globe for its self-destruct sins,
and then flung open the Hammer House gates
of my Rocky Horror Hades,
and tossed the key.

Ablaze with the sharp and the syrup, yeh!
I sozzle whisky mixed with Drambuie, neat, just
a tot, a pint, two litres, ta, topped up, topped up,
on brassic days Mr Gordon's Dry Gin, on the rocks,
rocky, slippery, slippery, o hickory, six bottles Bells
under the sofa, in the sink, in the bin, under the stairs,
a little drop 'ere, a little drop there, droppy droppy
everywhere, now! ready to paint a masterpiece, oops!
mistresspiece, yeh! I mean ten gallons whisky on a drip,
drop, hit the high spot, tick tock, 12 o'clock, havin' a ball,
ready, steady, do a splishy sploshy 'ere, a splish splash
whoopshy! Ah! the bluesy woes of a suffrin' artist!
Why did you trip me up, Mr Easel? Come here now!
groove on down with Leonard Cohen, hit the floor
with Simone, Bach, a little light Gregorian chanting,
stumble to the loo, prop up, eyes open, keep 'em open
or the bath'll spin n' spin, I feel like, don't wanna feel,
wanna chuck up, eyes shut, in bed, room whirls, upside
down, downside up, wideways in, I weep, I weep, I weep,
I am an old wound, I weep, that has not healed,

      shpin
shpin   and out.
   shpin.

I nightmare, damply scream into silence . . .
run backwards into childhood, down Arundel Road,
his Pinnocchio belt pursues, lassoos me, leather belted,
I am legless, my mother in the kitchen, cooks marshmallow
love on a ravioli of self pity, boils over, I skid on her tears –
all the way into the Eighties, Sainsburies, Stepford Wives
checkout, I find a bulging co-star, is he a computer
or just a print out? I sleazily X-ray his Uncle Tom, ding!
dong! 'That'll be six pounds and 69 pence, madam.'
I take him home, wardrobe him in leather jock strap,
gun holder, bikers' boots, baby oil his jet buns, play
Black Barbarella to his Kola The Cunt Controller,
he unzips my PVC mini, down the back! Black fishnet
stocks, crotchless satin knicks, red-light thigh highs, patent
I pant, trade entrance only, cat o' nine tails, 'On yer knees!'
Sweet Jesus! I play second fiddle to his diddle-daddle.
'Juice it, Bitch! More! Faster! Faster! You must obey!'
'I won't! I won't!' Swoosh! Swhop! Shlick! Tingle!
'Spread 'em, take it like a' . . . a witch, I . . . I . . . run screaming
on moors, scarecrowed by bibles in batted capes, coarse
cloth and clog villagers, I am stoned into rivers . . . a car
alarm goes off, I awake, relieved, moist, dehydrated.
Say ten Hail Marys, my child. Yes Father.

'You're an undressed genius! Lara!' Trish unwraps
my magnum opus on the floor of our latest makeshift
gallery, another empty shop in Marylebone High Street.
I laugh, proud of my painting, a life-size bottle, my naked
self going glug glug to the bottom. 'It's called Booze!' I say,
'Eat yer art out Jean Michel-Basket! This is London-stylee!
My influences are Hackney, Afro-beat and Blue Peter!'
I stand back, watch Trish contrast the freshly white walls,
'Never was the Nefertiti from Neasden so beautiful!'
I declare grandiloquently. 'Tis true! you know!' She grins,
'Many have commented on my timeless, regal, beauty!'
She spins the floor like a Whirling Dervish, ululating.
'I'm going away!' I call out. 'Yeh! Yeh! Another fancy!'
'No, for real this time! I'm hitting the road, Jack, Trish.
I've had it! Aint no Saatchi gonna doubloon my satchel.
I've hoarded some coppers in my piggy. It'll last a while.'
Trish stopped, then frowned, 'It's just escapism, Lara.
We're best friends. Don't bugger off now, you old cow!'
'I s'pose I am escaping. I'll soon know if it's from myself.
Come with me, live a little, leave this cage. Anyway,
when this show comes down, it's toodle-oo from me.
I'm going to trundle my way across Europe.'

It's pissing down, out the jeep, out the door, pissoir,
perched for a pee, cloth over knees, secrete, number twos,
mobile loo, out of view, 'cept for spyin' lorries, who honk
and perv and rev on down the slick autobahn – wet wipes,
towels, maps, stanley knife, ice box, cassettes, the long
and winding, yellow brick, to follow, wherever I lay my,
home, hat, the road, we spiral around, gorge on satay chips,
salami, Belgian chocs, sauerkraut, Austrian beer, vin,
brie slabs in French sticks, olives, artichokes, a million
pastas, dip doughnuts in cups of hot thick chocolate,
we brawl, sulk, make up, Trish and I, hold our breaths
as borders fly into blurs, black geese flying amid white,
will they stop us? our passports wave us through, phew!
my geriatric jeep, Bess, pipped by sleek Mercs, Heinzes
in huge homobiles, and on down Spain's dry African spine,
we overheat, slow down, rest, renew, stagger farting
up the package Costas, ex-pat colonys, retired colonels,
fish'n'chips, Brit bars, we flee, exhilarate, compass the sun,
tunnel the mountainous Med, zipped nights on sand,
or reclined in Bess, morning scrub with halved lemons,
Brindisi, Patras, Piraeus, Heraklion, Rhodes, Marmaris,
we edge, we ease, we secure Bess onto ferries,
chug, we sail the clean Aegean, east.

Empty roads guzzle us up, frazzled tarmac,
smoking horizons, lunar mountains, ploughed land, we
snipe, bicker, sweat, Bess grunts, spits, aches as we fizz
east, yavaş, yavaş, slowly, slowly, shallow breathing,
fantasizing baths of iced water, dream of a full Sunday roast,
all of a sudden: spuds, cabbage, gravy, salivate, PG Tips,
in the heat, fried breakfast? ketchup, even. We become
more British, Trish and I, darker with the Turkish sun,
yet less aware of race for we are simply: İngiltere.
Our tracks lead to dusty villages, musty beds, my brain
contains three thoughts, only – petrol, food, shower.
London retreats, a dislocated memory, immaterial now.

Finally,
    I flop on an old hippy beach for a year,

                           and stop.
Under the Asian sun my armour roasts,   rusts,
falls off in bits,
is swept out by the tide.   I watch it bob off,

                           new

flotsam,
study the twinkles in the firmament at night,
go for a midnight dip,   and emerge,

                        the sum of all my parts.

He smelt of the sea. Haakan. And fish –
during the day. Bedtime of Imperial Leather soap
and at midnight we discharged semen and come.
A fisherman, he stitched nets, the far side of the beach,
I watched his back, stripped, hairless, brown, broad
from rowing boats. I left my tent, early morning,
swam over, tiny fish slipping down my costume.
He poured thick coffee, outside his cabin – spent summers
near the sea, he said, winters in his mountain village.
Haakan, Tartar-man, sharks flecked in his narrow eyes.
Some nights he rowed me out to sea, Mehmet II,
a larger boat, awaited, and nets spread for a wide catch.
I lay on deck, cushioned against salted wood, waves
licked, caressed, the moon, lolling of the sea. Perfect.
I was whole. I closed my eyes, tried to picture my real
life but only sky appeared. He worked silently, oblivious,
almost. I was seasonal, perhaps. It was safe to love Haakan,
in a capsule, both knowing I would not stay forever.

For a while I was a fisherman's moll,
by the sea, on beaches, on the fallen stone plinths of ruins,
in a cabin, the woods, by the Med. And when I left,
Haakan did not look up, from mending his nets.

MEILING JIN

Meiling Jin was born in Guyana in 1963 to a Chinese family. She has travelled widely, taking in various Chinese diasporic communities around the world. She is the author of a volume of poetry, *Gifts From My Grandmother*, a children's novel, *Thieving Summer*, and a book of short stories. She is also a playwright.

'Goodnight, Alice' is taken from *Song of the Boatwoman*, a collection of short stories set in a variety of locations – London, China, California, Malaysia and the Caribbean. They focus strongly on the lives of women and explore sexual identities.

from *Song of the Boatwoman*
Goodnight, Alice

She drove all the way along the coast from Oakland to Santa Cruz, and when she got there she stopped at the Boardwalk and bought herself a hot dog. It was early. There was plenty of time to relax and then go and register. She saw a couple of women with spiky hair, maybe gays, maybe going to the retreat. She ignored them in case they weren't.

She thought once more about the weekend and considered going home again – back to Kay. She'd never been to anything like this before. And never again, please god. Hell. All the bitching and politicking. What am I doin' here?

She turned and wandered into the arcade. If she left straight away, maybe she could catch Kay before she left. Maybe they could make a weekend of it in Sacramento, Labour weekend after all. She looked at her watch. Kay would already have left.

She found herself in front of a game machine and automatically began to feed it with money. Racing was her passion – anything from the cars to bikes to horses. 49, 48, 47, 46, 45 Blip! How could she miss? 43, 42, 41, 40 Blip! She grabbed the wheel grimly. She was losing her grip; 39, 38, 37, 36, 35. That's better.

She emerged from the Boardwalk an hour later. Glancing once at the sea, she strode to the car. She might as well get it over and done with. She drove slowly up to the University. Asian Pacific Lesbian retreat. Huh! How many Asians were there going to be? Maybe ten or eleven, all blind as bats and spouting rubbish.

The road curved up to the University and afforded her a view of the sea.

'My god this place is like a holiday camp! Don't tell me people actually study here with all those trees and this scenery.'

She saw the sign APL and turned left. Asian Pacific Lesbian. Huh! This had better be good.

Women. All shapes, sizes.

Don't let it get to your head, Al. Take it easy. Walk slowly to the registration desk, and take the stupid grin off your face. You're cool.

'Hi, are you registered yet?'

She looks down at a pair of horn-rimmed glasses.

'No, er, I wasn't sure I could make it.'

'Glad you made it. Did you hit a lot of traffic?'

'Sort of.'

'Haven't I seen you around before?'

'Rapture maybe, or did you ever try for a loan at the Western Fed? I work there.'

The woman laughs. 'No I didn't. Rapture I guess. What's your name?'

'Alice. Alice Lee.'

'Mine's Julie. You can fill in the form and pay over there. I'll just make you a badge while you're doin' that.'

'Thanks.'

She moves along to another face with spiky hair and sunglasses.

'Hi, you staying for the whole thing?'

Nope. I'm outa here as soon as you can say, kiss my— 'Maybe.'

'Okay, fine. Sort out the accommodation over there.' She turns to another desk and steps back in astonishment. Christ!

'Fraid you'll have to share. It's all twin-bedded rooms.'

Alice stares at the woman. 'Really? Can I share with you?'

The woman smiles. 'I already have a room-mate. But I'm on the same floor. Here's your keys.'

Alice grins and takes the keys. If they're all like you, honey, I'm staying.

The woman adds, 'You'd better go eat right now. Dinner finishes at 7.00.'

'Thanks! Thanks a lot.'

She follows a couple of women to the dining room. The noise hits her as soon as she opens the door. Holy Jane Ann! Look at all those dykes: Filipinos, Japanese, Indian as well. Not a white woman in sight. And all looking so intense. Ha! Maybe it was a good thing I came without Kay. Not that she coulda come.

'Hi, Alice!'

'Gracie!' She puts the tray down and gives Gracie a hug.

'Easy honey, I might like it! What brings you here anyway? Thought this was too intellectual for you?'

She shrugs. 'Maybe.'

'Watcha doin these days. Hiding out at Oakland?'

She grins. 'Maybe.'

'How's Kay?'

'She's gone to Sacramento for the weekend.'

'So you're free.'

'Maybe.'

'Look, is that all you can say? I expect at least a one line answer after ten months?'

'Come and eat with me.'

Gracie laughs.

Later that evening Alice walks to the car and collects her case. That wasn't too bad. Gawd, I didn't realize I hadn't seen Gracie in ten months. Must be the married life. She recalls the time when she used to nod at Gracie at Anna's night spot. Gracie had been the only other Asian gay around. Must have been all of – fifteen years ago!

She slams shut the trunk and makes her way towards the dormitories. As she rides the elevator to the fourth floor, she stares critically at her reflection in the mirror. Alice, you're getting crow's feet around your eyes and your jacket's looking a bit, well, old. One thing I hate is a dyke in old leather. Huh! Let me see room 412, 405, 403, 401. Oops, wrong way.

She hesitates in front of 412. Here I am at the screwball retreat. Might as well have fun while I'm here. I've never been with an Asian before. I wonder what they're like in bed?

As she puts the key in the door someone opens it from the inside.

'Ooops, excuse me.'

'S'okay. Hi, I'm Alice, your room-mate. You're—?'

The woman smiles and backs away. 'Jeanie.'

Alice walks forward. 'Good ta meet you, Jeanie. Lemme see now, do you snore?'

Jeanie smiles. 'I don't think so.'

'Good. I'm a light sleeper.'

Alice dumps her bag on the chair, pokes around the room and decides it will do.

'Single beds and a desk each. Christ, these students have fun. Oh and a lamp!'

Jeanie laughs. She fiddles around awkwardly in the wardrobe then goes back and flops on the bed.

'Whew, I'm beat and I haven't done anything yet.'

Alice's turn to smile. 'Wait till after the Social on Saturday night and see how you feel.' She opens her bag and starts unpacking.

'Where are you from, Jeanie?'

'New York.'

'That's a long way to come for a retreat.'

'I guess.'

'How did you know about it?'

'May Young told me about it last year. She's on the planning group. I came with her and her girlfriend, Kit. I've been looking forward to it all year, and now I'm here, I can't believe it. How about you?'

Alice looks up from her unpacking. She decides not to mention Kay to her new room-mate yet.

'Oh, someone told me, and I figured I'd check it out. I live in Oakland so it wasn't far.'

'You must know a lot of the women here.'

'No, I don't.'

'How come?'

'Don't get around much.'

'Funny, I thought if I lived here, I'd go to everything. I mean look at all the women.'

'Yeah, now that *is* a surprise.'

There's a knock on the door.

'Come in!'

Two women enter.

'You coming down to the plenary, Jeanie?'

'Yeah, sure. Alice, this is Kit and Gail.' Alice looks up to see the woman from the accommodation table. She goes into her routine: an admiring look, followed by a swift grin, then rapid conversation. 'Hi, you gave me a good room and a great room-mate. What more do I need?'

Gail laughs. 'You're easy to please, right?'

'That's me. Say, are you next door?'

'No, I'm along the corridor, number 405.'

'I'm on the right floor anyway,' says Alice, cheerfully.

Jeanie puts on her sweater and turns to Alice. 'You coming down now?'

'Sure.'

Alice leaves the room last so she can check herself in the mirror. Tall. Short hair, round chalky face, leather jacket. Looking good. Good looking.

She sits at the back of the lecture hall with Gail and Jeanie.

'I want to say this is a fine coming together. There's plenty of workshops. And space for more if you want to suggest one. Everything will take place in this part of the campus, apart from eating and sleeping.'

God this is boring.

'And also I wanna say how pleased I am to be here and to see so many Asian faces. I lived in a place where there was only me and well, me. I never dreamed I'd sit in a room with more than a hundred like me. Even if I don't go to anything else, I feel positive.'

Cut the crap.

Later that night, Alice lies in bed, staring at the ceiling. Suddenly, Jeanie's voice comes out of the dark. 'What did you think of the plenary, Alice?'

'Okay. A bit boring, but OK.'

'What did you expect?'

'I'm not sure. I've never been to anything like this before. I'm not political and I don't talk much.'

'Being a gay is political, isn't it?'

'No it's not. It's different, but it ain't political.'

'Why did you come then?'

'Dunno really. Someone, Kay actually, told me about it. I saw the stuff and decided to come.'

'Something must have attracted you.'

'Yeah, the women.'

'You're on the cruise for women?' says Jeanie, indignantly.

'Sure.'

'Wouldn't you be better off in the bars?'

'More choice here.'

'You might be wasting your time.'

Alice turns over and nestles down snugly. 'I don't think so. I bet most of the women here are on the make. Why else would they come? I know they spout this stuff about coming together and moving forward. But I bet, underneath, they're eyeing each other up to see who they can score with.'

'You're joking!'

'No. Okay, that's too crude. They're on the look out.'

'Are you on the look out?'

'Yes and no. I'm married see. To Kay. But there's no harm in looking.'

'Alice, you're weird.'

'No more than you, honey. Why did you come then?'

'I came to meet other women. Share experience. Talk about what it's like being gay in New York. A Chinese gay who doesn't fit in. I grew up in Delaware with no other Asians around. I want to talk about it. Talk about being part Filipino. Why I hate my father. Why I can't talk to my mom. How hard it is to find other Asians.'

'Kid, you need a shrink for all that, not a retreat.'

Jeanie laughs. 'Maybe.'

There's a long silence.

'Don't you have anything you wanna talk about, Alice?'

'Nope.'

'Are you happy with who you are?'

'Yep.'

'I envy you.'

'Know something, Jeanie?'

'What?'

'You think too much.'

'Goodnight, Alice.'

'G'nite, Jeanie.'

Alice sleeps in the next morning well up to 11 o'clock. She manages to make the second round of workshops and chooses the one on 'safer sex'. Her attention is caught, but she comes out not having contributed to any of the discussion. She meets Jeanie on the stairs.

'Hi, Alice. You woke up at last. What did you think of the work-shop?'

'Okay I guess. Kinda crowded, but interesting.'

'I thought it was fun, but I guess we always laugh about sex to cover the embarrassment.'

'Yeah, I didn't realize other people did that tongue thing too.'

They both start laughing.

'Say, do you want to come swimming this afternoon?'

'No. I want to go to the adoption workshop.'

Alice shakes her head. 'I say this for you, kid, you got stamina.'

'Not really. How many times in my life do I get to sit in a room full of Asian Pacific lesbians?'

Alice shrugs. 'Once a year if it keeps going, I guess.'

They head for the dining room.

Alice chooses not to disappear after lunch. Instead she goes to another workshop on relationships with white women. She feels personally challenged even though she knows no one in the workshop. She comes out angry and goes off to play tennis with Gracie. She lets off steam in the changing rooms.

'You know some of those women have a nerve. All of twenty-four and they think they know everything.'

'Yes, O aged one.'

'Come on, Gracie, we're fifteen to twenty years older than some of them. That counts for something.'

'Leave me out, honey, I'm only thirty-seven.'

'That makes you thirteen years older.'

'Yeah, well don't remind me. How come you're so mad anyway?'

'I was mad at that young kid for saying we should only go with Asians.'

Gracie picks up her racket and takes a quick look at herself in the mirror.

'Maybe we should. That at least would cut the crap, and we have enough of it as it is.'

'But what if you don't know any other Asians? What if you don't like any? What if you grew up in a place where you were the only one, and the only other one was so and so's sister and, God, she was ugly?'

Gracie laughs. 'Then you got yourself a problem.'

'All I can say, it was different in those days. You were glad enough to spot another gay of whatever colour. Besides, I never liked a woman because she was gay. I always liked first and found out later.'

'Maybe that's your trouble, Al.'

Alice shakes her head and walks out onto the court.

Later that evening, Alice finds Gail stitting on her own outside the Social and manages to talk to her without going into her routine. She discovers that Gail is with Susan but continues anyway.

'Don't you find it a little hard having a relationship with someone in Hawaii?'

'I guess so. I call once a week and so does she. It used to be every day, but like, it was costing a fortune. There's the time difference too. They're three hours behind so I'd have to wait until it was cheap time, but late enough for her to get home. Now we save everything for the weekend, but we talk a long time.'

'Why doesn't she come over here?'

'Hawaii is her country. She loves it there. She's in the middle of a degree, so she'd have to finish that first.'

'Why don't you go over there?'

'She never asked me.'

'Christ.'

'No, it's not true. She did; I guess I'm a little scared of it. Every time I've stayed there for more than a month I get this isolated feeling. She lives in Kilua, you know, it's north of the island. I guess I'm town bred.'

Alice finds herself thinking Susan must be mad. She keeps her thoughts to herself and stares at Gail's profile in the dark.

'She plans to come over when she's got her degree.'

'Who?' says Alice, absentmindedly.

'Susan. It's only another eight months.'

Meanwhile anything can happen, thinks Alice.

Suddenly, Susan comes walking across the courtyard.

'Gail?' The two women look up. 'I've been looking for you all over.'

'We've been sitting right here. I thought you said meet outside the Social.'

'No. We've been watching slides and having a Lua. I thought you were going to come along.'

Gail springs up and follows Susan. 'I'll see you later, Alice.'

Alice sits and stares into the night. Boy, these two have got trouble. She gets up slowly and walks towards the dining hall where the Social is being held.

The Social turns out to be an anti-climax as far as Alice is concerned, especially since no smoking and no alcohol is allowed. Alice finds it impossible to cruise without a beer in her hand. She ends up talking to Jeanie instead.

'You look kinda dreamy and spaced out, kid.'

'I guess it was the workshop this afternoon. It was really emotional.'

'Yeah, well this is the time to relax and forget it.'

Jeanie continues almost to herself, 'You know this place is like a mirror, you see reflections of yourself all over, and some parts you like and some parts you can't stand, and it's all a kinda shocking.'

'Yeah, and way too deep. This is the Social, remember?'

'Hmmm.'

Alice waves a hand in front of Jeanie's face. 'Anybody home?'

Jeanie laughs, 'When did you come out, Alice?'

'Look, we're not in the workshop now.'

'I know, I just wanted to know. You're so cool and cynical and—'

'If you really want to know, I'm not cool at all and I'm scared shitless of getting old. And if you really want to hear another coming-out story, I'll tell you later.'

'Okay, let's dance then,'

Alice stands up. 'Honey, I thought you'd never ask.'

Just as Alice is about to fall asleep that night, Jeanie's voice floats through the dark.

'So when did you come out, Alice?'

'Oh gawd, this woman,' groans Alice.

'You said later.'

'I didn't mean 4 o'clock in the morning.'

Jeanie turns over and pumps her pillow up. 'That's the best time for coming out stories.'

Alice groans again, wrestles with the blanket and gives up in disgust. 'I thought folks didn't use blankets anymore. Okay, lemme see. The first love of my life was Stacey.'

Jeanie nestles down to listen. 'Who was Stacey?'

'Stacey was in 7th grade. But even before that, I think I was always gay. I mean I always liked girls. I was a tomboy myself. I have three brothers and we were always swinging from trees and getting into trouble. I played with the boys but always liked girls. I liked them soft and pretty because that always made me feel strong. I used to thump them one; that was how I expressed myself. I guess I was awkward as a kid, you know, big and gawky. I didn't fit the Asian stereotype of petite and feminine.'

'So you were aware of a stereotype?'

'Hell, from my own mother. She used to despair over the size of my feet. I'm sure she would have bound them if she could.'

'When did you find out you were attracted to women?'

'Well, Dr Jeanie.'

Jeanie giggles.

'The first girl I fell for was Stacey. She was petite and blonde; quiet and sort of timid; although I got the feeling she was no way as timid as me on the inside. I followed her around like a dog and offered her things from my lunch box. She even liked noodles, so I got my mom to put that in all the time. One day she let me carry her books home and I was her servant for life. Her folks thought I was some weird Asian kid their daughter picked off the streets. Or maybe even the errand girl from the grocer shop. I never went inside their house though. I knew my place, see.'

'And what happened?'

'Nothing much. I mooned over her, got passionate, carved a heart on the only tree in our block – Alice and Stacey. Ha! When Stacey got another friend I was jealous. Supremely jealous. I used to take the other kid's coat off the hook and trample all over it. Then I'd hang it up again so there were foot prints up and down. Stacey herself blew hot and cold. Sometimes she'd let me walk home with her, other times, she didn't care for the attention. One day I got in a rage with her and thumped her one. She never told her folks, but she wouldn't talk to me again. Stubborn. But that's what I liked about her.'

'Poor Alice.'

'Poor Alice nothing. I made up for it since.'

Silence.

'Jeanie?'

'Hmmm.'

'Goodnight.'

Both Alice and Jeanie sleep in late the next morning. They get up and struggle to the open forum. By afternoon, they've both had enough and decide to go swimming with Gail and Gracie. It turns out that half the Retreat have the same idea because they meet more and more women on the beach, and it becomes a celebration.

Alice looks at the groups of women dotted around her and sighs.

'Say, you know I'm going to miss all this next week.'

'You don't mean to say you like being here with us, Alice,' says Jeanie.

'That's exactly what I do mean. Who else is going to wake me up at 4 o'clock in the morning, asking for my coming-out story?'

'What about Kay?' says Gracie.

Alice looks suspicious. 'What do you mean, what about Kay?'

'Don't you miss her?'

Alice looks uncomfortable.

Gracie laughs and adjusts her shades. 'It's okay, you don't have to miss her; you don't have to feel guilty either. How long have you been together now?'

'Three and half years.'

'Did she mind you coming away?'

'No. It was she that told me about it. We sort of do our own thing, Kay and me.'

'Modern, huh?'

Alice laughs. 'Maybe.'

They go back to the Campus and spend a quiet evening playing cards and talking. After a few hours everyone disappears and just Jeanie and Alice remain in the room. Jeanie stifles a yawn and deals another round to Alice.

'Do you speak Chinese, Alice?'

Alice barely looks up. Instead she lays down an ace and says, 'There you go again.'

'There I go again what?'

'There you go, asking me all these questions.'

'I'm only asking cos' I don't know you well, and—'

'Yes? And?'

'And you seem to know lots of things.'

Alice throws down her hand of cards and rolls over on her back. 'Come on, do I look like your mother?'

Jeanie starts to laugh. 'Not really.'

Alice continues. 'Let me ask you a few questions for a change.'

Jeanie sits up. 'Okay go ahead.'

Alice collects the cards together slowly, giving herself time to think. 'Okay, er, what you doin' Tuesday night?'

Jeanie laughs.

Alice grins shame-faced. 'Okay no I mean, how old are you Jeanie?'

'What if I said, I'm doing nothing, Alice, just waiting for you. That'd blow you away, wouldn't it?'

'Ah, Jeanie, you know me too well. But I was serious anyway.'

'What – about my age?'

'No about Tuesday night.'

'I'm twenty-three, and Tuesday night I'll be staying at Gail's and flying out Wednesday morning.'

Alice gets up, stretches and gets into bed with her clothes on. 'Good, then you can come and have dinner with me.'

'What about—'

'Kay?'

'No, what about Chinese,' says Jeanie. 'Do you speak Chinese?'

'Yes I do. We'll go for a Chinese meal, and I'll tell Kay.'

'Yummm, yeah Chinese; it'll be like an antidote for the poison they've been feeding us here.'

'Why did you want to know whether I speak Chinese?'

'Cos I don't, and I envy you. I feel less Chinesey, know what I mean?'

Alice begins to laugh, 'Hell, that's the funniest thing I heard all weekend. How can not-speaking Chinese make you less Chinese?'

'That's because you speak it. I don't. And it makes me feel, well, you know, like I'm not Chinese or something. When I first met May Young (you know May Young?), she used to take me to meet her folks, and her mom would try to speak to me in Cantonese. I used to get dead embarrassed. I told her I was half Filipino anyway, because I think my dad was. She thought I spoke Tagalog so I lied and said I did. I tried to learn once, but every time I open my mouth to practise every one falls about in hysterics.'

'Yeah, but some people are weird. And you don't need to take any notice of them. Anyway, look how good your English is. I bet you got straight A's.'

Jeanie pulls the cover over her head in disgust. 'That's what white people say to me, Alice.'

'Gee I'm sorry, Jeanie, I only meant I'd be proud if I spoke like you and to hell with all the others. Anyway how can you be less Chinese? There's no such thing along a scale of ten.'

'But, Alice, you do speak like me, and you also speak Chinese. And I'm just telling you how I feel; and that's stupid; especially when I go into a Chinese restaurant and I can't order, and the waiter looks at me like I'm nothing.'

'Didn't your ma speak Chinese?'
'No my mom's white. I was adopted.'
'Oh.'
Silence.
'Jeanie, I'm sorry. For being such a dope.'

The next morning, Alice goes to the last plenary and then packs her car ready to leave. She hates saying goodbye so she tries to slip away. Gracie spots her and runs over. 'Alice! you're not going without saying goodbye, are you?

'Er, no, I was just packing the car, Gracie.'
'Am I gone get to see that silly grin of yours, sometime?'
'Sure.'
'Why don't you come over and I'll cook you dinner?'
'Sure.'
'How about Friday?'
'Great.'
They hug.
Alice tries to slip away a second time.
'Alice!'
'Gail?'
'I'm having a party on Thursday. Nothing special, maybe some Japanese food. Will you come?'
'Sure.'
'Give me your number and I'll ring you.'
Gawd, these women are fast! Alice takes out her card and scribbles her home number on the back.
'I'll see you Thursday.'
'Sure.'

Slowly, she drove back along the coast to Oakland, her mind caught in images of the Retreat, talking to Gail, dancing with Jeanie, arguing with Gracie in the workshop. She retraced all the conversations in her mind and wondered how she was ever going to be the same again.

Alice, you're being overdramatic. A weekend with a hundred and fifty Asians and you've gone off the rails. So . . . anyone would go off the rails with that many women. Asian Pacific, hmmm.

As she drove along, she glanced at the sea. It was the first time she was really aware of it. She pulled the car over and got out to admire the view. The wind was strong on the cliffs, but instead of making her feel cold, it filled her with energy. She gazed at the sea: sunlight glinting on green crystal. She thought about Jeanie. Jeanie was right about the reflections. She had caught a glimpse of herself reflected in a hundred and fifty women. And she was shocked. Take it easy Alice. You're forty-eight. She laughed. All the more reason for going off the rails.

She thought of Kay. What was she going to tell Kay? Nothing, she supposed. Suddenly, she felt like a bird in a cage with the door open. Was she going to fly out? She opened her arms as if she was about to soar from the cliffs into the sea. 'Alice, my girl, this is just the beginning,' she said, flapping her arms.

VICTOR HEADLEY

Victor Headley was born in Jamaica but grew up in London. His first novel, *Yardie*, became an instant bestseller, exposing in graphic details the world of drugs and violence that underscore the marginal existence of a small minority of the black community. *Yardie* was the first in a trilogy, which concluded with *Excess* and *Yush*. *Yardie* opened the market for a popular genre of novels about the black experience – a market which has been brilliantly captured by the publishing company X Press.

Yardie describes a frightening journey through the world of the 'frontlines' and the various drugs barons or dons who control them. D arrives at Heathrow Airport from Jamaica, strolling through customs with a kilo of top-grade cocaine strapped to his body. He is a courier for one of the big Posse dons in Jamaica. But he has other plans, such as setting himself up as a freelance, and the Frontline's newest don. But his treachery is not easily forgotten – or forgiven. In the extract below, D has begun to establish his territory, but is aware that there is a price on his head.

from *Yardie*

The atmosphere was hot and smoky in the basement room. The set always played a revival selection in the early morning hours, to allow the dancers to cool off after the heavy dancehall music. Couples were lined up against the walls, tightly swaying to the rhythm of the Studio One bass line. Standing beside a speaker-box, D was busy drawing on a spliff of prime sensimillia. He and Leroy had arrived at the shebeen about two hours earlier. After spending some time near the bar, drinking beer with two of Leroy's associates, D had chosen to settle in this corner opposite the door, from where he could see the entrance, through the corridor. The place was full almost every night, peaking at about five in the morning when all the ravers, hustlers, and players, all the regulars of the North London night scene had arrived.

High Noon, the top sound for the last three years, attracted so many people that it was often a problem to fit everyone in. Tonight, the two rooms and the corridor were full, with people rocking lazily in the confined space, amidst the sweat, perfume, and smoke. The over-crowding was too much to bear sometimes and, in the general state of intoxication from liquor and other substances, arguments and fights were not uncommon. Yet, no matter how crowded the place, no matter how long the queue outside, High Noon was a must for anyone involved in the night life. Only the mighty Jah Shaka could rival it.

D first came to know the sound through Leroy who had taken him there about a week after his arrival. He had gotten acquainted with a few of the DJs and usually spent some time at the shebeen most nights. It was a similar scene to the one he had left in Jamaica, except that there the dances were held outdoors. Recently settled Yardies were numerous in this part of London and kept the Jamaican-style sounds such as High Noon in business. Besides the Yardies who had obtained legal resident status many had come into the country on a visitor's visa and simply 'extended' their stay, unofficially and indef-initely. For anyone coming from a poor background in Kingston's tenements, England, no matter how tight things were getting, was still a more comfortable environment to live in.

The high proportion of newly arrived Jamaican youths in the area had adversely affected the local hustlers; the competition was now tougher. Furthermore, the newcomers didn't operate by the same principles as their UK counterparts. They were totally ruthless; they didn't respect the established hierarchy, and were not prepared to allow anything like friendship or allegiances to stand in their way. They were hungry, and wanted money. Lots of it, and now. As a result, in the last five years, the atmosphere in the area had become more tense, even more volatile, than before. The use of violence in settling 'trade' disputes had now become common practice.

D took a deep draw from the spliff and glanced at the girl to his right. For the best part of an hour, she had been trying to attract his attention. She had asked him for a light twice. He didn't mind the attention but had played it cool so far. The girl was looking fine, about medium height and wearing a light-coloured dress. She had the sort of haircut that was in vogue for young Black women – short at the back. In the six weeks that he had been in England, D had avoided getting involved with any of the local girls, spending his time between Donna's flat, the shebeen, and Leroy's record shop. He had made a few contacts which he cultivated cautiously; he didn't intend to sell the bulk of his merchandise until he had found a source of supply, one unconnected to his former outfit.

The Spicers had managed in the last two years to gain control of nearly all the channels feeding the Black community in London. They had also succeeded in setting up bases in several of the main country towns. In Manchester, Birmingham and Bristol violent skirmishes had occurred between local 'soldiers' and the few independent dealers who still refused to pay dues to the organization.

D had found himself an associate. Charlie had been in England less than two years but was already nicely set up. Leroy had introduced him to D, having explained that he wasn't connected in the drugs business, but that Charlie would help him. As it turned out, Leroy was right; Charlie was the right man to meet for someone newly arrived and independent. The tall brown-skinned man knew everything about the trade and everyone involved in it in town. At first, D had treated him in a friendly but cautious manner. He was naturally suspicious, particularly because Charlie had previously lived in New York. He observed his new friend carefully for several weeks until, finally, he accepted that Charlie had started out in a very similar position to his own.

Having grown up from an early age in the Bedford-Stuyvesant area of New York, Charlie had found himself a virtual outsider on the London scene. After a while, he succeeded in setting up a chain of supplies that allowed him to make a name for himself; everyone knew now that Charlie's stuff was top quality. Nobody had forgotten either the way he had dealt with two young Yardies who had attempted to rob him one night outside the shebeen. After sticking a gun in his stomach and taking three ounces of cocaine from him, they had been foolish enough to hang around in the dance, getting high and boasting. They never really saw what happened . . . Charlie had walked in, found them amongst the dancers, and shot each one in turn, in the legs. He then coolly searched them, retrieved most of his property, and left the pair bleeding and groaning on the floor. Since that day, no one else had tried anything against him.

Charlie had politely but firmly rejected several offers from the Spicers to go into partnership. He had managed to keep them out of his business in New York and intended to do the same here.

D and Charlie struck a closer friendship when they discovered that they had lived only a few streets from one another in Greenwich Farm, back in Jamaica. They were also about the same age.

Charlie was the kind of example D planned to follow; he had a nice house, wore stylish clothes and drove a new-model black BMW. All this from starting out two years before with only one pound of Colombian cocaine out of New York!

D finished the spliff and took a sip from his Budweiser. He knew that Charlie would show up sooner or later, but punctuality, a rare commodity amongst Jamaicans, was not one of his qualities.

Studio One selection after Studio One selection. The selector had the dancers where he wanted them, begging for more. Nobody who understood the history and roots of reggae could resist any record on the legendary Studio One label. From its Brentford Road head-quarters in Kingston, Studio One and its founder, Clement Dodd, had encapsulated every form of reggae expression. His were the original bass lines, the original drum patterns still borrowed from heavily by contemporary reggae producers and US rappers. Somehow, no other rhythms in reggae seemed to swing as perfectly as a Studio One rhythm.

In response to the shouts of 'forward' and 'lift it up', the operator started the tune again from the top. The punch of the bass line got the couples straight back in the groove.

D looked to his right; the girl in the white dress was rocking slowly, arms outstretched and head bowed, enjoying every beat of the music. He reached out and touched her left arm. The girl raised her head, her eyes searching his before she stepped towards him. He held her waist lightly in his right arm and they started rocking, tuning to each other's slow gyrations. He could feel the girl's face tight against his and her hands holding him lightly. She was a good dancer, fol-lowing him around the beat, answering every slight move of his hips with a slight sway of her own. The song finished.

'Dat tune yah short,' he whispered in the girl's ear before letting go of her.

She smiled at him, staying close. Her eyes were slightly slanted, her skin a shiny dark brown hue. D smiled back. As the beat of the next song surged from the speakers, she came against him of her own accord and put her arms around his shoulders. They began to sway together, slower and tighter this time. They rocked through two more tunes, exchanging few words, absorbed in the rhythm patterns of their welded bodies. Then the selector decided to change the mood. The heavy thump of a ragamuffin bass line shook the crowd, couples let go of each other and before long the whole venue was stepping and jumping wildly.

D and his partner started to dance side by side. She had told him her name was Jenny. The music was stirring the dancers into a frenzy, the beat bouncing from wall to wall. As the tune ended and another hot rhythm began to pound, he leaned towards her.

'Go and buy some drinks for you and your friend, and get me a Budweiser,' he said in her ear, handing her a £10 note.

Jenny took the money and headed for the bar. D peeled off some sheets of Rizla paper and was about to build a spliff when he saw them. Against the opposite wall, near the door, he recognized the face of the tall, dark youth who had been watching him for several nights. Wearing a white Kangol flat-cap and half hidden by rows of dancers, he was staring at D intensely. His partner, a shorter man with a near-shaven head and sporting several large gold chains, was leaning against the door, sipping from a bottle.

D proceeded to build his spliff, slowly sticking the paper together, apparently oblivious to the two pairs of eyes fixed on him. They had a certain attitude about them, which suggested who they were even before D enquired about them. Charlie had told him that the taller one with the dead face was Blue, a soldier for the Spicers who had settled in England five years ago. Alfie, his companion, was the brother of a Miami *ranks*, something of a singer, and a show-off.

Charlie had dismissed Alfie as an 'idiot', but told D to watch out for Blue; he was an experienced knifeman, a bad *bwoy* from his early days in the Waterhouse area of Kingston. He was known for his lack of humour and his inclination towards violence.

D lit up the spliff, his mind alert, while he blew out a cloud of smoke with apparent nonchalance. He knew the two soldiers wouldn't make a move until they had orders to do so. He also knew that as much as Joseph wanted him dead, he also needed to take the rest of the merchandise from him. He just had to stay on his guard until they made their move.

Anyone associated with D was bound to become a target eventually, but Charlie didn't mind that. He had listened to D's story and, concluding that it was a smart move, had elected to stick by his new friend through trouble. Besides, Charlie had no love for the Spicers, suspecting them of having been behind the robbery attempt on him the year before.

Jenny came back with the drinks. D opened the can, took a sip of the beer, and placed it on the speaker box next to him. He was keeping an eye on the two men across the room, while talking in Jenny's ear. They were getting on fine; D found that she was easy to talk to

and seemed to like him. She wasn't stuck up in the way he had been
told many English-born girls were.

He was telling Jenny how pretty he thought she was when, from
the corner of his eye, he saw Blue making his way through the crowd
towards him. His smile vanished and his face became expressionless,
as he felt the surge of energy through his body. Without a word, he
pulled Jenny gently but firmly backwards, placing her behind him.
The girl noticed the change in him and didn't ask any questions.
Slowly, D took the ratchet knife from his back pocket and dropped
his hands loosely by his side. He saw Leroy talking to a friend near
the bar ten yards away. D took his breath and blew the air through his
mouth, slowly. He was ready.

Blue was coming right at him. A sharp flick of the wrist; the blade
of D's knife was out. Two yards in front of him, Blue stopped. Two
pairs of steely eyes locked into each other, a silent duel . . .

'My boss wan' fe talk,' Blue said after a few tense seconds,
making himself heard over the din of the music.

Suddenly there was space around the two men. Even for those who
didn't know anything about them, it was plain to see that some kind
of confrontation was at hand.

'I don't need fe talk to nobody,' D retorted sharply. He didn't want
this conversation to last too long.

Blue looked down, and then straight back into D's eyes. Stone-
faced he delivered his message.

'Star, hear wha' now . . . I supposed to arrange a meeting. Any
time, any place.'

D's brain was working fast. He knew that, one way or another,
they would try to set him up. This was the first play and he had to be
sharp.

'Tell your boss I'm not interested. The way I see it, dem owe me.
Mek we call it quit, seen?!'

Blue's face broke into a vicious grin. He nodded slowly, then the
frozen look reappeared.

'I will give dem your answer.' The voice was like the face – cold.
He turned and walked back into the crowd. D watched him make his
way out the door followed by his accomplice. Slowly, he closed the
blade of the knife and slipped it back in his pocket. With the 'meeting' now over, the dancers had reclaimed the dance space around
him. No one in their right mind hung around in this type of situation;
innocent casualties all too often resulted from dancehall fights. The

music hadn't stopped pumping. Only the subtle change of atmosphere had warned those in the close vicinity of the challenge of the impending danger.

Jenny was back by D's side. She observed him, unsure whether she should ask him about the incident. Yet he seemed relaxed, sipping his drink slowly. He turned to her with the mischievous grin which was one of his trademarks.

'I t'ink seh you gone,' he said in her ear.

'What was that about?' she ventured, half expecting a scolding reply.

But he didn't mind her question.

'Jus' business, man. Everyt'ing cool.'

She looked into his face, serious, but decided against questioning him further and simply shook her head to let him know that she didn't believe that everything was 'cool'.

ANDREA LEVY

Andrea Levy was born in London to Jamaican parents. Her father came to England on the *Empire Windrush* in 1948. Her well-received first novel, *Every Light in the House Burnin'*, published in 1994, is set in the early 1960s and provides a rich portrait of two Jamaicans and their families.

Never Far From Nowhere, set in the 1970s, tells the story of two sisters, Olive and Vivien, born to Jamaican parents and brought up on a council estate in north London. They go to the same grammar school, but while Vivien's life becomes a chaotic mix of friendships, youth clubs, skinhead violence, A Levels, discos and college life, Olive, three years older and a skin shade darker, has a very different tale to tell. In the following extract, Vivien has gone away to art school. Her boyfriend, Eddie, comes to stay.

from *Never Far From Nowhere*
Vivien

Eddie used to come and visit me at weekends. Every weekend he'd turn up on the doorstep in his white afghan coat with his acoustic guitar over his shoulder and a grin on his face. I was pleased to see him after a week of college. A week of conversations about art; discussing the merits of the Impressionists, the Fauvists, the Cubists. Of listening to classical music during life drawing, and theories of why Sibelius symphonies always sound familiar. 'He repeats his initial refrain, de da, de da, de da, de da. Can you hear it Vivien?' Or talk of missing mothers or brothers or washing machines or gardens to sit in.

There was no one in my group who was from a dilapidated council estate, who liked to eat Mother's Pride white sliced loaves and was more than used to washing all their clothes by hand. Who liked Radio One and knew what was top of the pops and said 'ain't' and 'blimey' when they forgot. There was no one who looked around themselves every morning and wondered how they got there. How they managed to be living in a flat that was nicer than one their parents could provide, with a woman who could rustle up something called a lasagne and got upset when she remembered that her father wouldn't let her have a pony when she was young.

Eddie would come down with tales from back home. Telling me about all the beer he had drunk: 'You could have lit my burps with a match,' or about the places we used to go: 'King's Arms is still the same. I'm jamming there next week. Doing someone a favour really, 'cause their guitarist got sent down for drunk and disorderly.' Or stories about Olive learning to drive in his van. 'We had to tie the exhaust on with a pair of your sister's tights – I hope you're not jealous.' Or: 'She's having trouble with the social, but you know Olive, she gives as good as she gets.'

'So what's been happening at college?' he'd ask, and I'd just shrug.

Eddie had never met Victoria because she went back to Northumberland every weekend for a party or a 'gathering of the clan' or just to get away from 'this bloody dump'. She'd pack her bag on Friday morning and sneak out of college at four. Then turn up on Monday looking flushed pink, well-fed and usually driving a different car.

Then one weekend she stayed. 'Everyone's away – I'm going to sample the delights of Herne Bay.' She invited three people from college round for Saturday lunch. So have you got it now, Vivien, lunch is in the afternoon and dinner is at night. We didn't spend a lot of time together, Victoria and me. She'd stay out until late at night during the week, at a pub or club which I was never invited to. I'd stay at home in front of one bar of an electric fire watching *Sale of the Century* on television.

'So you're the mysterious Eddie,' Victoria said.

'That's me,' Eddie replied, 'dark and mysterious.' He flashed a smile at Victoria who looked at me and said, 'I should stay here more often – see what you two get up to when I'm away.'

Eddie began to get more and more cockney as the evening wore on. Victoria looked enthralled and laughed at his jokes. By ten o'clock he was talking about having a pig's ear in his whistle and flute down the rub-a-dub-dub when he was boracic lint, but still managed to come out Brahms and Liszt.

'I know "up the apples and pears",' Victoria said.

'Yeah, but you don't say it right – you're too posh. But stick with me – I'll make a cockney of you yet,' Eddie promised.

'He's so earthy,' Victoria said to me when Eddie went out of the room to warm up some 'loop-de-loop'.

But then on Saturday morning Victoria wouldn't get out of bed. She was in one of her moods. She often got into moods. The first time it happened she was at college, scratching through wax on an etching plate, talking loudly about her brother's misdemeanour at Oxford involving a punt and a pole, when a phone call came for her. When she came back her face was stone grey. She picked up her bag and walked out of college. She wouldn't get out of bed for two days and she wouldn't speak to me at all. She just lay in bed smoking joint after joint until her room smelt like every Bonfire night I'd ever had. I thought I was going to have to phone her mum and dad, the Right Honourable Something or the Sir and Lady This and That, I couldn't remember. But then she emerged on the third day looking pert and pretty as if nothing had happened. 'I'm starving,' she said, and we never spoke about it again. I learnt to leave her alone.

'I'll get her up, I'll use my Eddie charm,' Eddie said. He walked into her bedroom before I could grab him back. 'What's up, Vic,' I heard him say. There was a bang and a shout of 'Victoria, you cretin,' and a red-faced Eddie rushed out again.

'What's up with her?' he said.

'Just leave her.'

'She's right down in the dumps. I know, I'll tell her a joke.'

He went to walk in the room again. 'Leave her, Eddie.'

'It never fails. I will not admit defeat – I'll put a smile on her face if it's the last thing I do.' He began straightening his shirt.

'Leave her alone,' I shouted.

I walked into the kitchen. 'I'll have to make the lunch,' I said. It was the last thing I wanted to do. I hadn't invited any one round. I never did. I occasionally went round to other students' houses and ate spaghetti bolognese. And after we'd play a game of Botticelli, where someone would hold forth, thinking they were Napoleon, and everyone else would try to guess who they were with questions like 'Are you a nineteenth-century philosopher beginning with N?', to which the answer would be 'Ummm . . . no, I'm not Nietzsche.' I'd try to avoid most of the game by staying in the toilet, only coming out in time for my Earl Grey tea. 'Really, milk and sugar in Earl Grey, Vivien, are you sure?'

'Don't worry,' Eddie said putting his arm round me, 'I'll do one of me fry-ups.' Eddie's fry-ups consisted of egg, bacon, sausage, mushrooms and tomato, all fried to a charred mass until the different items were indistinguishable from one another. He served it on to plates before slapping bread into the cinders in the frying-pan and making it squelch up the remaining fat. Eddie would eat a mouthful then wipe the grease from his face with a tea towel.

'No you can't,' I snapped.

'Why not?'

'They won't like it.'

'Everyone loves a fry-up.'

I started to cry.

'Come on,' Eddie said. 'Well, what was her ladyship making?'

'I don't know – quiche or something.'

'What?' he asked.

'Exactly.'

By the time the doorbell rang we'd settled on rounds of egg-and-salad sandwiches: 'No, the brown bread, Eddie.'

Only Chrissy and Jim turned up. The Scottish Margaret couldn't come because her parents had come down to surprise her and had caught her in bed with Ken the Japanese boy. Chrissy knew Victoria before college. 'Is she in one of her moods?' she said, when she noticed her absence. I nodded. 'Bitch,' she added.

Chrissy was born in Barbados, although she was porcelain-white with long brown hair that she kept plaited down her back. I liked her. She said she was a rebel, and on the first day we met she asked me if my parents came from Jamaica. I said yes, and she smiled and said, 'I love the Caribbean.' We spent an evening drinking in the college bar, her elbow propped on the counter, guzzling pints of beer with whisky chasers, her telling me about her expulsions from boarding schools. 'So I told the mayor on prize day to stop looking at my tits – dirty old bastard.' She said art college was her last chance. Her father had threatened to 'cut her off' if she didn't stop hanging about with 'undesirable left-wing weirdos'. Her ambition, she declared, was to become an alcoholic.

Eddie grabbed the six-pack of beer she brought and they opened a can each. 'Are you at college, Eddie?' she asked.

'University of life,' he replied.

'Much more interesting and no exams.' They laughed.

Jim looked concerned. 'Is Victoria all right?' he asked me. Jim adored Victoria. It was sad to watch. He badly wanted to go out with her. But he was too ugly for her. 'Ginger eyelashes,' Victoria would say with a shudder. He followed her around college and she would ask him to fetch and carry things for her which he would perform like an eager golden retriever. He obviously thought this invitation to lunch was his chance to woo. He stank so much of Aqua de Silva aftershave that I could tell what it tasted like.

'Jim – beer?' Eddie said, holding up one of Chrissy's cans.

I drank my can fast and enjoyed the warm, shaking feeling that came up through my legs and made things seem not quite so strange.

We listened to Jim talk about Victoria. About what a wonderful artist she was. How good a driver. How down-to-earth, despite her background. 'She'll talk to anyone,' Jim told us with admiration. We all listened and Chrissy rolled her eyes as Eddie handed round the sandwiches and I looked at my watch. 'So what do you do, Eddie?' Chrissy asked. My heart began to beat so loudly I covered my chest with my arms to muffle it.

'I'm a musician,' Eddie signalled to his guitar in the corner.

'Oh, give us a song then,' she said.

Eddie tipped his head and swaggered to his guitar like he was Bob Dylan asked to play 'Blowin' in the Wind' for an encore. I tried to stop him with a look, but he didn't notice. We sat and listened to Eddie tuning up, but then realized after about fifteen minutes that that was it.

'Do you know any Crosby, Stills and Nash?' Jim asked.

'I don't like that stuff,' Eddie said. He also didn't like the other requests for Donovan, James Taylor, Steven Stills, the Beatles and, in desperation, 'Where have all the flowers gone?' Eddie strummed a loud chord: 'I'm a rock musician,' he said. I went to the kitchen to get some more beer, stopping outside the door to Victoria's room to give her the V-sign, the finger and the 'up yours' fist.

When I came back Eddie's guitar was on the floor. I breathed out.

'Here, Vivien,' Eddie said, 'your friends here don't know you're a cockney like me. They thought you was posh.'

I laughed: what else could I do? I'd let people believe I was from Islington – one of the big houses near Gibson Square. My father was an engineer, I'd say, my mother's in catering. I went to a grammar school. I let them make up the rest. 'No, she's a good ole salt of the earth like me – council estate. She likes a knees up, don't you, Viv?' He sounded like his dad. I laughed again as Jim and Chrissy stared at me with indulgent grins. There was total silence.

'Do you go back to London much, Vivien?' Chrissy asked.

'Not a lot,' I said.

'Well if you're back next week there's a march you might want to go on.'

'What sort of march?'

'Protest march for abortion – the woman's right to choose.'

Jim groaned.

'Shut up, you,' Chrissy said to him. 'It's an important issue for women.'

'I don't believe in it,' Jim said.

'What do you mean?' Chrissy said, raising her voice. Eddie picked up his guitar again.

'I believe that life is sacred.'

'Oh for God's sake, what about women, what about their lives? All those women whose lives are ruined because they've had a baby too young. What about them?'

'They should be more careful.'

'What about the men? It takes two to tango.'

'Well, it's the women that get pregnant. And that's just a fact. If there was a contraceptive pill for men I'd take it.' Chrissy looked at me and raised her right eyebrow. Eddie strummed louder and Chrissy had to shout. 'Oh, sure, I'd trust you. Don't you think women should have the right to choose if they want to have a baby or not?'

'I don't believe in abortion, that's all.'

'But,' I started tentatively, 'what sort of a life would an unwanted child have?'

Chrissy touched my arm in agreement. 'Exactly,' she said. 'Every child a wanted child, every mother a willing mother. That's why there's a march.' Jim made a face.

'What do you think, Eddie?' Chrissy asked. Eddie stopped strumming his guitar.

'About what?'

'Abortion on demand.' He looked in the air and thought; then said, 'I don't agree with it.' I covered my heart with my arms again.

Jim patted Eddie. 'Good man,' he said.

'Oh God,' Chrissy moaned.

'No,' Eddie said, appealing for calm with his hands, 'hear me out.' My palms were making my jumper wet. 'I don't believe it should be on demand.'

'Well, do you agree with a woman's right to choose?'

'Yeah but listen,' Eddie carried on. 'I don't believe it should be on demand. I think you should have to say please.' There was another silence. Eddie expanded: 'I think a woman should go in and say nicely, "Could I have an abortion, please," not just run in and demand it.'

Chrissy began to laugh. 'You are joking, aren't you?'

But Eddie had a thoughtful face. 'No, I think it's very serious – I believe in good manners,' he said. Chrissy looked at me with her mouth open. So did Jim. And I would have died there and then on the lounge carpet if Victoria hadn't flung open the door and said 'Hi, everyone.'

Jim clapped at her entrance. She was in full make-up with her hair freshly Carmen-heated-hair-roller-curled. She sat on the settee.

'So, what have you been saying about me?' she said.

I stood up. 'I'm making some tea, does anyone want some?'

'Ooh lovely,' Victoria said, 'Earl Grey?' I grabbed Eddie's arm. 'Come and help me,' I said.

'Women,' Eddie said, rolling his eyes. 'Can't do anything.' I dragged him out of the room before there was another incident.

I closed the kitchen door behind me.

'Eddie, don't you understand?' I whispered. 'It's not that the woman is running in and demanding it.'

Eddie looked at me with a frown. 'What are you talking about?'

'Abortion.'

'Oh that – well it's not ladylike to go round demanding things, it's bad manners.'

'It's not about manners,' I tried to explain. 'Don't you get it?'

He shrugged it off, then smiled and came across the room and put his arms round me. I struggled out of his hug.

'What's the matter with you?'

'Nothing,' I said, filling the kettle with water.

'Well, come on then, give us a kiss.' He grabbed me again and squeezed me. 'Your friends are a bit . . . '

'A bit what?' I said, pushing him away again.

'I don't know – just not much fun – serious.'

'They were trying to have a conversation.'

'Yeah, but . . . '

'But what?' I snapped.

'What's the matter with you?' Eddie looked at me with a serious face.

'They were just trying to talk and you're playing your guitar and making stupid comments about women having manners and telling them things and talking in that stupid cockney accent—'

'Excuse me,' Eddie interrupted, 'that's the way I talk.'

'Going on about the rub-a-dub bleedin' dub and trying to impress everyone—'

'And you used to be cockney once. What makes you so good now?'

'It's so embarrassing. You don't get even simple things.'

'You've got so high and bloody mighty, Vivien, since you've been here.'

'Don't you want to learn anything, don't you want to get on in life – do something?'

'Don't forget where you come from – you're just a working-class girl. What you getting so worked up about? You're not one of them.' Eddie jabbed his thumb over his shoulder.

'They're my friends now. I live in this nice flat and go to college and everything. I'm getting on with my life.'

'So,' he spat.

'So . . . ' I was lost for words. 'So you're showing me up! I just wish you could be—'

'I'm me, Vivien. I can't be anyone else. I can't be all clever or arty. I'm me. So is that good enough for you or not?'

I looked in his brown eyes. The choice had become my old life or the new. I looked at him and said 'No, it's not good enough.'

Victoria opened the kitchen door with an 'Oops.' She looked from Eddie to me. 'Sorry, but there's a phone call for you, Vivien.'

'For me!'

The phone was in Victoria's bedroom. She had insisted on having one installed in the first few days we lived there, saying she'd die if she was incommunicado. I gave the number to my mum for emergencies.

'Yeah, and . . . could you make it quick – I need to make a call.' She smiled at me with only her mouth.

'Vivien, it's Olive.' Her voice sounded shaky, close to tears.

'What is it? Is it Mum – oh, not Amy?'

'I was arrested last night,' she said. For some reason I was relieved.

'Oh,' I said.

'What do you mean, Oh"? Didn't you hear me, I was arrested. The bastards! I can't believe it . . . I hadn't done anything . . . but the bastard said I had . . . called me a black slag.'

She was crying and rambling and I kept saying 'Calm down, Olive, I can't understand what you're saying.' But she went on, oblivious.

'They planted it . . . I don't take drugs, you know that . . . I don't do that . . . I smoked some tea leaves once but that's not illegal . . . but they thought that just because I was black I should have drugs . . . and when I didn't they just put some there . . . and no one believes me – no one . . . and they treated me like a criminal but I never did nothing – nothing . . . and I had to phone Mum, and she don't believe I didn't have them . . . she says she does but she doesn't . . . she keeps looking at me . . . and she said there's no smoke without fire . . . they took my fingerprints and everything . . . and I told them, I told them I hadn't done anything . . . that they were planted on me, but no one believes me . . . it's my word against theirs, and who's going to believe a black girl on benefits . . . nobody, nobody!' She stopped for a while. I could hear her sucking hard on a cigarette.

'So, are you in prison?' I asked.

'No, I'm not in prison,' she snapped. 'But I'm going to have to go to court.' She sniffed long and loud.

'But what happened?'

'I just told you,' she shouted, 'they stopped me in Eddie's van and made me empty my bag, which I did. Then they made me do it again and I thought it was odd and then there it was.'

'What?'

'The dope – a little round bit of dope all wrapped up.' She started to cry.

'Don't cry, Olive,' I said, patting my leg *there, there*, 'I'm sure it will be all right. I mean, if you're innocent then you'll be all right.'

Olive laughed a deliberate Ha! Ha! 'God, Vivien, you're so stupid.'

'I'm not – if you're innocent then just tell them.'

'They don't believe me.'

'Well, tell them again – tell them exactly what happened.'

'Grow up!' she shouted.

'Well, what can I do about it?' I quickly retorted.

'It's just,' Olive hesitated, 'it's just that I feel . . . I feel . . . scared here.'

There was silence.

'What do you mean?' I asked.

She took a trembling breath. 'Well, I can't go to Mum's, not the way she goes on, I'd go mad, and I don't like being in the flat on my own. I know it sounds stupid. I mean, it's not that I'm not a strong black woman. I am. I am!'

'So what do you want me to do?'

'I wondered if I could come down there, just for a few days, with Amy. A week maybe, no longer, I just want to get away, out of London – somewhere quiet and . . . safe.'

I looked out of the window at the sun setting over the sea. It was leaving a beautiful, impossible sky-blue pink horizon. But as I thought of Olive in my flat, in my life here, a grey cloud drifted across the scene.

'No, you can't,' I said. 'There's no room.'

'I thought you said it was a big flat.'

'Well, it's not that big and besides, I share it with someone and they don't like people coming to stay.'

'It wouldn't be for long.'

'No, I'm sorry, Olive.'

'Please.'

'No – I'll come back soon . . . '

She didn't let me finish before she started.

'That's so bloody typical of you. You little cow, you're so selfish, all you think about is yourself. What's the matter, do you think I'll be embarrassing? You make me sick, Vivien. You make me really sick. I knew you'd say that, I don't know why I asked. Now you've got all your college friends, now you've got your own flat, now you're all right. I knew you'd say that. Selfish, snotty cow.'

Suddenly I was shouting. 'Just leave me alone – just leave me alone Olive! I don't want you here – don't you understand – just leave me alone!' I began to sob from way down in my stomach and gasp for air like someone drowning. And I could hear Olive's small voice saying 'I don't feel sorry for you Vivien – cry all you want.' Then she put the phone down.

I wiped my eyes with my sleeve and the phone rang again. I thought it was Olive: I tried to take a deep breath, but it came in little staccatos and I quietly said 'Hello.'

'Hi,' a voice yelled, 'Vicky, it's Philip, you old tart.'

'I'll get her,' I said before the voice knew what was going on. I went into the hall and called Victoria. But there was no reply. I went into the front room which was empty – just cans of beer over the floor and an ashtray that was still smoking slightly. The kitchen was empty. There was a scrawled note on the table. *Gone to pub. You and*

Eddie come and join us. I called out for Eddie. There was no sign of him – no 'Up here, Viv,' no 'Yes, that's me.' I ran up to my bedroom. 'Eddie, Eddie!' All his things had gone – his holdall, his white afghan coat. I ran into the front room panting like a dog and looked for his guitar through tears. It had gone too. He had gone. I sat on the floor in the still and quiet of the empty flat and looked out at the horizon.

I was alone.

FERDINAND DENNIS

Ferdinand Dennis was born in Kingston, Jamaica, grew up in London, and attended the University of Leicester and Birkbeck College. He has worked as a lecturer in Nigeria, a journalist and a broadcaster. His first book, *Behind the Frontlines: Journey into Afro-Britain*, won the 1988 Martin Luther King Memorial Prize. *The Sleepless Summer* was his first novel.

The Last Blues Dance is the story of Boswell Anderson, a reformed gambler, now owner of the run-down Caribbean Sunset Café in Hackney. The café was once renowned for its bacchanalian blues dances. Now its former denizens have grown old, returned to the Caribbean, or dream of doing so, or have assumed married respectability. Boswell has a final chance to change his life when he is invited to a big poker game. As the game approaches, the lives of Boswell, the remaining customers of the Sunset Café, and their British-born children are thrown into sharp relief as they struggle to come to terms with the past. It is a funny, but sad, blues song about a period of missed opportunities and abandoned hopes.

from *The Last Blues Dance*

In that hazy moment between waking and rising, when receding memories of dreams seem like memories of real events, and reality seems like a new dream unfolding, Boswell could only smell Lorette's sleepy body mixed with a trace of her night perfume. The usual innocent scents of mornings that followed a physically passionless night. As he lay there wondering whether it, the odour of betrayed love, had all been a dream, Lorette stirred. And in the somnolent voice with which she made the same request every morning, she asked for a parting hug. He obliged dutifully but half-heartedly, but she held him with such desperate tenderness, such reassuring affection, that, to Boswell, his failure to reciprocate seemed cruel. Slowly, his torturous night now began to appear like the nightmare of a man afraid of losing the most precious thing in his life. He remembered how, in the first months of courting Lorette, insecurity so plagued him that each time they parted he feared he would never see her again, because all his adventures in love had ended disastrously. Locked in Lorette's arms after that night stained with the scent of betrayed love, he remembered the awesome power of dreams to unearth a man's worst fears. So he held her properly now, clasped her to his pulsating heart which overflowed with bountiful gratitude for the realization that it was only fear that had poisoned his night.

She murmured, 'What an awful night. Had all kinds of strange dreams but I can't remember them.'

'Me too,' Boswell whispered, kneading her coccyx, a spot he knew she liked massaged. Her skin had never felt softer to his fingers, her sleep-laden breath on his face sweeter, her love so strong. She rolled on top of him and Boswell, almost tearful with joy, did not care if the Caribbean Sunset Café opened late that morning.

By the time he reached the café, Boswell had resolved to cast aside his foolish suspicion, put the episode out of his mind. Another empty morning would have weakened this resolve, caused him to brood on his fear of losing Lorette, but fortunately the rain resumed with the working day, bringing in a steady flow of damp customers on whom Boswell – now the sympathetic listener, now the raconteur, now the complaisant waiter – bestowed his apparently undivided attention. When he thought of Lorette, he thought of the glorious reward awaiting him at the day's end.

He did manage to snatch a few minutes from this happily busy day to telephone Stone Mason and confirm his participation in the poker game with T-Bone Sterling, when it happened. Stone Mason was delighted. Boswell had to hold the telephone away from his ear, such was the torrent of swear words from his friend.

But the furious rhythm of the day conspired against him finding the peaceful moment he needed to read Cleo's letter. The next day he changed his suit, and Cleo's letter, forgotten, still in his pocket, was sent to the dry cleaner's. Until he rediscovered the letter, Boswell would occasionally pause in the middle of a task and try to remember something he should have done, yesterday or the day before. But in the busiest week the Caribbean Sunset Café had known for years the existence of the unread letter from his former lover was completely overlooked.

The weekend came, and if they had not had a prior engagement to attend the farewell party of Bobby and Marion Summers, who were returning to Jamaica after thirty years in London, Boswell and Lorette would have spent it in bed. But duty was duty. So on

Saturday night they deigned to go out into the world.

They almost didn't make it beyond the bedroom. Boswell, whose wardrobe was somewhat limited, had donned his best brown suit, and was heading for a drink to occupy himself while Lorette dressed. But she detained him in the bedroom by seeking his advice on which of two outfits she should wear. Boswell made his choice, then lingered by the door as she sat on the edge of the bed and began slowly to pull black tights over shimmering, shapely legs, which, like the rest of her body, were a dark reddish brown colour. He had seen her dressing on many occasions but he had never really watched. Now he noticed the methodical slowness with which she prepared herself; how she scrutinized her reflected body from head to toe, from front to side, to back; how she pinched and squeezed the rolls of fat around her midriff and scowled disapprovingly. Each gesture seemed to bury her deeper into this critical self-admiration. Boswell felt as though he were a stranger watching a deeply personal ritual. Desire stirred inside him. Bobby Summers' farewell party could wait, he decided, approaching her. She started, as though he had caught her unawares and shattered the moment of privacy. She laughed embarrassedly when he suggested that they dally a while, but did not resist his caress.

After they had showered, Lorette chased him out of the bedroom. When she reappeared Boswell was stunned. Lorette was wearing a plain, finely woven body-hugging black woollen dress, complemented by a fan-tailed, cream-coloured linen jacket with gold stitching. It was not the outfit he had chosen. But her jewellery – oval-shaped earrings of silver and malachite and a matching brooch, his present to her – appeased any annoyance he felt at his choice being ignored. Two grey streaks in her lightly permed hair, a narrow one running down the centre of her head, a broader band above her left ear, contrasted with her still youthful figure and face. For Boswell, she was a woman who had transmuted the ravages of time – without resort to the illusory disguise of heavy cosmetics; she wore only eyeshadow and lip gloss – into simple adornments. Without them she would be beautiful still; with them her beauty acquired subtle qualities of mystery and grace.

Boswell fell in love with his wife a second time that night. Only Lorette's reminder that he was supposed to speak at the party prevented him from delaying their departure yet again.

The valedictory party for Bobby and Marion Summers was held at a community centre near Hackney Downs. The occasion had flushed out an army of old friends and acquaintances whom Boswell had not seen in years. Men and women who used to frequent the Caribbean Sunset Café in its halcyon days. They had drifted away, claimed by the routines of ordinary domesticity, marriage and parenthood. Now and again he had seen them hurrying along Stoke Newington High Street or shopping in Ridley Road market. The women with resentful-looking children trailing behind them as they inspected the plantains and yams and sweet potatoes they were considering buying. The men tired and fretful, their faces etched with the lines of family responsibilities and burdens, their brief exchanges with him hinting that he belonged to a past they had left behind, irrevocably, thankfully. He had not seen them again in the Caribbean Sunset Café.

Somehow Boswell got separated from Lorette by these old-timers. They all seemed curious to find out what Boswell had been up to in the intervening years, whether he still ran the café. Boswell gradually became aware of who was there as much as who was not there. Dixie Peters, whom Boswell had allowed to sleep in the Caribbean Sunset Café while searching for a room, told him about attending Buzz Campbell's funeral. It had been a quiet subdued affair attended by a handful of mourners, who had not been especially close to the deceased. Buzz Campbell had died of loneliness in an unheated Finsbury Park bedsit six months after his wife decided that she could not face another London winter, could not wait for the end of the five years that she and Buzz had originally agreed to spend in England. The half-built house – windowless, doorless – in St Thomas, which represented their life's savings and dream, with its view of the blue, blue Caribbean Sea, would suffice for her. So she had left Buzz here and he had promised to join her in a year's time. But he had not made it. Instead his life had turned ice blue with death.

Before Boswell had fully digested Dixie Peters' tragic tale, another of the men, Frank Bailey, with whom he stood, said: 'You know when I first came to England that was my biggest fear, dying in some cold, lonely room. But last year I bought a house in Kingston. Plenty land around it. Plenty fruit trees, mango soursops. And a lovely pear tree; you know the one that bears them big purple pears. Lovely. That's where I'll die.'

Yet another man, Carlton Ricketts, said: 'It's the country for me. Got a cosy little cottage in Clarendon. The verandah's got a view of the hills and peace is all around.'

'By the way, Bosy,' Frank Bailey said, 'I ran into Lance Tomlinson, Rupert Phillips and Cuthbert Harrison last time I was in Kingston. They're all real Kingstonians now. Anyway, Tomlinson asked when you're coming home, Bosy; whether you're waiting for the Englishman to repatriate you?'

They all laughed good-heartedly, including Boswell, who simultaneously glanced around for Lorette. She was engrossed in conversation with a group of ladies. Boswell longed to be reunited with her. But his acquaintances detained him further when Frank Bailey said: 'But you know is true, Bosy. I've known you for over twenty years and I've heard you talk about home but never actually going home.'

This remark heightened Boswell's eagerness to escape from these men, with their discomforting talk of death and departure. He saw in the proud lined faces of those around him the contentment of men who had lived out most of their simple ambitions and now had one remaining: to live a good death. A spasm of sadness shook him, and he thought: so many people I knew have gone home or are going home. How could he tell these men that he was different from them, that he had always been different because he had never had a vision of a home to which he would one day return?

After a seemingly long pause, Boswell said: 'Home? Man, I'm like the spider. I carry my home on my back and spin my web in any dark warm corner, like Hackney, to make a home.'

'That's true,' Dixie Peters said. 'I could go away for twenty years and come back to find Bosy still running the Caribbean Sunset Café.'

They laughed again and with their laughter the apparent mystery of why Boswell did not talk about going home vanished. When Carlton Ricketts began talking about a friend who claimed to have seen a strange, disturbing figure late one night on Hackney Downs, Boswell seized the opportunity to escape. He went to join Lorette, whose own circle had thinned out. Reunited with her, he held her hand until the PA system cackled to life. The speeches were about to begin.

The first speaker, a former mayor of the borough, almost ruined the evening with a tedious and lengthy peroration. The spacious community hall in which they stood had been built during his tenure. His entire speech praised his own heroic role in helping to end the days when the only meeting places for West Indians were damp basement venues run by dubious characters. His very last sentence casually wished Bobby and Marion Summers, who stood beside him, a happy return to the Caribbean.

The next speaker was more focused, but almost as long-winded. The MC next called Boswell, introducing him as a pioneering black entrepreneur. Sensing the crowd's restlessness, Boswell was determined to make a short speech. Leaving Lorette at the side of the hall, he made his way to the front and took the microphone. Unfortunately, the PA system went awry with his first words and he had to stop. While two men worked to fix it, Boswell scanned over the pool of heads for Lorette. At first he could not see her, but he continued looking. Then he saw her smiling and patting her hair and talking to a stranger. The man hovered disturbingly close to her, the closeness of a man with unmistakable predatory designs. She was clearly enjoying his attention. Jealousy flared in Boswell, like the eruption of a volcano. He wanted to abandon the microphone immediately and intercede. He saw her laugh a coy laugh which he remembered from their first encounter. Suddenly, the microphone cackled back to life. For a fleeting second a distracted Boswell held the instrument as if uncertain of its purpose. It was Bobby Summers' cough which snapped him out of the hypnotic daze caused by witnessing a man sweet-talking his wife. He started, determined to make his speech even shorter.

'Ladies and gentlemen,' Boswell said, desperately trying to keep his eyes focused on the centre of the hall, rather than the side where Lorette was. 'Ladies and gentlemen, I've known Bobby Summers for nearly twenty-five years. There was a time, long ago, when me and Bobby were two lonely men, scouring these streets of London that were then strange and hostile, looking for our fortune, looking even for love. When Bobby met Marion in the Caribbean Sunset Café, he found love, and I encouraged their romance and marriage, though Bobby didn't think he was good enough for Marion. I'm happy to know that Bobby has also found the fortune that eluded us both years ago. Now I know why I haven't seen Bobby or Marion in the Caribbean Sunset Café for years. They've been saving up for the great day when they can see a real Caribbean sunset for ever and ever.

'Bobby and Marion, we will miss you. But we will always remember you both with warmth and joy. And as you sit on your verandah in the evenings watching the sunset over the Caribbean, remember those of us you left behind.

'A toast to Bobby and Marion Summers, and safe passage home, to their eternal happiness.'

Boswell raised his glass and the crowd followed, cheering and clapping tumultuously. Before the applause subsided, he handed the microphone to the MC and began making his way through the hall towards the place where he had last seen Lorette. But his progress was hampered by several appreciative guests who stopped and congratulated him for the exemplary brevity of his speech and the accuracy of its sentiments. These delays heightened his anxiety to get to Lorette. Who the hell is that man? was a question that resounded in his mind even as he accepted the compliments.

When Boswell, trembling with jealousy, finally reached the spot where he had left Lorette, where he had seen her basking in a strange man's attention, he found only the ghost of her absence.

E. A. MARKHAM

'Letter to Kate' is taken from *Living in Disguise*.

Letter to Kate

When imprisoned in 1979 for 'incitement and
obstruction', i.e. for having been a founder member
of Charter '77, Vaclav Havel was allowed to write
one four-page letter to his wife, Olga, under the
following restrictions: 'No crossings out or
corrections were allowed; no quotation marks, no
underlinings or foreign expressions. We could only
write about "family matters". Humour was banned
as well: punishment is a serious business, after all,
and jokes would have undermined the gravity.'

I reach for your name and then think
Better of it, but I'm not allowed
Crossings-out, so you must stand, my love.
Let me explain, not who I am –
For this being a family letter,
You must know me – but why you have been
Reacquainted with this lover. I am,
As they say, distanced from a more familiar
Kate – not her name, you understand –
And must not use life's mishap to deny
Things their consequences: you cannot recouple
For a jailor's convenience. Kate, the name,
Is less foreign than Medbh or Tracy; sufficiently
Far from earlier family and not likely
To be suspected as a joke. Dear Kate,
Though apart, we must thank our luck
To be living at the same time in history,
And as one of us is not attuned to jokes,

The ban on this right, sorry, rite (emphasized
Not underlined) is not, indeed, onerous.
There are games that we like, separately,
And by rehearsing play at times fixed
By some public clock – cockerel crowing-in
The day, or a blackout where I live –
We might win safe conduct for this letter.
Or the next. Carnal matters I dare not
Hint at publicly. I should lose you then,
And be claimed by some professional wife
With your name. My love, I count your lashes –
Sorry, no private joke of bedrooms,
Just the miniature fans that frame your eyes;
And no hint, truly, of the days crossed off my back.

HANIF KUREISHI

Hanif Kureishi was born and brought up in Kent. He read philosophy at King's College, London. Novelist and playwright, he was awarded the George Devine Award in 1981 for his play *Outskirts*. In 1984, he wrote the Oscar-nominated screenplay for the ground-breaking film *My Beautiful Laundrette*. His second film was *Sammy and Rosie Get Laid*, followed by *London Kills Me*, which he also directed.

The Buddha of Suburbia is a bittersweet exploration of the early life of mixed-race boy Karim Amir, as he makes the transition to adulthood in suburban London. In the extract below, Karim introduces himself, his family and the limitations he is rebelling against.

from *The Buddha of Suburbia*

My name is Karim Amir, and I am an Englishman born and bred, almost. I am often considered to be a funny kind of Englishman, a new breed as it were, having emerged from two old histories. But I don't care – Englishman I am (though not proud of it), from the South London suburbs and going somewhere. Perhaps it is the odd mixture of continents and blood, of here and there, of belonging and not, that makes me restless and easily bored. Or perhaps it was being brought up in the suburbs that did it. Anyway, why search the inner room when it's enough to say that I was looking for trouble, any kind of movement, action and sexual interest I could find, because things were so gloomy, so slow and heavy, in our family, I don't know why. Quite frankly, it was all getting me down and I was ready for anything.

Then one day everything changed. In the morning things were one way and by bedtime another. I was seventeen.

On this day my father hurried home from work not in a gloomy mood. His mood was high, for him. I could smell the train on him as he put his briefcase away behind the front door and took off his raincoat, chucking it over the bottom of the banisters. He grabbed my fleeing little brother, Allie, and kissed him; he kissed my mother and

me with enthusiasm, as if we'd recently been rescued from an earth-
quake. More normally, he handed Mum his supper: a packet of
kebabs and chapatis so greasy their paper wrapper had disintegrated.
Next, instead of flopping into a chair to watch the television news and
wait for Mum to put the warmed-up food on the table, he went into
their bedroom, which was downstairs next to the living room. He
quickly stripped to his vest and underpants.

'Fetch the pink towel,' he said to me.

I did so. Dad spread it on the bedroom floor and fell on to his
knees. I wondered if he'd suddenly taken up religion. But no, he
placed his arms beside his head and kicked himself into the air.

'I must practise,' he said in a stifled voice.

'Practise for what?' I said reasonably, watching him with interest
and suspicion.

'They've called me for the damn yoga Olympics,' he said. He
easily became sarcastic, Dad.

He was standing on his head now, balanced perfectly. His stomach
sagged down. His balls and prick fell forward in his pants. The considerable muscles in his arms swelled up and he breathed energeti-
cally. Like many Indians he was small, but Dad was also elegant
and handsome, with delicate hands and manners; beside him most
Englishmen looked like clumsy giraffes. He was broad and strong too:
when young he'd been a boxer and fanatical chest-expander. He was
as proud of his chest as our next-door neighbours were of their kitchen
range. At the sun's first smile he would pull off his shirt and stride out
into the garden with a deckchair and a copy of the *New Statesman*. He
told me that in India he shaved his chest regularly so its hair would
sprout more luxuriantly in years to come. I reckoned that his chest was
the one area in which he'd been forward-thinking.

Soon, my mother, who was in the kitchen as usual, came into the
room and saw Dad practising for the yoga Olympics. He hadn't done
this for months, so she knew something was up. She wore an apron
with flowers on it and wiped her hands repeatedly on a tea towel, a
souvenir from Woburn Abbey. Mum was a plump and unphysical
woman with a pale round face and kind brown eyes. I imagined that
she considered her body to be an inconvenient object surrounding
her, as if she were stranded on an unexplored desert island. Mostly
she was a timid and compliant person, but when exasperated she
could get nervily agggressive, like now.

'Allie, go to bed,' she said sharply to my brother, as he poked his head around the door. He was wearing a net to stop his hair going crazy when he slept. She said to Dad, 'Oh God, Haroon, all the front of you's sticking out like that and everyone can see!' She turned to me. 'You encourage him to be like this. At least pull the curtains!'

'It's not necessary, Mum. There isn't another house that can see us for a hundred yards – unless they're watching through binoculars.'

'That's exactly what they are doing,' she said.

I pulled the curtains on the back garden. The room immediately seemed to contract. Tension rose. I couldn't wait to get out of the house now. I always wanted to be somewhere else, I don't know why.

When Dad spoke his voice came out squashed and thin.

'Karim, read to me in a very clear voice from the yoga book.'

I ran and fetched Dad's preferred yoga book – *Yoga for Women*, with pictures of healthy women in black leotards – from among his other books on Buddhism, Sufism, Confucianism and Zen which he had bought at the Oriental bookshop in Cecil Court, off Charing Cross Road. I squatted beside him with the book. He breathed in, held the breath, breathed out and once more held the breath. I wasn't a bad reader, and I imagined myself to be on the stage of the Old Vic as I declaimed grandly, 'Salamba Sirsasana revives and maintains a spirit of youthfulness, an asset beyond price. It is wonderful to know that you are ready to face up to life and extract from it all the real joy it has to offer.'

He grunted his approval at each sentence and opened his eyes, seeking out my mother, who had closed hers.

I read on. 'This position also prevents loss of hair and reduces any tendency to greyness.'

That was the coup: greyness would be avoided. Satisfied, Dad stood up and put his clothes on.

'I feel better. I can feel myself coming old, you see.' He softened. 'By the way, Margaret, coming to Mrs Kay's tonight?' She shook her head. 'Come on, sweetie. Let's go out together and enjoy ourselves, eh?'

'But it isn't me that Eva wants to see,' Mum said. 'She ignores me. Can't you see that? She treats me like dog's muck, Haroon. I'm not Indian enough for her. I'm only English.'

'I know you're only English, but you could wear a sari.' He laughed. He loved to tease, but Mum wasn't a satisfactory teasing victim, not realizing you were supposed to laugh when mocked.

'Special occasion, too,' said Dad, 'tonight.'

This was obviously what he'd been leading up to. He waited for us to ask him about it.

'What is it, Dad?'

'You know, they've so kindly asked me to speak on one or two aspects of Oriental philosophy.'

Dad spoke quickly and then tried to hide his pride in this honour, this proof of his importance, by busily tucking his vest in. This was my opportunity.

'I'll come with you to Eva's if you want me to. I was going to go to the chess club, but I'll force myself to miss it if you like.'

I said this as innocently as a vicar, not wanting to stymie things by seeming too eager. I'd discovered in life that if you're too eager others tend to get less eager. And if you're less eager it tends to make others more eager. So the more eager I was the less eager I seemed.

Dad pulled up his vest and slapped his bare stomach rapidly with both hands. The noise was loud and unattractive and it filled our small house like pistol shots.

'OK,' Dad said to me, 'you get changed, Karim.' He turned to Mum. He wanted her to be with him, to witness him being respected by others. 'If only you'd come, Margaret.'

I charged upstairs to get changed. From my room, the walls decorated ceiling to floor with newspapers, I could hear them arguing downstairs. Would he persuade her to come? I hoped not. My father was more frivolous when my mother wasn't around. I put on one of my favourite records, Dylan's 'Positively Fourth Street', to get me in the mood for the evening.

It took me several months to get ready: I changed my entire outfit three times. At seven o'clock I came downstairs in what I knew were the right clothes for Eva's evening. I wore turquoise flared trousers, a blue and white flower-patterned see-through shirt, blue suede boots with Cuban heels, and a scarlet Indian waistcoat with gold stitching around the edges. I'd pulled on a headband to control my shoulder-length frizzy hair. I'd washed my face in Old Spice.

Dad waited at the door for me, his hands in his pockets. He wore a black polo-neck sweater, a black imitation-leather jacket and grey Marks and Spencer cords. When he saw me he suddenly looked agitated.

'Say goodbye to your mum,' he said.

In the living room Mum was watching *Steptoe and Son* and taking a bite from a Walnut Whip, which she replaced on the pouf in front of her. This was her ritual: she allowed herself a nibble only once every fifteen minutes. It made her glance constantly between the clock and the TV. Sometimes she went berserk and scoffed the whole thing in two minutes flat. 'I deserve my Whip,' she'd say defensively.

When she saw me she too became tense.

'Don't show us up, Karim,' she said, continuing to watch TV. 'You look like Danny La Rue.'

'What about Auntie Jean, then?' I said. 'She's got blue hair.'

'It's dignified for older women to have blue hair,' Mum said.

Dad and I got out of the house as quickly as we could. At the end of the street, while we were waiting for the 227 bus, a teacher of mine with one eye walked past us and recognized me. Cyclops said, 'Don't forget, a university degree is worth £2,000 a year for life!'

'Don't worry,' said Dad. 'He'll go to university, oh yes. He'll be a leading doctor in London. My father was a doctor. Medicine is in our whole family.'

It wasn't far, about four miles, to the Kays', but Dad would never have got there without me. I knew all the streets and every bus route.

Dad had been in Britain since 1950 – over twenty years – and for fifteen of those years he'd lived in the South London suburbs. Yet still he stumbled around the place like an Indian just off the boat, and asked questions like, 'Is Dover in Kent?' I'd have thought, as an employee of the British Government, as a Civil Service clerk, even as badly paid and insignificant a one as him, he'd just have to know these things. I sweated with embarrassment when he halted strangers in the street to ask directions to places that were a hundred yards away in an area where he'd lived for almost two decades.

But his naïveté made people protective, and women were drawn by his innocence. They wanted to wrap their arms around him or something, so lost and boyish did he look at times. Not that this was entirely uncontrived, or unexploited. When I was small and the two of us sat in Lyon's Cornerhouse drinking milkshakes, he'd send me like a messenger pigeon to women at other tables and have me announce, 'My daddy wants to give you a kiss.'

Dad taught me to flirt with everyone I met, girls and boys alike, and I came to see charm, rather than courtesy or honesty, or even decency, as the primary social grace. And I even came to like people who were callous or vicious provided they were interesting. But I was sure Dad hadn't used his own gentle charisma to sleep with anyone but Mum, while married.

Now, though, I suspected that Mrs Eva Kay – who had met Dad a year ago at a 'writing for pleasure' class in an upstairs room at the King's Head in Bromley High Street – wanted to chuck her arms around him. Plain prurience was one of the reasons I was so keen to go to her place, and embarrassment one of the reasons why Mum refused. Eva Kay was forward; she was brazen; she was wicked.

On the way to Eva's I persuaded Dad to stop off at the Three Tuns in Beckenham. I got off the bus; Dad had no choice but to follow me. The pub was full of kids dressed like me, both from my school and from other schools in the area. Most of the boys, so nondescript during the day, now wore cataracts of velvet and satin, and bright colours; some were in bedspreads and curtains. The little groovers talked esoterically of Syd Barrett. To have an elder brother who lived in London and worked in fashion, music or advertising was an inestimable advantage at school. I had to study the *Melody Maker* and *New Musical Express* to keep up.

I led Dad by the hand to the back room. Kevin Ayers, who had been with Soft Machine, was sitting on a stool whispering into a microphone. Two French girls with him kept falling all over the stage. Dad and I had a pint of bitter each. I wasn't used to alcohol and became drunk immediately. Dad became moody.

'Your mother upsets me,' he said. 'She doesn't join in things. It's only my damn effort keeping this whole family together. No wonder I need to keep my mind blank in constant effortless meditation.'

I suggested helpfully, 'Why don't you get divorced?'

'Because you wouldn't like it.'

But divorce wasn't something that would occur to them. In the suburbs people rarely dreamed of striking out for happiness. It was all familiarity and endurance: security and safety were the reward of dullness. I clenched my fists under the table. I didn't want to think about it. It would be years before I could get away to the city, London, where life was bottomless in its temptations.

'I'm terrified about tonight,' Dad said. 'I've never done anything like this before. I don't know anything. I'm going to be a fuck-up.'

The Kays were much better off than us, and had a bigger house, with a little drive and garage and car. Their place stood on its own in a tree-lined road just off Beckenham High Street. It also had bay windows, an attic, a greenhouse, three bedrooms and central heating.

I didn't recognize Eva Kay when she greeted us at the door, and for a moment I thought we'd turned up at the wrong place. The only thing she wore was a full-length, multi-coloured kaftan, and her hair was down, and out, and up. She'd darkened her eyes with Kohl so she looked like a panda. Her feet were bare, the toenails painted alternately green and red

When the front door was safely shut and we'd moved into the darkness of the hall, Eva hugged Dad and kissed him all over his face including his lips. This was the first time I'd seen him kissed with interest. Surprise, surprise, there was no sign of Mr Kay. When Eva moved, when she turned to me, she was a kind of human crop sprayer, pumping out a plume of Oriental aroma. I was trying to think if Eva was the most sophisticated person I'd ever met, or the most pretentious, when she kissed me on the lips too. My stomach tightened. Then, holding me at arm's length as if I were a coat she was about to try on, she looked me all over and said, 'Karim Amir, you are so exotic, so original! It's such a contribution! It's so you!'

'Thank you, Mrs Kay. If I'd had more notice, I'd have dressed up.'

'And with your father's wonderful but crushing wit, too!'

GRACE NICHOLS

'Hurricane Hits England' is taken from *Sunris*.

Hurricane Hits England

It took a hurricane, to bring her closer
To the landscape
Half the night she lay awake,
The howling ship of the wind,
Its gathering rage,
Like some dark ancestral spectre,
Fearful and reassuring:

Talk to me Huracan
Talk to me Oya
Talk to me Shango
And Hattie,
My sweeping, back-home cousin.

Tell me why you visit
An English coast?
What is the meaning
Of old tongues
Reaping havoc
In new places?

The blinding illumination,
Even as you short-
Circuit us
Into further darkness?

What is the meaning of trees
Falling heavy as whales
Their crusted roots
Their cratered graves?

O why is my heart unchained?

Tropical Oya of the weather,
I am aligning myself to you,
I am following the movement of your winds,
I am riding the mystery of your storm.

Ah, sweet mystery,
Come to break the frozen lake in me,
Shaking the foundations of the very trees
within me,
Come to let me know
That the earth is the earth is the earth.

COLIN PRESCOD

Colin Prescod was born in Trinidad Tobago and educated in Britain. He has followed a dual career in academia and media. He was Senior Lecturer in Sociology at the Polytechnic of North London for some two decades and Editor of the African Caribbean Unit at the BBC. As an editorial board member of the influential journal *Race and Class* (Institute of Race Relations, London), he has been actively involved in the discourse around racism and community in Britain.

Dealing with Difference Beyond Ethnicity was a paper presented to the Royal Tropical Institute in the Netherlands as part of a discussion on museums, arts education and the cultural policies of municipal authorities.

Dealing with Difference Beyond Ethnicity

Just two weeks ago, I went to see a marvellously theatrical play, written by a very special English dramatist – a woman called Caryl Churchill. The production was at The Cottesloe, the little space at the National Theatre in London. The play was *Light shining in Buckinghamshire*, set in England in the 1640s – the period of the aftermath of the great Civil War. The main action of the play concerns the attempt by the still radical popular social forces in England to push the democratic English revolution even further. The names that we now have for these social groups are wonderfully graphic. The Levellers, who were the foot-soldiers of Parliament's New Model Army. What they wanted at this point was the vote for all men (note, only men!) over twenty-one years old. The Diggers, another group of social forces, who literally dug up common land to reclaim it for farming so that poor people could feed themselves. And the religiously zealous Ranters, who, amongst other things, wanted free access to as many women as they liked, and who challenged the very idea of sin. Gradually all of these social forces and their demands were defeated. Oliver Cromwell and the new establishment heard but dismissed their ideas, and executed the leaders who would not submit. This was England in the 1640s.

In the little theatre I sat next to two tourists from the USA, who told me that they were looking at the play for its production style and values – not for its content, therefore. I, on the other hand, was really moved by the piece. While the rest of the audience applauded, politely, at the end of the play, I cheered and shouted my appreciation. No one around me shared my enthusiasm. I was alone in that audience.

I am suggesting that Caryl Churchill's play can be read as a play about multicultural or intercultural England in the 1640s. And it served to remind me that when a genuinely multicultural space is opened up, when people who don't normally have a significant voice in the big affairs of a society, manage to raise their voices and have them heard – there is always a challenge which disturbs the culturally dominant, hegemonic voices in that society. The play served to remind me too, that the 'Establishment' response can and does tend to see to it that the voices for multiculture, although heard, are not heeded – tolerated, but not engaged with, or embraced, or acted upon. Further to all this, Caryl Churchill's play about seventeenth-century England reminded me of nothing so much as our contemporary late-twentieth-century European cultural turmoil. Here, once again, multiculture and interculturality have been placed on the policy agendas of governments and municipalities, by challenges so loud that they have to be given a hearing. Let us be clear – it is not the municipal officers and bureaucrats who have thought to place multiculturalism on the late-twentieth-century social agenda. Rather it is the new social forces – the migrant communities, women, the working class – and the challenges they have made, that have pushed the municipalities to place multicultural concerns on their agendas.

An All-Change World

Current European concern with multiculturalism is constituted then from a series of layered challenges for change, which are articulated by a variety of late-twentieth-century social forces.

First of all there is the challenge from 'without', which has put a stop to Europe ruling the world: from the ex-colonized, in Europe's ex-colonies; and from those in the ex-Third World, pressuring for a New World Order. Secondly we see a challenge from 'within': from the class, and gender and ethnically oppressed, excluded and marginalized; and from those, marginalized according to age status, that is to say, those in 'youth' and increasingly 'oldie' social categories; and from members of the ex-colonized, now moved from the colonized peripheries to the metropolitan centres – the Third World now resident in the First World. Thirdly we register the challenge against dominant and long-standing ideologies – against imperialism, progressivism, male chauvinism. This is a challenge that is reflected in the deep philosophical controversies of postmodernist discourse – just as it is reflected in 'decolonizing the mind' discourses of ex-colonials. And finally we are becoming more and more aware that the sum of these challenges is part and parcel of a grand questioning of the relevance of most of our dominant social and political institutions. Virtually everything, from the nuclear family to the nation, is being actively questioned in our time. So, then, we live in an 'all-change' world. A world forced to change by a new technological industrial revolution; a new world order; the collapse or the collapsing of an old world order; the increasing irrelevance of the old nation states and of narrow nationalisms – and so on, and so on. Now, if we make, or discuss, or critique municipal policy and formal education, in the arts, or in any other area, without giving our discussion and planning this all-change context, I believe that our efforts will be exposed as irrelevant and/or laughable.

Dangerous Crossroads

In the face of all this complexity of social forces and challenges, I would warn against taking it for granted that we are automatically on the right policy track, merely by putting multi- and interculturality on our agenda. And in order to do this, there are some major themes that I want to put to you, relating to the all-change context.

– Europe is now not so much a place as a changing environment. And the rather simplified 'ethnic' interculturality axis of new Europeans/old Europeans is but one of the indicators or signs of this changed and still rapidly changing environment.

– Even the most progressive municipal arts policies are but part of the many, official, attempts (just) to catch up with the rapid changes in our new cultural environment. The increasing municipal policy focus on multicultural and intercultural arts and arts culture, reflects the fact that this 'arts' area is one of the few relatively free, public or social spaces open to the new social forces now acting on old Europe.

– The abstract concept of interculturality only hints at the extra-ordinary, rapid and largely under-theorized cultural mix that characterizes our contemporary European and indeed global sociology. The metaphor 'dangerous crossroads', borrowed from the American cultural analyst George Lipsitz, might present us with a better image for apprehending this historic moment of accelerated cultural mix and confrontation.

– If we study any one municipal policy (for the arts or wider), with regard to this accelerated cultural mix and confrontation – we will find it consists of a mêlée or confusion of objectives. (a) There will be apartheid-like objectives – which seem to be aimed at preserving separate ethnicities. (b) There will be assimilationist objectives – which tend to neutralizing new cultural interventions that confront old Europe. (c) There will be what I want to call disablement objectives – which define or design 'difficult' areas of society or culture as in some way, effectively, disabled 'ghettoes of disadvantage' – in order to justify compensating or supporting them! (d) There will be what I want to call, with deliberate linguistic clumsiness, liberal-radicalism objectives. These are often seen as the most progressive or daring policy objectives – aiming at active and genuine interculturality or transculturality.
My argument is that all of these distinct and conflicting objectives will probably exist, simultaneously, in any one municipal policy dealing with the new cultural mix and challenges in our new Europe.

– Arts education in schools and academies, in the context of celebrating interculturality at our 'dangerous crossroads' of accelerated mix and disturbing challenges, cannot be cosy or safe in establishment terms. We need only remind ourselves that formal school education, for example, is always being challenged by the informal education of playground, street, home, neighbourhood, and popular edu-tainment culture.

Multiculturalism, Beyond Ethnicity

I was invited to this symposium because I have been at the centre of developing what is commonly referred to as a multicultural arts intervention: the 'DRUM', in Birmingham, England. The 'DRUM' is an arts and culture initiative dedicated to celebrating and supporting the new awakening of confident contributions to British cultural diversity – by the society's Asian, African and Caribbean communities, for the whole community, black and white. It emerges out of a history of social and artistic pressures and demands to which the Birmingham City Council, West Midlands Arts, and the West Midlands Probation Service have responded. These are the bodies that have provided the initial funding base for the 'DRUM' development – from a combination of political will, enlightened arts commitment, and concern for what might be termed 'communities at risk'. Such are the real convergences of interest that fuel policy. For those of us who have taken on the responsibility of delivering this ambitious project, though, the 'DRUM' is an act of the imagination – simultaneously a tool of black liberation and a national focus for interculturality.

The 'DRUM' is in and of Birmingham – just as Birmingham is in and of Britain. Birmingham has the same 'race and class' history as Britain. Within this history, Birmingham's factories were still producing shackles used to hold and restrain African slaves in the New World in the late nineteenth century – decades after Britain had officially abolished slavery and emancipated slaves in its colonies. In more recent times, Birmingham, like Britain, has had its massive 'riots' and its urban uprisings of disenfranchised and disgruntled, mainly young, mainly black citizens – from the 1970s into the 1980s. And it is these 'riots', part and parcel of the insistent settlement of major communities of black ex-colonials (Indian, Pakistani, Caribbean, African), that have placed dealing with difference on the political and policy agendas in Birmingham, as in Britain.

Birmingham and its region has produced some of Britain's most exciting and popular new art and culture. In the 1970s and 1980s, for example, the world-famous band Steel Pulse came out of Birmingham – inventors, of urban reggae, from the First World, as distinct from reggae from the Third World. UB40, a massively popular band, mixing black and white personnel and black and white lyrical and musical forms, came out of Birmingham in the same period. In the 1990s Birmingham and its region has thrown up the pop phenomenon Apache Indian, with a transcultural mix of Asian, African-American and Caribbean musical art forms. And perhaps most distinctively, through Goldie, amongst others, the region has been at the centre of the 1990s invention, *jungle* – a musical form that is created, uniquely, out of Britain's new multicultural mix.

Subversive Cultural Enclaves

I want to make three bold observations related to the broader implications of these Birmingham and British developments. First of all I
believe that this black British cultural intervention is at the centre of
what makes multiculturalism, or interculturality, most concrete,
most real, in contemporary Britain. Secondly I want to contend that
the dangerous cutting edge of this new black British cultural intervention is seriously subversive in its intent – and this makes it
unlikely that it can be grasped by the establishment. Often, what is
there at the cutting edge of new culture is so seriously disturbing
that we couldn't expect it to be grasped by the municipalities. To
illustrate this with examples from popular musical interventions:
young blacks, normally excluded from mainstream participation, are
making their interventions using, and sometimes abusing or 'liberat-
ing' other-purpose technologies. Record-player turntables, ordinarily
used to put a record on, so that they play music to us, now become,
through the technique of *scratching*, musical instruments in themselves. That is an abuse of the technology, in a way a subversion of
its first purpose. Synthesizers and mixing desks in recording studios
are deliberately made to distort, to make new noises – in order to
make new musics. This is subversive activity. This is not something
you expect the establishment of the academic conservatoire to be
able to accept.

Finally, the most disturbing observation that I want to make is
that quite a lot of the new cultural milieu, animated by these black
popular interventions, opens out into what, hitherto, has been seen
as crime. To illustrate once again with examples from the world of
popular culture: at the core of much of the new, popular black music
is a compositional process called *sampling*. Sampling is taking bits
from other people's music, or sound forms from other people's products and using them in any manipulated form that you want to. From
the perspective of official, legal frameworks, this is wrong. This is
breaking the law. There are currently huge copyright debates about
all this. But sampling is deliberately done, it is stealing and the new
composers know that it is. But they don't care. And then there is the
rave. Rave culture is propelled by techno, jungle and other new
musics. It throws up spontaneous disco-clubs – raves attended by
masses of people, in their tens of thousands. And this phenomenon, by
and large, has been seen, by the authorities, as an unwelcome addition

to our cultural scene. Our municipal leaders want them shut down, because 'anything could happen in those kinds of places'. A radical philosopher-analyst, Hakim Bey, is talking about this rave culture as creating what he calls 'temporary autonomous zones', TAZs, which terrify the authorities. In his book, *The Temporary Autonomous Zone, Ontological Anarchy and Poetic Terrorism*, Bey argues that, for those who have given up the idea of being able to make old-fashioned, lasting revolution, the TAZ is a cultural space in which moments of social freedom can be seized. And the authorities sense this. I am pointing out that much of this new, 'cutting edge', urban, cultural intervention, is culturally, *not ethnically*, challenging to our established status quo – and I am arguing that these interventions must be included in our engagement with multiculturality.

Now, I am aware that the picture that I have been painting, or maybe I should say, the jazz score that I have been drafting here, looks like and sounds like the characterization of some kind of revolutionary age – a changing environment, in which everything is being challenged and fought against. But it is a revolutionary age with no revolutionary parties, and with no revolutionary leaders! Historically though, we note that revolutions and revolutionaries are always resisted and often driven back(wards) – so we must always anticipate the neutralizing and levelling inclination of the establishment's responses to cultural challenge. And from history we note too, that revolutions always overtake the revolutionaries – so we must know that the challenges and calls for change, coming from the marginalized, do not provide social solutions, in themselves. Ironically, in our time, it is in fact the policy-makers, and not revolutionary leaders or parties, who find themselves on the front line – obliged to provide ways forward, at our taxing, 'dangerous crossroads'.

SALMAN RUSHDIE

'Is Nothing Sacred?', a passionate plea for literature to occupy 'a privileged arena', was the Herbert Read Memorial Lecture for 1990. It was delivered on the author's behalf by Harold Pinter at the Institute of Contemporary Arts, London, on 6 February 1990, and reprinted in *Imaginary Homelands, Essays and Criticism 1981–1991* (Granta Books in Association with Penguin Books, 1991).

Is Nothing Sacred?

I grew up kissing books and bread.

In our house, whenever anyone dropped a book or let fall a chapati or a 'slice', which was our word for a triangle of buttered leavened bread, the fallen object was required not only to be picked up but also kissed, by way of apology for the act of clumsy disrespect. I was as careless and butter-fingered as any child and, accordingly, during my childhood years, I kissed a large number of 'slices' and also my fair share of books.

Devout households in India often contained, and still contain, persons in the habit of kissing holy books. But we kissed everything. We kissed dictionaries and atlases. We kissed Enid Blyton novels and Superman comics. If I'd ever dropped the telephone directory I'd probably have kissed that, too.

All this happened before I had ever kissed a girl. In fact it would almost be true, true enough for a fiction writer, anyhow, to say that once I started kissing girls, my activities with regard to bread and books lost some of their special excitement. But one never forgets one's first loves.

Bread and books: food for the body and food for the soul – what could be more worthy of our respect, and even love?

It has always been a shock to me to meet people for whom books simply do not matter, and people who are scornful of the act of reading, let alone writing. It is perhaps always astonishing to learn that your beloved is not as attractive to others as she is to you. My most beloved books have been fictions, and in the last twelve months I have been obliged to accept that for many millions of human beings, these books are entirely without attraction or value. We have been witnessing an attack upon a particular work of fiction that is also an attack upon the very ideas of the novel form, an attack of such bewildering ferocity that it has become necessary to restate what is most precious about the art of literature – to answer the attack, not by an attack, but by a declaration of love.

Love can lead to devotion, but the devotion of the lover is unlike that of the True Believer in that it is not militant. I may be surprised – even shocked – to find that you do not feel as I do about a given book or work of art or even person; I may very well attempt to change your mind; but I will finally accept that your tastes, your loves, are your business and not mine. The True Believer knows no such restraints. The True Believer knows that he is simply right, and you are wrong. He will seek to convert you, even by force, and if he cannot he will, at the very least, despise you for your unbelief.

Love need not be blind. Faith must, ultimately, be a leap in the dark.

The title of this lecture is a question usually asked, in tones of horror, when some personage or idea or value or place held dear by the questioner is treated to a dose of iconoclasm. White cricket balls for night cricket? Female priests? A Japanese takeover of Rolls-Royce cars? *Is nothing sacred?*

Until recently, however, it was a question to which I thought I knew the answer. The answer was No.

No, nothing is sacred in and of itself, I would have said. Ideas, texts, even people can be made sacred – the word is from the Latin *sacrare*, 'to set apart as holy', – but even though such entities, once their sacredness is established, seek to proclaim and to preserve their own absoluteness, their inviolability, the act of making sacred is in truth an event in history. It is the product of the many and complex pressures of the time in which the act occurs. And events in history must always be subject to questioning, deconstruction, even to declarations of their obsolescence. To respect the sacred is to be paralysed by it. The idea of the sacred is quite simply one of the most conservative notions in any culture, because it seeks to turn other ideas – Uncertainty, Progress, Change – into crimes.

To take only one such declaration of obsolescence: I would have described myself as living in the aftermath of the death of god. On the subject of the death of God, the American novelist and critic William H. Gass had this to say, as recently as 1984:

The death of god represents not only the realization that gods have never existed, but the contention that such a belief is no longer even irrationally possible: that neither reason nor the taste and temper of the times condone it. The belief lingers on, of course, but it does so like astrology or a faith in a flat earth.

I have some difficulty with the uncompromising bluntness of this obituary notice. It has always been clear to me that God is unlike human beings in that it can die, so to speak, in parts. In other parts, for example India, God continues to flourish, in literally thousands of forms. So that if I speak of living after this death, I am speaking in a limited, personal sense – my sense of God ceased to exist long ago, and as a result I was drawn towards the great creative possibilities offered by surrealism, modernism and their successors, those philosophies and aesthetics born of the realization that, as Karl Marx said, 'all that is solid melts into air.'

It did not seem to me, however, that my ungodliness, or rather my post-godliness, need necessarily bring me into conflict with belief. Indeed, one reason for my attempt to develop a form of fiction in which the miraculous might coexist with the mundane was precisely my acceptance that notions of the sacred and the profane both needed to be explored, as far as possible without pre-judgement, in any honest literary portrait of the way we are.

That is to say: the most secular of authors ought to be capable of presenting a sympathetic portrait of a devout believer. Or, to put it another way: I had never felt the need to totemize my lack of belief, and so make it something to go to war about.

Now, however, I find my entire world-picture under fire. And as I find myself obliged to defend the assumptions and processes of literature, which I had believed that all free men and women could take for granted, and for which all unfree men and women continue every day to struggle, so I am obliged to ask myself questions I admit to finding somewhat unnerving.

Do I, perhaps, find something sacred after all? Am I prepared to set aside as holy the idea of the absolute freedom of the imagination and alongside it my own notions of the World, the Text and the Good?

Does this add up to what the apologists of religion have started calling 'secular fundamentalism'? And if so, must I accept that this
'secular fundamentalism' is as likely to lead to excesses, abuses and
oppressions as the canons of religious faith?

A lecture in memory of Herbert Read is a highly appropriate occasion
for such an exploration, and I am honoured to have been asked to
deliver it. Herbert Read, one of the leading British advocates of the
modernist and surrealist movements, was a distinguished representative of the cultural values closest to my heart. 'Art is never transfixed,'
Read wrote. 'Change is the condition of art remaining art.' This
principle is also mine. Art, too, is an event in history, subject to the
historical process. But it is also *about* that process, and must constantly strive to find new forms to mirror an endlessly renewed world.
No aesthetic can be a constant, except an aesthetic based on the idea
of inconstancy, metamorphosis, or, to borrow a term from politics,
'perpetual revolution'.

The struggle between such ideas and the eternal, revealed truths of
religion is dramatized this evening, as I hope I may be excused for
pointing out, by my absence. I must apologize for this. I did, in fact,
ask my admirable protectors how they would feel if I were to deliver
my text in person. The answer was, more or less, 'What have we done
to deserve this?' With regret, I took the point.

It is an agony and a frustration not be able to re-enter my old life,
not even for such a moment. However, I should like to thank Harold
Pinter, through his own mouth, for standing in my place. Perhaps this
event could be thought of as a form of secular revelation: a man
receives a text by mysterious processes from Elsewhere – above?
below? New Scotland Yard? – and brings it out before the people,
and recites . . .

More than twenty years ago, I stood packed in at the back of this
theatre, listening to a lecture by Arthur Koestler. He propounded
the thesis that language, not territory, was the prime cause of aggression, because once language reached the level of sophistication at
which it could express abstract concepts, it acquired the power of
totemization; and once peoples had erected totems, they would go to
war to defend them. (I a: '. pardon of Koestler's ghost. I am relying on
an old memory, and the 's an untrustworthy shoulder to lean on.)

In support of his theory, he told us about two tribes of monkeys living on, I think, one of the northern islands of Japan. The two tribes lived in close proximity in the woods near a certain stream, and subsisted, not unusually, on a diet of bananas. One of the tribes, however, had developed the curious habit of washing its bananas in the stream before eating them, while the other tribe continued to be non-banana-washers. And yet, said Koestler, the two tribes continued to live contentedly as neighbours, without quarrelling. And why was this? It was because their language was too primitive to permit them to totemize either the act of banana-washing or that of eating bananas unwashed. With a more sophisticated language at their disposal, both wet and dry bananas could have become the sacred objects at the heart of a religion, and then, look out – Holy war.

A young man rose from the audience to ask Koestler a question. Perhaps the real reason why the two tribes did not fight, he suggested, was that there were enough bananas to go round. Koestler became extremely angry. He refused to answer such a piece of Marxist claptrap. And, in a way, he was right. Koestler and his questioner were speaking different languages, and their languages were in conflict. Their disagreement could even be seen as the proof of Koestler's point. If he, Koestler, were to be considered the banana-washer and his questioner the dry-banana man, then their command of a language more complex than the Japanese monkeys' had indeed resulted in totemizations. Now each of them had a totem to defend: the primacy of language versus the primacy of economics: and dialogue therefore became impossible. They were at war.

Between religion and literature, as between politics and literature, there is a linguistically based dispute. But it is not a dispute of simple opposites. Because whereas religion seeks to privilege one language above all others, one set of values above all others, one text above all others, the novel has always been *about* the way in which different languages, values and narratives quarrel, and about the shifting relations between them, which are relations of power. The novel does not seek to establish a privileged language, but it insists upon the freedom to portray and analyse the struggle between the different contestants for such privileges.

Carlos Fuentes has called the novel 'a privileged *arena*'. By this he does not mean that it is the kind of holy space which one must put off one's shoes to enter; it is not an arena to revere; it claims no special rights *except the right to be the stage upon which the great debates of society can be conducted.* 'The novel,' Fuentes writes, 'is born from the very fact that we do not understand one another, because unitary, orthodox language has broken down. Quixote and Sancho, the Shandy brothers, Mr and Mrs Karenin: their novels are the comedy (or the drama) of their misunderstandings. Impose a unitary language: you kill the novel, but you also kill the society.'

He then poses the question I have been asking myself throughout my life as a writer: *Can the religious mentality survive outside of religious dogma and hierarchy?* Which is to say: Can art be the third principle that mediates between the material and spiritual worlds; might it, by 'swallowing' both worlds, offer us something new – something that might even be called a secular definition of transcendence?

I believe it can. I believe it must. And I believe that, at its best, it does.

What I mean by transcendence is that flight of the human spirit outside the confines of its material, physical existence which all of us, secular or religious, experience on at least a few occasions. Birth is a moment of transcendence which we spend our lives trying to understand. The exaltation of the act of love, the experience of joy and very possibly the moment of death are other such moments. The soaring quality of transcendence, the sense of being more than oneself, of being in some way joined to the whole of life, is by its nature short-lived. Not even the visionary or mystical experience ever lasts very long. It is for art to capture that experience, to offer it to, in the case of literature, its readers; to be, for a secular, materialist culture, some sort of replacement for what the love of god offers in the world of faith.

It is important that we understand how profoundly we all feel the needs that religion, down the ages, has satisfied. I would suggest that these needs are of three types: firstly, the need to be given an articulation of our half-glimpsed knowledge of exaltation, of awe, of wonder; life is an awesome experience, and religion helps us understand why life so often makes us feel small, by telling us what we are *smaller than*, and, contrariwise, because we also have a sense of being special, of being *chosen*, religion helps us by telling us what we have been chosen by, and what for. Secondly, we need answers to the unanswerable: How did we get here? How did 'here' get here in the first place? Is this, this brief life, all there is? How can it be? What would be the point of that? And, thirdly, we need codes to live by, 'rules for every damn thing'. The idea of god is at once a repository for our awestruck wonderment at life and an answer to the great questions of existence, and a rule book, too. The soul needs all these explanations – not simply rational explanations, but explanations of the heart.

It is also important to understand how often the language of secular, rationalist materialism has failed to answer these needs. As we witness the death of communism in Central Europe, we cannot fail to observe the deep religious spirit with which so many of the makers of these revolutions are imbued, and we must concede that it is not only a particular political ideology that has failed, but the idea that men and women could ever define themselves in terms that exclude their spiritual needs.

It seems obvious, but relevant, to point out that in all the countries now moving towards freedom, art was repressed as viciously as was religion. That the Czech revolution began in the theatres and is led by a writer is proof that people's spiritual needs, more than their material needs, have driven the commissars from power.

What appears plain is that it will be a very long time before the peoples of Europe will accept any ideology that claims to have a complete, totalized explanation of the world. Religious faith, profound as it is, must surely remain a private matter. This rejection of totalized explanations is the modern condition. And this is where the novel, the form created to discuss the fragmentation of truth, comes in. The film director Luis Buñuel used to say: 'I would give my life for a man who is looking for the truth. But I would gladly kill a man who thinks he has found the truth.' (This is what we used to call a joke, before killing people for their ideas returned to the agenda.) The elevation of the quest for the Grail over the Grail itself, the acceptance that all that is solid *has* melted into air, that reality and morality are not givens but imperfect human constructs, is the point from which fiction begins. This is what J.-F. Lyotard called, in 1979, *La Condition Postmoderne*. The challenge of literature is to start from this point, and still find a way of fulfilling our unaltered spiritual requirements.

Moby Dick meets that challenge by offering us a dark, almost Manichean vision of a universe (the *Pequod*) in the grip of one demon, Ahab, and heading inexorably towards another; namely the Whale. The ocean always was our Other, manifesting itself to us in the form of beasts – the worm Ouroboros, Kraken, Leviathan. Herman Melville delves into these dark waters in order to offer us a very modern parable: Ahab, gripped by his possession, perishes; Ishmael, a man without strong feeling or powerful affiliations, survives. The self-interested modern man is the sole survivor; those who worship the Whale – for pursuit is a form of worship – perish by the Whale.

Joyce's wanderers, Beckett's tramps, Gogol's tricksters, Bulgakov's devils, Bellow's high-energy meditations on the stifling of the soul by the triumphs of materialism; these, and many more, are what we have instead of prophets and suffering saints. But while the novel answers our need for wonderment and understanding, it brings us harsh and unpalatable news as well.

It tells us there are no rules. It hands down no commandments. We have to make up our own rules as best we can, make them up as we go along.

And it tells us there are no answers; or, rather, it tells us that answers are easier to come by, and less reliable, than questions. If religion is an answer, if political ideology is an answer, then literature is an inquiry; great literature, by asking extraordinary questions, opens new doors in our minds.

Richard Rorty, in *Philosophy and the Mirror of Nature*, insists on the importance of historicity, of giving up the illusions of being in contact with Eternity. For him, the great error is what he calls 'foundationalism', which the theologian Don Cupitt, commenting on Rorty, calls 'the attempt, as old as (and even much older than) Plato, to give permanence and authority to our knowledge and values by purporting to found them in some unchanging cosmic realm, natural or noumenal, outside the flux of our human conversation.' It is better, Cupitt concludes, 'to be an adaptable pragmatist, a nomad.'

Michel Foucault, also a confirmed historicist, discusses the role of the author in challenging sacralized absolutes in his essay, 'What is an Author?' This essay argues, in part, that 'texts, books and discourses really began to have authors . . . to the extent that authors became subject to punishment, that is, to the extent that discourses could be transgressive.' This is an extraordinary, provocative idea, even if it is stated with Foucault's characteristic airiness and a complete absence of supporting evidence: *that authors were named only when it was necessary to find somebody to blame.* Foucault continues:

In our culture (and doubtless in many others), discourse was not originally a product, a thing, a kind of goods; it was essentially an act – an act placed in the bipolar field of the sacred and the profane, the licit and the illicit, the religious and the blasphemous. Historically it was a gesture fraught with risks . . .

In our beginnings we find our essences. To understand a religion, look at its earliest moments. (It is regrettable that Islam, of all religions the easiest to study in this way, because of its birth during the age of recorded history, has set its face so resolutely against the idea that it, like all ideas, is an event inside history.) And to understand an artistic form, too, Foucault suggests, look at its origins. If he is right about the novel, then literature is, of all the arts, the one best suited to challenging absolutes of all kinds; and, because it is in its origin the schismatic Other of the sacred (and authorless) text, so it is also the art mostly likely to fill our god-shaped holes.

There are other reasons, too, for proposing the novel as the crucial art form of what I can no longer avoid calling the post-modern age. For one thing, literature is the art least subject to external control, because it is made in private. The act of making it requires only one person, one pen, one room, some paper. (Even the room is not absolutely essential.) Literature is the most low-technology of the art forms. It requires neither a stage nor a screen. It calls for no interpreters, no actors, producers, camera crews, costumiers, musicians. It does not even require the traditional apparatus of publishing, as the long-running success of samizdat literature demonstrates. The Foucault essay suggests that literature is as much at risk from the enveloping, smothering forces of the market economy, which reduces books to mere products. This danger is real, and I do not want to seem to be minimizing it. But the truth is that of all the forms, literature can still be the most free. The more money a piece of work costs, the easier it is to control it. Film, the most expensive of art forms, is also the least subversive. This is why, although Carlos Fuentes cites the work of film-makers like Buñuel, Bergman and Fellini as instances of successful secular revolts into the territory of the sacred, I continue to believe in the greater possibilities of the novel. Its singularity is its best protection.

Among the childhood books I devoured and kissed were large numbers of cheap comics of a most unliterary nature. The heroes of these comic books were, or so it seemed, almost always mutants or

hybrids or freaks: as well as the Batman and the Spiderman there was
Aquaman, who was half-fish, and of course Superman, who could
easily be mistaken for a bird or a plane. In those days, the middle
1950s, the superheroes were all, in their various ways, hawkish law-
and-order conservatives, leaping to work in response to the Police
Commissioner's Bat-Signal, banding together to form the Justice
League of America, defending what Superman called 'truth, justice
and the American way'. But in spite of this extreme emphasis on
crime-busting, the lesson they taught children – or this child, at any
rate – was the perhaps unintentionally radical truth that exceptionality was the greatest and most heroic of values; that those who were
unlike the crowd were to be treasured the most lovingly; and that this
exceptionality was a treasure so great and so easily misunderstood
that it had to be concealed, in ordinary life, beneath what the comic
books called a 'secret identity'. Superman could not have survived
without 'mild-mannered' Clark Kent; 'millionaire socialite' Bruce
Wayne made possible the nocturnal activities of the Batman.

Now it is obviously true that those other freakish, hybrid, mutant,
exceptional beings – novelists – those creators of the most freakish,
hybrid and metamorphic of forms, the novel, have frequently been
obliged to hide behind secret identities, whether for reasons of gender
or terror. But the most wonderful of the many wonderful truths about
the novel form is that the greater the writer, the greater his or her
exceptionality. The geniuses of the novel are those whose voices are
fully and undisguisably their own, who, to borrow William Gass's
image, *sign every word they write*. What draws us to an author is his
or her 'unlikeness', even if the apparatus of literary criticism then sets
to work to demonstrate that he or she is really no more than an accu-
mulation of influences. Unlikeness, the thing that makes it impossible
for a writer to stand in any regimented line, is a quality novelists
share with the Caped Crusaders of the comics, though they are only
rarely capable of leaping tall buildings in a single stride.

What is more, the writer is there, in his work, in the reader's hands,
utterly exposed, utterly defenceless, entirely without the benefit of an
alter ego to hide behind. What is forged, in the secret act of reading,
is a different kind of identity, as the reader and writer merge, through
the medium of the text, to become a collective being that both writes
as it reads and reads as it writes, and creates, jointly, that unique
work, 'their' novel. This 'secret identity' of writer and reader is the
novel form's greatest and most subversive gift.

And this, finally, is why I elevate the novel above other forms, why it has always been, and remains, my first love: not only is it the art involving least compromises, but it is also the only one that takes the 'privileged arena' of conflicting discourses *right inside our heads.* The interior space of our imagination is a theatre that can never be closed down; the images created there make up a movie that can never be destroyed.

In this last decade of the millennium, as the forces of religion are renewed in strength and as the all-pervasive power of materialism wraps its own weighty chains around the human spirit, where should the novel be looking? It seems clear that the renewal of the old, bi-polar field of discourse, between the sacred and the profane, which Michel Foucault proposes, will be of central importance. It seems probable, too, that we may be heading towards a world in which there will be no real alternative to the liberal-capitalist social model (except, perhaps, the theocratic, foundationalist model of Islam). In this situation, liberal capitalism or democracy or the free world will require novelists' most rigorous attention, will require reimagining and questioning and doubting as never before. 'Our antagonist is our helper,' said Edmund Burke, and if democracy no longer has communism to help it clarify, by opposition, its own ideas, then perhaps it will have to have literature as an adversary instead.

I have made a large number of sweeping claims for literature during the course of this piece, and I am aware of a slightly messianic tone in much of what I've written. The reverencing of books and writers, by writers, is nothing particularly new, of course. 'Since the early 19th century,' writes Cupitt, 'imaginative writers have claimed – have indeed enjoyed – a guiding and representative role in our culture. Our preachers are novelists, poets, dramatists, film-makers and the like, purveyors of fiction, ambiguous people, deceivers. Yet we continue to think of ourselves as rational.'

But now I find myself backing away from the idea of sacralizing literature with which I flirted at the beginning of this text; I cannot bear the idea of the writer as secular prophet; I am remembering that one of the very greatest writers of the century, Samuel Beckett, believed that all art must inevitably end in failure. This is, clearly, no reason for surrender. 'Ever tried. Ever failed. Never mind. Try again. Fail better.'

Literature is an interim report from the consciousness of the artist, and so it can never be 'finished' or 'perfect'. Literature is made at the frontier between the self and the world, and in the act of creation that frontier softens, becomes permeable, allows the world to flow into the artist and the artist to flow into the world. Nothing so inexact, so easily and frequently misconceived, deserves the protection of being declared sacrosanct. We shall just have to get along without the shield of sacralization, and a good thing, too. We must not become what we oppose.

The only privilege literature deserves – and this privilege it requires in order to exist – is the privilege of being the arena of discourse, the place where the struggle of languages can be acted out.

Imagine this. You wake up one morning and find yourself in a large, rambling house. As you wander through it you realize it is so enormous that you will never know it all. In the house are people you know, family members, friends, lovers, colleagues; also many strangers. The house is full of activity: conflicts and seductions, celebrations and wakes. At some point you understand that there is no way out. You find that you can accept this. The house is not what you'd have chosen, it's in fairly bad condition, the corridors are often full of bullies, but it will have to do. Then one day you enter an unimportant-looking little room. The room is empty, but there are voices in it, voices that seem to be whispering just to you. You recognize some of the voices, others are completely unknown to you. The voices are talking about the house, about everyone in it, about everything that is happening and has happened and should happen. Some of them speak exclusively in obscenities. Some are bitchy. Some are loving. Some are funny. Some are sad. The most interesting voices are all these things at once. You begin to go to the room more and more often. Slowly you learn that most of the people in the house use such rooms sometimes. Yet the rooms are all discreetly positioned and unimportant-looking.

Now imagine that you wake up one morning and you are still in the large house, but all the voice-rooms have disappeared. It is as if they have been wiped out. Now there is nowhere in the whole house where you can go to hear voices talking about everything in every possible way. There is nowhere to go for the voices that can be funny one minute and sad the next, that can sound raucous and melodic in the course of the same sentence. Now you remember: there is no way out of this house. Now this fact begins to seem unbearable. You look into the eyes of the people in the corridors – family, lovers, friends, colleagues, strangers, bullies, priests. You see the same thing in everybody's eyes. *How do we get out of here?* It becomes clear that the house is a prison. People begin to scream, and pound the walls. Men arrive with guns. The house begins to shake. You do not wake up. You are already awake.

Literature is the one place in any society where, within the secrecy of our own heads, we can hear *voices talking about everything in every possible way*. The reason for ensuring that that privileged arena is preserved is not that writers want the absolute freedom to say and do whatever they please. It is that we, all of us, readers and writers and citizens and generals and godmen, need that little, unimportant-looking room. We do not need to call it sacred, but we do need to remember that it is necessary.

'Everybody knows,' wrote Saul Bellow in *The Adventures of Augie March*, 'there is no fineness or accuracy of suppression. If you hold down one thing, you hold down the adjoining.'

Wherever in the world the little room of literature has been closed, sooner or later the walls have come tumbling down.

MIKE PHILLIPS

Mike Phillips is a Londoner and the author of several books, including the Sam Dean series of novels. The first of these, *Blood Rights*, was serialized for BBC TV; the second, *The Late Candidate*, won the Crime Writers' Association's Silver Dagger Award. His subsequent novels, *Point of Darkness*, *An Image to Die For* and *The Dancing Face*, received critical acclaim.

The following piece was commissioned for this anthology.

At Home in England

For most black people who grow up in Britain, normal life involves rubbing shoulders with people from a wide variety of ethnic backgrounds. For instance, in the district of North London where I live, it would be impossible to walk a hundred yards down the High Street without encountering men and women who have their origins in India, China, Greece, Turkey, Africa, the Caribbean and everywhere else in Europe that you can imagine. This apparent diversity – men in turbans, women wearing masks, the swishing of multi-coloured saris – has become a normal and inevitable feature of the urban landscape in Britain, and its absence becomes a fact filled with meaning.

In recent years, for instance, it's become a routine journalistic exercise to point out that there are at least two versions of Britain – the urbanized, multi-racial areas colonized by the ethnic minorities, and, all around them, another country, where the sight of a black or Asian person is so rare as to be startling.

In general, black people tend to echo this observation in their own perception of the British landscape. No need to run a poll to find out our opinion about this. We vote with our feet. Take the geographical centre of the country, the Lakes and the Peak District. These are sparsely populated, so the absence of a black community is no great surprise. But these areas are huge centres of internal tourism. On any given day during the summer coachloads of trippers arrive every hour, the streets are lined with bed and breakfast accommodation, and the most popular beauty spots are as crowded as Oxford Street during the Christmas shopping season.

Even in this mass of people from all over Britain you could search for weeks, months perhaps, without discovering more than the occasional single black or Asian face, and you could say the same for huge swathes of more densely populated towns and villages. But this isn't a simple case of a split between urban and rural population patterns. On a different scale the same effect can be seen in a number of cities throughout the North and the Midlands – Derby, Leicester, Nottingham, Sheffield. It would be hard to deduce from a quick survey of the centres or of the more prosperous areas, that there are sizeable black communities living within the city limits. In Nottingham, for example, young people crowd into the town hall square on Friday and Saturday nights as a preliminary to scattering into the clubs and pubs in the district. Given the popular notion that youth culture is focused on black music and black style, it is astonishing to observe that the crowds of teenagers on these occasions are almost exclusively white. This is a rule which seems to hold good for anywhere outside the major conurbations like London, Birmingham, Leeds and Manchester.

From one point of view you could argue that all this is a concrete reflection of the way that British society has contained and isolated black people. On the surface it also seems like evidence for the view that there is a parallel, larger Britain which has effectively insulated itself from the multi-racial society of recent years: and, leaving aside the effects of discrimination, this is a view which seems to be endorsed by the consistency with which black British people choose to stick to those quarters where they have an established and proprietorial presence.

At the level of the emotions it's easy to understand why. The prospect of a purely social isolation is bad enough, and, hidden in the imagination, the thought of being isolated in an angry mob, alone among a crowd of hostile, alien faces, provokes an atavistic flutter of anxiety. Black people in Britain, unlike African Americans, have no direct memory of lynch mobs, but the image is close to the bone. Our history as immigrants reinforces this feeling. As a schoolboy, during the decade of the fifties, the London in which I lived seemed a dangerous and violent arena where I was always conscious of hostile, angry vibes directed at me and anyone who looked like me. In my memory there is a clear sense of being under siege, as if my home was a miniature fortress which I reached each night with a feeling of relief. Among our circle of family and friends, every night was threaded through with recitals of a litany of threats and insults, our daily experience of what it meant to live in England. From that perspective we continue to live within a hugely extended and fortified pale within which we feel secure. Looking to the outside world we see a map embellished with threatening figures. Here be dragons.

In the circumstances, as I set out to drive to Scotland recently, intending to travel the length of the country, stopping in as many places as I could manage, I felt a certain wariness, a sense that I had to be prepared for whatever might happen. This wasn't merely the sort of low intensity paranoia which, from time to time, I recognize in myself and other immigrants. Isolated events, like the murder of Stephen Lawrence while he stood at a bus stop, are constant reminders that, beyond the headlines and all over the country, black and Asian people can be attacked, beaten or killed at random, for no apparent reason apart from the colour of their skins. On the other side of the coin, racist and violent policemen are said to be a tiny fraction of the force, but there is, of course, no guarantee that chance won't pitch you up against the baddest of the bad apples one dark night on a B road miles from anywhere. Being black in Britain confers a special vulnerability and the fears of black people are rooted in that knowledge. But truth is a much more complex affair.

After three days into my travels I was walking along a street in Jesmond when it occurred to me that I'd been out for more for than half an hour without seeing a black person or an Asian. I'd been more or less expecting this because Jesmond is a prosperous suburb of Newcastle, and, once you get past Leeds, going up the east coast of the country, black people are few and far between; but the sense of being the only one for miles around, a dark speck in the sea of white faces, was curiously dislocating, as if I had suddenly set foot in a foreign country, a tourist, tentatively surveying the language, the customs and the atmosphere round me.

The sensation was so strong that when I saw a newsagent's shop in the middle of a small parade I headed for it with a feeling of relief, as if the familiar act of buying my usual newspaper would ground me in reality, and restore my connection with everyday life. Instead, the experience made matters worse. Asian newsagents are a contemporary equivalent of Roman milestones, and the fact that this one was white heightened my feeling that I was in a foreign, slightly exotic place.

There was a time, not so many years ago, when I'd have reacted with an automatic caution, but, curiously enough, I felt nothing of the sort.

It was one of those bright sunny mornings late in the summer when there was still enough moisture left over from the night to give the grass a furtive sparkle, and there was something in the wind, a sort of tang, which seemed to hint that autumn was on its way. As I walked it struck me that the disorientation I felt was more to do with the look of the place rather than any uncertainty about the effect of my presence on the white people I encountered, the way I might have felt in Hamburg or Bratislava. On the contrary, my presence didn't seem to cause a single ripple, not even so much as a single curious look, and in return I didn't look over my shoulder once.

For some reason I found myself sorting through my memory, looking for an occasion in another country when I'd felt the same ease in an unfamiliar environment. It was hard to think of one. Nowadays in the Caribbean I feel wary, alien, an outsider in the region where I was born. In the USA, surrounded by black faces, it's easy to feel estranged, excluded by networks of idiom and manners which were not my own. In Africa I was a foreigner, belonging to nowhere and no one. In comparison it was only in Britain that I could stroll through unknown territory, with the same confidence, even in the whitest pockets of the country, as if this was where I truly belonged.

I found myself struggling against this conclusion. History again. Black identity is a complex and developing notion. The double ferment of Civil Rights in the USA and the anti-colonial struggle in the rest of the black world produced a psychological account of the relationship between blacks and whites. This hinged on the idea that black people had internalized the white view of their identity, the consequence being that they could only see themselves and each other as insignificant and inferior – the eternal *Other* of the white imagination. For black intellectuals and activists the struggles for self-government, and for equality in white societies, were inseparable from the struggle to invent and control their own identity. In Britain the spaces we inhabited also became territories of the soul, where it was possible to recreate and possess cultures, which, in defiance of white permission, would allow us to define and control our re-invented selves.

This was a crucial element of the background that has dominated black attitudes for the last three decades. In theory black people have squared the circle by recreating parts of the major inner city as bubbles within which it is possible to be the subject of our own invention rather than the reflected object of the white gaze. To step outside the bubble is, in a sense, to reject oneself. From this point of view there was something perverse about feeling almost as relaxed in a world of strange whites as I would have in my own London neighbourhood.

On the other hand, the simple equation that balances black self-assertion against white rejection is an inadequate explanation for the nature of the relationship between black British citizens and their environment. One element of the reality we lived was the porous quality of the barriers between blacks and white in Britain, and ironically, inside our inner city bubbles of territorial and cultural comfort the white population was always larger. In comparison, white faces are a rarity in an American 'ghetto', while geographical boundaries between the races are strictly drawn and socially policed in a fashion that would be impossible in Britain. Looking back at the progress of the arguments about identity within the black communities over the last thirty years it becomes more and more obvious that the idea of a black nation was never more than rhetoric. In the USA it drew its resonance from their history of segregation and the physical separation of cities into racial quadrants. In Britain it was a stark choice between joining up or getting out, and the solution had been a typical British compromise. We had declared the rescue of our identities from within an imagined culture, a Third World of the mind, the passport to which was a sort of diasporic style bible – music, language, hairstyles.

As it happened the real context was a fortunate historical accident. At the time when I arrived in this country, over forty years ago, British identity was still wrapped up in the concept of empire and imperial destiny. The gaze with which the English regarded us, the aliens, came from the eyes of colonial masters. But the mid-century saw the end of Empire and the beginning of an extended period of reassessment. During that time almost all the institutions and habits which underpinned whiteness and imperial certainty have withered or fallen apart, leaving British identity confused and fragmented: and in that time all the national and political crises around the issue of British citizenship have gone in one direction. Citizenship has slowly been decoupled from race, and the concept of the United Kingdom as a nation has loosened, almost imperceptibly at first, then in a rush of permission for a variety of identities to assert themselves. Part of the process has been the leakage of identity between the multi-racial bubbles of the inner cities and the world around them. In any case the geography of our cultures was never static and immovable. Both blacks and whites have moved in and out of these worlds with increasing ease, carrying with them new and more ambiguous outlines of identity.

Nowadays moving through the 'white' areas of the country what I feel is far from the anxiety of the past. Instead, I have the curious sense that I am in areas which have stayed stuck in the past, and somehow failed to catch up with the look and the atmosphere of modern Britain. What's even more curious is the impression that I get that this is a feeling which is overwhelmingly shared by the bulk of residents in the districts where it is a rarity to see a black or an Asian face. Local conflicts may remain, but for the English the mixture of races is now a real facet of their identity, whatever colour the family next door happens to be.

JOHN AGARD

'Equiano Beyond the Margins' is taken from *A Stone's Throw from Embankment*. Here, he is inspired by Out of the Margins, a four-day festival that celebrated the enormous contribution of black writers in Britain.

Equiano Beyond the Margins

'I have often taken up a book and have talked to it and then put my ears to it, when alone, in hopes it would answer me; and I have been very much concerned when I found it remained silent.'

From 'The Interesting Narrative of the Life of Olaudah Equiano, or Gustavas Vassa, the African' (1789)

I

When first I
shook their book
I heard no lion roar.
Their words were closed door.
No open savannah.
But did I not see
black words run like zebra
across a white page?

       So I chased words
       with the spear of my tongue
       following the footprints
       of words
       following the shadows
       of words/
       but whose words?

I wanted to set
fire to the grass of their vowels
but my tongue was numb with frost

Therefore I walked stealthy
between gain and loss
where all was made new
by the absence of name
and my curiosity
was the flame
to see me through
on a coldest winter night

Snow then I thought
was a gift of salt
from the sky
and I puzzled why
when I put my ears
to their book
their book did not reply

How could I snare
a flock of their consonants
between the trap of my teeth?

So in the gourd of my mouth
I stored the little sounds
that pleased my pulse/

I rattled pebbles of verbs
till nouns were so jealous
they wanted to join the dance of doing

Now some 200 years later
their words have sprung
new buds from
the tree of my tongue/

I am many-branched with utterance.
Africa gestures between the pages
Asia flavours the Queen's English
Caribbean breezes blow through libraries

where my eloquent ghost wanders at ease
with neither boundary nor margin

unlocking doors with word-keys
loosening lions among teacups

II

I saw John La Rose and John Figueroa
chatting on the South Bank balcony
like two elders in complicity

John La Rose gave a boyish kaiso grin.
I said Hello.
I'm Equiano. From Eboe.
He said I know. Not too far from Benin.
And don't you have a distant cousin somewhere in San
Fernando?

John Figueroa seemed like one from wisdom's school
who might have sat upon the golden stool.
I said Hello.
I'm Equiano. From Eboe. .
Man, your beard really grow
and it white for so. Is it the salt or the snow?

The man made me to understand
he was distantly related to the Norse god Odin
by way of Viking
and possibly to Obatala of Yoruba origin
not forgetting a hint or two
of Sephardic Jew.
And all that northern frost falling on his beard like dew.

I watched these two knowledgeable scribes
catch up on ole-talk on a november morn.
I asked myself will the second generation and the third
gather words from such elders of the tribe,
or will they turn their backs
on anecdotes that nourish
and are a beacon to the British Blacks?

Now I Equiano will do my divination. Eboe-born.
If I don't have cowrie shell, I turn to acorn.

Some things I write. Some things I tell.
My tongue is a pen I carry inside my mouth.
But ah how beautiful to see
John La Rose and John Figueroa
chatting on the South Bank balcony
like two elders in complicity.

Such timeless moments blessed beyond diasporic dawn.
So I walked on. Walked on.
Leaving John to converse with John.

III

Berry's bluefoot man
down railway track to centre stage/
Nichols' Fat Black Woman
stepping on the cosmic scale/
D'Aguiar's Mama Dot
oracle in rocking chair/

THE WEATHER COLD
BUT THE WRITING HOT

Selvon's Moses crossing red sea
(that is metaphorically)
Beryl Gilroy stirring the pot of psychology
Aunty Kailash Puri handling the agony
Emecheta, yes, the same Buchi,
she too telling the settlers' story

THE WEATHER COLD
BUT THE WRITING HOT

Mapanje and Namjoshi
riding on the back of fable riddle an ting-
He on a chattering wagtail wing
She on a blue donkey
small tales stretching to infinity
THE WEATHER COLD
BUT THE WRITING HOT

Diversity of sound/ bridging sky and ground-
Sujata Bhatt buttering English words
with Hanuman honey
Debjani Chatterjee following language-thread
through labyrinth of identity
Martin Glynn (alias Doctor G)

in jazz/rap
swing
warning that language-trap
could do yo head in

THE WEATHER COLD
BUT THE WRITING HOT

History is a weight
to break a back
unless you create
a crick or a crack/
crick of light   crack of hope

one day one day soon come
cow buss rope
        remember monkey slip
on rotten pomerack/
let Merle Collins take you on that Antillean trip.
Her proverbial grandmother have the knack
of boiling history
down to low gravy/
for let it be said again
the canefields were no bed of roses.
Lives drained at the green altars
        of standing sugar.
Bodies once ornamented with tribal marks
        now tormented with scars.

        Who can recall all those mothers
        like David Dabydeen's Jasmattie
        and all those fathers
        lost to El Dorado's golden daggers?

But now ain't time to dwell on history's sins.

> Now gather stars
> from among the sky's unfathomable margins/
> now rise beyond the hurricane's havoc
> keened in Markham's elegies/
> that's right Binta shower us with a breeze
> of red rebel songs to heal/
> that's right John Lyons season your lines

with a bouquet garni of trini talk/
Charm us Errol Lloyd with colours of childhood/
Arm us Grace Hallworth with stories that jump out/
Is that you John Hendrickse? Thought
I recognized you by your Khoi clicks

Our hearts ready for the alchemy of Anansi tricks
and blissful morning mantra Mantis.

THE WEATHER COLD
BUT THE WRITING HOT

Zephaniah prancing higher with he locks of fire/
Jackie Kay exploring the land of other loves and desire/
Lemn Sissay going his way down rhythm highway/
LKJ looking back on things and times
with a blam-blam of dreadbeat rhymes/
Firdaus Kanga from his wheelchair chariot
throwing darts of wicked satire
taking the mickey out of empire/

and like Amryl Johnson's granny in the market square
we questioning the universe with a curse
we harvest love with baskets of air
we add our branches to the language-tree

David Dabydeen

'London Taxi Driver', taken from *Coolie Odyssey*, reproduced by kind permission of the author. Copyright © by David Dabydeen, 1988

Ferdinand Dennis

Extract from *The Last Blues Dance* reproduced by kind permission of the author and the publishers HarperCollins. Copyright © by Ferdinand Dennis, 1996

Buchi Emecheta

Extract from *Second Class Citizen* reproduced by kind permission of the author. Copyright © by Buchi Emecheta, 1974

Bernardine Evaristo

Extract from *Lara* reproduced by kind permission of the author and the publishers Angela Royal Publishing Ltd. Copyright © by Bernardine Evaristo, 1997

Beryl Gilroy

Extract from *Boy-Sandwich* reproduced by kind permission of the author and the publishers Heinemann Educational Books. Copyright © by Beryl Gilroy, 1989

Paul Gilroy

Extract from *Small Acts* reproduced by kind permission of the author. Copyright © by Paul Gilroy, 1993. All rights reserved

Stuart Hall

'The Formation of a Diasporic Intellectual', taken from *Stuart Hall: Critical Dialogues in Cultural Studies* (edited by David Morley & Kuan-Hsing Chen), reproduced by kind permission of the publishers Routledge. Copyright © by David Morley & Kuan-Hsing Chen, 1996

Wilson Harris

Extract from *The Palace of the Peacock* reproduced by kind permission of the author and the publishers Faber & Faber Ltd. Copyright © by Wilson Harris, 1960

Victor Headley

Extract taken from *Yardie* reproduced by kind permission of the author and the publishers Dotun Adebayo/The X Press. Copyright © by Victor Headley, 1992

Roy Heath

Extract from *Kwaku – Or the Man Who Could Not Keep His Mouth Shut*